AF607954

OUT OF DUE TIME

OUT OF DUE TIME

Wilfrid Ward and the *Dublin Review*

DOM PASCHAL SCOTTI

THE CATHOLIC UNIVERSITY OF AMERICA PRESS
Washington, D.C.

Copyright © 2006
The Catholic University of America Press
All rights reserved

The paper used in this publication meets the minimum requirements of American National Standards for Information Science—Permanence of Paper for Printed Library Materials, ANSI Z39.48-1984.
∞

Photo on cover and frontispiece by Frank Scott Clark

LIBRARY OF CONGRESS CATALOGING-IN-PUBLICATION DATA
Scotti, Paschal, 1961–
Out of due time : Wilfrid Ward and the Dublin review / by Paschal Scotti.
p. cm.
Includes bibliographical references (p.) and index.
ISBN 13: 978-0-8132-1427-6 (alk. paper)
ISBN 10: 0-8132-1427-0 (alk. paper)
1. Ward, Wilfrid Philip, 1856–1916. 2. Dublin review (Dublin, Ireland) 3. Catholics—Ireland. 4. Ireland—Church history—19th century. 5. Ireland—Church history—20th century. 6. English literature—Irish authors—History and criticism—Periodicals. 7. Ireland—Civilization—Periodicals. I. Title.
BX4705.W297S36 2006
282′.092—dc22

2005000845

CONTENTS

Preface vii

1. The Intellectual Politician 1

2. English Catholicism and the *Dublin Review* 29

3. Transcendence, Revelation, and Immanence 57

4. Politics 91

5. Society 121

6. Literature 168

7. Ireland 205

8. Foreign Affairs 226

9. The Great War 260

10. Conclusion 289

Appendix: Contents of the *Dublin Review*, January 1906–April 1916 295

Select Bibliography 309

Index 325

PREFACE

Looking back on the last century, so filled with war, pestilence, and famine, in which tens of millions were offered up on the pyres of competing ideologies, where every sort of evil received its followers and apologists, and even the ideas of a common culture and normative ethics were denied, the early years of the twentieth century look remarkably placid and unified.[1] For some a nostalgic glow colors them and a sense of loss clings to them. While it is true that the Edwardian Age was the final phase of that relatively long era of European peace that began with the fall of Napoleon in 1815 and continued, with brief interruptions, to the First World War, yet it did not seem as idyllic and peaceful to those who lived in it. The century began with the death of Queen Victoria (January 22, 1901), an event that led many to ponder the future in trepidation. Already, in his "Recessional," written for Queen Victoria's Diamond Jubilee in 1897, Kipling had recalled some of the great empires of the past whose pride had destroyed them, and warned Britain of hubris. Humility, however, was not in evidence at the coronation of Victoria's heir, King Edward VII, where the majesty of empire was displayed in all its grandeur, and for which A. C. Benson's famous anthem "Land of Hope and Glory," set to the music of Elgar, called upon God to make the great British Empire even greater. "God, who made thee mighty, make thee mightier yet."

The British Empire was still the greatest the world had ever seen, but doubts had begun. The Boer War (1899–1902), and the effort it took to defeat a rabble of backwoods Dutch farmers, had revealed

1. See Robert Conquest, *Reflections on a Ravaged Century* (New York: W. W. Norton, 2000); Stéphane Courtois et al., *The Black Book of Communism: Crimes, Terror, Repression* (Cambridge: Harvard University Press, 1999); and Gertrude Himmelfarb, *The Demoralization of Society: From Victorian Virtues to Modern Values* (New York: Knopf, 1995). "Contrary to its promise, the twentieth century became mankind's most bloody and hateful century, a century of hallucinatory politics and of monstrous killings." Zbigniew Brzezinski, *Out of Control: Global Turmoil on the Eve of the 21st Century* (New York: Scribner's, 1993), 4–5.

Britain's weakness; and the fact that so many of those who had tried to enlist were found unfit began a widespread discussion about national degeneracy. This sense of decline was only intensified by the phenomenal growth of Germany and the United States in trade and economic power, so that Britain's mercantile and industrial preeminence was no longer a given. To say that the age was one of transition and change is merely to state the obvious. Change is always with us and adaptation is as old as Adam. Yet at this time the pace of change did take on an intensity and depth all its own. While it may not be that human character changed "on or about December 1910," as Virginia Woolf maintained, many traditional assumptions about human nature and society were being challenged.[2] As Samuel Hynes has pointed out, it was an age that stood in an odd pivotal position between the nineteenth and twentieth centuries, not quite Victorian nor altogether modern.[3] While modernity has brought many benefits, it is not without its darker side. Its most dangerous characteristic is, in the phrase of the philosopher Leszek Kolakowski, "the disappearance of taboos," by which he means the application of a narrow rationality which cuts away at all inherited beliefs and customs.[4] Newman too had warned of the destructive power of modernity, though he had a different name for it. As the British Empire was undergoing change, so too was the English Catholic Church, but with her change had not led to a crisis of confidence but to a growth in it. Its members were becoming more numerous, more prosperous and educated, more cohesive, and more integrated and accepted into national life. The Church had finally reached the level where its corporate capacities were beginning to match its universalistic ambitions. While change can be a difficulty, it can also be an opportunity. Wilfrid Ward, remembered today for his biography of Cardinal Newman and a leading Catholic intellectual and man of letters of the day, saw in the times a great op-

2. See Virginia Woolf's "Mr. Bennett and Mrs. Brown," in *The Captain's Death Bed and Other Essays* (New York: Harcourt Brace Jovanovich, 1950), 94–119.

3. Samuel Hynes, *The Edwardian Turn of Mind* (Princeton: Princeton University Press, 1968), vii.

4. Leszek Kolakowski, *Modernity on Endless Trial* (Chicago: University of Chicago Press, 1990), 3–13. "The point is that in the normal sense of 'rationality' there are no more rational grounds for respecting human life and human personal rights than there are, say, for forbidding the consumption of shrimp among Jews, of meat on Friday among Christians, and of wine among Muslims. They are all 'irrational' taboos. And a totalitarian system which treats people as exchangeable parts in the state machinery, to be used, discarded, or destroyed according to the state's needs, is in a sense a triumph of rationality" (13).

portunity. In 1906 he took charge of the *Dublin Review,* the leading Catholic journal in the English-speaking world, believing that it provided the best means of achieving his long-held goals. He wished to bring the best of the Catholic mind to the nation at large, revealing the intrinsic power and beauty of the faith which alone, he believed, could counter the dissolving forces of modernity, and to expose the Catholic faithful to the best of the changing world around them. The story of this book is the story of these pursuits.

Assembling an exceptional group of contributors, Ward achieved something unique. Under his guidance the *Dublin* experienced a golden age, gaining for the Catholic side a hearing from the larger world rarely accorded it. An editor molds his journal by his selection of contributors and articles, and many of the *Dublin* authors are of more than historical interest. While a few names should be familiar to the reader, others deserve to be. This work is, therefore, not just about Ward but about the journal itself under his editorship, its tone and characteristics, its interests and opinions. The *Dublin* belonged to the belletristic tradition of the great English quarterlies in its desire to speak to the entire educated public on the whole range of topics without a narrow erudition and with literary style. It is for this reason that I have tried to let its authors speak in their own words as much as possible. (Also, for a better understanding of the journal's range, I have listed in the Appendix all the articles published in the *Dublin* during Ward's tenure.) This was probably the last generation to which such an attempt really seemed possible. Our own age has become far more specialized, and if that was to be expected, it has also led to a far more fragmented and disjointed world. I have great admiration for Ward and great sympathy for what he tried to do. Ward was a man much misunderstood in his own time and ignored in our own, and it is hoped that this work can partially rectify that situation. This is not a neutral work, but I hope that it is an accurate and objective one.

Many debts were incurred in the writing of this book. I wish to thank our school librarian, Mrs. Roberta Stevens; Vincent Martin, who faithfully drove me to the URI library; Fr. Ian Dickie, the archivist of the Westminister Archdiocese; Fr. Augustine Kelly, O.S.B.; Matthew Papi and Daniel Betz; Dr. M. N. E. Tiffany; Dr. John Haldane of St. Andrews University; the librarians of the British Library and the St. Andrews University Library; the Very Rev. Brian M. Canon Halloran for his great personal kindness to me during my month at St. Andrews; the administration of St. Andrews University for my accommodation there; and the graduate students of Deans Court who treated me so well. I wish also to thank the community of Ealing Abbey for their great kindness during the month I spent in London, and Dom Dunstan O'Keefe and the community of Downside Abbey for their few days of hospitality. I wish to thank Dr. Norman Reid, the Keeper of Manuscripts, University of St. Andrews Library, for permission to quote from Ward's letters, and Mr. Oliver Hawkins for permission to quote from a letter of Wilfrid Meynell; the Catholic University of America Press for permission to use material from my article, "Wilfrid Ward: A Religious Fabius Maximus," and the *Downside Review* for permission to use material from my article "Wilfrid Ward and the *Dublin Review.*" I wish to thank Dom Matthew Stark and Dom Edmund Adams for reading my manuscript and for their comments, and the unnamed reviewers who did the same. Finally, I wish to thank my editor, Suzanne Wolk, for the exemplary job she did. It is deeply appreciated. This book is dedicated to my parents, Patrick (†) and Rose Scotti, to whom I owe everything.

OUT OF DUE TIME

1 THE INTELLECTUAL POLITICIAN

In 1906 Mrs. Wilfrid Ward (as Josephine Ward signed herself) published a novel, *Out of Due Time.* Its hero was an English Catholic, a writer for the *Nineteenth Century* and *Quarterly* and the editor of a religious journal, named George Sutcliffe. While the story was inspired by the tragic career of Lamennais and the condemnation of his journal *L'Avenir* more than seventy years before, the characters and the issues involved bore an uncanny, if unintended, resemblance to contemporary figures and events. Sutcliffe is not a portrait of her husband Wilfrid, though there are enormous similarities.[1] Not only was Wilfrid Ward an English Catholic who wrote for the *Nineteenth Century* and *Quarterly,* and the editor of a Catholic journal, but, like Sutcliffe, his greatest desire was to see the reconciliation of the Church and the world.

Mr. Sutcliffe was by nature a man of action. But circumstances had made him realise that the field for action in the present day for all who were interested in

1. For Ward's life, see the two volumes by his daughter, Maisie Ward, *The Wilfrid Wards and the Transition,* vol. 1, *The Nineteenth Century* (New York: Sheed and Ward, 1934) and vol. 2, *Insurrection Versus Resurrection* (New York: Sheed and Ward, 1937), hereafter cited as *Wilfrid Wards* 1 and *Wilfrid Wards* 2. The Wilfrid Ward Papers (hereafter WWP) can be found at St. Andrews University Library, St. Andrews, Scotland. More material has been added since the catalogue was originally done by Mary Jo Weaver, "A Working Catalogue of the Ward Family Papers," *Recusant History* 15 (1979): 43–71, and a new catalogue has been put online at the St. Andrews University Library site, http://specialcollections.st-and.ac.uk/.

religion is an intellectual one. . . . And he found his co-religionists immensely blind to what he wanted them to do. He wanted them to understand that there was a world of thought, and of thinkers, almost unknown to them as they sat at home at ease in faith and plenty. He wanted them to understand how the usual text-books used by Catholics in this country, were not only inadequate to express the great truths of religion, but were almost unintelligible to those who had been educated in the language of a new civilization. That that civilization might be decadent and morbid was not the point, the point being that it was in possession of the minds of men. Greek may be a finer language than English, but it is not usually of so much use in dealing with the inhabitants of the British Isles. His practical English mind demanded that something should be done to bridge the chasm between the very rich in spiritual gifts and the very desolate.[2]

To understand why reconciliation was needed one could do no better than to turn to the *Syllabus of Errors.* Issued in 1864 as part of the encyclical *Quanta Cura* and taken from previous pronouncements of Pius IX, it caused profound consternation even among many of the faithful. When Pio Nono was elected in 1846 he seemed the most unlikely of beings, a liberal pope.[3] Greeted with acclaim throughout Europe and well known and popular in the Papal States, where his affability, kindness, and liberality contrasted sharply with the austere, reclusive, and stodgily old-fashioned Gregory XVI, he raised expectations that no pope, even the most liberal, could have met. The assassination of his prime minister, the layman Count Pellegrino Rossi, the Roman Revolution of 1848, and his flight to Gaeta ended whatever affinity he had for nineteenth-century liberalism; and the later attacks on the Church and the Papal States by the "enlightened" Piedmontese government only made things worse. The *Syllabus,* condemning in its eighty propositions the "chief errors of our times," covered a wide area, political, religious, intellectual, and moral. While many were unexceptional, such as condemning the denial of a personal God or of Christ's divinity, others, such as condemning the separation of Church and State or the freedom to adopt whatever religion one wished, seemed shocking. The most controversial was number eighty, which stigmatized the belief that the "Roman Pontiff can and should reconcile and har-

2. Mrs. Wilfrid Ward, *Three Novels* (London: Longmans, Green, 1933), 43–46. See also Peter Erb, "Some Aspects of Modern British Catholic Literature: Apologetic in the Novels of Josephine Ward," *Recusant History* 24 (July 1999): 364–83. *Out of Due Time* was reviewed favorably by R. B., *Dublin Review* (July 1906): 200–204.

3. See E. E. Y. Hales, *Pio Nono: A Study in European Politics and Religion in the Nineteenth Century* (London: P. J. Kennedy, 1954).

monise himself with progress, with liberalism, and with recent civilization." In their proper contexts they took on a much less radical edge, as their defenders later were to make clear, but the reception of the *Syllabus* in liberal Europe and in the English press was universally negative. It was seen as an absurd return to obscurantism and medievalism and as a rejection of modern civilization.[4] Later events further isolated the papacy and hardened its opposition to current trends. In 1870 the last remaining part of the Papal States, Rome itself, fell to the Piedmontese, and Pius became "a Prisoner of the Vatican." In the 1870s Bismarck began his *Kulturkampf* in Germany to subject the Church to the state. At Pio Nono's death in 1878 the Church was embattled and seemingly at war with the age.

Ward had been a seminarian in Rome in the final months of Pio Nono's reign, and while he admired him for his sanctity and his patience in suffering and had utter contempt for King Victor Emmanuel and the new Italian government, which had usurped the papal patrimony for its new capital, the isolation of the Church was painfully obvious. Nor was the estrangement just political. Ward found his studies lifeless and utterly unconnected with, and even contemptuous of, modern thought and conditions. Everything was learned by rote. Even philosophy was taught from authority, not by argumentation, and real philosophical thought only annoyed the teachers. In his younger days Ward applied himself as a philosopher of religion, but he was always more fascinated by persons and the workings of men's minds than by abstract theories. It was rather as an intellectual politician than as a speculative thinker that he would attempt to bridge the chasm between the Church and the world. His life work would not be the important task of developing a new synthesis himself but the equally necessary one of creating an opportunity and space for such a synthesis to come about, of creating room to maneuver and to find common ground where all sides could meet. As it was remarked in an article written after his death:

> And what concerned him most in regard to the human mind was that it should go forward in orderly activity: he was less concerned with the actual results of philosophic or scientific investigation, except in so far as they were evidences of intellectual activity. Hence he followed with a keenly appreciative interest the developments of thought in all manner of subjects—in theology and philosophy, in natural science and history, in literature and art; but always it was with the eye of the politician, fol-

4. See Damian McElrath, *The Syllabus of Pius IX: Some Reactions in England* (Louvain: Bibliothèque de l'Université, Bureau de la Revue, 1964).

lowing the movements of the time with a view to the welfare and evolution of the State. He belonged, in fact, to that class of thinkers who may be described as the politicians of the world intellectual.[5]

One cannot understand the *Dublin* during Ward's editorship until one understands his career as an intellectual politician—as a mediator both within the Church, between its rulers and thinkers, and outside the Church, between it and the larger world of thought. As a friend put it after his death, he was essentially a "liaison officer, one who links together by his knowledge, sympathy and wisdom many who would otherwise be apart, and helps them to work together for the common good."[6] His program of reconciliation began long before he took on the *Dublin Review,* and the *Dublin* was merely its culmination.

At first blush Ward would seem an unlikely candidate for such a position. His father, William George Ward (1812–1882), the most brilliant of Newman's Oxford disciples, was one of the most extreme and dogmatic of Catholics, a leading figure in that most papal and rigid school of Catholic thought called Ultramontane. In describing himself, he could say things such as, "You will find me narrow, and strong—*very* narrow, and *very* strong"; or, in discussing some point of Catholic doctrine, "There are two views, of which I, as usual, take the more bigoted."[7] His extremism, however, was intellectual, the outcome of an unusually logical mind, and on a personal level he was extremely friendly and dispassionate, amusing, and self-deprecating. Jowett compared him to Socrates in dialectical power and to Falstaff in his love of making fun.[8] Wilfrid's entirely Catholic and intensely religious upbringing also made him an unlikely mediator. As with so many of the children of Oxford Movement

5. Fr. Cuthbert [Hess], O.S.F.C., "Wilfrid Ward (I.)," *Dublin Review* (July 1916): 4. In a letter to Tyrrell (July 7, 1900) Von Hügel criticized Ward, obliquely but clearly, over his too-political manner and view of things. See Friedrich von Hügel, *Baron Friedrich von Hügel: Selected Letters, 1896–1924,* ed. Bernard Holland (London: J. M. Dent & Sons, 1927), 85–86.

6. Sir Michael Sadler to Mrs. Wilfrid Ward, cited in *Wilfrid Wards* 1:96.

7. Quoted in *Wilfrid Wards* 1:7. In *Unfinished Business* (New York: Sheed and Ward, 1964), Maisie said of her father's relationship with his father: "Papa loved him devotedly, disagreed with him vehemently, and talked of him incessantly" (15).

8. Wilfrid Ward, *William George Ward and the Oxford Movement* (London: Macmillan, 1889), 439. Chesterton said of W. G. Ward: "While he affirmed the dogmas of the believer with an apocalyptic absoluteness worthy of a pontifical throne, he also asked questions of the sceptic with a ferocious clarity which might have landed weaker minded people in a padded cell." G. K. Chesterton, "An Agnostic Defeat," *Dublin Review* (Jan. 1912): 171.

converts, whose parents had sacrificed their futures for a spiritual ideal, his early life, and that of his siblings, was much more a preparation for heaven than for earthly success. Three of Wilfrid's sisters became nuns, and his younger brother, Bernard (the future historian), entered the priesthood. Excluded from the great English universities, a fact which he always lamented, he spent the last three years of his education as a seminarian at Rome and at Ushaw, the great school and seminary near Durham.

Yet his father, for all his narrowness of adherence, was a man of great intellectual breadth and power. He was a leading figure and favorite in that most unlikely of discussion groups, the Metaphysical Society (1869–1880), which brought together most of the leading intellectual figures of Victorian England to talk about the great problems of human life.[9] He was also a friend, or at least genial sparring partner, to such unbelievers as Thomas Huxley, whose presence at the Metaphysical Society he quite enjoyed. Nor did he have any illusions about the quality of Catholic intellectual life. Having taught seminarians at St. Edmund's for seven years (1851–1858), he knew how little prepared they were intellectually. In a letter to Richard Simpson in 1856 he wrote: "I am most deeply convinced that the whole philosophical fabric which occupies our colleges is rotten from the roof to the floor (or rather from the floor to the roof). Nay, no one who has not been mixed up practically in a seminary would imagine to how great an extent it *intellectually debauches* the students' minds."[10] In another letter to Simpson, from 1858, Ward wrote that "as far as I can see, at the present time, the Catholic world to the Protestant world is in much the same relation as barbarians to civilized men."[11] And while there is more than a little exaggeration in these comments, there can be no doubt that years of isolation from English cultural life had left Catholics backward in comparison with their Protestant neighbors, who had access to the great universities. But, more than anything else, it was his father's example that showed Wilfrid that thought did not necessarily dissolve belief, and that faith could meet intellectually with unbelief on an equal footing.[12] It was this very confi-

9. For W. G. Ward's involvement in the Metaphysical Society, see Wilfrid Ward, *William George Ward and the Catholic Revival* (London: Macmillan, 1893), 296–318. For the Metaphysical Society, see Alan Brown, *The Metaphysical Society* (New York: Columbia University Press, 1947).

10. Quoted in Francis Aidan Gasquet, *Lord Acton and His Circle* (New York: Longmans, Green, 1906), xxxvii.

11. Ibid., 37n.

12. *Wilfrid Wards* 1:43–44.

dence which led him to the creation of the Synthetic Society (1896–1910), a newer and, he hoped, more constructive version of his father's Metaphysical Society.[13]

A deeply religious upbringing can be cramped and inhumanly austere, and the life described by Sir Edmund Gosse in his autobiographical *Father and Son* (1907) comes immediately to mind as such an example. But Catholicism is an incarnational religion that affirms as well as denies, and W. G. Ward, with his love of French plays and Italian opera, was no puritan or philistine. Wilfrid's childhood, though narrow, was happy and secure. It was this very security in the faith, he thought, which made for his later large-mindedness.

> Anxiety about the fundamentals of faith leads some persons to be nervous of relinquishing any beliefs hitherto entertained—lest it may prove the first step towards a more general denial. When one has no doubt that in fundamentals one is right and secure, one shrinks the less from complete candour. One does not tremble lest to face a new fact may mean to dissolve one's faith. This feeling of perfect security was engendered by the nature of our life as children. Thus in a sense the very narrowness of my early training told for breadth in the long run—because the narrowness meant the exclusiveness which gives depth and stability to belief.[14]

But if it was his father's example that confirmed his faith both in Catholicism and the life of the mind, it was his father's sometime foe, Cardinal Newman, who supplied him with the manner and the themes of such a life.[15] While Wilfrid was also greatly influenced by Baron von Hügel, particularly in his younger days, this identification was never as complete, and over time they drifted apart intellectually.[16] Newman remained Ward's intellectual guide to the end of his days.

But, along with the disadvantages already mentioned, Wilfrid also had certain advantages. Son of one of the most important figures in the English Catholic intellectual world, by his marriage to Josephine Hope (1864–1932), niece of the 15th Duke of Norfolk, he was connected to the leader of the

13. For Ward's involvement in the Synthetic Society, see ibid., 344–79, and *Wilfrid Wards* 2:412–17. In Appendix B of the former, 417–20, can be found the rules and a nearly complete membership list of the Synthetic Society.

14. *Wilfrid Wards* 1:35.

15. See Sheridan Gilley, "An Intellectual Discipleship: Newman and the Making of Wilfrid Ward," *Louvain Studies* 15 (1990): 318–45.

16. See Jo Ann Eigelsbach, "The Intellectual Dialogue of Friedrich von Hügel and Wilfrid Ward," *Downside Review* 104 (July 1986): 144–57.

Catholic laity and one of England's leading peers.[17] Through his father, especially while writing his father's biography, he came into contact with many of the major figures of English life. Well connected and of independent means, with leisure to read, think, write, and meet people, blessed with a sincere and sympathetic personality, a keen intelligence, and the ability to enter other men's minds, he soon expanded the list of his friends and acquaintances. Ward inhabited a world where it would not have been out of place for him to breakfast with Hutton, the influential editor of the *Spectator,* lunch with Ruskin, spend the weekend in Oxford with Jowett, and go out on long walks with Tennyson.[18] While some of this was due to the stratified nature of English society and the relative smallness of its upper class, it was primarily due to Ward's personal and intellectual gifts. An elderly Catholic lady was once shocked to find on Mrs. Ward's table photos of the Anglican R. W. Church, the well-known dean of St. Paul's, and the agnostic Thomas Huxley, the "Pope of Science." She should not have been. While Ward's religion was certainly of no help in this world, where anti-Catholicism was far from dead, religious belief was of less significance than social and personal connections.

While Ward was open and sympathetic to all the world had to offer, he was not uncritical in his acceptance. His liberalism (and he resented being called a Liberal Catholic) was always of a rather conservative kind, and among his associates in this program of "mediating liberalism," such as Fr. George Tyrrell, S.J. (1861–1909) and Baron Friedrich von Hügel (1852–1925), he was always the least adventurous.[19] Like his father, his mind was firmly grounded in dogma and first principles; he disliked flabbiness and muddled thinking and was

17. When Josephine Hope's father, James Hope-Scott, died in 1873, her mother, Lady Victoria Howard, already being dead, Josephine was raised by her grandmother, the Dowager Duchess of Norfolk. "Uncle Henry," the 15th Duke, remained close to her and her family. See *Wilfrid Wards* 1:130–56.

18. Tennyson was a friend of his father's from the Metaphysical and Wilfrid's neighbor on the Isle of Wight. Richard Holt Hutton (1826–1897) was an important guide in Wilfrid's early career. Ward wrote of him and his *Spectator:* "It is very rare that a weekly journal should be the *medium* whereby a great thinker and spiritual leader exercises his power over his generation. It was so in Hutton's case. Much of the influence on human lives which a great teacher of philosophy exercises in a university, or a great preacher from his pulpit, was exerted week by week by Richard Hutton in *The Spectator* for the space of thirty-five years on a large number of English readers." See Wilfrid Ward, "Three Notable Editors: Delane, Hutton, Knowles," *Dublin Review* (July 1908): 168.

19. For Tyrrell, see David G. Schultenover, *George Tyrrell: In Search of Catholicism* (Shepherdstown, W.Va.: Patmos Press, 1981). For von Hügel, see Lawrence Barmann, *Baron Friedrich von Hügel and the Modernist Crisis in England* (Cambridge: Cambridge University Press, 1972); and

unmoved by sentimentality and emotionalism. While he appreciated the achievements of the nineteenth century, with its expansion and development of all the sciences, the accumulation and classification of facts, the application of the scientific method to the whole spectrum of human life and the concomitant development of new specialized fields of study, he could also be skeptical of them.[20] In an 1890 article in the *Nineteenth Century,* "New Wine in Old Bottles," he used the example from Mark 2:22 of the folly of putting new wine into old bottles to criticize the attempt to synthesize Christian belief with modern science too quickly.[21] While Ward did not ignore the great boons and advances that science had presented to mankind, he was leery of the exaggerations this explosion of knowledge had made possible.

> We hear a good deal in the present day of the love of truth which animates the explorers of physical or historical science; and those who do not unreservedly sympathise with them are said to be indifferent to truth—or even to be its enemies. It is perhaps worth while to remind ourselves that truths may be lost as well as gained; that there are old truths to preserve as well as new truths to learn; that scientific discovery is concerned only with new truth; that though all truth is intrinsically consistent, it may not always appear so in the course of its attainment; and that at a given stage a too exclusive concentration on steps towards new truth may obscure for the individual mind its perception of truths already possessed.[22]

Ward cautioned that it was the nature of great intellectual movements to exaggerate their own importance and belittle what had come before them. Therefore, it was important that this pursuit of novelty should not endanger what was already gained. Though time would prune away the excesses of these enthusiasms, removing what was fallacious and restoring what was of permanent value, many things were too important to wait for future generations to achieve, the truths of religion and all that they entailed being one of them. He saw this most clearly in the various modern attempts to find a *modus vivendi* between Christianity and modern science, where, it seemed, that Christianity was clearly the loser. "The new wine has been poured bodily into the old bottles, and the bottles have burst forthwith." The result was usu-

---

Thomas Michael Loome, *Liberal Catholicism, Reform Catholicism, Modernism: A Contribution to a New Orientation in Modernist Research* (Mainz: Matthias-Grünewald Verlag, 1979), 123–92.

20. For Ward's final view of the nineteenth century, see "The Time-Spirit of the Nineteenth Century," in *Problems and Persons* (London: Longmans, Green, 1903), 1–65.

21. Wilfrid Ward, "New Wine in Old Bottles," *Nineteenth Century* 27 (June 1890): 942–56, reprinted in *Witnesses to the Unseen and Other Essays* (London: Macmillan, 1893), 68–97.

22. Ibid., 68–69.

ally a watered-down Christianity of the *Robert Elsmere* variety. Robert Elsmere, the main character of the 1888 best-selling novel by Mrs. Humphry Ward, was an Anglican cleric whose orthodox Christian belief, destroyed by the modern science of biblical criticism, had been transformed into a new religious synthesis of theism and social concern. For Ward such a capitulation to modern science was not acceptable. While the difficulties of individual believers were genuine and should be taken seriously, doubt over the accuracy and stability of ever-growing, ever-changing scientific opinion was also valid. Neither had said its last, so patience had to be the watchword; nor could any precipitate unity be attempted. "Let the two be kept apart until the new is ripe for assimilation with the old."[23]

Ward thought that in the churches that had no living voice of authority, no tribunal of judgment, the voice of the expert or scholar would prevail. The recent (1889) publication of *Lux Mundi* by a new generation of High Church Oxford dons, the most eminent being the future Anglican bishop of Oxford, Charles Gore (1853–1932), was a good example of this.[24] "A book with the weight attaching to *Lux Mundi,* from the ability and position of its writers, is as near an approach to an *ex cathedra* decision as to what are within the limits of Anglican orthodoxy as the case admits." Ward had the greatest respect for the seriousness and high intellectual attainments of the *Lux Mundi* theologians, and he was well aware that it was written for just such troubled consciences; but such a voice, having no internal principle of recovery, tended to

23. Ibid., 73, 70. For *Robert Elsmere,* see William S. Peterson, *Victorian Heretic: Mrs Humphry Ward's Robert Elsmere* (Leicester: Leicester University Press, 1976); and Bernard Lightman, "*Robert Elsmere* and the Agnostic Crises of Faith," in *Victorian Faith in Crisis: Essays on Continuity and Change in Nineteenth-Century Religious Belief,* ed. Richard J. Helmstader and Bernard Lightman (Stanford: Stanford University Press, 1990), 283–311. For Mrs. Humphry Ward's life, see John Sutherland, *Mrs Humphry Ward: Eminent Victorian, Pre-eminent Edwardian* (Oxford: Clarendon Press, 1990).

24. In a letter to Ward about the article, sent through his aide, Fr. Neville, Newman wrote, "I think the argument of Lux Mundi is in substance the old story of Private Judgment." And, according to Neville, Newman remarked of the book: "It is the end of Tractarianism. They have given up everything." See Newman, *The Letters and Diaries of John Henry Newman,* ed. C. S. Dessain and Thomas Gornall (Oxford: Clarendon Press, 1977), 31:294. Ward remembers him as being more divided in his views: sympathetic to the attempt to deal with real needs but dreading that this would let in rationalism. See *Wilfrid Wards* 1:182–83. For a discussion of Gore and this new Tractarianism, see James Carpenter, *Gore: A Study in Liberal Catholic Thought* (London: Faith Press, 1960); Peter Hinchliff, *God and History: Aspects of British Theology, 1875–1914* (Oxford: Clarendon Press, 1992), 99–121; and Aidan Nichols, *The Panther and the Hind: A Theological History of Anglicanism* (Edinburgh: T. & T. Clark, 1993), 130–46.

be seen as final, and was prone to follow whatever was dominant at the moment, "the tyranny of the Zeitgeist." There had to be something for the individual conscience in difficulty which did not at the same time commit the faith to what was particular and provisional. In Ward's judgment, Catholic pastoral practice and Church history supplied examples of just this sort of thing. Just as the confessor applied the Church's universal principles to a particular case, so theologians did the same in answer to new questions. "So the individual teacher looks at the analogies in Church history and at the general principles laid down by theologians, and to their treatment of similar cases, and decides to the best of his power what is tenable by a Catholic with respect to a new scientific hypothesis; but he does not and cannot commit the Church to the conclusion he draws except so far as he may say he thinks it is the true conclusion." Precluding an authoritative judgment, a variety of opinions was possible. "While her caution protects her against those whims of the Zeitgeist which prematurely claim the title of discoveries, the activity of her life enables her *in the end* to find a *modus vivendi* with what is really valuable in intellectual movements, or really true in scientific achievement."[25]

It was a difficult task because it was not always clear what was essential and what not. Also, there was the danger that this process might lead to a loss of faith, especially by the multitude who were not prepared to distinguish in the traditional interpretation what was accidental and what was essential. Ward heartily agreed with Newman's dictum that truth often appeared as error to those who were unprepared for it. Sometimes, for their sake, repression was necessary. "The primary duty of protecting religious belief in the mass of Christian souls may have called for a check on the propagation of an imperfectly ascertained discovery for which the minds of the faithful were unprepared, and which seemed to impugn the authority of Holy Scripture."[26] The general movement of the Church was one first of prudential condemnation, then of assimilation. The acceptance of Aristotle was a perfect example of this. The dangerous rationalism inherent in Aristotle was at first condemned, then accepted only in stages, and finally absorbed by St. Thomas Aquinas. "Years had passed, and the details of Aristotelianism had been discussed and weighed in the academic circles of the *Schola Theologorum.* Albert the Great and Alexander of Hales had adopted such of its principles as were consistent with

25. Ward, "New Wine in Old Bottles," 90, 82, 83.
26. Ibid., 86.

Christianity, and interwoven them with the ethics of the Fathers, texts of Holy Scripture, and the decisions of Church authority. In this new garb and surrounded with these new associations and safeguards, the condemned *Metaphysics* lost their terrible character."[27]

Rome could be patient because she was eternal. Time was on her side, and time would smooth out the difficulties and create a new synthesis. It was a difficult process, tentative, with much to-ing and fro-ing, an advance here, a setback there; but through it all further analysis and development went on, and discussion clarified the hypotheses. "Thus when finally the truth emerges with scientific certainty, a double office has been performed—minds have been familiarised with an hypothesis, and prepared for its reconciliation with Christian teaching should it prove true, and at the same time positive assent on the part of the Church herself has been withheld to what may after all prove to some extent false." The Church's manner was ever cautious: "It combines readiness to consider the working of every possible hypothesis with great slowness in ultimate decision on its limits or on its truth at all."[28]

In a later piece Ward would call this double activity of resistance and assimilation "the conservative principle of the Church."[29] Authentic conservatism could not be purely negative, a mere resistance to innovation, but must also have a constructive and adaptable side. "To preserve a building we must indeed resist those who would pull it down. But we must also repair it, replace what is worn out by what is new, and fit it to last in the varying conditions of life. True conservatism involves constructive activity as well as resistance to destructive activity. Periodical reform and reconstruction belong to its very essence."[30]

The task of resistance was the work of authority; the task of assimilation was primarily the work of individuals whose work the Church would ratify if it proved successful. This was a difficult process, but it was made even more difficult by the fact that various historical circumstances had moved the Church into a purely defensive position. The intellectual adaptability characteristic of the Church in earlier centuries had been lost in the need to defend herself at the Reformation. And this defensive posture, which Ward called

27. Ibid., 89.

28. Ibid., 93, 94.

29. Wilfrid Ward, "The Conservative Genius of the Church: An Address to the Catholic Conference of 1900," published in *Men and Matters* (London: Longmans, Green, 1914), 301–18.

30. Ibid., 304.

"the state of siege" in his essay "The Rigidity of Rome," had not been lost in the intervening centuries, despite the changing environment.[31]

In the time of siege, court-martial supersedes trial by jury; the cultivation of the arts is less important than the training of good soldiers; the workmen who had been occupied in building museums and lecture halls are drawn off to repair fortifications, which, though indispensable for preserving the city, are useless for the general culture of its citizens. The length of the siege is likely to be the measure of the completeness of the transformation from the industrial and peaceful to the military state, of the concentration of all forces in the city on its defence, and of the neglect of those merely intellectual or artistic or scientific pursuits which make a full and refined life.[32]

Rome's very adaptability had led to her rigidity. Ward believed that the state of siege should come to an end, and that the polemical and apologetical mind that had been necessary at the time of the Reformation had to be abandoned. First, because it distorted the full nature of Christian revelation, and its attractiveness. Second, because it was no longer necessary. The battle was no longer between Protestant and Catholic, but between religion and infidelity. "When we see around us a civilization in which belief in theism and immortality is becoming perilously weak and vague, in which Christian education is threatened, in which a positive caricature of forces destructive of social order shows itself in Anarchism and Nihilism, there is surely enough for all lovers of religion to work for together, while they agree to differ on further questions, pending, at all events, the arrival of that calmer and more sympathetic temper which would make discussion more fruitful."[33]

In any case, the conflict was less necessary because even in the Protestant world there had been a movement toward Catholic ideals and principles (which the Catholic Church had preserved alone these many centuries), the Oxford Movement being only one aspect of a general Catholic revival throughout Europe and America. While reunion was now not possible, it might not always be so as cooperation and understanding developed, and as what was temporary and exceptional, owing to the state of siege, was abandoned. Only then would Roman claims be taken seriously. Only then would Rome's exclusiveness, in both her rigidity and her adaptability, be appreciated.

To Ward's mind the world needed the Church, and this was most suc-

31. Wilfrid Ward, "The Rigidity of Rome," *Nineteenth Century* 38 (Dec. 1895): 786–804, republished in *Problems and Persons,* 66–98.

32. Ibid., 76.

33. Ibid., 96.

cinctly and powerfully described in the epilogue to his biography of Cardinal Wiseman, "The Exclusive Church and the Zeitgeist." There, reiterating the themes seen earlier concerning the twofold nature of the Church to be both exclusive and inclusive, to resist all that is opposed to its supernatural nature and to conciliate and assimilate all that was good and true outside herself, he ended with this little reverie:

> Our own countryman, Roger Bacon, was the first to suggest a beautiful medieval dream, of a golden age in religion. Papa Angelico, the ideal pope, was to come some day—a pope of wisdom and of holiness. He was to heal schisms, to encourage science, to win all peoples to trust in his comprehensive wisdom and respect for his beneficent authority. He was to be a pope of "peace," but not of the "peace" of indifferentism or sentimentalism. His was to be a reign of wise and tolerant rule on the one part, and of grateful obedience on the other.
>
> A century of revolution has done something towards renewing medieval dreams. We have not seen the end of the revival of the Romantic School of Novalis, the Schlegels and Chateaubriand. Will Europe ever again pray for a Papa Angelico?[34]

Was the reigning pontiff, Leo XIII, this ideal ruler, this Papa Angelico? Certainly, in many ways he was. While he continued the ban on allowing Italian Catholics to be involved in the new Italy, his conciliatory policy did achieve an end to the *Kulturkampf* in Germany; and his failure to rally French Catholics to the Third Republic (the *ralliement*) was due more to the intransigence of others than to any lack of adaptability in himself. He approved and encouraged the very successful International Scientific Congresses started by Mgr. d'Hulst to which Ward so often referred in his articles. He opened the Vatican Archives to scholars and elevated such scholars as Hergenröther and Newman to the Sacred College. Most important of all, perhaps, he promoted the revival of scholastic philosophy with *Aeterni Patris* (1879).[35]

34. Wilfrid Ward, *The Life and Times of Cardinal Wiseman* (London: Longmans, Green, 1897), 2:582–83. In a letter that Wilfrid wrote his son Leo (c. 1915) he admitted that this epilogue had little to do with Wiseman: "the introduction of Wiseman's name is mere Jesuitry, the thoughts which fill the bulk of the epilogue are totally outside Wiseman's purview." Quoted in Mary Jo Weaver, ed., *Letters from a "Modernist": The Letters of George Tyrrell to Wilfrid Ward, 1893–1908* (Shepherdstown, W.Va.: Patmos Press, 1981), 6n2. The idea of Catholicism and the papacy leading modern European society was not as strange as it might seem at first sight. A number of secular English thinkers, seeing the amazing resilience of institutional religion and the growth of Catholicism and Anglo-Catholicism, feared that just such a thing might come to pass. See Jeffrey Paul von Arx, *Progress and Pessimism: Religion, Politics, and History in Late Nineteenth-Century Britain* (Cambridge: Harvard University Press, 1985).

35. For the revival of scholasticism, see Gerald A. McCool, *Catholic Theology in the Nineteenth*

As a seminarian Ward had not been impressed by the scholasticism he experienced; and certainly those who were most opposed to current intellectual trends usually were so from a rigid scholastic position, often contemptuous of other approaches and seeing no need for any other. Ward believed that scholasticism was not enough. He appealed for a "medicinal philosophy" that was in contact with modern trends, as well as a purely scholastic one.[36] Since the language and principles of scholasticism, however good in themselves, were not attractive or understandable to many in a world "infected" by the unhealthy intellectual atmosphere of the age, something else was needed, a different kind of philosophy. The purpose of such a philosophy was not to take the place of scholasticism but to prepare minds for the traditional works of the Fathers and the great scholastics. "No one can feed on medicine. Medicine prepares the organs to receive nourishment; but it cannot nourish itself."[37] He also believed that scholasticism could not turn in upon itself, becoming merely a timid "archaeological study," but had to adapt itself to contemporary concerns and thought.[38]

Ward was to write many years later that Pope Leo XIII was not "a Liberal Pope," either in his theories or in his temper of mind. "Sanguine and conciliating in method, indeed, he was. Liberalistic or confident in the tendencies of the age he was not." Ward did not think that Leo really believed in free discus-

Century: The Quest for a Unitary Method (New York: Seabury Press, 1977), reprinted as *Nineteenth Century Scholasticism: The Quest for a Unitary Method* (New York: Fordham University Press, 1989).

36. Wilfrid Ward, "The Healing Art in Philosophy," *Dublin Review* (Jan. 1885): 30–49.

37. Ibid., 49.

38. Wilfrid Ward, "The Scholastic Movement and Catholic Philosophy," *Dublin Review* (April 1891): 255–71. "St. Thomas's example in this matter should teach Catholic writers not to give their chief attention to questions foreign to contemporary thought, but to questions which occupy the mind of the age; not to adhere jealously to phrases and forms of the past, but to be ready, as he was, to assimilate modes of speaking and thinking which we find in use, clothing old principles if needs be in a new dress; not to be shy of great thinkers, because they are not Catholics or even Christians, but to treat them in that calm, kindly, candid, and philosophical spirit in which he and his greatest fellow-scholastics treated Aristotle, Plato, Avicenna, and Maimonides; not to fear a great thought, or a happy solution of a contemporary controversy, because the thinker who first expressed it was not a Catholic; not to hesitate, if philosophy is our vocation, to study fully, carefully, dispassionately all sides of crucial problems and discussions; to be quite prepared to find a great movement of modern thought outside the Church as compatible with the faith which is handed down to us as portions of the philosophy of the Neo-Platonists were with the teaching of St. Augustine, and the essential features of Aristotelianism with that of St. Thomas; not to view tentative expressions of even the greatest Catholic thinkers as final analyses of philosophical truth" (270–71).

sion or untrammeled criticism in either history or biblical research, but that he was only pragmatically liberal. "But the wisdom of the statesman, who knows that to rule effectively the ruler must often tolerate what he does not approve, that you must be conciliatory and considerate if you hope to win conciliation and consideration—these are the essence of Pope Leo's policy."[39]

Ward's hope for reconciliation depended on the continuation of these policies of openness, but his hopeful confidence in authority was weakened throughout the 1890s because of a series of actions by the Roman authorities that did not bode well for broader views. In 1893 the relatively conservative encyclical on biblical studies, *Providentissimus Deus,* appeared. Then in 1899 there was the condemnation of "Americanism" for its excessive adaptation of the faith to modern American tastes.[40] And, finally, there was a series of actions against the idea of human evolution, which, excluding the origins of the human soul, had been an open question among Catholics throughout the nineteenth century.

Earlier in the century the eminent English zoologist and Catholic convert St. George Jackson Mivart (1827–1900) had worked to reconcile evolution with Catholic belief and had achieved some success, winning the praise of the Catholic press and theologians, and even being awarded a doctorate from Pope Pius IX in 1876.[41] While an evolutionist, he was not a Darwinian, and it was his criticisms that caused Darwin and Huxley the greatest trouble. Others followed him, of which the most significant were the French Dominican theologian M.-D. Leroy and the American scientist and Notre Dame professor John Augustine Zahm (1851–1921).[42] Leroy had published *Evolution des espèces organique* in 1887, with a second edition entitled *L'Evolution restreinte aux espèces organiques* in 1891; and Zahm had published *Evolution and Dogma* in 1896. Both defended Mivart's theories. Zahm's book became an international best-seller and was soon translated into Italian.

39. Wilfrid Ward, "Leo XIII," in *Ten Personal Studies* (London: Longmans, Green, 1908), 192–93.

40. See Thomas Timothy McAvoy, *The Americanist Heresy in Roman Catholicism, 1895–1900* (Notre Dame: University of Notre Dame Press, 1963).

41. See Jacob W. Gruber, *A Conscience in Conflict: A Life of St. George Jackson Mivart* (New York: Columbia University Press, 1960).

42. For Zahm, see Ralph Weber, *Notre Dame's John Zahm: American Catholic Apologist and Educator* (Notre Dame: University of Notre Dame Press, 1961); and R. Scott Appleby, *"Church and Age Unite": The Modernist Impulse in American Catholicism* (Notre Dame: University of Notre Dame Press, 1992), 13–52.

The attack on Catholic evolutionism only generally became known in January 1899 when the Jesuit *La Civiltà Cattolica,* an influential Roman newspaper with close ties to the Holy See, attacked a *Dublin Review* article by Bishop Cuthbert Hedley of Newport that had favorably reviewed Zahm's book.[43] Hedley, a former editor of the *Dublin Review* and a highly respected theologian among the English bishops, had been an early defender of attempts to reconcile Catholicism and evolution, his article "Evolution and Faith," in the July 1871 issue of the *Dublin,* being an impressive and judicious handling of the topic.[44] The *Civiltà* article also revealed that earlier (1895) Leroy had been called to Rome and that his thesis on the compatibility of man's bodily evolution with Catholic belief had been secretly judged "untenable" by "competent authority." Leroy had made a public retraction in a letter in *Le Monde* (March 4, 1895), but it seems to have escaped the attention of many, including Bishop Hedley. In a letter to the *Tablet* (January 11, 1899), Hedley guessed that the "competent authority" must have been the Holy Office and stated that "the 'Mivartian' theory, therefore, can no longer be sustained."[45] Later, in 1902, in a letter to written to the Anglican Rev. Spencer Jones that was published in many journals, Catholic and other, Hedley challenged the accuracy of the *Civiltà* on the Leroy case, and denied that there had been any condemnation of him by the Holy See or any tribunal of it, since there was no public act. In April 1902, and very obviously working from greater knowledge of the case than Hedley, the *Civiltà* made clear that he was wrong, that the Holy Office had indeed condemned Leroy and that if Hedley would just write to that "competent authority" he would find out, though perhaps only confidentially, that this was the case.

Leroy was quietly condemned in 1895 and he removed his book from publication. In September 1898 the Congregation of the Index secretly banned Zahm's book and he also removed his book from publication. Zahm's letter (May 16, 1899) asking his Italian translator to withdraw the book on the orders of the Holy See appeared in the *Gazzetta di Malta* (May 31, 1899) and was reprinted in full by the *Civiltà* on July 1. In neither case was there any

43. Hedley's article, "Physical Science and Faith," appeared in October 1898. For Hedley's life, see J. Anselm Wilson, *The Life of Bishop Hedley* (New York: P. J. Kennedy, 1930).

44. The article was reprinted in *Evolution and Faith, with Other Essays* (London: Sheed and Ward, 1931), 1–56. For Hedley on this topic, see ibid., xiii–xxvii, and Wilson, *Life of Bishop Hedley,* 169–72, 179–80, 211–12.

45. For the full text of the letter, see Wilson, *Life of Bishop Hedley,* 170–71.

public act that could point to an official condemnation. Recent research in the now open archives of the old Holy Office (at present called the Congregation for the Doctrine of the Faith) makes a very strong case for the direct involvement of the *Civiltà Cattolica* in the condemnation of both.[46] It also points to why a public condemnation of Catholic evolutionism was thought inopportune: their fear of rousing the opposition of many "weighty" theologians who would have not supported them in this.

These actions by the Roman authorities led to a series of articles and letters to the editor in the next year and a half, mostly critical of the Holy See, that would end only with the publication of the English bishops' Joint Pastoral condemning Liberal Catholicism. One such critic was William Gibson, who, in an article in the *Nineteenth Century,* strongly attacked the Vatican for its obscurantism and foresaw new curial acts of aggression.[47]

Ward wrote a reply to this article in the same journal that, while it did answer many of the arguments made by Gibson, was primarily an attack on his method. "If the theologians are told that the whole authorised theological system is absurd from the standpoint of modern science and criticism, they may be excused if they are slow to believe, from *their* standpoint, that it is worth their while seriously to consider science or criticism of so aggressive and controversial a character." Gibson's tone and absurd demands made it impossible even for the experts (which Ward made clear Gibson was not) to be allowed

46. See Barry Brundell, "Catholic Church Politics and Evolution Theory, 1894–1902," *British Journal for the History of Science* 34 (March 2001): 81–95.

47. William Gibson, "An Outburst of Activity in the Roman Congregations," *Nineteenth Century* (May 1899): 785–94. Gibson (1868–1942), from 1913 2nd Lord Ashbourne, was the author of *The Abbé de Lamennais and the Liberal Catholic Movement in France* (London: Longmans, Green, 1896), converted to Catholicism on Comtist principles while at Oxford, and became a good friend to Ward despite their great differences. See *Wilfrid Wards* 2:21, 121–24. Merry del Val, in a letter to Ward (June 5, 1899), wrote: "Gibson, of course, is only a *minimal* Catholic, and no loyal son of the Church can sympathise with and much less accept his principles, his utterances or his attitude. One can't help wondering what he is doing in the Church even *nominally;* it would be more honest and more consistent were he to sever the outward link. There exists unfortunately in England as well as in France, Germany, the United States and even here a group of traitors in the camp and it would be better were they quickly to go 'out from us' for they are 'not of us' 'that they may be *manifest* that they are not all of us.' Gibson found one day that he was a Catholic; perhaps if he examines things a little more closely he will find that he is not one. He seems to be walking thro' the Church on his way elsewhere, like people walk to and fro thro' S. Stefan's Cathedral in Vienna, going in by one door and out by the other to make a short cut. It is much to be regretted that some Catholics, unwittingly I dare say in many cases, countenance men like Gibson and play with their ideas. They appear to be attracted by the glamour and popularity of appearing what is so vaguely described as *broad* mindedness." See WWP VII/205a (3).

the provisional intellectual liberty which was as necessary as the "wise conservatism" of authority. "We are slow to allow liberty to those who abuse it."[48]

But this was just the beginning. In the opening months of 1900 a far more significant event occurred that would rock the Church: the excommunication of Mivart.[49] While Mivart had been lauded in the 1870s, in the 1880s he had begun to move away from traditional Catholic positions, particularly in the area of Scripture interpretation and in his attempts to reconcile science with religion. In 1893 his articles on hell (where he defended an ameliorative hell) were condemned by the Holy Office and put on the Index. He submitted, though without changing his opinions or retracting what he had written, seeing his submission rather as a matter of obedience than as a matter of faith, and remained publicly quiet. However, shocked by the Dreyfus Affair in France, inspired by Gibson's article, realizing that he did not have long to live, and, finally, seeing that his name remained in the new edition of the Index, Mivart publicly attacked Church authority and traditional views of Catholic doctrine in letters to the *Times* and in articles published in respected secular journals, the ferocity and extremism of which surprised even his closest friends and supporters.[50] As Mivart's biographer Gruber has pointed out, by these articles Mivart "was no longer a Catholic critic; he had become a critic of Catholicism."[51]

The main focus of his attacks was the Roman Curia (and its mindset "Curialism") which he thought corrupt and unscrupulous, willing to use any deceit to gain power over "weak, credulous minds and tenderly scrupulous consciences." The tone was bitter and mocking, full of righteous indignation. But it was not only the Curia, with its "broken teeth" and "blunted claws," that was the object of his scorn; its apologists also were to blame, especially Wilfrid Ward.[52] It was a challenge that Ward could not ignore, especially as others

48. Wilfrid Ward, "Catholic Apologetics: A Reply," *Nineteenth Century* (June 1899): 959, 956. In a letter to Ward (June 1, 1899) Gibson wrote that he had no disagreement with the Church or Catholic apologetics per se but that he was worried over recent Vatican policy, and that he was pleased with Ward's article, for, though it criticized his article, it had made such a strong protest against unwise Church interference. See WWP VII/121/5.

49. See John D. Root, "The Final Apostasy of St. George Jackson Mivart," *Catholic Historical Review* 71 (Jan. 1985): 1–25; and Paschal Scotti, "Happiness in Hell: The Case of Dr Mivart," *Downside Review* 119 (July 2001): 177–90.

50. Mivart's articles were "The Continuity of Catholicism," *Nineteenth Century* (Jan. 1900): 51–72, and "Some Recent Catholic Apologists," *Fortnightly Review* (Jan. 1900): 24–44.

51. Gruber, *Conscience in Conflict*, 198.

52. Mivart, "Some Recent Catholic Apologists," 24–44, where Mivart, among others, attacked

soon became involved who associated "Liberal Catholicism" with ideas far too extreme for Ward and his friends.[53] In reply to Mivart's theological points Ward wrote his essay "Unchanging Dogma and Changeful Man," while in response to the other Catholic critics he wrote "Liberalism and Intransigeance."[54]

For Ward, Mivart's failure was primarily a failure of imagination. First, Mivart had an inability to see into other minds and understand their reasonings and that they had real points to make. Second, Mivart could not see that dogmas were not exhaustive expressions of reality. So for him all change must be a change in essence, a transformation, not a development. Finally, this lack of imagination was manifest in his distaste for the technical vocabulary of theology and its subtleties. Every attempt by Catholic theologians to defend and explicate official statements he could only see as duplicitous, an explaining away rather than an explanation. Ward thought his mind, in its ahistorical theological and philosophical reasoning, was "purely, almost touchingly medieval." This last point was remarkably similar to von Hügel's opinion: he also saw a remarkable similarity in tone and method between Mivart and his neo-scholastic opponents.[55]

Mivart claimed that radical dogmatic change had occurred, and would

---

Ward's reply to Gibson ("Catholic Apologetics: A Reply"), and an unsigned Ward article, "The Ethics of Religious Conformity," *Quarterly Review* (Jan. 1899): 103–36. In a letter to Ward, Tyrrell wrote (Feb. 4, 1900): "I fear now that Mivart will throw everything back at least a decade unless reasonable people combine in some way to keep up a steady stream of healthy literature. . . . so the ark must pass into the hands of the Philistines for the present." See Weaver, *Letters from a "Modernist,"* 25.

53. Among the many articles by Catholics calling for adaptation of Church teaching were Robert Dell, "A Liberal Catholic View of the Case of Dr. Mivart," *Nineteenth Century* 47 (April 1900): 669–84, and "Mr. Wilfrid Ward's Apologetics," ibid., 48 (July 1900): 127–36; two articles in the *Contemporary Review* by Fidelis [Dell], "A Convert's Experiences of the Catholic Church," 77 (June 1900): 817–34, and "The Movement for Reform within the Catholic Church," 78 (Nov. 1900): 693–709. Robert Edward Dell (1865–1940), a journalist and convert to Catholicism, was editor of the liberal Catholic *Weekly Register* (April to September 1899) and a highly intemperate proponent of liberal ideas.

54. Wilfrid Ward, "Unchanging Dogma and Changeful Man," *Fortnightly Review* 67 (April 1900): 628–48, reprinted in *Problems and Persons*, 99–132. The later version dropped the introductory material on Galileo. "Liberalism and Intransigeance," *Nineteenth Century* (June 1900), 960–73. In the first footnote Ward did not include Mivart in that number of Catholic critics because his letters "in defence of his articles showed that he was not a Catholic at all."

55. See the letter of von Hügel to Ward, Feb. 8, 1900, quoted in Root, "Final Apostasy," 21: "Two things have particularly struck me,—the close resemblance between the intellectual tone and method, between Mivart and his Neo-Scholastic antagonists."

continue to occur, in conformity with the advancement of the sciences. Seemingly nothing was closed to dramatic reinterpretation, neither the traditional account of Christ's virginal conception and birth nor the traditional account of his resurrection. Mivart catalogued a whole series of areas where significant change had happened and was happening, and all, he believed, were excellent examples of the Church's Catholicity ("which desires all truth, justice, and rational liberty in religion"), which was essential if the Church were to regain the acceptance "of the civilized world and by men of light and leading."[56] As he wrote in an article defending his January articles: "After mature reflection and many struggles, I had come to the conclusion that the Roman Catholic Church must tolerate a transforming process of evolution, with respect to many of its dogmas, or sink, by degrees, into an effete and insignificant body, composed of ignorant persons, a mass of women and children and a number of mentally effeminate men."[57]

Ward thought that Mivart failed to understand how change occurred in the Church, which remained *semper eadem* (always the same). "It was not the Divine revelation which changed. It was man with his equipment for its explication and expression which changed." The process of resistance and assimilation manifested itself over and over again in the Church's history, and would continue to do so. "They are instances of growth in our understanding of what practically follows from, or is involved logically in, dogma; or of increased precision in our discrimination of the essence of dogma from its form; or of the readiness of the Church to express dogmatic truth in the terms supplied by the science or thought of the day; or all of these phenomena." This would certainly affect the belief of Catholics ("We do not now necessarily believe, with St. Thomas or St. Gregory, that hell is in the bowels of the earth"), but it would not necessitate a change in the essence of what was to be believed. ("If the wicked go to hell, it matters little whether hell be in the center of the earth or no.")[58] Mivart could see only duplicity in this explication because he did not realize that all human language and every human concept falls short of the dogmatic reality, and therefore that dogmatic language could not be unequivocal and ultimate in its meaning.

In "Liberalism and Intransigeance" Ward turned to the "Liberal Catholics"

56. Mivart, "Continuity of Catholicism," 72.

57. Mivart, "Roman Congregations and Modern Thought," *North American Review* 170 (April 1900): 571, quoted in Root, "Final Apostasy," 11.

58. Ward, *Problems and Persons,* 104, 106.

who had arisen in the wake of the "Mivart Affair," attacking the "Roman Curia, the Jesuits, the whole Ultramontane party (whatever that may mean), the scholastic system, the temporal power, the Roman Congregations" as all a part of a corrupt system—a system that was "hard to distinguish from the existing Catholic Church." These Catholic writers, these extremists of the left, Ward wrote, with their intemperate and impractical grumbling and violence of expression, with their claims to be "in common cause" with the leading Catholic intellectuals of the period, were only playing into the hands of the extreme right ("the enemies of all change—including the changes which mark off the living being from the fossil"), and they gave the word "liberalism" a bad name, it being a word already "steeped in an anti-Catholic connotation." They tried "to identify their excesses with the programme of the wise—destructive liberalism with the plea for reality and life" just as much as "the extreme right try to identify the programme of the wise with the excesses in question—adaptation to the times with destruction of the faith."[59]

These critics did not try to put themselves in the place of the authorities and understand their situation or appreciate their difficulties, so it was not surprising that they were not taken seriously. The danger was that their criticism would be taken too seriously, not distinguishing them from the true scholars who wished to serve the Church:

> It is all-important that authority should know its own friends. In an age which is pre-eminently one of transition—when new lights on matters scientific, historical, critical; new points of view and new overmastering impulses on matters social, political, philosophical are making their appearance year by year, it is only those few who have made these subjects specially their own, and who, at the same time, have the interests

59. Ward, "Liberalism and Intransigeance," 960, 961, 969. Ward scathingly described the extreme right: "They include certain types not so much of Catholicism as of human nature. They include the mere lovers of the existing state of things. . . . They include also the fanatical devotees of ancient forms and those unable to look beyond the interests of their party or order—not the Dominics and the Loyolas or their true representatives in our own time, but those who fossilise their words and lose their spirit—the Dominican who resents the addition of a word to the teaching of St. Thomas Aquinas; the Jesuit who burlesques the splendid military discipline to which great saints, a Xavier and a Borgia, owed their character and their victories, by attachment to the minutiae of an intellectual drill, whose rules were made for the warfare of three centuries ago. And closely allied to these are the Professors who treat a stereotyped neo-scholastic text-book as the final and exhaustive expression of the teaching of the Catholic Church. There are also the born obscurantists who love to believe the incredible; the martinets whose pleasure it is to crush genius or originality; the petty tyrants who look jealously at promise in the young; the devotees of sheer absolutism—some characterised by heroism and piety, but blind to modern conditions; some the flatterers of the powers that be" (968–69).

of the Church at heart, who can be, in the nature of the case, equal to the situation. They alone have the perceptions and knowledge needed to see how Catholic thought can deal with and assimilate what is sound or true, can effectively resist what is dangerous. They are the natural eyes of those in power. . . . And when the ruling power is really alive to the situation, its first wish is to find such assistants. If on the other hand it is not alive to the situation . . . the Church loses for the time the active principle of intellectual progress. Catholicism may lose touch with the age, and forfeit much of its influence. And this may happen although the Church is not internally corrupt.[60]

No longer, Ward believed, could controversial matters be limited to the few, restricted to the Latin of the learned. All classes could now read, and so it was in the best interest of both Church and State to educate them, creating a moderate, disciplined and responsible public opinion, friendly to authority. They would have to be given some voice and influence (though indirect and unofficial), and since Catholics were at present both zealous and loyal, they could be of great service to the Church. He believed that a repressive policy would not be in the Church's best interests and in fact would be sterile, driving many to more radical positions.

Unfortunately, authority did not always know its friends. Ward had sent a copy of "Liberalism and Intransigeance" to Rafael Merry del Val, the president of the Accademia dei Nobili Ecclesiastici and a rising star in Rome.[61] In a letter of June 17, 1900, to Cardinal Vaughan, Archbishop of Westminster, Merry del Val revealed his negative view of Ward, and also the difficulties that Ward would eventually find.

I do not feel safe with [Ward] . . . I need hardly tell you what I thought of the article when I read it. I was horrified. . . . Moreover, as you say, it is deplorable that he should speak from such a platform. . . . I fancy W.W. will come to grief unless he is humble enough to acknowledge his mistake and allow himself to be taught by the Church instead of trying to be the *"Ecclesia docens"* himself. He will not satisfy the extreme liberals because as yet he does not go far enough, and he falls out with the orthodox feeling by going much too far, and like the *"doctrinaire"* liberals in politics he will fall between two stools or save himself by entirely siding with one or other. . . . In

60. Ibid., 962.

61. Rafael Merry del Val (1865–1930), son of a Spanish diplomat and an English-born mother, educated at Ushaw and the Accademia dei Nobili Ecclesiastici, where select priests were trained for the Vatican's diplomatic service, and ordained for the Archdiocese of Westminster, was very involved in affairs back home. As the secretary of state under Pope Pius X (1903–1914), he would have a profound influence in the modernist crisis. For his life, see Marie Cecilia Buehrle, *Rafael Cardinal Merry del Val* (London: St. Martin's Press, 1957).

some respects I consider W.W.'s action more harmful than Mivart's, because it steadily weakens all the screws and prepares the way for many more Mivarts in the future. It is very insidious and among many converts it does incalculable harm.[62]

Nor were all of Ward's friends entirely happy with his response to Mivart and the other writers. While von Hügel praised "Unchanging Dogma and Changeful Man" in a letter to Ward, he also noticed a certain deficiency in it.

The progress of all science and philosophy necessarily spring from earnestness and enthusiasm, from some keen sense of the defectiveness of an existing position, or some deep instinct or intuition of further or new truth; without heat or passion, no more will be achieved, than without light and self-repression. We must then, somehow, get a general view and tone, which will not only tolerate but will encourage this necessary heat; without drama, conflict, tragedy, life will be correct only to be barren. And so I would want the theory on the whole to sympathise with friction, up to the point when it would no more favour healthy motion, but would clog it. . . . Nothing but a very deep and constantly pressing reason can suffice . . . and this *pressingness* I do not feel in your pages to the extent to which I should like to feel it there.[63]

Neither by temperament nor by conviction was Ward inclined to the necessity of conflict, friction, drama, tragedy, and enthusiasm to achieve growth. He was an instinctual conservative who saw growth as organic, not dialectical. Conflict would arise, and when it did the goal of the individual was to try to resolve it, not push it further till it clogged things. Ward believed that von Hügel did not really appreciate the situation, and judged too indulgently the Liberal Catholics who were disrupting the scene. "I think much the greatest practical difference between us is that you more or less *welcome anything* on the left side though you yourself may not agree with it, while I feel that there is a species of agitation so indiscriminate and unintelligent that it simply injures the cause of progress and justifies the reactionaries."[64]

Mivart's decree of excommunication was published in the *Tablet* on January 21, and he died excluded from the sacraments on April 1, 1900. Because of the enormous amount of attention his case received in the press, Cardinal

62. I have conflated the citations of the letter in Root, "Final Apostasy," 22n113, and J. Derek Holmes, "Cardinal Raphael Merry del Val—An Uncompromising Ultramontane: Gleanings from His Correspondence with England," *Catholic Historical Review* 60 (Jan. 1974): 60–61. See Gary Lease, "Merry del Val and Tyrrell: A Modernist Struggle," *Downside Review* 102 (April 1984): 136–37.

63. Von Hügel to Ward, Feb. 18, 1900, quoted in *Wilfrid Wards* 1:323.

64. Ward to von Hügel, June 28, 1900, quoted ibid., 332. For a good comparison of Ward and von Hügel, see Eigelsbach, "Intellectual Dialogue of von Hügel and Ward."

Vaughan issued a pastoral letter (dated February 22) demanding that Catholic journals follow the Church's lead in all religious matters. Vaughan sought Merry del Val's advice on what was to be done and received the reply that the English bishops should take a stand against the Liberal Catholic movement with a doctrinal pronouncement that, to give it greater weight, would receive public approval from the Holy See. He even offered to have such a document written for him and sent for his approval. On December 29, 1900, the bishops of England and Wales issued "The Church and Liberal Catholicism: A Joint Pastoral Letter." Its principal authors were the Jesuits Salvatore Brandi of *La Civiltà Cattolica* and Thomas A. Hughes, an American working in the Roman Curia. Its origins, however, were kept secret.[65]

The Joint Pastoral, as it stood, was a paean to authority and left no place for the laity, for the expert, or for anyone for that matter, between the small body of bishops who were the teachers (*Ecclesia docens*) and the very large body of everyone else (*Ecclesia discens*), who were to submit their minds and wills to the bishops in matters of religion. According to the bishops the source of the evils afflicting society was the principle of private judgment, with the concomitant idea that "all power and authority in civic, political, and religious matters are ultimately vested in the people" who are therefore the final tribunal in all questions. It was from this infectious idea that Liberal Catholics got the idea that they could publicly discuss Church matters:

> They take leave to discuss theology and the government of the Church with the same freedom of speech and opinions that they are accustomed to use in launching new theories on social science, political economy, art, literature, or any other subject. Being wanting in filial docility and reverence they freely dispose of doctrine, practice, and discipline upon their own responsibility and without the least reference to the mind of the Church or to her ministers. This is to be liberal, indeed—with the rights and the property of another—with the sacred prerogatives of Christ and His Church. It is the exercise of liberality of this counterfeit sort that characterises what is known as "the liberal Catholic."[66]

The proclamation of true doctrine by the Church was not exercised "because specialists in divinity, philosophy or the natural sciences have been con-

65. The Joint Pastoral was published in the *Tablet* 62 (Jan. 5 and 12, 1901): 8–12, 50–52. It can be more conveniently read in Weaver, *Letters from a "Modernist,"* Appendix B, 131–57. The letter of congratulations from Pope Leo was published in the *Tablet* (March 23, 1901): 441. For the background to the pastoral, see David G. Schultenover, *A View from Rome: On the Eve of the Modernist Crisis* (New York: Fordham University Press, 1993), 131–58.

66. Weaver, *Letters from a "Modernist,"* 132, 133.

sulted, or have lent their assistance" but belonged to her by divine right, and it was the duty of the bishops to exercise this right. "The Church indeed may encourage even the faithful laity to write, and lecture upon matters relating to religion, when she sees that they are fit to serve her in these ways; not, however, in their own right, but in strict subordination to her authority." The key virtues for the laity could only be humility and obedience.[67]

The Joint Pastoral attacked many other theories "advanced in the name of science, criticism and modern progress" in reference to the immutability of doctrine and its development, to Church government, and to the respect given to Church decisions and censures, including those of the Roman congregations, many of which Ward would also have attacked. There was much that Ward agreed with and had even spoken about himself, such as the tendency to give excessive credence to scholars because they are scholars, even to the detriment of the faith. "The bold assertions of men of science are received with awe and bated breath; the criticisms of an intellectual group of *savants* are quoted as though they were rules for a good life, while the mind of the Church and her guidance are barely spoken of with ordinary patience."[68] But he also had respect for intellectuals and was aware of the genuine difficulties that these thinkers were trying to resolve. The Joint Pastoral clearly did not.

Ward was very disturbed by all this. What disturbed him most were not the things it said but all the things the Joint Pastoral did not say, and the negative and discouraging tone, especially for those who wished to use their talents in the service of the Church. Also, it made it seem that there was no limit to what authority could demand. He was worried that the Pastoral would be taken as the full exposition of Church teaching. In an article signed by Lord Halifax but really written by Tyrrell, the Joint Pastoral was attacked as ecclesiastical absolutism.[69] Ward wrote a short article, "Doctores Ecclesiae," in the Anglican *Pilot* (June 22, 1901)—it was unlikely that it could have been published in a Catholic journal after Vaughan's earlier pastoral letter—to explain what the Pastoral had left unsaid, stating that the reason why these limitations were not discussed in the Joint Pastoral was that they were already

67. Ibid., 136–38.

68. Ibid., 144.

69. George Tyrrell, "The Recent Anglo-Roman Pastoral," *Nineteenth Century* 49 (May 1901): 736–54. For Tyrrell's authorship, see Thomas Michael Loome, "A Bibliography of the Published Writings of George Tyrrell, 1861–1909," *Heythrop Journal* 10 (1969): 305. For Tyrrell's response to and campaign against the Joint Pastoral, see Mary Jo Weaver, "George Tyrrell and the Joint Pastoral Letter," *Downside Review* 99 (Jan. 1981): 18–39, and Schultenover, *George Tyrrell,* 143–65.

present in Catholic theology. "The teaching of a Pastoral does not supersede on any point of doctrine the universal teaching of the theological schools. It presupposes that teaching." He also made clear the distinction in function between the Church's pastors and her thinkers:

> I mean the distinction in the history of the Church between the bishops or pastors whose duty it has been to guard the faith in their flocks, and the Doctores Ecclesiae who have elucidated it theologically in successive ages in view of the circumstances of the time. The faith and morals of the many are protected by the Episcopate. But Catholic thought has been elaborated through successive ages mainly by the individual Catholic thinkers of genius or learning, who in the spirit of loyalty to the Church have developed her theology. . . . Looking back now at the great Doctores Ecclesiae, with the halo round their brows, we may forget to separate their position from that of the pontiffs and bishops who in the long run have sanctioned the results of their labours. But in their own lifetime they did their work not, for the most part, in virtue of any position as members of the *Ecclesia docens,* but prompted by their loyalty, devotion, and genius, and sometimes in spite of opposition on the part of unworthier holders of official status.[70]

A great pastor was not necessarily a great teacher. Even in these days, Ward wrote, this distinction was recognized in the fact that it was the theologian who gave a new work its *nihil obstat,* which would then be ratified by the bishop with his *imprimatur.* And while the Reformation had led us to forget this need for the individual teacher, it was still necessary: "If individual initiative were crushed in matters intellectual, humanly speaking, the best intellectual life within the Church would be killed."[71]

Ward received many congratulations on his article but, as a letter from a friend very much in sympathy with him pointed out, "It is an ungrateful task to be continually protecting those in authority from the consequences of their own utterances—and, after all, *they* do mean what they say, and the average man knows they do, even if he does not accept it as binding upon him to accept it."[72] Nor were others unaware that Ward had done the very thing that the Joint Pastoral had condemned, and had found distinctions there that had no foundation in the document itself. But whatever the bishops may have thought about what he had done, they never publicly disavowed him.

Tyrrell was not happy with Ward's response, and continued his pseudony-

70. Quoted in *Wilfrid Wards* 2:139–140.

71. Ibid., 141.

72. James Britten to Ward (n.d.). See WWP VII/50a (2).

mous attacks. The clear break with Ward was to come only in 1904, when Tyrrell published a review of Ward's *Problems and Persons* in an article in the *Month* entitled "Semper Eadem." In this article he stated that Ward's attempt to reconcile Catholic theology with modern thought was a failure. There was no *via media* between "the Scylla of the old theology and the Charybdis of the new," for they mix as well as oil does with water, a combination of incompatible principles. Tyrrell seemed to associate Liberal Catholicism and Ward with the more extreme "liberal theology" of Sabatier, which he was also criticizing. The article was seen as an attack on Ward for being too liberal, and Tyrrell received letters of approval from delighted conservatives ("innocent as serpents, wise as doves") who had come to the conclusion that he had seen the light. Tyrrell tried to explain in letters to Ward that he was being ironic, but these same letters also made clear that he did feel that Ward was in an unstable position and had not sufficiently separated himself, in principle, from the extreme right.[73]

The year 1905 was to be a turning point in Ward's life. When Cardinal Newman died in 1890 he left Fr. William Neville as his sole literary executor. Despite the need for a full-scale biography based on his papers, while Neville lived he allowed no one full access to them, nor did he invite anyone to write the cardinal's biography. In 1905 Neville died and Ward was asked by the new executors to use the papers and write the biography of the man he most admired and upon whose mind he had modeled his own. The Newman biography was to be Ward's crowning achievement and his greatest claim to fame. The year 1905 was also the year that Ward was asked to be the editor of the *Dublin Review,* the oldest and most prestigious of the English Catholic periodicals. The *Dublin Review* was owned by the Archdiocese of Westminster (now under Archbishop Bourne since the death of Cardinal Vaughan in 1903) and shared its aura of authority as a semi-official organ. It was a clear sign of public recognition, of Ward's ability and his orthodoxy. Ward was now in an ideal position to implement his vision more broadly, and with greater official sanction, and the *Dublin Review* was to be the vehicle for all this.

The success of his Wiseman biography, published in 1897, had led to his

73. George Tyrrell, "Semper Eadem," *Month* 103 (Jan. 1904): 1–17, reprinted in *Through Scylla and Charybdis: Or the Old Theology and the New* (London: Longmans, Green, 1907), 106–32. For these letters of Tyrrell, see Weaver, *Letters from a "Modernist,"* 92–101, 158–61. As Weaver points out, it was not Ward's intention to find a final synthesis but "to use the *via media* idea to argue for moderation from all sides" (93).

election to the Athenaeum, under Rule II, the category reserved for those of "distinguished eminence in Science, Literature, or the Arts, or for Public Service."[74] His admission to "that Pantheon of earned eminence in Waterloo Place" showed his acceptance into a different social elite, that of the public intellectual.[75] His sphere was now much larger than just the Catholic body. The intellectual politician had come into his own, and Ward could look forward to the future with a certain satisfaction and expectation. But to understand Ward's task one must better understand the recent history of English Catholicism and the important place the *Dublin Review* played in it, and to this we now turn.

74. For a discussion of the significance of being elected to the Athenaeum under Rule II, see Stefan Collini, *Public Moralists: Political Thought and Intellectual Life in Britain, 1850–1939* (Oxford: Clarendon Press, 1991), 13–21.

75. Martha S. Vogeler, *Frederic Harrison: The Vocations of a Positivist* (Oxford: Clarendon Press, 1984), 181.

2 ENGLISH CATHOLICISM AND THE *DUBLIN REVIEW*

My Fathers and Brothers, you *have seen it on one side, and some of us on another; but one and all of us can bear witness to the fact of the utter contempt into which Catholicism had fallen by the time that we were born. . . . No longer the Catholic Church in the country; nay, no longer, I may say, a Catholic community;—but a few adherents of the Old Religion, moving silently and sorrowfully about, as memorials of what had been. . . . Here a set of poor Irishmen, coming and going at harvest time, or a colony of them lodged in a miserable quarter of the vast metropolis. There, perhaps an elderly person, seen walking in the streets, grave and solitary, and strange, though noble in bearing, and said to be of good family, and a "Roman Catholic." . . . Such were Catholics in England, found in corners, and alleys, and cellars, and the housetops, or in the recesses of the country; cut off from the populous world around them, and dimly seen, as if through a mist or in twilight, as ghosts flitting to and fro, by the high Protestants, the lords of the earth.*

John Henry Newman, "The Second Spring"[1]

Newman's great sermon "The Second Spring," preached in 1852 at the first meeting of the restored Catholic hierarchy of England, the First Provincial Council of Westminster, despite its eloquence and

1. John Henry Newman, *Sermons Preached on Various Occasions* (London: Longmans, Green, 1900), 171–73.

beauty has had a distorting effect on our perceptions of English Catholic history. This view gives an exaggerated importance to Catholic Emancipation in 1829, to the restoration of the hierarchy in 1850, and to the statistical boom of the 1840s, a boom that was due primarily to the influx of the Irish, not to conversions from Anglicanism. In reading this sermon one must not be led astray by Newman's rhetoric or by the rhetoric of others who are followers of what might be called the "second-spring" view, "the most persistent of all historical orthodoxies about English Catholicism in the nineteenth century."[2] While it cannot be denied that Catholics were a distinct minority in the early nineteenth century, despised when not ignored, they had won a certain degree of acceptance and freedom in England even before the Relief Acts of 1778 and 1791.[3] As Bossy shows, taking advantage of the substantial removal of penalties by the Catholic Relief Act of 1791 and the opportunities created by the Industrial Revolution, English Catholicism had been expanding long before Catholic Emancipation and the Oxford Movement.[4] As he puts it, "the early nineteenth century was in many respects a period of take-off for English Catholicism, the period in which, perhaps for the first time, the mission evoked a response commensurate with the effort put into it; and for the community as such an age of quantitative expansion and qualitative maturity, when it managed to combine fidelity to its tradition and openness to its environment with a rare, and certainly so far unequalled, measure of success."[5] The Industrial Revolution, with its demographic shifts, had removed interior constraints and created a real opportunity for the spread of the faith. As one missionary wrote: "In the manufacturing districts there is found a greater spirit of enquiry, and a greater freedom of thought and expression, than in the less populous parts of the country, and consequently the pastor who avails himself of this opportunity is sure to find his zeal rewarded with many conversions, and an abundant harvest of souls."[6] In 1770 there were probably eighty thousand Catholics in England, and by the time of the restoration of the hierarchy perhaps three-quarters of a million in a population a little under

2. Mary Heimann, *Catholic Devotion in Victorian England* (Oxford: Clarendon Press, 1995), 5.

3. See John Bossy, "English Catholics after 1688," in *From Persecution to Toleration: The Glorious Revolution and Religion in England,* ed. Ole Peter Grell et al. (Oxford: Clarendon Press, 1991), 369–87.

4. John Bossy, *The English Catholic Community: 1570–1850* (New York: Oxford University Press, 1976), 295–322.

5. Ibid., 297.

6. *Catholic Magazine* 5 (1834): 310, quoted in Bossy, *English Catholic Community,* 316–17.

eighteen million.[7] The restoration of the hierarchy was merely the confirmation of this progress. While anti-Catholicism (No Popery) remained a deep-seated element of English life, its influence and violence declined.[8] The growth of Catholicism was to continue, so that by the early twentieth century Catholics were about 5 percent of the population, in certain areas, particularly cities, much more. By the time Wilfrid Ward became editor of the *Dublin Review* in 1906, there were about one and a half million Catholics in England and Wales. Three strands made up the English Catholic body: the old Catholic families, descendants of the recusants who had survived penal times, the converts, and the Irish. One cannot understand English Catholicism in the nineteenth and twentieth centuries until one understands them.

The old Catholic families supplied continuity to the ancient heritage and rights that the English Catholic Church proudly asserted.[9] Their existence was originally due to the influence of powerful aristocratic families who had maintained the faith on their estates and among their dependents. There were strong concentrations of them in Lancashire, Staffordshire, Worcestershire, Monmouthshire, and Yorkshire, in Northumberland and Durham, and in London. And while it was originally gentry dominated, in the early nineteenth century a Catholic middle class was coming into influence. Their piety was traditional, unobtrusive, and restrained: they were the "Garden of the Soul" Catholics, after Challoner's book of devotion (1740), so widely used among them. There was also a certain reserve, even antipathy, displayed by old Catholics to those outside their circle. While the majority seemed happy in their loyalties, there were those who sought a Catholicism more congenial to English and modern tastes, the so-called Cisalpines.

Among the converts, the second strand, the most important were those connected with the Oxford Movement. This Catholicizing movement within the Church of England to restore apostolic authority and tradition, to emphasize the freedom of the Church from the state and the primacy of the spiritual, led both to a renewal of the Church of England and to numerous con-

7. See ibid., 298.

8. See Edward R. Norman, *Anti-Catholicism in Victorian England* (New York: Barnes and Noble, 1968); Walter L. Arnstein, *Protestant versus Catholic in Mid-Victorian England: Mr. Newdegate and the Nuns* (Columbia: University of Missouri Press, 1982); John Wolffe, *The Protestant Crusade in Great Britain, 1829–1860* (Oxford: Clarendon Press, 1991); and D. G. Paz, *Popular Anti-Catholicism in Mid-Victorian England* (Stanford: Stanford University Press, 1992).

9. For the aristocratic old Catholic families, see Mark Bence-Jones, *The Catholic Families* (London: Constable, 1992).

versions to the Catholic Church throughout the century, including that of its greatest figure, John Henry Newman. The converts were generally better educated and more aggressive in their belief than the old Catholics, and there was much friction between them in the initial decades.

The Irish, the third strand, were important to English Catholicism in a number of ways. The 1801 union of a predominantly Catholic Ireland with England made Catholics a force to be reckoned with. While it is likely that Catholic Emancipation would have come about eventually, in point of fact it came about only because of the agitation of Daniel O'Connell (1775–1847). His mass movement for Catholic political inclusion made change inevitable if Ireland was to be pacified. Most of the remaining limitations still placed on English Catholics—the most important being the inability to hold political office—were removed only because of a man whom English Catholics generally mistrusted and some even feared. The massive Irish emigration to England in the nineteenth century changed the nature of that body dramatically. While there had been emigration before, it was only after the Napoleonic Wars that it became heavy, growing in volume till it peaked during and right after the Great Famine of 1845–1849, though the numbers remained substantial for decades to come. In 1841 there were 419,256 Irish-born residents in Britain; a decade later there were 727,326; and in 1861 the number stood at 806,000.[10] By the late nineteenth century, the great majority of English Catholics, perhaps as many as 80 percent, were Irish-born or of Irish descent. Largely poor, uneducated, and unskilled, most of them settled in the industrial towns of Lancashire and Western Scotland, and in London, with smaller groups in the North and the Midlands. In Liverpool they made up a quarter of the population, and in London a little less than 5 percent. This put an enormous burden on the Church and called forth from its clergy genuine heroism.[11] Nor was it just the poverty of so many of its members that the clergy had to deal with. While the bulk of the Irish were Catholic, their Catholicism was almost a folk religion, centered on shrines and holy wells, short on formal instruction and regular sacramental practice.[12] Their knowledge of

10. M. A. G. O'Tuathaigh, "The Irish in Nineteenth-Century Britain: Problems of Integration," in *The Irish in the Victorian City*, ed. Roger Swift and Sheridan Gilley (London: Croom Helm, 1985), 14. In their preface, Gilley and Swift give different numbers: 291,000, 520,000, and 602,000 for those corresponding dates (1).

11. See Raphael Samuel, "The Roman Catholic Church and the Irish Poor," ibid., 267–300.

12. See Gerard Connelly, "Irish and Catholic: Myth or Reality? Another Sort of Irish and the Renewal of the Clerical Profession among Catholics in England, 1791–1918," ibid., 225–54.

doctrine, often patchy and confused, was touched by superstition. Their low levels of religious observance, which looked especially bad when compared with the high levels among the native English Catholics, improved greatly over time but never reached the levels of success achieved in Ireland during this period.

The English Catholic world was changing in other ways. In the late eighteenth and early nineteenth centuries, influenced by the Enlightenment and Gallicanism, there developed in England a movement known as Cisalpinism.[13] Its main focus was its desire to limit the influence of the papacy so as to show national loyalty and thus gain greater relief for Catholics in England. Their name, Cisalpine, locates them on this side of the Alps, on the side beyond Italy and Roman influence. Their opponents, those who desired greater unity with the papacy beyond the Alps, were called Ultramontanes. But there was more than this: they also had a different worldview. Cisalpinism was an attempt to adjust the Church to the "modernity" of the day, that is, to the currents of thought of the Age of Reason. However, the two did not always mix. While the Enlightenment emphasized man's untrammeled reason (Kant's *sapere aude*) and the necessity of intelligibility, the Church was built on the superiority of revelation, the authority of tradition, and the intrinsic value of mystery. The Enlightenment virtues of orderliness and moderation are fine things, but they fall short of the fullness of Christian life, which is modeled on the folly of the Cross and the radical witness of the saints. This desire for accommodation with the dominant culture that was such a strong part of Cisalpinism, therefore, could endanger the distinctiveness of the faith and empty the gospel of its power. Nor was its desire for accommodation with the dominant English and Protestant culture just the manifestation of a dislike of new or foreign developments and devotions, as some have suggested. It was a general antipathy toward baroque Catholicism in general, even its traditionally English "Garden of the Soul" variety. They found Bishop Challoner's classic prayer book, *The Garden of the Soul*, obscure, and disliked its use of specifically Catholic forms. Their emphasis was on intelligibility and irenicism, and their whole pastoral program was an attempt to make the faith as accessible to Protestants as possible, even if it made it less Catholic.[14] The late

13. For a recent and generally favorable evaluation of Cisalpinism, see Joseph P. Chinnici, *The English Catholic Enlightenment: John Lingard and the Cisalpine Movement, 1780–1850* (Shepherdstown, W.Va.: Patmos Press, 1980).

14. See ibid., 142–43, 145–46, 164–75.

eighteenth and early nineteenth centuries were marked by conflicts between the Cisalpines and the more traditional Catholics such as Bishop Milner ("the English Athanasius") and William Eusebius Andrews, the editor of the *Orthodox Journal.* By the 1820s the environment that had nurtured the Cisalpine outlook was gone, as the Age of Reason passed into the Romantic Revival, and its greatest figures, except for the highly respected historian John Lingard (1771–1851), were passing away. Politically and culturally the Cisalpines had been overtaken, but through the *Catholic Magazine* (1831–1836) their influence continued. By the 1830s the English Catholic world was ready for a new lead, and the *Dublin Review* would supply it.

The key figure in the founding of the *Dublin* was Nicholas Wiseman (1802–1865). Born in Spain of Irish parents, educated for nine years in England at Ushaw, Wiseman was sent to the restored English College in Rome in 1818, where he blossomed. He won his doctorate in 1824, was ordained a priest in 1825, was named vice-rector of the English College in 1827, and in 1828 became its rector. He gained a European reputation as an Orientalist, and with his skill in languages (he spoke half a dozen) he was in contact with scholars throughout Europe. From his position in Rome he was also in contact with leading figures within the Church, not just from the Curia but men like Lamennais of France and Döllinger of Germany, leaders of the Catholic revival and important Ultramontanes. Lifted out of the insularity of a purely English education, coming into maturity in the full grandeur of papal Rome, in contact with the best in European scholarship and Catholic thought, Wiseman saw the Church in a very different light from the Cisalpines. He was also a child of his time, when the cultural tide had turned against the Enlightenment. Romanticism was dominant and it was much more sympathetic to traditional Catholicism.

When several English priests formed the *Catholic Magazine* in 1831, Wiseman was enthusiastic about it, even offering to be a contributor, but by 1833 he had withdrawn himself from its pages. Under the editorial guidance of Cisalpines its tone soon began to offend Wiseman: its critical spirit, with its animus toward the miraculous and traditional devotion, left him cold. It was the debate over the inclusion of the Litany of Loreto in a prayer book that proved the end for Wiseman. Lingard, under the guise of a new convert from Protestantism, "Proselytos," had argued that the Litany of Loreto was not appropriate for use in an English prayer book: "every rational man will deem it preferable to put his petitions in language which he can understand, than to employ for that purpose a jargon of mysterious, unintelligible, aye, even 'portenous sounds.'"[15] Wiseman was scandalized by this cast of mind and wrote in a letter to his friend, William Tandy (December 3, 1833): "What could give greater offense at Rome or in any Catholic country than to denounce the Litany of the B. Virgin as unfit for public use and as mere unintelligible nonsense. . . . God knows devotion towards her is sufficiently cold in England without the clergy throwing water upon it."[16] In another letter to Tandy (February 2, 1834) Wiseman wrote:

I have not as yet written to Mr. Kirk about the Magazine. I hardly have courage to do so, from fear of some pettish or secondary motive being attributed to me for an act proceeding from pure conscience. A propos of the controversy on the Loreto Litany some man said that its beautiful mystic terms were not "suited to the taste of the present age." Who so wrote thus knew but little of the taste of the age, but moreover must have a soul devoid of poetry, and be ignorant that there is such a thing as poesy in prayer. I read the other day the *Iambes* of Auguste Barbier a young poet now rising in France to the first eminence. . . . Only note the words underlined, compare them with the Litany, then remember that they were written and published in wicked, infidel Paris in 1833, that so you may compare the taste of the age and time *there* and among *some catholics* in England.[17]

It was against such a mindset that the *Dublin* was founded, as the editors of the *Catholic Magazine* clearly perceived. When the *Dublin* came out the editors of the *Catholic Magazine* showed their distaste by refusing to accept a complimentary copy of the new review. When Daniel O'Connell, one of the co-founders of the *Dublin,* wrote to the Irish bishops to gain their support for the journal, he contrasted it with other publications, the *Catholic Magazine* in particular: "The other quarterly publications are in the hands either of avowed and malignant enemies of Catholicity, or—what is worse—insidious and pretended friends, who affect a false liberality at the expense of Catholic doctrine."[18]

In 1835–1836, fresh from the Continent, where the Catholic revival was in the ascent, helped along by the romanticism that was inspiring all Europe, even England, with a love of the medieval past, respect for ancient forms, and a fascination with the mysterious, Wiseman visited England and lectured

15. Quoted in Richard J. Schiefen, *Nicholas Wiseman and the Transformation of English Catholicism* (Shepherdstown, W.Va.: Patmos Press, 1984), 39.

16. Ibid.

17. Quoted in Chinnici, *English Catholic Enlightenment,* 141–42.

18. Quoted in Bishop L. C. Casartelli, "The First Sixty Years," *Dublin Review* (April 1936): 201.

publicly on the Catholic faith with great success, many non-Catholics coming to hear him. The Catholic Church never looked so attractive. It was at this time that he was approached by Michael Quin about creating a new journal. Quin, a journalist from Thurles in Tipperary now practicing law in London, and a political associate of Daniel O'Connell, joined O'Connell and Wiseman in creating the *Dublin Review,* the first number coming out in May 1836.[19] In the preface to a collection of his essays, Wiseman gave two reasons for founding the *Dublin.* First, he wrote, with the flourishing of the Catholic Church in England the times seemed propitious.

> Signs of a more active circulation had shown themselves: communities were springing up; schools were beginning to be multiplied; new missions were opened; churches, upon a scale of size and of embellishment previously unknown, were contemplated or begun; and the people were evidently manifesting more interest in our religion, and a more fair disposition to hear and judge it justly. . . . The Catholic religion, as she is in the fulness of her growth, with the grandeur of her ritual, the beauty of her devotions, the variety of her institutions, required to be made more known to many who had never seen her other than she had been reduced by three hundred years of barbarous persecution.[20]

Second, Wiseman cited the development within the Church of England of a movement open and congenial to Catholicism, the Oxford Movement. In 1833 he met J. H. Newman and Hurrell Froude in Rome and was impressed by their sincerity and Catholic temper. As he wrote in a letter of 1847: "From the day of Newman and Froude's visit to me, never for an instant did I waver in my conviction that a new era had commenced in England. . . . To this grand object I devoted myself. . . . The favorite studies of former years were abandoned for the pursuit of this aim alone."[21]

19. The last issue was the one for winter 1968–69. For a list of early English Catholic periodicals, see John R. Fletcher, "Early Catholic Periodicals in England," *Dublin Review* (April 1936): 284–310. For a survey of later English Catholic periodical literature, see J. J. Dwyer, "The Catholic Press, 1850–1950," in *The English Catholics: 1850–1950,* ed. George Andrew Beck (London: Burns, Oates and Washbourne, 1950), 475–514. For a survey of all British religious periodicals, see Josef L. Altholz, *The Religious Press in Britain, 1760–1900* (New York: Greenwood Press, 1989). There is a very brief overview to the *Dublin* in Alvin Sullivan, ed., *British Literary Magazines,* vol. 2, *The Romantic Age, 1789–1836* (Westport, Conn.: Greenwood Press, 1983), 114–119, and a much more in-depth entry listing all the articles and their authors in the *Dublin* up to 1900 in Josef L. Altholz, "The Dublin Review, 1836–1900," in *The Wellesley Index to Victorian Periodicals, 1814–1900,* ed. Walter E. Houghton (Toronto: University of Toronto Press, 1972), 2:11–128.

20. Nicholas Wiseman, *Essays on Various Subjects* (New York: P. O'Shea, 1853), 1:ix.

21. Quoted in Ward, *Life and Times of Cardinal Wiseman,* 1:119.

> The moment when I was invited to join in this new review appeared to me most critical and interesting. Three years before, had begun to manifest themselves the germs of that wonderful movement which, originating at Oxford, was destined to pervade and agitate the Anglican Establishment, till it should give up many of its most loving and gifted sons to the Catholic Church . . . and I have been surprised, on visiting England in 1835, to find how little attention it had excited among Catholics. . . . For Catholics to have overlooked all this, and allowed the wonderful phenomenon to pass by, not turned to any useful purpose, but gazed at till it died out, would have been more than stupidity,—it would have been wickedness. To watch its progress, to observe its phases, to influence, if possible, its direction, to move it gently towards complete attainment of its unconscious aims; and, moreover, to protest against its errors, to warn against its dangers, to provide arguments against its new modes of attack, and to keep lifted up the mask of beauty under which it had, in sincerity, covered the ghastly and soulless features of Protestantism; these were the duties which the new Review under took to perform, or which, in no small degree, it was expressly created to discharge.[22]

Wiseman believed that a quarterly was best suited to the promotion of his tasks, since it would allow far more depth than a newspaper or magazine while allowing him to return to the same subject when appropriate. He wanted it to promote Catholic progress in every way, desiring that it "should treat of living questions and existing controversies, should grapple with real antagonists, wrestle with tangible errors." In taking on this journal, though, he had to turn away from his previous studies and works long contemplated, "attention being more required for passing events and current literature." Though originally he was to take on only its theological direction, his work soon encompassed more than that. He and Dr. Charles William Russell (1812–1880), professor and later president at Maynooth, the Irish national seminary, were to write the lion's share of the articles for the first series (May 1836 to April 1863), so much so that it has been dubbed the Wiseman-Russell Series.[23]

In an age replete with party organs, it was to be the Catholic voice of Great Britain, in contrast to the Whig *Edinburgh Review* and the Tory *Quarterly* and the various Protestant periodicals. Nor was it the first or only Catholic periodical, but most of the others had narrow interests, small circulations, and brief existences. For O'Connell there was very little to be gained by his involve-

22. Wiseman, *Essays on Various Subjects,* 1:vii–viii.

23. Ibid., x. For Russell, see Ambrose Macaulay, *Dr. Russell of Maynooth* (London: Darton, Longman and Todd, 1983). Russell contributed at least one article for almost every number at this time and sometimes as many as four.

ment in the *Dublin.* By agreement with Wiseman, no "extreme political views" were to be introduced into the journal. Neither O'Connell's political views nor his campaign for the repeal of the union of Ireland and England were to be promoted there. As Altholz points out, O'Connell's role in the founding of the *Dublin* was a generous and genuine act of Catholic solidarity.[24] Religious publications generally did not make money (highbrow quarterlies least of all), so being a proprietor gave him only one privilege: "it conferred an unlimited right to lose money." Without O'Connell's name, involvement, and financial backing, the *Dublin* never would have been founded and survived its early years. Despite its green cover, the frequent articles on Ireland or by Irish authors (it is estimated that at least half of the first series was produced in Ireland), and even its name, it was always published in London and its focus, though broad, was clearly English.[25] It is not clear how it gained its name. Perhaps it was to compliment and curry the favor of O'Connell and the Irish, who were certainly the largest and most powerful part of the Catholic body in the realm; perhaps to contrast it to the *Edinburgh.*

The *Dublin Review* did have its desired effect upon the Oxford Movement. The Oxford divines certainly read it, and it was an article by Wiseman that started Newman toward Rome. Wiseman's article destroyed the claims of the ancient schismatic Donatists (and thereby the Anglicans) by denying that those who cut themselves off from the universal Church could be right, using St. Augustine's appeal to the judgment of the universal Church *(Securus judicat orbis terrarum).*

Hardly had I brought my course of reading to a close, when the Dublin Review of that same August was put into my hands, by friends who were more favourable to the cause of Rome than I was myself. There was an article in it on the "Anglican Claim" by Dr. Wiseman. This was about the middle of September. It was on the Donatists,

24. See Josef L. Altholz, "Daniel O'Connell and the *Dublin Review,*" *Catholic Historical Review* 74 (Jan. 1988): 1–12.

25. Casartelli, "The First Sixty Years," 199. Until 1878 the *Dublin*'s cover had the Irish national arms with an Irish motto in Irish characters on it. Unfortunately their knowledge of Irish was not equal to their Irish enthusiasm, and instead of the motto saying "Ireland Forever" (as they clearly intended) it said something like "Ireland unto a shroud" or "Ireland unto a flag." See Owen Dudley Edwards and Patricia J. Storey, "The Irish Press in Victorian Britain," in Swift and Gilley, *Irish in the Victorian City,* 160. In 1961 the *Dublin* changed its name to the *Wiseman Review,* but it reverted to its old title in 1965. In announcing the first name change, the proprietor, Cardinal Godfrey, gave two reasons. First, to honor Wiseman, who was one of its founders. Second, because it "has been found that there is a widespread and mistaken impression that the Review treats largely of Irish affairs and interests." See *Wiseman Review* (spring 1961): 4.

with an application to Anglicanism. I read it, and did not see much in it. . . . But my friend, an anxiously religious man, now, as then, very dear to me, a Protestant still, pointed out the palmary words of St. Augustine, which were contained in one of the extracts made in the Review, and which had escaped my observation. "Securus judicat orbis terrarum." He repeated these words again and again, and, when he had gone, they kept ringing in my ears. "Securus judicat orbis terrarum"; they were words which went beyond the occasion of the Donatists. . . . They gave cogency to the Article, which had escaped me at first. They decided ecclesiastical questions on a simpler rule than that of Antiquity. . . . What a light was hereby thrown upon every controversy in the Church![26]

In 1840 Wiseman was named coadjutor to Bishop Walsh of the Midland District and president of Oscott College. In 1847 he was named Vicar Apostolic of the London District. With the restoration of the hierarchy in 1850 he was made Archbishop of Westminster and head of the Catholic Church in England. In his later years, distracted by the burdens of office and sickness, the quality of the *Dublin* declined. He contributed infrequently after 1850, nor did he have much money with which to pay contributors. The founding of the *Rambler* in 1848 by the convert parson, John Moore Capes, was another reason for the *Dublin*'s decline.[27]

The Oxford Movement drew into the Church many educated men, especially clergymen, and while some could continue their careers as Catholic priests, the married could not. Nor were their talents much appreciated by many of the old Catholics. When W. G. Ward was received into the Church by Bishop Griffiths, Vicar Apostolic of the London District, he was told: "We are glad to welcome you, Mr. Ward. Of course we have no work for you."[28] In the clerical world of English Catholicism there were not many options for such men, but writing was one. The *Rambler* became their main organ and it soon overshadowed the *Dublin,* which had become too cautious and safe. However, used to the standards of the great universities and the freer ways of the *Ecclesia Anglicana,* these men tended to see the old Catholics as intellectually and socially backward, too timid to enter English public life as they should. While not trying to create controversy within the fold or come into

26. See Newman's *Apologia Pro Vita Sua,* ed. Martin Svaglic (Oxford: Clarendon Press, 1967), 109–10. The article was "Tracts for the Times (Part III)" (Aug. 1839), 139–80, reprinted in *Essays on Various Subjects,* 3:199–271.

27. See Josef L. Altholz, *The Liberal Catholic Movement in England: The "Rambler" and Its Contributors, 1848–1864* (London: Burns & Oates, 1962).

28. See Ward, *William George Ward and the Catholic Revival,* 8.

conflict with the bishops, they often did. This was especially true after another convert parson, Richard Simpson, joined the journal in 1854. As Newman was later to write of Simpson: "He will always be flicking his whip at Bishops, cutting them in tender places, throwing stones at sacred Congregations, and, as he rides along the road, discharging pea-shooters at Cardinals who happen by bad luck to look out the window."[29] In December 1856 Wiseman publicly criticized the *Rambler* in the *Dublin,* stating that the *Rambler* authors were setting themselves apart from and above other Catholics, creating division within the Church between old Catholics and converts. He also defended those Catholics, of whom he counted himself one, whom the *Rambler* had condemned as ignoring difficulties and seeing everything through rose-colored glasses. The *Dublin* had been founded "upon a *couleur de rose* principle," he maintained, for the successes of the faith were real if imperfect. Such an attitude was also in keeping with Christian hopefulness, which even in the greatest difficulties blessed what God had given and was sanguine as to the final results.[30]

In 1858 Simpson became editor of the *Rambler.* In the same year Sir John Acton, scion of an old Catholic family with cosmopolitan connections, looking for an outlet for his talents and desirous of bringing the fruits of German historical science into the English Catholic world, became a partner in the *Rambler.* In an article he wrote for the February 1859 number he outlined his ideals and severely criticized the *Dublin* for the dearth of serious Catholic literature.[31] Its narrowness, its exclusivity and jealousy of other journals, and its failure to keep up with the times, he charged, disqualified it as an outlet for Catholic talent and left Catholics ignorant and lazy. Intellectual indolence was the cause of the inferiority of Catholic literature, and the scientific studies that should be the glory and the support of the faith were instead used against her. Acton believed that science (in the broad sense of the word) was the best hope for the Church's victory over her enemies, for by its impartiality it would in the end bear witness to her truth. Religion could not be served by ignoring or smothering facts, or by defending false opinions in the pretense of defending faith, so the principle of the *Rambler* would be the principle of free inquiry.

29. Newman to Sir John Acton, July 5, 1861, in Newman, *Letters and Diaries of Newman,* 20:4.

30. Wiseman, "The Present Catholic Dangers," *Dublin Review* (Dec. 1856): 441–70.

31. Sir John Acton, "The Catholic Press," *Rambler* (Feb. 1859): 73–90, reprinted in *Essays on Church and State,* ed. Douglas Woodruff (London: Hollis and Carter, 1952), 260–78.

That principle was to lead to endless trouble, and in February 1859, to prevent censure by the bishops, Simpson resigned and Newman was brought in to moderate the journal and steer it away from controversial matters. But after two issues he resigned and Acton became editor, with Simpson a major contributor. Acton's lack of zeal for Catholic causes such as the temporal power of the pope remained a sore point, and in 1862, to preclude a formal censure by the bishops and perhaps even by Rome, the journal was renamed the *Home and Foreign Review.* It also became a quarterly, coming into direct competition with the *Dublin,* the only other Catholic quarterly. The *Home and Foreign Review* broadened its interests and began to rival the great secular quarterlies in quality and influence. In an 1865 essay Matthew Arnold would lament its loss. "Perhaps in no organ of criticism in this country was there so much knowledge, so much play of mind; but these could not save it. The *Dublin Review* subordinates play of mind to the practical business of English and Irish Catholicism, and it lives."[32]

The change of the *Rambler* into the *Home and Foreign* did not mollify Wiseman. In a letter sent to his clergy in 1862 he attacked it for "its absence for years of all reserve or reverence in its treatment of persons or things deemed sacred, its grazing over the very edges of the most perilous abysses of error, and its habitual preference of uncatholic instincts, tendencies, and motives."[33] Other bishops shared this condemnation with their clergy, but their disapproval was not a prohibition and the journal continued. In 1862, in an attempt to revive the *Dublin,* Wiseman gave it to Manning, who appointed William George Ward editor. Cardinal Wiseman had offered it to Ward in 1858 and, despite misgivings about his ability and about his working under Wiseman, whom he considered even more unfit than himself for such a post, Ward accepted. His desire to serve the cardinal and his detestation of the *Rambler* won out. Later, however, when he learned that Newman was to edit the *Rambler,* he removed himself from the burden. As he wrote in a letter of March 8, 1859: "On public grounds I don't care one button for having a good *Review,* nor do I see who would be better for one, in our miserable state of intellectual degradation. But I am *perfectly certain* that the *only* chance of our having one, would be that you should throw aside scruples *which are most misplaced,* and simply take the editorship of the Rambler, working it into a

32. Matthew Arnold, "The Function of Criticism at the Present Time," *Essays in Criticism,* 1st ser. (London: Macmillan, 1902), 20.

33. Quoted in Altholz, *Liberal Catholic Movement in England,* 188.

regular Quarterly. The Dublin then must die, and I should with great delight dance at its funeral."[34]

The *Dublin* did not die, for Newman's editorship of the *Rambler* did not last very long. Ward now had no choice but to become its editor. Ward was well aware of his deficiencies when he took over the *Dublin.* In a letter to Newman of October 16, 1862, he wrote: "It is certainly a new phenomenon to have an editor of a quarterly profoundly ignorant of history, politics, and literature. . . . But it was really a Quintus Curtius affair, and the only apparent alternative was the Tories seizing it and making it a political organ. I think even my editorship is better than that. I am very desirous to avoid . . . all appearance of *cliquiness,* and my notion is when I go back to town to call on as many different kinds of people as I can."[35] While Wiseman would not interfere, one of his conditions was that there be three theological censors, approved by him, for theological topics. Ward's first number was July 1863. His conciliatory policy, however, did not last long. His good intentions were soon overtaken by events that pushed him in a very different direction: the Catholic Congress held in Malines, Belgium, in August 1863, and a similar one held in Munich a month later.

At the first, Montalembert, the leading French Liberal Catholic, spoke twice. In one speech he called for liberty of conscience and religious tolerance, and in another for a complete separation of Church and State as the ideal, using the phrase "a free Church in a free State" (a slogan generally used by anticlericals to despoil the Church). At the Munich Congress, Döllinger, the great German Catholic historian under whom Acton had studied, gave an inaugural address on the history, condition, and duties of Catholic theology. Two years earlier, Döllinger's lectures on the temporal power, where he stated that the Papal States were not essential to the Church and that their loss might even be a good thing, had caused an enormous stir and much denunciation. In the address Döllinger made clear that he did not believe that scholastic theology could present Catholic doctrine in all its organic completeness and in its connectedness to religious life; he also praised German theology for its scientific qualities and called for great freedom if scientific theology was to flour-

34. Quoted in Maisie Ward, "W. G. Ward and Wilfrid Ward," *Dublin Review* (April 1936): 236–37. In the same letter Ward said of Wiseman: "Abounding (as I think) in most admirable *instincts,* but not a *reasonable being* in any shape."

35. Ward, *William George Ward and the Catholic Revival,* 155.

ish.[36] In March 1864, in the wake of the Munich Catholic Congress, the apostolic letter *Tuas Libenter* (the so-called Munich Brief), sent to the Archbishop of Munich by Pope Pius IX, was published. It denied the complete freedom of research from ecclesiastical authority, and, while not censuring Döllinger, it was a clear criticism of his address. With this Acton closed the *Home and Foreign,* since he no longer believed it possible for its principles to continue.[37]

The provocations of Montalembert and Döllinger could not be ignored, least of all by William George Ward. While Ward was restrained by Wiseman from writing against Montalembert in the *Dublin Review,* he was not restrained in other ways.[38] Under him the *Dublin* waged war against liberalism in all its forms and exalted the decisions, and even the desires, of the pope and the Roman congregations to a whole new level. He once wrote: "Unity can be found only in subjection to Rome: hearty and profound unity only in hearty and profound subjection."[39] He was strongly allied to Henry Edward Manning, a converted Anglican clergyman who succeeded Wiseman at Westminster in 1865 and who was instrumental in the definition of papal infallibility at the First Vatican Council in 1870. Ward became one of the leading European advocates for papal infallibility, and the *Dublin,* widely read by Catholics on the Continent at this time, one of its leading organs. He also became engaged in a running controversy with Father Ignatius Ryder, superior of the Birmingham Oratory, claiming that all doctrinal instructions in the pope's official public letters were strictly infallible. With Manning, he also opposed allowing Catholics to go to Oxford and Cambridge. As his granddaughter Maisie Ward put it, he turned the review into "a kind of theological battering-ram."[40] After 1870 that changed, and the *odium theologicum* that had marked the journal tended to disappear. Part of this was due to the fact that with the definition of papal infallibility and the loss of the temporal power by the conquest of Rome by a unified Italy, those issues had become more or less settled. Part was also due to a serious illness that Ward suffered that year. He turned

36. See Sir John Acton, "The Munich Congress," *Home and Foreign Review* (Jan. 1864): 209–44, reprinted in *Essays on Church and State.*

37. Sir John Acton, "Conflicts with Rome," *Home and Foreign Review* (April 1864): 667–96, reprinted in *The History of Freedom and Other Essays,* ed. J. N. Figgis and R. V. Laurence (London: Macmillan, 1907), 461–91.

38. Altholz, *Liberal Catholic Movement in England,* 220.

39. Ward, *William George Ward and the Catholic Revival,* 193.

40. Maisie Ward, "W. G. Ward and Wilfrid Ward," 237. For Ward's editorship, see also Leo J. Walsh, "William Ward and the *Dublin Review*" (Ph.D. diss., Columbia University, 1962).

to more abstract philosophical topics, writing against the theories of John Stuart Mill, Bain, and Huxley. In 1878 the *Dublin* was given to Herbert Vaughan (1832–1903), Bishop of Salford, another Ultramontane and a friend of Manning and Ward, who appointed Bishop Hedley editor.

John Cuthbert Hedley (1837–1915), a Benedictine monk and an auxiliary bishop to Bishop Brown of Newport and Menevia, had not experienced the rich cultural and intellectual life of Rome (as had Wiseman) or the intellectual give-and-take of Oxford (as had Ward).[41] His education had been entirely English and insular. He went to Ampleforth, in an isolated part of Yorkshire, where he also did his novitiate and priestly studies, and was ordained in 1862. Blessed with a fine mind and some excellent teachers, among them Abbot Bury, who had mastered St. Thomas Aquinas while studying in Italy at the University of Parma, Hedley was sent within a month of his ordination to the English Benedictine Congregation's house of studies at Belmont in rural Hereford, where he taught for the next eleven years. Thoroughly grounded in scholastic philosophy and theology, he was also knowledgeable on patristic literature, Church history, and mysticism. To this theological culture he added a good knowledge of literature and science. Wilfrid Ward later praised Hedley for the depth and openness of his mind, his sensitivity to modern ways of thought, and his understanding sympathy toward the doubter.[42] While still a professor at Belmont he wrote a series of articles on the Fathers of the Church for the *Dublin Review* that were extremely well received, for he was a fine stylist as well. He was a frequent contributor to the *Dublin* in this period, primarily on early Church history, though he also wrote on St. Thomas and on prayer and contemplation. Perhaps the most important of these articles, though, dealt with science, his discussion of evolution considered from the point of view of faith, "Evolution and Faith," published in the July 1871 number. "It has been too hastily assumed that the 'evolution' theory is a smashing assault upon orthodoxy that is carrying terror and confusion into the ranks of all believers in Revelation. It is nothing of the kind."[43] Excluding the separate and special creation of the soul, and of its spirituality, the denial of which is contrary to the faith, he did not see any problem with evolution up to, but not including, man. And even in reference to the evolution

41. For Hedley's tenure at the *Dublin,* see Abbot Matthews, "Bishop Hedley as Editor," *Dublin Review* (April 1936): 253–66.

42. Wilfrid Ward, "Bishop Hedley," *Dublin Review* (Jan. 1916): 1–13.

43. See Hedley, *Evolution and Faith,* 3.

of man's body he only called the idea "rash, and, perhaps, proximate to heresy." This was hardly the most damning of judgments, and in his 1898 article "Physical Science and Faith" he was even stronger in recognizing the probable truth of evolution. Made an auxiliary bishop in 1873, Hedley split his time between the demands of a large though sparsely populated diocese, preaching and giving retreats (at which he was excellent) and editing the review. Hedley's goal was to broaden the *Dublin*'s appeal. Under Ward it had become both narrower and too abstract. In a letter to Hedley, Bishop William Bernard Ullathorne of Birmingham wrote:

> I am very glad to see that the Dublin Review has come into your hands. It is high time it became a Catholic instead of a party review. What an influence it had under its first management, when it interpreted the Tractarians to themselves, and let nothing of moment pass in the world of letters that struck at the Faith without an attractive reply! when, also, we had pleasant articles that suited the general reader, and secured it a place on the drawing-room table; and when we looked to its notices of books as a guide and a security against purchasing rubbish![44]

The *Dublin* did not reject its past, for Ward continued to contribute articles, though not so many of them got published, as did Cardinal Manning (the very first number included an article by him). Also, though Hedley was favorable to removing the prohibition on Catholics attending Oxford and Cambridge, the *Dublin* was guided by the views of its proprietor, Herbert Vaughan, who followed Manning and Ward in opposing the removal of the prohibition.[45] What was different, however, was the absence of the bitter party spirit that often animated Ward's journal. Thus Hedley rejected an article of Ward's attacking Newman, and at Newman's elevation to cardinal in 1879 Hedley wrote a fulsome article on him, though he personally disagreed strongly with Newman's philosophical views.[46] The goal of the *Dublin* under Hedley was stated in the final number of the Ward series. "The work of the *Dublin Review* will be, as heretofore, to deepen Catholic intellectual life; to promote Catholic interests, to enlighten and assist those who are seeking for Catholic truth; to utter warnings against dangers to Faith and practice; and to diminish as far as possible that friction, arising from national, local or personal narrowness, which retards the onward march of Catholic principle. Its mot-

44. Quoted in Wilson, *Life of Bishop Hedley*, 193.

45. Vincent Alan McClelland, *English Catholics and Higher Education, 1830–1903* (Oxford: Clarendon Press, 1973), 334.

46. Wilson, *Life of Bishop Hedley*, 199 and 205–206.

to, as that of all Catholic journals, must be—Truth, Culture, and Conciliation."[47] There would be more articles of a popular nature, with greater focus on historical, literary, and political topics, and the tone would be much more irenic. The *Dublin* followed this pattern for the rest of the century.

It has been the tendency to see English Catholic history of the nineteenth century as one of disputes, conflict, and polarization, with a particular focus on the conflict between Catholic liberals and Ultramontanes. For some this period marks the victory of an authoritarian Ultramontanism, "the triumph of the Holy See," a time when English Catholicism became "more Roman than Rome."[48] This seems exaggerated. Mary Heimann has shown how foolish it is to use such categories in reference to the devotional life of English Catholics; it was "an invigorated English recusant tradition, not a Roman one," that dominated the period after the restoration of the hierarchy.[49] She also points out that it would be equally wrong to believe that either the *Dublin* under Ward or the *Rambler* and *Home and Foreign* under Acton were representative of English Catholicism.

> The silence of the vast majority of English Catholics on issues which, to judge by contemporary issues of the *Rambler* or *Dublin Review,* or from modern historians' accounts, amounted to a subversion of liberty by the ultramontanes must surely strike any student of English Catholicism. Why should only a few English Catholics—most notably Manning on the ultramontane side and Acton on the liberal—have spoken out about such issues as the imminent threat of Gallicanism to undermine the orthodoxy of Catholicism in England, or the sinister moves of the ultramontanes to subvert English freedoms through a sweeping definition of papal infallibility?[50]

The bulk of English Catholics eschewed the extremes; and to Heimann, and many others, it is a man like Ullathorne, with his distaste for the distorting and uncharitable aspects of both sides, who perhaps best symbolizes the English Catholic mainstream.[51] As we have seen, Ullathorne valued Hedley's judicious and traditional orthodoxy, and under Hedley the *Dublin Review* again became a good reflection of English Catholicism.

In 1881 Hedley succeeded Bishop Brown, and, overburdened by his pas-

47. Quoted in Casartelli, "First Sixty Years," 216.

48. See J. Derek Holmes's books *More Roman Than Rome: English Catholicism in the Nineteenth Century* (London: Burns & Oates, 1978), and *The Triumph of the Holy See: A Short History of the Holy See in the Nineteenth Century* (Shepherdstown, W.Va.: Patmos Press, 1978).

49. Heimann, *Catholic Devotion in Victorian England,* 137–73.

50. Ibid., 20.

51. Ibid., 24.

toral obligations, he resigned as editor at the end of 1884. However, because of the weight he carried in the Catholic intellectual world, he was sometimes forced to write again, his articles in late 1887 and early 1888 criticizing Dr. Mivart's exaggerated views of science being the chief example of this. Despite his dislike of controversy and his personal friendship with Mivart, and because of the pleadings of others, he spoke out in as conciliatory a vein as possible, trying to show that science could never be "free" from revelation since in an incarnational religion it was inevitable that the two should overlap at points.

> Does Dr. Mivart mean to assert that there are no matters of chemistry or biology which are so intimately bound up with revealed truth that the pastorate of the Church may not be divinely protected in pronouncing upon them? Most people know that the miraculous conception of our Lord Jesus Christ has been asserted to be impossible on physiological grounds. The Real Presence has been rejected for reasons connected with chemistry. The Resurrection is pronounced by the "critical" school to be a myth, because it conflicts with the laws of nature. The whole of the miraculous aspect of Christianity is swept away by a reference to the demands of science. To maintain that the divine guardian of revelation, in teaching the world what is the truth on these and similar matters, cannot at the same time indirectly decide with unerring accuracy the "scientific" doctrine involved in such teaching, is to *dissolve* the power of teaching altogether. The Christian revelation embraces not merely spiritual and mental ideas, but facts and physical occurrences. The sphere of "science" is to investigate facts and physical occurrences; but when these things have become the subject of Revelation, there is no room left, on those particular questions, for any further investigation, and science must simply bow to the teaching of God's witness. This seems to be elementary Christianity.[52]

Mivart replied, but he never dealt with the serious questions Hedley raised; and no retraction followed, either in public or in private correspondence. Mivart learned nothing from this encounter and continued on to his tragic end.

When Hedley resigned, Vaughan became editor. Known not as a scholar but as a particularly effective administrator, he had no time to spare for the journal, so the sub-editor, Fr. W. E. Driffield, took on much more of the work. At the beginning of 1892 James Moyes (1851–1927), a close friend of Vaughan and the Canon Theologian of Salford, became editor. A controversialist, particularly against Anglicanism, and a narrow, unimaginative conservative, he followed Vaughan to London when he was translated to Westminster, becoming the Canon Theologian of Westminster in 1895. He was one of

52. *Dublin Review* (Oct. 1887): 402–3.

the three Englishmen appointed on Vaughan's nomination to the Papal Commission on Anglican Orders in 1896. While he was editor for thirteen years, he was probably known more for his frequent contributions to the *Tablet* (another Vaughan organ), writing a series of thirty-one articles on Anglican orders between February and December 1895 and another series of nineteen articles, from February to July 1897, defending the Papal Bull *Apostolicae Curae* condemning Anglican orders. While the *Dublin* under Moyes may not have been, as a recent historian described it, "an organ for narrow, dogmatic pieces on Catholic minutiae and antiquarianism," it was still a much diminished journal in comparison to its past.[53] Many able scholars, among them Cuthbert Butler, John Chapman, Aidan Gasquet, and Edmund Bishop, were contributors at this time. But by the end of Moyes's editorship the *Dublin*'s decline became so noticeable that when Tyrrell heard that Ward was taking it on he wrote to him warning about it: "I am afraid that the *Dublin* will give you more trouble than it is worth. One has seen death in the eyes this many a day."[54]

When Ward was asked to take over in 1905 he felt honored, but the honor was not without its risks. First of all, by focusing all his energies in a purely Catholic enterprise there was the danger that his influence would be lessened. Up to that point his articles had been primarily in the major secular journals such as the *Nineteenth Century* and the *Quarterly*, where they could have a significant influence on the general educated public. By 1905 he had written more than a hundred articles, yet only four had been for the *Dublin*, and none recently.[55] Second, beyond the normal difficulties of editors, there was the added difficulty that he was the editor of a semi-official journal (it was owned by the Archbishop of Westminster) and would, therefore, have to contend with the different shades of Catholic opinion, and with authority itself. While Ward had so far successfully navigated through the shoals of ecclesiastical authority, there was no telling when he might still hit a rock. Despite all this, Ward decided to take it on. He was uniquely prepared to be the editor of such a journal by his vast contacts and interests. He was well connected and had a gift for friendship, and friendship could be useful for attracting sub-

53. Nadia M. Lahutsky, "Wilfrid Ward: Roman Catholic 'Modernism' between the Modernists and the Integralists," *Downside Review* 103 (Jan. 1985): 36.

54. Tyrrell to Ward, Aug. 4, 1905, in Weaver, *Letters from a "Modernist,"* 102.

55. For a complete listing of Ward's works, see Mary Jo Weaver, "A Bibliography of the Published Works of Wilfrid Ward," *Heythrop Journal* 20 (Oct. 1979): 399–420.

scribers and contributors. Certainly Ward actively solicited subscriptions for the *Dublin* from among friends such as Arthur Balfour, the prime minister and fellow member of the Synthetic.[56] If this seems odd, one must remember that the subscription costs of quality journals were relatively high (the annual subscription to Ward's *Dublin* was a guinea, slightly above the weekly wage of a town laborer), and their circulation was usually low, even the successful ones generally having a circulation in the thousands rather than in the tens of thousands. What was important was to connect with the right people, "the upper ten thousand" who formed the governing and educated class and who wielded the greatest influence.

While Vaughan had been a family friend for whom Wilfrid had the highest respect and affection, it was highly unlikely that Vaughan would have ever let him run the *Dublin,* as Ward's daughter admits.[57] Nor would Canon Moyes have been happy to be succeeded by Wilfrid, whom he considered unsound and intellectually restless.[58] But with Vaughan's death in 1903, and the succession to Westminster of Francis Bourne (1861–1935), the Bishop of Southwark, the way was open. Even Merry del Val, now Cardinal Secretary of State to Pope Pius X, appeared to be open to the idea. In a letter to the Duke of Norfolk dated January 7, 1905, Ward wrote: "I talked to Cardinal Merry del Val about the *Dublin* and he seemed quite satisfied with the line I propose to take. It came at the end of a long discussion on other subjects, and he did not

56. In a letter of August 17, 1905, to Arthur Balfour, he wrote: "I am asking some of my Synthetic colleagues to patronize the *Dublin Review* which I am going to edit next year. A good many of the old Metaphysical Society subscribed to it under my father's editorship. I need not say that if you are disposed to take it in we should feel honoured, and it would help to bring the Review under the notice of the class of people to whom I wish to appeal outside the Catholic communion. George Wyndham is subscribing, and a good many more of his sort. Reggie Balfour is my sub-editor—whom I think you know. I enclose an order form in case you are disposed to take the Review in." See WWP II/3 (119). Balfour replied (Aug. 23, 1905) that he would be delighted to subscribe. See WWP II/3 (120). Balfour's friendship with Ward is remarkable considering his strong dislike of Catholicism. See *Wilfrid Wards* 1:373, and Kenneth Young, *Arthur James Balfour* (London: G. Bell, 1963), 159.

57. *Wilfrid Wards* 2:212–13.

58. Ibid., 154–55. In an undated letter to Bourne from J. G. Snead-Cox (1855–1939), editor of the *Tablet* from 1884 to 1920 and a director of Burns & Oates, we read: "I have had a long talk with Monsignor Moyes. I explained fully what was proposed in regard to the Dublin. He took it all very well and I think has no personal feeling in the matter. He does not disguise his distrust of our proposed editor, but said that of course everything rests with you." See WWP VII/43e (9). Maisie Ward clearly understands this letter as referring to Ward's taking up the editorship. See *Wilfrid Wards* 2:213.

commit himself to any very definite opinions, but he seemed perfectly satisfied and he said not one word expressing any doubt or anxiety on the subject."[59]

By 1905 English Catholicism had reached a certain level of maturity. In a few years (1908) this would be recognized by the Holy See in the removal of England from the jurisdiction of the Congregation de Propaganda Fide, ending its missionary status. Its numbers, its tight organization, its integrated system of institutions, and its theological and doctrinal discipline had put it in a position of great strength.[60] By the end of the Victorian period the Catholic Church "was poised to become the principal religious alternative to the established church."[61] By this time also Catholics had become much more a part of British national life. In 1886 the prime minister, Lord Salisbury, appointed Henry Matthews (later 1st Viscount Llandaff) home secretary, the first Catholic cabinet minister since the reign of James II; and from 1895 to 1900 the 15th Duke of Norfolk, Wilfrid's good friend and confidant, served as postmaster general in Lord Salisbury's government.[62] Salisbury also appointed the first Catholic ambassador since the Glorious Revolution: Sir Nicholas O'Conor, ambassador at St. Petersburg and, later, at Constantinople, and Wilfrid's brother-in-law.[63] In a society where the aristocracy still maintained great political and social authority the conversion between 1850 and 1900 of some seventy-six aristocrats, of which the most prominent were the 3rd Marquess of

59. See WWP VII/43c(1).

60. Hugh McLeod, "Building the 'Catholic Ghetto': Catholic Organizations, 1870–1920," in *Voluntary Religion,* ed. W. J. Sheils and Diana Wood (Oxford: B. Blackwell, 1986), 411–44.

61. Gerald Parsons, "Victorian Roman Catholicism: Emancipation, Expansion and Achievement," in *Religion in Victorian Britain,* ed. Gerald Parsons (Manchester: Manchester University Press, 1988), 1:181.

62. Newman's friend, the convert William Monsell (1812–1894), later Lord Emly, had served as postmaster general in Gladstone's government from January 1871 to November 1873, but this was not a cabinet position. Henry Matthews (1826–1913), from an old Catholic Herefordshire family on his mother's side and educated at the University of Paris *(bachelier-ès-lettres)* and the University of London (B.A. and LL.B), achieved great success at the bar and served in the Commons from 1868 to 1874 and from 1886 to 1895, when he was elevated to the peerage. He was home secretary from 1886 to 1892. Henry Fitzalan Howard (1847–1917), 15th Duke of Norfolk, hereditary Earl Marshal of England, a major benefactor of British Catholicism and its leading lay figure, was postmaster general until he resigned to serve in the Boer War. For Norfolk, see John Martin Robinson, *The Dukes of Norfolk: A Quincentennial History* (Oxford: Oxford University Press, 1982), 212–37.

63. O'Conor (1843–1908), from an ancient Irish family, educated at Stonyhurst and at Munich under Döllinger, entered the diplomatic service in 1866, served as British envoy to the emperor of China from 1892 to 1895, and then was British ambassador to Russia (1895–1898) and to the Sultan of Turkey (1898–1908). He was married to Josephine's sister, Minna.

Bute and the 1st Marquess of Ripon, was also of great significance.[64] In other ways, too, Catholics had become more involved in national life. In 1895, with Ward playing a significant role, the prohibition on Catholics going to Oxford and Cambridge, the seedbeds of the governing class, was removed.[65] While Catholicism was able to retain a large working-class constituency, it was also able to make some inroads in the middle and professional classes. The different segments of English Catholicism had also begun to fuse. Certainly the distinction between old Catholic and convert had largely disappeared, and to a certain extent even the distinction between Irish and English Catholics had begun to fade. Archbishop Bourne himself had a convert English father and an Irish mother. This fusion was certainly helped by the more enthusiastic Catholic piety of the nineteenth century, which transcended the different groups and seemed to bring together every class of Catholic.[66]

Ward's view of the importance of having a respected Catholic periodical and of what should constitute it can be found in an essay about Lord Acton and the *Rambler* which appeared in the January 1907 issue of the *Dublin,* and which, though unsigned, is certainly by Ward.[67] There he quotes approvingly a letter that Newman wrote (February 26, 1865) to one of the founders of the *Month,* Fr. Peter Gallwey, S.J.

As secular power, rank and wealth are great human means of promoting Catholicism, so especially in this democratic age is intellect. Without dreaming of denying the influence of the three first-named instruments of success, still I think the influence arising from repute for ability and the cultivation of science, in this age, is greater than any one of them. The Catholic body in England is despised by Protestants from their (unjust) idea of our deficiency in education, and in that power which education gives of bringing out and bringing to bear natural talent which Catholics have, as others. They have an idea that few Catholics can think justly or explain themselves suitably. A first-rate journal then, of which the staple was science, art, literature, politics, etc.,

64. Sheridan Gilley, "The Years of Equipoise, 1892–1943," in *From without the Flaminian Gate: 150 Years of Roman Catholicism in England and Wales, 1850–2000,* ed. Vincent Alan McClelland and Michael Hodgetts (London: Darton, Longman and Todd, 1999), 25. Lord Bute (1847–1900), the figure who inspired Disraeli's *Lothair,* was enormously wealthy and a great benefactor of the Church. Lord Ripon (1827–1909), son of a prime minister, a former Liberal minister and grand master of the English Freemasons, went on to become the only Catholic viceroy of India and served in Campbell-Bannerman's Liberal government.

65. See McClelland, *English Roman Catholics and Higher Education.*

66. See Sheridan Gilley, "Vulgar Piety and the Brompton Oratory, 1850–1860," in Swift and Gilley, *Irish in the Victorian City,* 255–66; and Heimann, *Catholic Devotion in Victorian England.*

67. [Wilfrid Ward], "Lord Acton and the 'Rambler,'" *Dublin Review* (Jan. 1907): 1–19.

would be worth more to the Catholic cause than half a dozen noblemen, or even a millionaire.[68]

Newman's letter cautioned that the journal should not teach Catholic truth directly for fear that it would be considered an "Ultramontane organ" and so lose the broad appeal that would be necessary for its success. In another letter (June 1865) quoted by Ward, to the Jesuit Fr. Henry Coleridge, the editor of the *Month,* Newman wrote that if theology were to be brought into such a publication it should be done in the least technical and most approachable way possible, in a way most open to English common sense.[69]

Ward was impressed by the ability of Acton, for both of his journals were far superior to other Catholic periodicals in intelligence, candor, and style, as well as in the notice they gained from educated Protestants. He was, however, also critical of him (as was Newman), because, by his lack of sensitivity to the feelings of the ordinary faithful and his lack of respect for authority and past theology, he unnecessarily alienated many. "Hundreds who would accept it if it came in the dress of loyal Catholic sympathies, will reject it if it is accompanied by a disloyal tone, or even by an ill-mannered disregard of the external respect due to ecclesiastical authority. This is the one all-important distinction between 'Liberal' Catholicism in the invidious sense and the spirit which animates really progressive thought in theology—the spirit of the great schoolmen of the thirteenth century."[70]

Inspired by Newman, Ward's vision was clear: "a Review, marked by general culture, literary and scientific, technical theology being reduced to a minimum."[71] If the Catholic vision was universal, as Ward certainly believed it was, then all aspects of human culture were within its purview. It had to be a

68. Ibid., 12. The complete text can be found in Newman, *Letters and Diaries of Newman,* 21:422–23.

69. [Ward], "Lord Acton and the 'Rambler,'" 13. The full text can be found in Newman, *Letters and Diaries of Newman,* 21:496–97. In an earlier letter to Coleridge (June 14, 1865) Newman wrote that he was sorry theology was being introduced into the *Month:* "I don't see theology is wanted, whereas literature etc is—nor do I think it the instrument of conversions—and it will deprive the Magazine of the chance of influence in the Protestant world" (ibid., 494).

70. [Ward], "Lord Acton and the 'Rambler,'" 16. Though Acton was severe in his historical moral judgments and assaulted what he considered the mendacious use of history by the Ultramontanes, his own prejudices against them undermined his scholarly objectivity. See Hugh Tulloch, *Acton* (New York: St. Martin's Press, 1988), 49–55. Ward could not write biographies of those to whom he was not sympathetic, and when Lord Acton's son asked him to write one on his father after his death, Ward declined.

71. [Ward], "Lord Acton and the 'Rambler,'" 13.

journal of general culture, accessible to the general reader. It would also be a journal loyal to the Church and aware of the sensitivities of the faithful; yet not skirting the hard truth to preserve communal *esprit de corps.* All he demanded was that the articles be well written, intelligent, loyal to the Church, understanding of the world, and sympathetic to whatever was valuable outside the household of faith. The tone was to be proudly Catholic and intelligently irenic. This, by definition, excluded the more intransigent Catholics, who were still in a siege mentality, and the "Liberal Catholics," whom Ward thought were too contemptuous of the institutional machinery of the Church, with its cautious conservatism and interfering ways.

Ward was a Tory, and while the general political tone of the journal reflected this, on purely political topics he included articles on both sides of an issue. This was not to say that the *Dublin* would be bland or colorless. Ward believed that the success of the journal depended on its taking a definite line on current topics, and that line would certainly reflect Ward's own views.[72] In an undated letter to the editor of the *Times,* Ward expressed his views on the responsibility for the opinions of the *Dublin*'s signed articles and reviews. Unlike the *Nineteenth Century,* which accepted all articles as personal, or the *Edinburgh,* where the editor accepted all responsibility, the *Dublin* followed a middle course. "Incidentally expressed opinions will be found to the writers, but articles and reviews will not as a rule be admitted advocating in important points views *materially* different from those which the editor desires to maintain in the Review." Besides articles, mostly signed, there was an extensive section, "Some Recent Books," for shorter reviews, always forty or fifty pages of each number, with reviews from a paragraph to four or five pages in length, containing some of the *Dublin*'s best work.[73]

He also wished to include the full range of the Catholic mind: there were men and women, lay and clerical, members of the religious orders and diocesan priests, converts and cradle Catholics. Even Jesuits, who had their own journal, the *Month,* to support, contributed, among them Herbert Thurston (1856–1939), and C. C. Martindale (1879–1963).[74] Ward's view of the Church

72. "I believe the strength of the Review and its source of success will largely be that it represents *conviction.* . . . And I believe that the best chance I have of making the Review a success is by taking a definite line on current topics, and not by trimming or being colourless." Ward to his publishers, cited in *Wilfrid Wards* 2:210.

73. For the *Times* letter, see WWP VI/25d. For the "Some Recent Books" section, see *Wilfrid Wards* 2:207–8.

74. Thurston entered the Jesuits in 1874, was ordained in 1890, and joined the staff of the

was always triumphalist: no matter her human imperfections, she was the ark of salvation and the locus of divine truth, and nothing could diminish his respect and loyalty to her. But the journal was not meant to be exclusively Catholic. Non-Catholics such as Lord Hugh Cecil, Lord Halifax, G. K. Chesterton (who was only received into the Church in 1922), and W. H. Mallock (who entered the Church on his deathbed in 1923) could be found in its lists. The *Dublin* attracted many readers from outside the Church, and it was the non-Catholics, especially, whom Ward wished to influence. What chiefly drew them, according to Ward's daughter, were the articles on pure literature and politics, both home and foreign.[75]

Ward always tried to stress the positive, so it is not surprising that his journal did the same, particularly in reference to Catholic works. In Ward's editorial correspondence we see a good example of this. Ward had asked the learned Benedictine Dom John Chapman to review *The Greek Fathers* (1908) by the English Catholic priest-scholar Adrian Fortescue (1874–1923). Ward found the review too negative, however, and wanted it rewritten in a more positive vein. Chapman could not oblige. "I do not admit that I wrote in the spirit of a Saturday reviewer; I should not think of slashing out at the faults of a fairly good book; nor should I treat a poor book as a very bad one. In this case I simply said what I thought: the book is astoundingly bad."[76] In the end, a damning review did appear, though it was only a few pages long and attempts were made to soften the blow with some kind words ("he has put together much interesting material, and has written some charming descriptions").[77] If Ward wished to stress the positive, it did have limits, and scholarship was certainly one of them.

While the following chapters will discuss some of the journal's particular areas of interest and their authors, it would be well to briefly look at some others that will not be given such attention.

Month in 1894, remaining there until his death. Known for his critical, even skeptical, cast of mind, his main areas of research were history, hagiography, and the liturgy. For Thurston, see Joseph Crehan, *Father Thurston: A Memoir with a Bibliography of His Writings* (New York: Sheed and Ward, 1952). Cyril Charles Martindale was received into the Church on leaving Harrow. After entering the Jesuits he went to Oxford, where he received a first in *Litterae Humaniores* (1905) and a slew of prizes and scholarships. Ordained in 1911, he was an able preacher, writer, and spiritual guide. For his life, see Philip Caraman, *C. C. Martindale: A Biography* (London: Longmans, 1967).

75. *Wilfrid Wards* 2:207.

76. Chapman to Ward, Oct. 30, 1908, WWP VII/60/1/5.

77. John Chapman, "Some Recent Books," *Dublin Review* (Jan. 1909): 206–8.

A good portion of the journal dealt with philosophy, both modern and scholastic. Ward was very impressed by what Désiré Mercier had achieved with his *Institut Supérieur de Philosophie* at Louvain, with its study of modern science and modern philosophy and their integration of these with the principles of St. Thomas Aquinas. He not only included an article on it but he put John Vance, with a Louvain D.Ph., in charge of a specialized periodic column reviewing philosophy books beginning with the January 1914 number.[78]

In the area of the natural sciences, particularly biology, the most eminent and prolific contributor was Sir Bertram Windle (1858–1929), who, besides writing articles, wrote an enormous number of reviews in "Some Recent Books" under the initials B.C.A.W.[79] Windle, a fellow of the Royal Society educated at Trinity College, Dublin, where he received his M.D. in 1883, and a convert to Catholicism after a period of agnosticism, was an able teacher, researcher, and administrator. It was largely through his work that Birmingham University was created in 1900. In 1904 he was made president of Queen's College, Cork, and he was knighted in 1911. As he wrote in his initial letter to Ward, he wished primarily to write on scientific matters "of present-day interest" so as "to give Catholics the most recent information available on burning questions."[80]

Finally, critical work on Scripture and early Church history was also given extensive coverage, particularly in the "Some Recent Books" section. In the area of Scripture, Canon William Barry (1849–1930)[81] and Hugh Pope, O.P.

78. John G. Vance, "Science and Philosophy at Louvain," ibid. (July 1913): 27–52. The founder of the Institut was Désiré Mercier (1851–1926), Archbishop of Malines in 1906 and a cardinal in 1907. Georges van Riet, *Thomistic Epistemology: Studies Concerning the Problem of Cognition in the Contemporary School,* vol. 1 (St. Louis: B. Herder, 1963), 124–63, has a good account of what Mercier did at Louvain as well as of his philosophical views. John G. Vance (1885–1968) was ordained in 1911 and was a professor at Westminster's St. Edmund's, Ware. In a letter to Lord Halifax, Oct. 1, 1907, Ward praised Mercier, who had given evidence when Ward was on the Irish Universities Commission. See WWP VI/13 (85).

79. See Monica Taylor, *Sir Bertram Windle: A Memoir* (London: Longmans, Green, 1932).

80. Windle to Ward (Oct. 23, 1905), WWP VII/319.

81. Dr. William Barry, ordained a priest in 1873 for Birmingham, was a prodigious author of novels, books, and articles on a vast range of subjects. In the *Dublin*'s review of his *Tradition of Scripture: Its Origin, Authority and Interpretation* (London: Longmans, Green, 1906) (part of the Westminster Library's "Series of Manuals for Catholic Priests and Students," edited by Bernard Ward and Herbert Thurston), the reviewer, W. H. K. (W. H. Kent), praised it as "a dispassionate examination of modern Biblical literature" that separated the "real results of scientific research from the crude speculations of individual critics" and kept a fine balance between the "temerity of critics" and "the intolerant temper of ultra-conservative theologians." "The book is thus a Biblical Eirenicon; and, if it cannot bring about absolute peace, it may be hoped that it will at least do

(1869–1946)[82] were major contributors. But the greater part of the writing in this area was done by John Chapman, O.S.B. (1865–1933) and later by John P. Arendzen (1873–1954).[83] Later on, beginning with the July 1908 issue, a specialized periodic column was set aside, first for Chapman and then for Arendzen, just to review recent biblical literature. In the area of patristics and early Church history there was Chapman (again) and Hugh Connolly, O.S.B. (1873–1948), a monk of Downside and an authority on Syriac and the early Christian liturgy.

something to still the storm." See "Some Recent Books," *Dublin Review* (April 1906): 407–9. For Barry's life, see his *Memories and Opinions* (New York: G. P. Putnam's Sons, 1926) and Sheridan Gilley, "Father William Barry: Priest and Novelist," *Recusant History* 24 (Oct. 1999): 523–51.

82. Hugh Pope received a doctorate in sacred Scripture in Rome (1909) and was professor of New Testament exegesis at the Angelicum, Rome, from 1909 to 1913, when he was accused of being a modernist, removed from his post, and sent back to England. For Pope's life, see Kieran Mulvey, *Hugh Pope* (London: Blackfriars Publications, 1954).

83. John Chapman was a convert from Anglicanism who joined the Belgian Benedictine monastery of Maredsous, helped found an English house at Erdington, and eventually transferred to Downside Abbey (1919) where he was abbot from 1929 to 1933. He was a member of the Commission for the Revision of the Vulgate from 1914 to 1923. Arendzen, ordained a priest in 1895 for Westminster, had a D.D. from Munich University and a Ph.D. (Semitic philology) from Bonn University, and was professor of holy Scripture at Old Hall. For Chapman's life, see Cuthbert Butler, "Abbot Chapman," *Downside Review* 52 (Jan. 1934): 1–12; and Chapman, *The Spiritual Letters of John Chapman,* ed. Roger Hudleston (London: Sheed and Ward, 1935), 1–19.

3 TRANSCENDENCE, REVELATION, AND IMMANENCE

Ward's particular interests were apologetics and theology. The most important and consistent theme in his writing, indeed, central to his life's work, was the reconciliation of Catholicism with the mind of the age. Catholic apologetics and theology in the late nineteenth and early twentieth centuries were dominated by a neo-scholasticism focused on extrinsic and objective factors, which stressed the supernatural, the rational, the logical, and the deductive, and was free of any historical sense.[1] The age, however, was strongly focused on intrinsic and subjective factors, on the personal, interior, and moral dimension of knowledge, guided by a strong sense of the historical. While all transcendence (the reaching beyond ourselves, particularly the experience of the abiding and infinite by the contingent and finite) includes both transcendent and immanent elements (things external to us and things internal to us), this is especially true of faith, which, while purely supernatural and gratuitous, is still rooted in our own natural powers and their capacities. A hallmark of modernity is the acquisition of historical consciousness, an awareness that things exist in a dynamic of becoming, in the particularity of the situation, embodied in some historical and cultural form, not in some timeless and universal essence. Revelation also existed in history and therefore shared in the problems of historicity. Neo-scholasticism, in contrast, saw revelation in essentialist and ahistorical terms. This new historical understanding had a profound effect upon apologetics and theology.[2] Ward's goal with the

1. See Gabriel Daly, *Transcendence and Immanence: A Study in Catholic Modernism and Integralism* (Oxford: Clarendon Press, 1980), 7–25.

2. See Hinchliff, *God and History.*

Dublin was to keep the transcendent supernatural reality of the Catholic faith on speaking terms with a world conditioned by a historical, personalistic, and subjective mindset.

To Ward's mind, the finest example of how Catholics should meet the intellectual challenges to their faith was the response of St. Thomas Aquinas and the great scholastics to the arrival of the full thought of Aristotle in the West. Ward turned to this example in the first article of the first number of his *Dublin.*[3] Ward compared the Oxford of the nineteenth century, with its clash of liberal and conservative, its defenders of reason and its defenders of faith, to the experience of the medieval universities at the time of the rediscovery of Aristotle and the use of dialectic as a means of knowledge. The medieval Church had only two options available: it could simply ignore the new learning and by the use of authority put an end to it; or it could use the new methods and authorities, purge them of their dangerous qualities, and so attempt to stem the tide of extreme rationalism. The first was tried and failed, while the second, under men like St. Thomas, was ultimately successful. Ward thought the same should be true of the present, and with the intellectual difficulties Catholics were experiencing. Proscription would inevitably fail, but "a strenuous effort to deal with modern criticism, to keep it within reasonable limits, to restrain by its own principles a method which professes to be cautious and experimental, but which is constantly proving itself in the highest degree theoretical, speculative and adventurous, is just the medicine which will remedy the ills of the hour after the manner of Albertus and Thomas."[4]

In the lead article of his second number, "Cardinal Newman and Creative Theology," Ward looked at the wider history of Christian thought.[5] He found in Christian theology the interaction of two elements: the conservative "Roman" element, embodying tradition, rule, and uniformity, which was represented especially by the authorities who sought to guard the original revelation, and the "Greek" element, which embodied "vital thought," that intellectual *élan* that pressed for a further elaboration of Christian revelation in relation to the thought of the age, and that could result either in heresy or in creative theology. He saw that the history of theology could be divided into

3. [Wilfrid Ward], "St Thomas Aquinas and Medieval Thought," *Dublin Review* (Jan. 1906): 1–27.

4. Ibid., 21.

5. [Wilfrid Ward], "Cardinal Newman and Creative Theology," ibid. (April 1906): 233–70.

periods of receptivity, where the teaching of the past was loyally adhered to, inculcated, and transmitted, and periods of creativity, depending upon which of these two elements was predominant. Periods of creativity included such eras as the patristic golden age and medieval scholasticism, while periods of receptivity included the monastic "Dark Ages" and the time from the Reformation till the early nineteenth century. While periods of receptivity, with their "normal and desirable Christian attitude of unquestioning belief," were good for the "restful life of devotion," their lack of critical awareness made it much more difficult for the faith to adjust and so to maintain its appeal. In the nineteenth century the conflict was not so much in philosophy as in the hard sciences and in historical criticism. While the Church had found many able apologists, the figure who best understood what must be done and who supplied the best model on how to deal with these topics, according to Ward, was Newman.

Ward believed that men like Acton exaggerated the impartiality of modern research. Acton believed that it was free of all party spirit, presuppositions, and bias, and had become dispassionate and impersonal. Therefore, it could be no danger to the Church or to the Christian faith. That is why he found the conservatism of the Church's authorities irksome and, outside the definitions of faith, demanded an absolute liberty of thought. It was skepticism about this very point that Ward found so attractive in Newman. For Newman, despite his sympathy with Acton's ideals of research, this mindset approximated closely that rationalistic liberalism which he had given his whole life to combating. Ward maintained that Newman's views were far more materially useful to our times in defining the scope and method of creative theology. They included "a profound sympathy with the plea for thoroughness, impartiality and freedom of research" with an awareness "that freedom of intellect, in its survey of the whole range of knowledge and of life," was unlikely to produce impartiality or lead to the highest truth. Newman believed that the natural man, fallen man, does not possess a pure unbiased intellect, nor are assumptions and presumptions the monopoly of the narrow or the ultra-orthodox. He thought that the modern spirit which inspired the liberal writers, because of its belief in the absolutely free exercise of human reason, was, in its *general* tendency, irreligious: self-confident in its all-encompassing science, consumed by the knowledge of the external senses, deaf to the subtle inner voice of conscience or any other intimation of the divine. Ward wrote: "As the heart of man must be renewed to make it love what is good and pure and congenial to our higher nature, so the intellect must be disciplined and purified to enable it to keep the simple eye for truth."[6] Newman's attack, however, was not on the lawful use of reason but on its constant abuse by fallen human nature, which could not see its limitations and was easily impressed by its successes in the visible world. For both Newman and Ward there was only one power that could spare man from the tyranny of the world of science and of the senses—the Catholic Church. No other institution, and certainly not the Bible, had been able to remain a bulwark against the corrosive skepticism of the unrestrained intellect. For Ward its office was twofold: "Firstly it reminds men of truths which the atmosphere of secular thought leads them to forget or ignore. It 'bathes' the human reason in a new atmosphere and new associations. But it has another also, which he [Newman] insists on in some detail—namely, the healthy *restraint* of the speculative intellect, which is as prone to excess as any other faculty."[7] Newman was not opposed to free discussion; he even saw its absolute necessity, but it should be limited to those prepared for it by the proper training and moral temper. He warned against attaching finality to existing forms of theological reasoning since that might check the pursuit of true lines of research and set up the faithful for a shock when a particular statement, having been identified with revealed truth, itself had to be dropped or explained away. This resistance to premature dogmatism, however, had to be allied with a deep respect for past theology and the inherited wisdom of the Church.

Newman's respect for the Christian past and his awareness of human limitations made him a defender of prejudice, an aspect of Newman's thought that Ward discussed in "The Functions of Prejudice."[8] Ward maintained that there were really two Newmans: the man whose intelligence was keen to all the beauties of the world and to every movement of thought, and the mystic who was absorbed in the consciousness of God's presence and for whom reality was solely in the things of the spirit. "He tasted—and no one more keenly or accurately—of all that is interesting and beautiful in life: he tasted, but he

6. Ibid., 256.

7. Ibid., 262.

8. [Wilfrid Ward], "The Functions of Prejudice," ibid. (Jan. 1906): 99–118. In a letter to Maud Petre (April 17, 1906), von Hügel mentioned that Ward had visited him, worried over the announcement by the *Tablet*'s Roman correspondent that "quite a number of English Catholic *lay* writers" were about to be condemned and that Archbishop Bagshawe had denounced both his article "The Functions of Prejudice" and the epilogue to his biography of Cardinal Wiseman. See British Library, Petre Papers, Add. 45361.

did not drink."[9] He entered into everything but was never absorbed by it. This duality in Newman was also apparent in his intellectual life. He had a keen appreciation of the movement of thought in theology and, at first, was inclined toward the liberalism of the Oriel Noetics, to which many of his sympathies pointed and whose theology was to lead to a full-blown rationalism. But his philosophy of faith, deepened by the death of his favorite sister and his study of the early Fathers, checked this inclination and threw him into the camp of the "two-bottle orthodox," the unintellectual conservatives whose faith was founded more on inherited and unreflective belief, on prejudice, than on any rational basis. This duality of attitude helps explain why Newman could enter into the premises of rationalistic thinkers so well, even as he denied their conclusions and even while, as a life-long opponent of liberalism in religion, he was sometimes called a Liberal Catholic. The key to Newman's shift to a conservative philosophy, Ward believed, was his new understanding that prejudice had preserved the truth far better.

> A legacy of important truths had been committed to the race by the primitive teaching of unsophisticated nature, by the experience of ages, by the wisdom of the few giants among thinkers and seers of the past, and by the revelation of Christ Himself. The acute and highly-trained nineteenth-century thinkers might be unequal to the justification of truths, which far greater minds than theirs had seen indeed, but which they had never proved by a process which could become private property. . . . The rationalist dismisses as below his intellect, as vain superstition, what may be really the vision of a mind that is above his own. The dogged persistence of the prejudiced and bigoted, and the faith of the simple, on the other hand, preserve such truths as a sacred tradition, not fathomed by their defenders, but undestroyed. Thus prejudice becomes the guardian of truth.[10]

Burke had also defended prejudice, but since his focus was on politics he was concerned mainly with the accumulated wisdom and experience of the race. Newman, concerned with religion, thought more about preserving man's primitive instinctual apprehension of the divine, the intuitions of the seer and prophet, and the unique revelation of Christ himself. Yet while prejudice was the conservator of this wisdom, of the sacred mysteries whose full comprehension was not possible, it could not be the only thing. As a Catholic, Newman did not have to worry about excessive rationalism, since the Church's institutional nature preserved traditional dogma from the dissolving

9. Ward, "The Function of Prejudice," 100.
10. Ibid., 102–3.

power of reason, but he saw a new danger and new worries. The danger was now the opposite: that the untenable elements of an earlier uncritical age, which the tradition had carried forward in its conservatism, should be confused with the essential truths of this wisdom. Yet Newman was hesitant about change, even as he saw its "sad necessity." As Ward wrote:

> The sanguineness of the typical liberal thinker, to whom the "march of mind" is so inspiring, was wholly alien to his nature. And his sense of the sacredness of the existing theological structure as symbolizing Divine Truth was such as to make him averse from all tampering with it. . . . The change had to be made but it was a thankless work, for the new theology was still, like the old, but an inadequate symbol of the Divine; and he did not share the enthusiasm of sanguine specialists whose imaginations and hopes painted in such glowing colours the glories of a Divinity which should be "up to date."[11]

Despite Newman's fear that change might rend the whole fabric of ancient dogma (he was even willing to leave some inaccurate statements in place for a while if that was necessary for the stability of the whole), change would come. He believed that a certain degree of openness, therefore, was necessary, and that all interests, and not merely the intellectual, had to be considered. "Consequently discussion must neither be burked nor allowed to lead to hasty changes. Minds must be gradually accustomed to the points at issue as being subjects for debate, before being forced into a definite direction. The new questions must be opened and allowed for a time to remain open."[12]

In his article "For Truth or for Life" Ward discussed man's two basic needs: the needs of the intellect, which seeks whatever is true, and the needs of our deeper nature, our spiritual or devotional nature, which go further than our discursive reason, which he referred to as the "needs of life."[13] He also considered the tension between them and elaborated on how much of our piety was tied to beliefs that, while not in any way essential to the faith, yet gave it a certain concreteness and specificity, and that, with the development of criticism, could no longer be held—much to the loss of piety and of life.

> The man who has gone on a yearly pilgrimage to the Holy Shroud at Turin feels himself to have derived no benefit from the news that the experts have given up its authenticity. He has lost a source of devotion to gain a barren truth. So too one who has had a devotion to the sixth Station loses much and gains nothing by learning that the

11. Ibid., 117–18.

12. Ibid., 112.

13. [Wilfrid Ward], "For Truth or for Life," ibid. (Oct. 1906): 233–51.

story of Veronica is not critically tenable. The Roman pilgrim loses much and gains nothing by being unable any longer to ascend the Scala Santa with the belief that it is identical with the steps of the Pretorium.[14]

Such was the human mind that some truths could be presented only with alloy, embedded in a mass of traditions of unequal value. Ward believed that the mass of Christian tradition was such a compound. While change was unsettling, if adjustments were not made in accordance with the certain fruits of criticism the rising generations would think Christianity untenable ("cannot face the problems of the day"). Change was, therefore, inevitable, but one had to be very careful in separating the true from the false for fear of destroying the hidden springs of religious life, of destroying a deeper and latent truth in the reckless pursuit of another. Because of this he thought that this change should be gradual and piecemeal so as not to shock the faithful too severely. The Christian critic was not in the same position as the non-Christian, for the Christian critic believed "that truth is for the Christian in possession, though bound up with incidental illusion and inaccurate knowledge," and that therefore he should avoid "dislocating the existing mental equipment of the Christian, while correcting it." In the area of biblical studies he thought that the great Anglican critics, Hort, Lightfoot, and Westcott, were exemplary in preserving the needs both of truth and of life.

Following Newman's 1877 preface to his *Via Media,* Ward described the Church's polity as being represented by three interests: the interests of truth, of devotion, and of stable and wise rule. At certain times in the Church's history a particular interest would gain an exaggerated preeminence over the others, and when that happened all one could do was be patient, knowing that the imbalance was only temporary.

Ward recognized that sometimes authority acted in ways that offended scholarly minds. In reviewing the published correspondence of Baron von Hügel and the American Protestant biblical scholar C. A. Briggs on the decision of the Pontifical Biblical Commission, on June 27, 1906, affirming the Mosaic authorship of the Pentateuch *(The Papal Commission and the Pentateuch),* Ward pointed out that it was the nature of such a conservative institu-

14. Ibid., 236. To look at an example that Ward himself uses, the Shroud of Turin, one can compare the dismissal of it by someone such as Fr. Herbert Thurston, S.J. (in his article on it in the *Catholic Encyclopedia,* ed. Charles G. Herberman et al. [New York: R. Appleton, 1907–14], 13:762–63), with the more ambiguous comments of the Cambridge Egyptologist James Ray in his article in the TLS ("The Turin Shroud Now," *Times Literary Supplement* [Oct. 18, 1996]: 3–4).

tion as the Church to be behind the scholarly curve.[15] It changes by degrees, beginning with small openings and suggestions that then can be explored further, until, bit by bit, over time, the truth becomes clear to everyone and acceptance is possible. He also pointed out that von Hügel seemed to attach to the commission's decrees a more conservative interpretation than did M. Mangenot, a professor at the Paris Institut Catholique and a member of the commission, whose book *L'Authenticité Mosaïque du Pentateuque* he was also reviewing. Mangenot maintained that the decree was not *de fide* and that Mosaic authorship did "not necessarily involve more than the attribution to Moses of *la rédaction ou le fond de la majeure partie de l'ouvrage.*"[16] As Ward pointed out later, in the continuation of "For Truth and for Life," acts such as that of the Pontifical Biblical Commission were generally not dogmatic statements of scientific fact but political statements whose aim was to regulate the too facile acceptance of critical ideas. Ward thought that von Hügel did not understand this. "He [von Hügel] interprets them indeed, as we pointed out in January, in a more conservative sense than M. Mangenot, himself a member of the Biblical Commission. . . . He treats the conclusions of the Commission as strictly scientific conclusions. A Professor at one of our leading

15. W. W. [Wilfrid Ward], "Some Recent Books," *Dublin Review* (Jan. 1907): 214–17. For the Briggs and von Hügel collaboration, see Gerald Fogarty, *American Catholic Biblical Scholarship: A History from the Early Republic to Vatican II* (New York: Harper & Row, 1989), 140–54. See also Mark Massa, "'Mediating Modernism': Charles Briggs, Catholic Modernism, and an Ecumenical 'Plot,'" *Harvard Theological Review* 81 (Oct. 1988): 413–30; and William J. Hynes, "A Hidden Nexus between Catholic and Protestant Modernism: C. A. Briggs in Correspondence with Loisy, von Hügel and Genocchi," *Downside Review* 105 (July 1987): 193–223. Von Hügel wrote to Ward (Jan. 26, 1907): "I have to thank you for three things. Your *notice of Dr. Briggs and me* was thoroughly kind and very acceptable in its personal tone to us both, I am sure. I doubt whether, even if you *had* felt more strongly as to the necessities of the situation *hic et nunc,* you could, in the 'D.R.' and as its Editor, have said more in this direction. And the notice will, probably, get us more readers. Thank you then in Dr. Briggs name as well as my own. The further questions, we have often talked over; they can await their solution on the painful, costing battle-field of time, and of life on the largest scale." See WWP II/170. In a letter to Ward ("3/6/1907") from David Fleming (1851–1920), who was a consultor of the Biblical Commission in Rome, Ward was told that things were now "satisfactory" in Rome, and that people there perceived that progress must be allowed, although some sort of condemnation was in the works. "The *Dublin* is doing well. Von Hügel is hopeless! His letter to Briggs gave great offence. He should not have mentioned *R. Simon* and Loisy. He is *absurd* in his conceit. I do not know anything very definite about the *Syllabus.* Anyhow, *you* need not be afraid, but von Hügel and the Subjectivists must be kept aloof. The whole philosophical question must be handled with great delicacy and accuracy in itself and in relation to history, exegesis and dogma. Some writers have made a hash all around." See WWP VII/105.

16. W. W. [Wilfrid Ward], "Some Recent Books," *Dublin Review* (Jan. 1907): 214.

Seminaries in this country said to the present writer: 'If you want scientific conclusions, you must go to the Universities; the decrees of a Roman Commission, ratified by the Pope, are *from the nature of the case* largely diplomatic.'"[17]

Ward wrote a second part to his article "For Truth or for Life" because it had been criticized by some as being too indulgent of the weaknesses of the unintellectual and by others as conceding too much to scientific criticism. In 1906–1907 Ward was attacked in the *Catholic Times*, the *Catholic Fireside*, and in a journal called *Rome*, and denunciations and strictures, some anonymous, were sent to Archbishop Bourne, who passed them on to Ward. Among those who criticized Ward's articles was Archbishop Bagshawe, the retired Bishop of Nottingham. The famed convert priest, preacher, and spiritual writer Basil Maturin wrote Ward (June 18, 1907) a very supportive letter at this time:

I cannot tell you how much I reject and deplore the proposed strictures on the *Dublin* article "For Truth or for Life." It appears to me if such an article is to meet with disapproval from those in authority then there be no place for the *Dublin* or indeed for a Catholic review of any intellectual standard in England under the present regime. That English Catholics must confess themselves unable to deal with modern thought at all. In the few months you have had the *Dublin* you have raised it to a position in which it can *hold its own* amongst the leading reviews of the day. Before you took it, it was moribund. If it cannot deal with questions that are disturbing men's minds in the very temperate and reverent way in which you did in your article, it must sink back into the *position* in which you found it.[18]

17. [Wilfrid Ward], "For Truth or for Life," ibid. (April 1907): 278.

18. WWP VII/199a (2). Basil Maturin (1847–1915) died tragically on the *Lusitania.* Maturin was the only other priest besides Bremond to attend Tyrrell's funeral, though he was unsympathetic to his positions. He only attended because Tyrrell was an old friend of his family; he had not known that there was any difficulty about the burial until he got to Storrington. Ward wrote of Maturin after his death: "He was wholly out of sympathy with the excesses of Modernism. The publication of Father Tyrrell's Life was a deep grief to him, for he had greatly admired the spiritual lessons contained in Father Tyrrell's early books, and he had an old family friendship with the man himself. 'I shall nevermore take any interest in anything Tyrrell has said,' was his deliberate utterance after reading Tyrrell's Life. On the other hand, Father Maturin detested the narrow anti-Modernists and was keenly alive, just as Cardinal Newman was, to the necessity of facing new facts which must affect our view of the universe, and of saying old things in a new way for a new generation." Wilfrid Ward, "Father Maturin," *Dublin Review* (July 1915): 15. In two letters (June 6 and 7), Bishop O'Dwyer, while saying that he found nothing worthy of condemnation in the "For Truth or for Life" articles and in fact found them very valuable, mentioned that he did notice an "uncatholic" flavor or tone in them that grated upon him. He also strongly condemned von Hügel's setting himself up over the Church and pope, and he did not like the line of excuse for him adopted by the *Dublin.* See WWP VII/226a (47) and (48). For Ward's reply to O'Dwyer, see WWP VI/25c (2).

For Ward the real test was the modernist crisis.[19] It is unfortunate that insofar as Ward receives any attention from contemporary scholars it is usually in relation to modernism. But since the modernist crisis almost ended his career as editor of the *Dublin* and endangered his life's work, it is something that must be discussed at some length. While the *Dublin* was not the mouthpiece of the more critical Catholic thinkers, Ward did not ignore them. After he became editor he asked Baron von Hügel if he could publish a paper, "Experience and Transcendence," that von Hügel had given at the Synthetic Society in 1903.[20] A significantly changed version of this paper appeared in the April 1906 number, and while its appeal to human experience as a locus of theological reflection may have disturbed some, most must have found it impenetrable.[21] Maisie Ward wrote of it: "My mother wrote to my father that she and Reggie Balfour had read it with wet towels round their heads trying to understand it."[22]

Despite the recent coldness in their relations, Ward did ask Tyrrell to review Oscar Wilde's *De Profundis* for the *Dublin,* but Tyrrell declined.[23] He spoke of Tyrrell's "invaluable contributions to Catholic thought" in his review of Charles Devas's book *The Key to the World's Progress.*[24] But he spoke most fully in his review of Tyrrell's *Lex Credendi.*[25] After commenting that a new book from Tyrrell was "an event of real importance" and praising Tyrrell's unrivalled ability and genius in using aphorisms and short essays to analyze the

19. The literature on modernism is immense. For a good general introduction and bibliography, see Bernard M. G. Reardon, "Roman Catholic Modernism," in *Nineteenth Century Religious Thought in the West,* vol. 2, ed. Ninian Smart et al. (Cambridge: Cambridge University Press, 1985), 141–77. See also Darell Jodock, ed., *Catholicism Contending with Modernity: Roman Catholic Modernism and Anti-Modernism in Historical Context* (Cambridge: Cambridge University Press, 2000). For the English scene, see William J. Schoenl, *The Intellectual Crisis in English Catholicism: Liberal Catholics, Modernists, and the Vatican in the Late Nineteenth and Early Twentieth Centuries* (New York: Garland, 1982). For the theological side, see Daly, *Transcendence and Immanence.*

20. For a discussion of this paper and the article that followed, see James Kelly, "Experience and Transcendence: An Introduction to the Religious Philosophy of Baron von Hügel," *Downside Review* 99 (July 1981): 172–89.

21. Friedrich von Hügel, "Experience and Transcendence," *Dublin Review* (April 1906): 357–79.

22. *Wilfrid Wards* 2:215. Oddly enough, Bishop O'Dwyer read it "with great admiration and a good deal of assent." O'Dwyer to Ward, April 30, 1906, WWP VII/226a (40).

23. Tyrrell to Ward, Aug. 4 and 11; see Weaver, *Letters from a "Modernist,"* 58–59. Before this request Ward had not written to Tyrrell for nearly a year after their falling out over Tyrrell's "Semper Eadem" article, which Ward took as a clear criticism of himself.

24. W. W. [Wilfrid Ward], "Some Recent Books," *Dublin Review* (April 1906): 409.

25. W. W. [Wilfrid Ward], "Some Recent Books," ibid. (July 1906): 182–87.

religious or psychological life of man or to criticize current popular theological exaggerations, he began his critique.

He is less reliable as a constructive thinker, partly because the extreme suppleness of his mind leads him to regard some of the problems with which he deals from very different points of view at different times. And the different aspects are often presented by him with so much force and brilliancy that his readers may identify what is only one aspect of a large question, or even the expression of a passing mood, with his mature and complete verdict. Nothing would be easier than to find passages in his more constructive writing which, taken by themselves, do not fairly represent his real mind. He has that quality, moreover, of the critic or zealous reformer, that he is more ready to dwell on defects in the existing state of things than to realize adequately the true principles underlying what is unsatisfactory—principles which may have been pressed out of due proportion or imperfectly realized.[26]

While lauding Tyrrell's attempt to show the fundamental connection between devotion and dogma, he lamented the fact that Tyrrell did not insist more clearly on the historical reality of the dogmas that underlie devotion. "It was the passionate belief in the fact of our Lord's Resurrection which lay at the very root of the hopeful prayer of St Paul and his contemporaries. If the historicity of the facts is disbelieved in or doubted, the prayer-value of the dogma is gone."[27] And while Tyrrell had a knack for finding what was good and helpful for Christian thought in nonbelievers, still Ward did not believe that Tyrrell sufficiently understood or appreciated Newman's theory of the development of doctrine and the physiological analogy underlying it.

The analogy does not, as Father Tyrrell says, either "degrade the present to exalt the past," or "degrade the past to exalt the present," though we fancy we recall both views of it suggested at different times in earlier works of Tyrrell. On the contrary, the conception of the Church as a living and growing organism and of its dogmatic theology as developing, presupposes that divine truth, which it does unreservedly exalt, is never *adequately* represented by human language either in the present or the past. If it so far exalts the Apostolic *depositum* as to find in it the unchangeable essence of Christianity, it also exalts the work of later teachers in excluding error. If, on the other hand, it finds early theological forms wanting in intellectual completeness, it still attaches authority to later and more complete definitions only because they express what was implicitly contained in the original *depositum.*[28]

26. Ibid., 182–83.

27. Ibid., 184.

28. Ibid., 186–87. For a good discussion of Tyrrell's view of the idea of development, see Aidan Nichols, *From Newman to Congar: The Idea of Doctrinal Development from the Victorians to the Second Vatican Council* (Edinburgh: T. & T. Clark, 1990), 114–35. Wilfrid Scawen Blunt, himself a

He was even more lavish in his praise for *Newman, Pascal, Loisy and the Catholic Church* (1906), by his friend and minor modernist figure, William J. Williams (1858–1930), which he considered "a most remarkable work, a veritable treasure-trove of deep thought on the foundations of religious belief," and "a very powerful *Apologia* for the Catholic Church."[29] The book conveyed Williams's intellectual journey to Catholicism in all its immediacy and candor, giving a frank story of his reasoning, some of which might startle the orthodox unused to his approach or unacquainted with his circumstances. Williams, however, did not intend to be provocative or unorthodox, in Ward's view. "There is no trace of that bias against the current language of orthodoxy, that desire to belittle ecclesiastical authority and Catholicism, that Little-Englandism of the Church, which is sometimes called Liberal Catholicism." Nor was Ward entirely negative toward the French biblical critic Alfred Loisy (1857–1940). "We are quite in accord with Mr Williams' view as to the place which Abbé Loisy's ostensible aim—namely a careful analysis of the results of modern criticism—would occupy in the carrying out of theological development on the lines of Newman's *Essay*." But he regretted that Loisy should even be included in the title since so little of the book was devoted to him. And considering the criticism his work had received and his censure by the Holy Office (December 1903), a brief treatment of his position was "unsatisfactory," raising greater expectations than could be met and prejudicing many against the volume.[30]

---

materialist at that point and very sympathetic toward Tyrrell after a lunch with him (Aug. 5, 1907), judged Tyrrell's views "quite incompatible" with any Church teaching he had ever heard of. See Wilfrid Scawen Blunt, *My Diaries: Being a Personal Narrative of Events, 1888–1914* (New York: Knopf, 1921), 2:176–77.

29. W. W. [Wilfrid Ward], "Some Recent Books," *Dublin Review* (Jan. 1907): 178–83. For Williams, see John D. Root, "William J. Williams, Newman, and Modernism," in Mary Jo Weaver, ed., *Newman and the Modernists* (Lanham, Md.: University Press of America, 1985), 69–95.

30. W. W. [Wilfrid Ward], "Some Recent Books," *Dublin Review* (Jan. 1907): 179, 183. In "For Truth or for Life" (Oct. 1906), Ward had mentioned that "a great authority on the subject" had said to him that if Newman were still alive he "would have entered into Loisy's views with special interest, although he would not have accepted them" (112). In a letter of Sept. 10, 1907, to Lord Halifax, Ward wrote of Loisy: "It is one thing to admit that we don't quite know what Our Lord's Glorified Body was, and that some mystery shrouds the Resurrection; quite another to formulate a startling theory which denies that the Body which was on the cross was buried and rose. It is reckless and rash and shallow French logic. Hügel goes further with these people than I like." See WWP VI/13 (83). The only other major reference to Loisy in the *Dublin* was a review of a book by M. Lepin criticizing Loisy, written by C. [Chapman], "Some Recent Books" (April 1909): 417–19. Chapman praised the work for showing how profoundly destructive Loisy's views really were in reference to the most fundamental beliefs of the faith.

Later that year he returned to Williams's book and *The Mystery of Newman* by the French Jesuit Henri Bremond.[31] He again praised Williams for his profound insight into Newman's thought, but he also faulted him for his lack of "intellectual self-restraint," in that he was "without that habitual sense of the effect of words or propositions on readers of different kinds" that was so characteristic of Newman. "There is much which Newman would not have maintained without explanation and qualification—much especially which he would not have said publicly during his life. For it was not his habit, without good reason, to raise problems and suggest difficulties before their time."[32] Ward thought Williams's book a "powerful and original" one even if it lacked literary style; and in view of the present weakening of all belief in the supernatural, one could not afford to lose such a work merely because it did not conform to the "etiquette of theological phraseology" or because of incidental statements that genuinely were open to criticism. Ward believed that Bremond's book, on the other hand, while it was extremely well written, lacked a real understanding of Newman and his thought. In reading it one would have thought its Newman an entirely different person from the Newman presented by Williams. "M. Bremond has taken as a model for his work a smaller man cut out of the real Newman—and a good deal altered and damaged in the cutting. From this model he has designed the figure which he gives us in his book. He has dressed him partly in French clothes and partly in raiment supplied by his own exuberant fancy. I am bound to add that he has constructed so lively a marionette that at moments one thinks he is really a living being."[33] Bremond's discussion of Newman's work was extremely inadequate. Nor was his portrait of his personality insightful, often seeing faults where there were none and ignoring his virtues, treating what was "not at once obvious as insoluble" and so as part of the "mystery of Newman." "It is not a psychological study, it is a novel suggested to a very imaginative writer by a personage who fascinates him, but who puzzles him still more, and who has very little in common with the French critic in intellect and character."[34]

For Ward, Newman was the key, and there was a certain proprietary quality to his defense of Newman.[35] It came as a shock to him, therefore, when the

31. Wilfrid Ward, "Two Views of Cardinal Newman," *Dublin Review* (July 1907): 1–15.

32. Ibid., 14.

33. Ibid., 2.

34. Ibid., 9. See also Roger Haight, "Bremond's Newman," *Journal of Theological Studies* 36 (Oct. 1985): 350–79.

35. For a study of Ward's Newman, see also Mary Jo Weaver, "Wilfrid Ward's Interpretation

encyclical *Pascendi Dominici Gregis* was promulgated by Pope Pius X in September 1907. (A few months earlier the decree *Lamentabili* had been issued, primarily against Loisy.) This document condemned modernism as the "synthesis of all heresies," and among those heresies were propositions that he thought clearly belonged to Newman. As he wrote to the Duke of Norfolk on October 10, 1907: "I don't believe the Pope *meant* to condemn Newman. But he has done so beyond all doubt so far as the words of the Encyclical go—not only on development but on so much else."[36] Ward's initial reaction was shock, then anger and dejection. He was upset and expressed this rather freely to those around him—he had a tendency to be as rash in person as he was careful in his public writing. He was angry at the use of authority and of censure to do theology, at the encyclical's lack of awareness of current difficulties and its use of incredibly violent language, and finally at the lack of precision in the formulation of what it was condemning. In a letter to Bishop O'Dwyer of Limerick (November 1, 1907), he commented that if the encyclical had condemned only subjectivism, immanence over transcendence, and the denial of Christ's divinity, he would have welcomed it despite its strong language, but "through an initial misconception and undervaluing of the motives both intellectual and moral of the chief modernists, it has condemned apparently, though I do not believe it really, just the thoughts and views which are indispensably necessary as a reasonable basis for Christianity in view of modern difficulties."[37]

The appeal of Catholicism to human nature is surely simply the old "Testimonium animae naturaliter Christianae" if Catholicism is the genuine version of Christianity. This is to all appearances most clearly condemned, and with it goes half the argument

---

and Application of Newman," in Weaver, *Newman and the Modernists,* 27–46. While an admirable essay, I disagree with Weaver's view that Ward had "misread the signs of the times" and "misread the issues." I think he understood them very well. It was just that he could not respond to them in the way some would have liked.

36. See WWP VI/24 (36). In the same letter Ward elaborated on where the encyclical had gone wrong and where Newman's positions had been touched, and called the use of papal encyclicals for intellectual instruction itself a kind of modernism, unknown before Pius IX. He lamented the effort that would be needed to extricate the pope from condemning a man he really did not intend to condemn. In his letters to Ward, Norfolk admitted that he was confused by the encyclical (he thought it would have dealt with more everyday issues instead of philosophical ones, and wasn't sure what it was the modernists held) and was disappointed in its tone. "Then as to the manner in which this is being done. To me as a man in the street it seems appalling. The language used, the methods presented fill me with dismay and hesitation. I cannot but feel this myself." Duke of Norfolk to Ward, Oct. 2 and 10, 1907, WWP VII/222a (101) and (102).

37. See WWP VI/25c (3).

of Newman's "Grammar of Assent." The proof of Christianity from the need of religion—again one of Newman's constant contentions in his sermons—seems to be excluded. The whole of Newman's account in the "Arians" and the last of the University Sermons of the origin of dogmatic formulae is swept away. Yet history absolutely demands it. The doctrine that the dogmatic propositions concerning God are symbols of a reality far exceeding them, which is taught by St. Thomas, as clearly as by Newman, is also apparently swept away. I could add very considerably to the list. I have felt very keenly, and so have others, that while all these things have prevented the Encyclical from helping those Catholics who most need help and have been a stumbling block with well-disposed Protestants, the "Tablet" has written as though they were simply non-existent, and as though the Encyclical contained merely a reassertion of the acknowledged truths of Catholicism. I cannot, having spoken as I have on this subject, do the same in the "Dublin Review."[38]

In the same letter he took up Bishop O'Dwyer's proposal to write an article on the encyclical for the *Dublin* and agreed with the line O'Dwyer was going to take. The authority of a bishop of O'Dwyer's position and name would be very helpful in calming individual consciences. He also wrote that Fr. Bidwell ("an intimate friend of Cardinal Merry de Val") had said that "if it were desirable some kind of sanction could be obtained at Rome for the kind of explanation" he was suggesting. Ward believed that O'Dwyer could save the situation for all the perplexed people whom Ward had especially in mind in editing the *Dublin.* "I cannot throw them over or cease to consider them. I am very anxious not to resign the editorship, but to bow beneath the storm and resume my work on these questions, perhaps more prudently, a little later. I fancy that not to treat the Encyclical would involve my having to resign. On the other hand if I write on it myself, any concessions to wider thought would be suspect in a moment of excitement. Moreover, I speak with no authority. From you they would, from both these points of view, come with infinitely greater effect." In the end Ward rejected O'Dwyer's article because he found the first eight pages too harsh and condemnatory, and because they ignored the fact that the encyclical contained real difficulties for the inexperienced layman due to its theological intricacies and the surface similarity of condemned and orthodox positions. Bishop O'Dwyer refused to have the pages cut and he published the article as a pamphlet.[39]

38. Ibid.

39. Edward T. O'Dwyer (1842–1917), whom Ward once called "a regular little fighting cock," was a complex and often contrary figure among the Irish bishops; he was also highly intelligent, independent, and fiery of temperament. For a fuller discussion of the O'Dwyer affair, see *Wilfrid*

Ward's relationship with Archbishop Bourne had been relatively good. Part of the agreement that Burns & Oates (the publishers) had with Bourne in "taking over the property" was a free hand in selecting an editor and writers—subject to the archbishop's veto, of course.[40] And Bourne was very good at not interfering. When complaints reached him about the *Dublin* he passed them on to Ward, not as a criticism but as a help. This is seen, for example, in a letter Bourne wrote to Ward on May 31, 1907:

I do not wish to hurry you in any way, but the papers which I enclose will show you that the concern created by your articles is, perhaps, more far-reaching than you have imagined. I am very anxious not to be forced into the position of seeming publicly to question either the orthodoxy or the prudence of the Editor of the Dublin Review. It would be a very serious matter were your name ever to appear in a letter such as that which has recently been issued by the Cardinal Prefect of the S.C. of the Index, and it is important that you should avoid even the possibility of such a contingency.[41]

After Bourne passed on criticism of his articles "For Truth or for Life," Ward wrote two letters on July 29, 1907, defending himself.[42] In the first he attacked the spirit of the criticisms as being not "worthy of the great subjects which are in question" and expressed his frustration. "When a writer has been doing his best to deal with real and urgent difficulties felt by many Christians, he may, I think, fairly look for some attempt on the part of his fellow-Catholics to appreciate and understand his writing before criticising it adversely." In the second letter (some forty-five pages long) he gave a detailed defense of his articles. In a letter to Ward of January 26, 1908, four months after *Pascendi,* Bourne wrote:

Wards 2:282–89, 312–13. For his life, see Thomas J. Morrissey, *Bishop Edward Thomas O'Dwyer of Limerick, 1842–1917* (Dublin: Four Courts Press, 2003). Maisie Ward writes that when the pamphlet *Cardinal Newman and the Encyclical Pascendi Dominici Gregis* (London: Longmans, Green, 1908) was published, it included in a brief preface what her father had vainly asked him to do in his article—advert to the difficult passages of the encyclical.

40. See Ward to Bourne, Jan. 22, 1905, WWP VII/43c (2).

41. See WWP VII/43a (5).

42. See WWP VII/43c (3) and (4). In a letter of July 31, 1907, Bourne, much disappointed with the letters he had received from Ward, wrote that he passed these criticisms on to him out of friendliness, so that he would be aware of what was going on, and so as to allow him an opportunity to prepare a statement, "calm and impersonal," which could be given to his critics. Unfortunately, Bourne complained, Ward had taken this to mean that Bourne had identified himself with these criticisms. "Neither to you nor to anyone have I passed judgment on those articles or their critics." See WWP VII/43a (6).

You have asked for and been allowed a greater liberty of control of the Review than is usual when the Editor is not at the same time the Proprietor. I do not wish to lessen this liberty, but things can only remain as they are on condition that you quite openly bear all responsibility, and preclude any one from imagining that your views are necessarily shared by the Proprietors or Lessees. In theological and philosophical matters the Dublin now hardly represents the ordinary views of Catholics in this country: it is representative rather of that particular school of thought which has your sympathy. As Ordinary I am not called upon to intervene, as long as you remain within the bounds of Catholic Orthodoxy, whatever my private opinions may be. Were I, however, to exercise rights of proprietorship my intervention might be more insistent and more frequent. And the existing state of things can evidently continue only on the understanding that the peculiar nature of your editorship is made quite manifest and that the views in the Review accepted as the views which you personally hold, and not the opinions of the Proprietors, still less of the Archbishopric. The Dublin must either be an organ of representative opinion in England or be representative of your personal views. You prefer to make it the latter, and this preference carries with, I think, the duty of leaving no one in doubt as to the real character of this periodical. If this be not made quite plain, there will be endless complications for every one.[43]

Ward's position was made more difficult by the public comments of those who claimed that Newman had been clearly condemned in the encyclical, as Tyrrell and Williams had done in the *Times.* While Ward was originally of the opinion that they were right, the views of such competent theologians as Hedley, O'Dywer, and Bidwell (Bourne's chancellor) that this was not true allowed him in good conscience, though he did not see it himself, to minimize the difficult points of the encyclical.[44] While he felt justified in his program of

43. See WWP VII/43a (9). In a letter to Bourne, Jan. 14, 1908, Ward had stated that his own interpretation of the encyclical was scarcely different from that of the *Tablet.* The *Tablet* was a reliably conservative journal owned by the archbishop. See WWP VII/43c (5).

44. In a letter to Williams (Nov. 18, 1907) Ward wrote: "Directly I read the Encyclical I was appalled at the apparently wide extent of the positions branded as parts of 'modernism'—including of course much of J.H.N. . . . My feeling was that the facts of the situation must be faced, and the authorities made to face them. I half thought of writing myself—not in the form of an attack, but as calling attention to an urgent difficulty which had to be met. . . . Then in the midst of these operations came your letter to the 'Times' and then Father Norris' disclaimer from Rome. This did somewhat change the situation. . . . It gave potentially the authority I had desired: to minimise on the difficult points the outcome of the Encyclical in interpreting it. This would appear disingenuous if there were no authoritative sanction; but with such sanction it would only be to bring the interpretation of the document into accord with its intention. I should add that all theologians whose opinion I obtained—Bidwell, Myers, Bishops Hedley and O'Dywer—*denied* that any of J.H.N. was censured—this before Norris' communication—therefore I supposed that such an interpretation was possible to the specialist though *I* did not see it." Quoted in *Wilfrid Wards* 2:271–72.

minimalism, he did not feel happy about it, and said he would resign if he were not allowed to intimate his lack of appreciation for the encyclical even as he accepted it. He wrote to Williams:

The very narrowness of the document justifies the view of the theologians that *technically* speaking the only *censure* is on the *whole* system—which includes sheer subjectivism and a God immanent and not transcendent. A different view from this would make havoc with all theology and not only with Newman. This view in my experience (or something very like it) theologians have held with practical unanimity. . . . I told our censor that I must resign unless I could intimate for those who read carefully that while I accept the Encyclical as a pontifical act, I do not in my own mind like it. . . . I think theological minimalism a necessity. Yet it is now getting to a point when it runs very close to sheer equivocation.[45]

It was in reply to Williams's first letter to the *Times* (November 2) that Fr. Norris, the head of Newman's Birmingham Oratory, wrote the *Times* (November 4) saying that he had it "from the highest authority that the 'genuine doctrine and spirit of Newman's Catholic teaching are not hit by the Encyclical, but the theories of many who wrongly seek refuge under a great name are obviously censured.'"[46] *L'Osservatore Romano,* the Vatican newspaper, in an article of November 5, said the same, and on March 10, 1908, Pope Pius X himself issued a letter praising Bishop O'Dwyer's pamphlet on Newman, praising Newman, and approving of how O'Dwyer showed the harmony between *Pascendi* and Newman's thought.[47]

It was impossible for Ward not to respond to and accept the encyclical

45. Ward to Williams, Dec. 14, 1907, WWP VI/38 (b).

46. In a second letter (Nov. 7) Norris said that it was Williams's letter of Nov. 2 that had led the Birmingham Oratorians to seek an authoritative disclaimer on Newman's censure. In a letter to W. S. Lilly (Nov. 5, 1907) Ward wrote that he believed that Merry del Val was the "highest authority" mentioned by Norris (WWP VI/16). In a letter to George Tyrrell of Nov. 28, 1908, von Hügel praised Williams's letters as "interesting and logical" but said he was disappointed in Ward: "As to the latter [Ward], it is abundantly clear from what he told me in the strand the other day that he most clearly realizes the general situation. But I find, even there, what I have now felt for a long time with him—not only that there is no getting him *publicly* to stand up and fight with sufficient openness for anything; but that even *privately* it cannot always be for *him* to say liberal things—these things are too subtle, dangerous, etc., for any one to touch and express but himself. It is indeed a pity, for he is so truly clever; and this now chronic lie of his, does not really make him happy within himself, it makes him shrivel inside, and leaves him practically without a friend or ally—on all these subjects—in the world. He is such a good husband and father, and as I have found in my own long experience with him, a good friend, outside of the religious battle matters." See British Library, George Tyrrell Papers. Add. MSS. 44930.

47. See Gary Lease, "Newman: The Roman View," in Weaver, *Newman and the Modernists,* 172–74.

publicly, but he would respond and accept it in his own way. His public response to *Pascendi,* mellowed by the intervening time between quarterly issues and by the care with which he always measured his public utterances, written after much consultation and with the help of Fr. Bidwell as his theological advisor and censor, appeared in the January number of 1908.[48]

While the secular press had severely criticized the encyclical, Ward stated that it was the "duty of every Catholic Reviewer at once to signify his acceptance of, and obedience to, this utterance of the Supreme Authority." "The present writer has been urged to enter on the full discussion of these questions more especially in their relation to the work which many Catholic thinkers have for years pursued in this Review and elsewhere. But he holds that the moment for this is certainly not the present. Such a discussion, involving, as it necessarily must, the weighing of *pros* and *cons* in a grave matter of ecclesiastical policy, might take place earlier or later, but not now." Public discussion of this matter at this time was "no more compatible with discipline and loyalty than would have been the public discussion of the tactics of Lord Roberts or General Buller by their subordinates during the Boer War." And while Catholic loyalty precluded such a discussion, there were a number of misrepresentations he wanted to clarify. His main concern was that the document had been read and discussed by the press as if it were a popular one and not a technical and theological one whose real interpreters were the theologians who understood the context and distinctions it was making, and who could associate it with the whole theological tradition. He believed that many of the criticisms of the encyclical were really misunderstandings brought about because it was read as if it were "a newspaper article," or because "scraps or isolated passages are read, and their *prima facie* meaning, if each be taken alone, is flourished before the world as the real one, and as containing a position which opposes what all great Catholic theological thinkers have taught."[49]

According to the encyclical, Ward wrote, the root of modernism was sub-

48. [Wilfrid Ward] "The Encyclical 'Pascendi,'" *Dublin Review* (Jan. 1908): 1–10. Fr. Bidwell was made the censor for this article. He had seen Archbishop Bourne before he returned it to Ward with only minor changes. See *Wilfrid Wards* 2:288. Bourne himself seems not to have been favorable to the encyclical: "6th June [1908]. . . . In the afternoon [Wilfrid] Meynell arrived, having spent all the morning with Archbishop Bourne. . . . His (Bourne's) position, in regard to Modernism is, contrary to what I imagined, one of disapproving the Papal Encyclical as unnecessary in England and ill-timed, and this, Meynell says, is the general opinion regarding it, so much so that Wilfrid Ward has been able to persuade the Duke of Norfolk to write in that sense to the Pope." Blunt, *My Diaries,* 2:203.

49. [Ward], "Encyclical 'Pascendi,'" 2, 5–6.

jectivism in religion, which resulted in a loss of belief in objective truth, reducing religion to sentiment or emotion, of a deity immanent in man but not transcendent, and the idea that dogmatic formulae were merely the reflection of the mind on its subjective religious experience. Its most conspicuous offense, however, was its attempt to explain away Christ's divinity. He found it very strange that Newman's name should be associated with such ideas, since it was against this antidogmatic principle that he had waged a lifelong battle. Dogma was the fundamental principle of Newman's religion, and while he held that dogmatic formulae were "symbols of divine fact," he did not mean that they were without truth as "empty symbols" (which the encyclical was attacking) but as shadows of the infinite and absolute Being whose description in human words would always fall short. In this he was only agreeing with St. Thomas, who saw dogmatic statements as *analogically* true: true as far as they go but falling short of the fullness of the reality. "Every false system has flourished in virtue of the truths it has used and abused."[50] Just as the Jansenists used much of St. Augustine's actual teaching and from it led others to error, so many have used Newman's actual teaching, but by exaggeration and exclusion have perverted its meaning. The encyclical's analysis of the modernist system, for the sake of completeness, included in it both the good and the bad elements of the system. "It is then censured, but not every proposition in the system is reflected on apart from the use of it. This part of the summary of 'Modernism' in the Encyclical is to Newman's works what *Augustinus* [the main Jansenist work] is to those of St Augustine."[51] The intervention of the "highest authority," having made clear that Newman was not condemned, was a sure proof that this was true, and this was already the position held by "theologians of weight."

The pope's reference in the encyclical to an earlier case of such an intellectual crisis—that caused by the introduction of Aristotle into the West in the thirteenth century—allowed Ward to return to one of his favorite historical examples of how the Church should meet new intellectual currents, and he talked about how the unorthodox excesses of the "Modernists" of the thirteenth century were met by such men as St. Thomas Aquinas, who drew all that was good from Aristotelian rationalism and purged it of its erroneous tendencies. The encyclical was a warning, Ward wrote, against the danger of unchastened and irresponsible speculation, and authority must be obeyed

50. Ibid., 6.

51. Ibid., 7.

even if it involved temporarily and publicly abstaining from those questions—which must be faced eventually—raised by the new sciences. "Toleration and sympathy for the attempt to accomplish what may be a pressing necessity in the interests of Catholic thought, can only be won now by scrupulously preserving the attitude of loyalty without which such work is disintegrating and cannot be assimilated by Catholic theology."[52]

While the article was generally praised, not all were happy about it. Bishop Hedley thought it good and even obvious, but complained of its lack of warmth toward the encyclical.[53] Baron von Hügel, on the other hand, who thought the encyclical terrible, wrote to Ward (February 10, 1908) that he could hardly have done less or written less favorably and still remain the editor of the *Dublin,* and, considering the unsatisfactory arguments he was forced to use, he wondered whether Ward's resignation would not have been "more simple and strong," more satisfactory to his conscience, and "more useful to the cause." "But all this does not prevent my being glad that you have not done more to content the unscholarly conservatives; and the announcement of Longman's [*sic*] list of Bp. O'Dwyer's rejected article shows me plainly that you have indeed not maintained your present condition without cost and danger." Von Hügel did, however, mention that, considering the already large number of periodicals he received, he might cancel his subscription to the *Dublin,* "either if you had to resign, or if you were to come back to the Encyclical, to say more for it than you have now published."[54]

Tyrrell had a number of caustic comments to make about Ward's view of things. "Is it true that Ward says that if you read the Encyclical as it ought to be read, back before on to a looking-glass, it is really a very cautious approval of Newman and only a condemnation of Bremond and myself?" "I believe Ward says the *evolution* but not *development* of doctrine is condemned, and that we should distinguish between mod*erns* and modern*ists;* and between Newman*ites* and Newman*ists,* as is quite plain if you read between the lines and alter the punctuation."[55] Nor was Ward *persona grata* among the powers

52. Ibid., 10.

53. *Wilfrid Wards* 2:290.

54. WWP II/6 (177). Von Hügel was pleased by what followed in the *Dublin,* though he still counseled resignation if Ward should be forced to concede more. See his letters of May 27 and June 5, 1908, WWP II/6 (180) and (181).

55. Tyrrell, respectively, to Mrs. William Gibson (Oct. 13, 1907), WWP VII/294h (2), and Mr. William Gibson (Oct. 28, 1907), WWP VII/294g (3). For Tyrrell and Newman, see Nicholas Sagovsky, "'Frustration, disillusion and enduring filial respect': George Tyrrell's Debt to John

in Rome. In a letter to Mgr. Joseph Broadhead, vice president of Ushaw, discussing the celebrations to be held there for its centenary, Merry del Val was happy that Ward was not to be one of the speakers: "I am glad to see that among your speakers you have not W. Ward who is so unsafe. He is an acrobat and performs the trick of teaching or insinuating unsound doctrines and of wriggling out of them within twenty-four hours, and then he tells everybody that all that is Newman. Poor Newman. We don't want this humbug at Ushaw where we like the genuine article in everything."[56]

The whole period after *Pascendi* was for Ward a period of great difficulty. Many suspected him of being a modernist himself. While it would have been much easier to resign, he believed that this would be seen as an admission of guilt, endanger the position he had won for the *Dublin,* hinder the conversion of many, and confirm the opinion that there was no intellectual Catholic opinion. Also, it would cast a shadow over the great biography of Cardinal Newman on which he had been working since 1905 and which would be published to great acclaim in 1912. So he consciously turned aside from theological topics to more literary, political, and philosophical ones (areas where he could not conflict with *Pascendi*), so that only two articles by him on these topics can be found in later issues of the *Dublin;* and both of these were in reaction to movements outside the Catholic Church to weaken the dogmatic character of Christianity so as to make it more acceptable to the modern age. His apologetics would now be mostly indirect, through a careful description of Newman's life and thought. His biography would be Newman's vindication, and his.[57]

Henry Newman," in Weaver, *Newman and the Modernists,* 97–115; and David G. Schultenover, "George Tyrrell: 'Devout Disciple of Newman,'" *Heythrop Journal* 33 (Jan. 1992): 20–44.

56. Ushaw College Archives, Jan. 17, 1908, quoted in Holmes, "Cardinal Raphael Merry del Val," 61. In fact, Ward did go to Ushaw for its centenary at the invitation of its president and gave an address on Wiseman. The text of it ("The Genius of Cardinal Wiseman") can be found in the *Dublin Review* (Oct. 1908): 229–43.

57. For Ward after *Pascendi,* see *Wilfrid Wards* 2:296–331, in a chapter aptly titled "A Time of Trial." As Maisie Ward makes very clear, this time was a trial of patience for her father, not a trial of faith. The modernist crisis made the writing of the Newman biography much more difficult and is one reason why Newman's own words are used so extensively in it. For the writing of the biography, see *Wilfrid Wards* 2:332–57; Sheridan Gilley, "Wilfrid Ward and His Life of Newman," *Journal of Ecclesiastical History* 29 (1978): 177–93; and Nadia M. Lahutsky, "Ward's Newman: The Struggle to Be Faithful and Fair," in Weaver, *Newman and the Modernists,* 47–67. In a letter to Ward dated Dec. 17, 1910, Wilfrid Meynell, the head of Burns & Oates, the *Dublin*'s publisher, complained that a recent decree forbidding seminarians to read periodicals would cost them thirty to fifty subscribers. Ward appealed to the Duke of Norfolk in a letter dated Dec. 18, 1910, in the

Ward's last words on the subject of modernism can be found in his article on the death of Pope Pius X.[58] While Ward had always thought of Pius X as a saintly individual, he had not always agreed with his policies. Ward set great store by his published words, and while he had a sharp political sense, he would never have written what he did not really believe. By 1914 his opinions had changed somewhat, certainly influenced by the oncoming war. Ward wrote that Pope Pius was not a patron of the arts, like some popes, or a thinker or man of letters, like others, but a "Holy Pontiff," and a "great priest, the personal embodiment of simple saintly heroism" who "stands forth as a beacon of light." In an age at war, when the peaceful arts are seen as inappropriate luxuries, it is the soldier and the saint to whom we look; "the soldier alone can stem the tide of evil." Among the litany of the pope's accomplishments, Ward brought up some of Pius's most controversial decisions, actions that had aroused great opposition in their time but were "justified in the event." One of these was his condemnation of modernism, against which he waged "a veritable crusade."

Ward had grown much less critical of *Pascendi* and had become more aware of the dangers condemned as modernism. Modernism was now described as "one of the most important and dangerous intellectual movements of our time," which Pius X, gifted as he was with "a sure instinct as to an intellectual attitude and spirit which was dangerous—even where his habit of mind and knowledge did not extend to all matters of detail," had broken before it could damage the Church. And while the full application of the encyclical was still to be worked out, and a calm and dispassionate shifting process between the truths and perversions of truth contained in these thinkers was still in the works, still, Ward considered Pope Pius's condemnation of modernism "the event in his Pontificate by which he will live in history."

On July 15, 1909, Tyrrell died in the small village of Storrington in Sussex at the home of Maude Petre, who had taken care of him in his last illness. Excommunicated and surrounded by some friends and his cousin William Tyrrell of the Foreign Office, he had made Petre his literary executor. She not only published his remaining works and defended publicly Tyrrell's work and reputation, she also finished *The Autobiography and Life of George Tyrrell*, pub-

hope that he could get the decree repealed. Both letters are at Downside Abbey in the Cardinal Gasquet Papers, 879b.

58. Wilfrid Ward, "Pope Pius X," *Dublin Review* (Oct. 1914): 217–25.

lished in 1912.[59] Petre had been a close friend of Mrs. Josephine Ward (whom she called "Joe"), had stayed at their house in Dorking, and when Ward's eldest son died tragically in 1902 it was to her that they turned, asking her to come and prepare the other children for the news, their eldest daughter Maisie being particularly left in her care.[60] Her views of Ward were mixed: while she respected him she thought him too hesitant to follow his theories to their logical conclusions, and too dependent on Newman.[61] In the intervening period Petre had published *Where Saints Have Trod* (1903) and *The Soul's Orbit* (1904), both of which had been severely criticized by the pre-Ward *Dublin* for their for "advanced views" and subjectivism.[62] This unorthodox reputation was probably the cause of a "little tiff" she had with Wilfrid, which seems to have been over his request that she not sign an article she had written for the *Dublin.* Later, when she saw that most of the articles of the April 1906 number were signed, she determined not to write for the journal.[63]

While Ward found Petre's work on Tyrrell interesting, skillfully done, and fair, he also found it extremely sad and "as a whole" not quite a true picture of him, particularly in the autobiographical part. Tyrrell was "a man of moods" and his account of things depended heavily on the situation or the person with whom he was corresponding. Also, for a true picture of the man a selection should have been made from works such as *Nova et Vetera* and *Hard Sayings,* where "the distinctive spiritual beauty of his mind" and the "attractive and more peaceful aspect of his thought and teaching" were best illustrated. What was noteworthy about the book was its revelation of the extraordinarily

59. The autobiography only reached to 1885, so Petre had to write the rest. Maude Petre (1863–1942), from the ancient Catholic Petre family and a friend to many of the leading modernist figures as well as a leading historian of the movement, was a member of the Society of the Daughters of the Heart of Mary from 1890 until 1907, when her unauthorized publication of *Catholicism and Independence: Studies in Spiritual Liberty* (London: Longmans, Green, 1907) led to her not being permitted to renew her vows. For her life, see Clyde F. Crews, *English Catholic Modernism: Maude Petre's Way of Faith* (Notre Dame: University of Notre Dame Press, 1984).

60. See Petre's diary entries in the British Library, Petre Papers, Add. MSS. 52372, for Sept. 14 and 15 and Oct. 6, 1900; Feb. 18 and 28, March 20, May 12, June 23, July 21, Aug. 4, and Dec. 19, 1901; and Feb. 4 (or 7), 12, and 13, 1902. The Wilfrid Wards even stayed with her after the funeral, as Maisie was not well enough to return home (Feb. 12, 1901).

61. Petre Papers, Add. MSS. 52372, diary, July 21, 1901. In her diary entry for Dec. 19, 1901, she wrote that she thought him "good" but "oppressive and antagonistic." "He seems, all the time, on the lookout to find one wrong in something."

62. See Crews, *English Catholic Modernism,* 27–34.

63. Petre Papers, Add. MSS. 52373, diary entries for Jan. 19, March 22 and 24, and April 5, 1906. Nor did she have kind words for Josephine's novel *Out of Due Time,* which she called "shabby" and "irritating throughout" (diary entries for March 24 and April 14, 1906).

inverted quality of his judging and analytical ability. For most people, Ward believed, the power of judgment was greater than the power to analyze.

With Tyrrell, on the contrary, the powers of analysis were quite abnormally strong; the powers of judgment comparatively weak. This was one cause of his constant variations in opinion. It was not the case of steady growth of the mind, of a gradual acquisition and digestion of fresh knowledge, but of over-rapid assimilation of any train of reasoning with which he was brought in contact, coupled with a sympathetic perception which enabled him to develop it with wonderful lucidity. . . . No doubt in highly subtle and speculative minds there is always, in dealing with complex problems a good deal of weighing and balancing before a decision is arrived at. But with Tyrrell the element of decision was reduced to a *minimum*. His was an unstable equilibrium, and his decision was often determined by accidents or keen and uncertainly balanced sympathies. It witnesses to no mental strength comparable to that often evinced in his analysis.[64]

Ward believed that Tyrrell had allowed his speculative reason to outrun his powers of judgment, so that while he left "contributions of the utmost value," they were "unfinished and undigested." Tyrrell's own conclusions were hard to discover, as they shifted from day to day, but the statements of his religious beliefs in his last years "appear to be the implied negation of any profession of the Catholic faith." "No doubt he may have hoped that some ideal Church of the future would endorse his views; but this, of course, was Luther's position also in his appeal to a future General Council. If he, moreover, deliberately rejected the definitions of the last two councils, as he declares in one of his later letters, that of course is decisive—unless indeed, which is possible, his illness had so far unhinged his mind that such sayings did not represent real convictions at all." He was lovable to his intimates, sincere, earnest (even when wrong-headed), and not self-seeking. "But the constant note of intellectual contempt witnesses to great limitations in his power of doing justice to the length and breadth of religious opinion. Moreover, he lacked mental stability and philosophical depth and patience, and without these it is difficult for a man of his extraordinary intellectual subtlety to be the adherent of any Confession—most of all of the Catholic Church. It was part of the tragedy of his life that while he craved for the sympathy and companionship of a Church, he could not submit to its necessary conditions, and his road was inevitably a lonely one."[65]

64. W. W. [Wilfrid Ward], "Some Recent Books," *Dublin Review* (Jan. 1913): 188.

65. Ibid., 190. It is interesting that the *Dublin* never reviewed Tyrrell's *Medievalism: A Reply to*

After the condemnation of modernism, Ward shied away from writing on theology and apologetics, focusing on other topics, but he did not give them up altogether. He was particularly impressed by the work of G. K. Chesterton, and his lengthy review of Chesterton's *Orthodoxy* (1908) could not have been more laudatory.[66] Ward admitted that opinions on Chesterton's writing were sharply divided. While all considered him brilliant, Ward thought him "penetrating" while Ward's friends thought him "superficial." Ward believed he was "pre-eminently the propounder of the maxims of common-sense" whose paradoxes startled the reader by their obvious truth; Ward's friends thought he was "primarily a purveyor of acrobatic feats of the intellect," an amusing show not to be taken seriously. While Ward thought that *Orthodoxy* was "a triumphant and irrefragable confutation of their view," his friends thought it a confutation of his. He could see why someone might think Chesterton frivolous.

"How can I take a man seriously," he will say, "who gives as the primary fact in all his philosophy the belief he has ever had in fairies (p. 85); who laughs at conscience and the inner voice, and tells you that the most horrible of all religions is the worship of the God within, (p. 136); who is so little alive to the history of all civilizations, except the Chinese, as to say that there is in the world no tradition of progress (p. 266); who tells us that if we credit any deviation from fixed law (and, of course, even free will is a deviation from fixed law), the most stupendous miracle is as easy of belief as the smallest; who takes his metaphors from taxicabs and tramcars in Battersea; from the Inner Circle trains and Gower Street Station and the Like—nay, who devotes half a page to explaining that seriousness is not a virtue, and that one should not take oneself seriously at all; that seriousness, moreover, is easy but undesirable? If such a man sums up on the side of obscurantism and against modern thought, it is just what was to be expected—it is all one huge paradox. He does not at bottom really believe what he says, or expect others to believe him. To unravel and refute his arguments is not worth while. It is as little worth while as to analyse the fallacies in Whately's proof that Napoleon I never existed."[67]

In fact, the only thing that should not be taken seriously in Chesterton, Ward thought, was the passage in which he seemed to say that he should not

---

Cardinal Mercier (London: Longmans, Green, 1908) or his posthumous *Christianity at the Cross-Roads* (London: Longmans, Green, 1909), probably because it was too close to the events and Ward had already had his say about modernism. Neither book could have received anything but the most negative review.

66. Wilfrid Ward, "Mr Chesterton among the Prophets," *Dublin Review* (Jan. 1909): 1–32.

67. Ibid., 2.

be taken seriously. Ward believed Chesterton to be profoundly earnest; the brilliant epigrams with which *Orthodoxy* was packed were a concession "which has become habitual on the part of the writer, to the taste of the age which loves to be amused and hates to being bored." "It is the administration of intellectual stimulants, or the application to a lethargic and tired and rather morbid world of a tremendous shower bath, in order to brace it and renew its normal activities. The net result, however, of Mr Chesterton's awakening treatment is not mere stimulating paradox, but, rather, a douche of startling common-sense."[68] While his views were not novel, his argumentation and mode of presentation certainly were. Never having read the chief books of Christian apologetics, Chesterton found his way to Christianity from agnosticism by arguments of his own devising. Unknown to him, and certainly in his own inimitable and striking style, he elaborated arguments that had been used in the past by some of the great Christian apologists.

We find, or instance, Butler's argument—urged in his sermons—on the adaptation of human nature to the Christian virtues. We find illustrations of Tertullian's *testimonium animae naturaliter christianae.* I do not say that Mr Chesterton gives us again all that Tertullian and Butler have given us. But in his record of the way in which these arguments presented themselves to him, and of the way they drove out modern theories too shallow to stand against them, we have most timely evidence of the ever-living power of thoughts not themselves new. . . . Again, when he mercilessly demolishes the confused thought which treats mathematical necessity and scientific uniformity as equally unalterable in the nature of things, he is saying over again what W. G. Ward and Dr McCosh said fifty years ago in answer to John Stuart Mill. . . . So, too, with Mr Chesterton's most important contention against naturalism, that reason cannot be the highest product of the evolution of merely non-rational forces—that there must be reason behind the process—we have an argument made familiar to our own generation by Mr Arthur Balfour's books and Archbishop Temple's Bampton Lectures; yet in Mr Chesterton it is original. So, too, is the view of skepticism as the suicide of thought. . . . In each case we have all the drama of personal conviction and history—and, in addition, the extraordinary richness and copiousness of illustration in which Mr Chesterton is unrivalled.[69]

While Ward believed that Chesterton should be taken seriously, he also singled out weaknesses in his presentation. Chesterton was very serious in his main purpose—and it was this very seriousness that helped make him "unconventional and startling"—yetl he had a tendency to say things ("violent

68. Ibid., 3.

69. Ibid., 4–5.

and exaggerated things") that were "false and indefensible" and weakened his case. At times he did not answer his enemy's position at all but only a caricature of it that no one worth convincing held. Ward believed that liberal theology was not as dogmatic in its unbelief as Chesterton claimed and that Chesterton's tirade against it missed the mark. He also thought that Chesterton sometimes ignored the real questions and made a joke of them. There were real difficulties and our understanding of dogma did change over time, and so it was dangerous to exaggerate the immutability of orthodoxy. Also, Ward was a great believer in the expert, and he didn't entirely care for Chesterton's appeal to popular belief over the opinion of the specialist. Sometimes his epigrams, despite their brilliance, were downright misleading. While Ward didn't want to cramp Chesterton's style, he feared that Chesterton might be inclined at some point to let the applause of the gallery be the test and spur for his writing. And he believed that Chesterton was better at attacking the popular excesses and defects of these general movements than at taking on their best exponents.

Taken as a whole, *Orthodoxy* is a timely warning given to his contemporaries with a youthful force and keenness by a convert to the aged creed of Christendom, which has passed its 1900th birthday. We learn how he has come to realize the inner force of its truth—"time-honoured" for some of the philosophers, "effete" for others, ever young for Mr Chesterton. His pages are marked by the freshness and often by the insight of genius—no other word can be used. They have not the balance of an all-round philosophy. They do not show the fastidious taste and discrimination characteristic of the typical scholar. They have not the artistic finish of the poet; and the true poetry of many a paragraph is marred by the transition from the sublime to the ridiculous. Yet in this there is meaning and method. It is carrying into action of the view expressed in the epilogue to Mr Chesterton's clever novel, the *Napoleon of Notting Hill,* that there are ever two aspects of the truth, the serious and the humorous. It is the utterance of a man in whom, to use Jowett's phrase, "things serious and profane lie near together, and yet are never confused." And the man who is more than his arguments must put himself into his writing. The book is the trumpet call of a reformer who, like all reformers puts his entire energy into his mission, and, therefore, cannot afford to be reflectively fastidious.[70]

In a later article, while discussing John Neville Figgis's *The Gospel and Human Needs* (1909) and Mrs. Humphry Ward's novel, *The Case of Richard Meynell* (1911), Ward again praised Chesterton's fresh apologetical style.[71] A jaded

70. Ibid., 29.

71. Wilfrid Ward, "Reduced Christianity: Its Advocates and Its Critics," *Dublin Review* (Oct.

world had ceased to realize that much of what was valued in contemporary civilization was really dependent on the "good news" of Christianity. Because Chesterton had himself been an agnostic, a modern pagan, he could experience the novelty of Christianity as the ancient pagans had. It was Chesterton's strength, Ward believed, that he appealed to the facts of experience, not to some ideal world.

It was this appeal to the facts of human experience that led Ward to consider the books by Figgis and Mrs. Humphry Ward. The title character of *The Case of Richard Meynell*, a sequel to *Robert Elsmere*, was like Robert Elsmere in that he was an Anglican cleric who has lost his belief in the creed; but unlike Elsmere he sought to remain within the Church of England and have it permit such comprehensiveness. Ward pointed out that life offered occasions where the problem of religious belief, "habitually regarded as tiresome and merely speculative," became "a most urgent and real matter." Misfortunes or the death of a loved one might lead one to ask ultimate questions about reality, and it was at such moments that one could genuinely judge the validity of the different prescriptions for life. He believed that there was a great resemblance between Figgis's thought and Chesterton's. While Figgis lacked the vividness of Chesterton's style, he was far more conversant with modern biblical and historical criticism, and faced more squarely the religious difficulties raised by them. There were those who believed that one must totally reject all modern criticism and critical thought of the day, or, if one gave it due weight, to accept a "Christianity so much reduced as to be revolutionized." This "reduced Christianity" (as it was called) eliminated miracles and much of the historical Christ. It emptied dogmatic formulae of their traditional content while keeping them for sentimental reasons—much as the old French cathedrals were kept as harmless monuments of the past as long as they no longer harbored "still living superstitions." To the followers of a reduced Christianity these could still inspire living a Christ-like life, "all the more happily because you have cleared the ground of superstitions and fables to which no thinking man can assent in his heart, and which clouded the best minds with secret suspicion of the whole system." Such was the opinion of Mrs. Ward's Richard Meynell.

Figgis, however, did not believe that these two options exhausted the alternatives available. One could accept modern criticism without rejecting tradi-

---

1912): 217–40. For John Neville Figgis (1866–1919), Anglican theologian and historian, see Maurice G. Tucker, *John Neville Figgis: A Study* (London: S.P.C.K., 1950). For *The Case of Richard Meynell*, see Peterson, *Victorian Heretic*, 190–206.

tional Christianity. He opposed the credulity of Mrs. Ward, "her wholesale and uncritical reaction from the credulity in old legends to credulity in brand new theories," and considered Richard Meynell's abandonment of the essence of the creed an irrational panic in the face of an aggressive and unwarranted criticism. He believed that the principles of "reduced Christianity," if realized, would lead simply to pantheism or even naturalism, and that many of its conclusions were really drawn not from sober criticism but from naturalistic presuppositions. Far from creating a deeper philosophy of life, it offered a shallower one. Christianity, tested by long experience and with its great record of beneficence and practical success, should be seen, he believed, as possessing the field until disproved. This was quite unlike the modernist, who began by displacing Christianity with naturalistic philosophical principles and "then places her on her knees as an outsider and a suppliant, asking only to reinstate a few unimportant, unintrusive survivals of her former self in a system of thought and belief to which she is on the whole quite alien." Like Chesterton, Figgis appealed to human experience and the practical needs of man. It was here that "reduced Christianity" showed its weakness and orthodox Christianity its strength. It was not just in the common man's sense of the miraculous, which confirms his sense of spiritual freedom amid the uniformity of the material universe, and of mystery. Nor was it simply the appeal to the ordinary man of the actual historical Christ whom the Christian believed died and rose again, and who because he still lived could succor those who called upon him—something an imagined ideal figure could never be. Most particularly, Figgis believed, it was in Christianity's belief in the reality of sin and the necessity of forgiveness that Christianity showed its practicality. The reality of sin, however, was most uncongenial to the modern temper, since it did not conform to the optimist philosopher's theory of life and of human nature.

> Mr Figgis quotes Sir Oliver Lodge as bidding sensible men "not to worry about their sins, but to be up and doing." All very well if men were so happily constituted that they could lead an ideal life of action untroubled by their lower nature. Such things as sin and the evil tendencies of nature were unseemly and depressing and undignified, and the philosopher looked away from them. They were too ugly a blot in any scheme of life for his complacency. The advocate of "reduced Christianity" also passed them by with scarcely a glance. Traditional Christianity on the other hand was too practical to ignore them, and brought from another world the mysterious explanations which enabled people frankly to face such mysteries as this.[72]

72. Ward, "Reduced Christianity," 229.

As Figgis pointed out, Christianity did not exist solely for the benefit of decent people and the cultivated classes (the kind of people to whom Mrs. Ward's concern was addressed), but primarily for the poor and sinners, who were not offended by the marvels recorded there, the marvels that Mrs. Ward found so distasteful. Ward did not think that there was enough belief left in this new Christianity ("mainly, so far as I can see, an enthusiasm for moral action—for the higher life of the spirit in its war against the animal life") to inspire great moral action.

> Certainly the ideal of self-denying charity towards our fellow-men is retained. But the complete other-worldliness of the Gospel ethics does not accord readily with Meynell's language. It would be rash to say that Richard Meynell accepts the unearthly teaching of the eight beatitudes, though he certainly accepts the ideal of cultivating the rational nature in man and fighting against sheer animalism. But when we ask for the *beliefs* which are to inspire the neo-Christians in this battle with some of the forces which made early Christians die rather than deny Christ our search is in vain. Sanctions we do not find in the system. It knows little of what Christ was in this world, nothing of his present existence in another. We find in it no tangible convictions to inspire our philanthropy and help us in the fight against the lower nature—not even a clear belief in a God accessible to prayer and ready to help us, still less in a future life in which we shall be rewarded or punished. It provides only an agreeable imaginative *stimulus* for refined minds and well-ordered characters—for those, that is, who stand least in need of religion.[73]

While Ward was sympathetic to the distress at being asked to part with these treasures of Christian memory, he did not believe that Mrs. Ward could claim a share in the associations and possessions which she had intellectually rejected, nor should Richard Meynell, her hero. It would be more reasonable and satisfactory, Ward believed, for her to frame a religion, much as Comte did, more in accord with her beliefs. If the Church of England could still share in the intellectual work of defending traditional Christianity, as Figgis believed it could, would it be wise to cripple her by admitting to her ministry those who came so close to the very attitude toward life that Christianity was set up to oppose?

Knowing that many Catholics might find Figgis's apologetic unfamiliar and even dangerous because of his loose use of language, Ward made clear that Figgis was neither a subjectivist nor a pragmatist with his talk of "life" and "experience." Though he did put a great emphasis on human psychology

73. Ibid., 232.

and the personal frame of mind of the individual approaching the proofs of religion, Ward thought no one more opposed to subjectivism than Figgis. Even Catholic theology recognized this personal, subjective element in religion, and while it would be dangerous to base belief on "religious experience," the opposite extreme of denying it would be "to discredit half our hagiography and to set down St Teresa and St John of the Cross as dreamers."

In 1912 "Seven Oxford Men" published a collection of essays, *Foundations,* which was, as its subtitle proclaimed, "a statement of Christian belief in terms of modern thought." It included such figures such as B. H. Streeter (1874–1937) and William Temple (1881–1944), the future Archbishop of Canterbury, and occasioned from a young Ronald Knox the brilliant parody "Absolute and Abitofhell" (a poem in the manner of Dryden's *Absalom and Achitophel*) and a more serious critique, *Some Loose Stones.*[74] This collection, written by a younger generation of Anglican theologians and scholars, was much like *Lux Mundi* (1889), both in its purpose and in its manner. Ward's response to it was also very much in the manner of his response to *Lux Mundi.*[75] He commended the authors for their concern with the intellectual difficulties of modern men toward traditional Christianity, but he thought that they were too concerned with these difficulties and so gave up too much. The process of adapting Christianity to new facts, of itself, he believed, should have no skeptical or paralyzing results. After all, our whole contact with the physical world involved a similar process. This process did not have to be unsettling for theology, as long as the mainsprings of faith were untouched and as long as it was done cautiously, so that every advance was a real one. He thought that an organized body was far better at resisting such unsettlement, and the conservatism of the Catholic body ("which would be excessive in a mere student of critical problems") was a far better protection against "the destruction of nerve," the "panic," and the "insecurity" that so often left Christianity desperately defensive before the world. The Church's official caution, "however un-

74. Ronald Knox (1888–1957), then an Oxford don and in Anglican orders, was well acquainted with the recipients of his satire, and they seemed to take it well. The poem seemed to get more attention than the book it made fun of, and *Some Loose Stones* (1913) also sold very well, more than four thousand copies. Knox believed that the authors were "worshipping an idol, or rather propitiating a bogy—that of the Modern Man with his Modern Mind." See his *Spiritual Aeneid* (London: Longmans, Green, 1918), 111–15 and 151–55. The poem was first published in the *Oxford Magazine* and reprinted in *Essays in Satire* (New York: E. P. Dutton, 1930), 79–88.

75. Wilfrid Ward, "Some Oxford Essays," *Dublin Review* (July 1913): 53–63. See Hinchliff, *God and History,* 232–44.

satisfactory at the moment to the merely intellectual," was part of its strength, for it kept away insufficiently proven novelties until they had been proven beyond a doubt and so were open to assimilation. This was not to say that the process worked perfectly or that authority was always up to the task. "In Nature much incidental waste attends on absolutely assured and far-reaching developments. In history the purposes of Divine justice are achieved amid the apparent failures mourned by Ecclesiastes. 'Though he slay me yet will I trust in him,' says Job. So too our trust in the Divine Power in the Church must rise above the mistakes of individual rulers in detail. Trust in their words and acts is measured by and limited by the teaching of theologians in the subject. Our trust in the divine indwelling spirit has no defined limitation."[76]

The death of Pius X and the election of Benedict XV in 1914 brought an end to the reaction against modernism. While Ward had survived it reasonably intact—neither the *Dublin* nor any of his works had been condemned—he did comply with the 1911 request of Cardinal Rampolla, secretary of the Holy Office, to remove the epilogue, "The Exclusive Church and the Zeitgeist," from his biography of Cardinal Wiseman.[77] Benedict's first encyclical, *Ad Beatissimi* (November 1, 1914), spoke of the need for concord within the Church, attacking any private person, "whether in books or in the press, or in public speeches," who took upon himself "the position of an authoritative teacher in the Church." He also made clear that "without harm to faith and discipline—in the absence of any authoritative intervention of the Apostolic See," there was room for divergent opinions in the Church and that all had the right to express and defend their own opinions. He called for charity and for an end of name calling and stigmatization of other Catholics, for Catholicism did not admit of degrees, of a more or a less.[78] In the description of Benedict XV written before the publication of *Ad Beatissimi,* J. S. Barnes gave a summary of a sermon he had heard when Benedict was still Archbishop of Bologna.

I remember the tenor of his peroration: The progress of science cannot harm the Church. It is on the progress of arts and sciences that the Church relies as on her foremost secular allies to bring mankind into the knowledge of the truth. The Church as in the past will never cease to help and encourage the production of all that is beauti-

76. Ibid., 62.

77. See *Wilfrid* Wards 2:318–25.

78. For the relevant sections (nos. 21–24), see Claudia Carlen, ed., *The Papal Encyclicals: 1903–1939* (Wilmington, N.C.: McGrath, 1981), 148–49.

ful and the attainment of all that is true. All she asks of science is to abstain from trading on the credulity of man, by setting forth theories as established facts under the seal of scientific authority, and so leading him into a maze of speculation, so teaching him an unworthy and unnecessary skepticism for no other purpose than to do honour to an aspiring professor with an ingenious hypothesis. Be honest with yourselves in the pursuit of truth and be honest to the public when you lay before them the fruits of your endeavours, and you may be sure that the blessing of the Church will rest upon your head.[79]

Barnes pointed out that Benedict was the first pope to choose that name since Prospero Lambertini, Benedict XIV, the learned and cultured pope of the eighteenth century, respected even by Voltaire and by Protestants. Benedict XIV also supplied a model and a name for the cultured and saintly figure of Fogazzaro's well-known 1906 novel *The Saint.* Barnes asked, "Will Fogazzaro's liberal Pope Benedict prove a prophecy?"[80] From Benedict XV's character and career Barnes implied that he would. He would be pious and a supporter of the arts and sciences; he would allow a certain freedom to his bishops and would let Italian Catholics elect and become members of parliament; he would reconcile with France while maintaining a friendly attitude toward Germany and Austria-Hungary; he would win the world by his charity and good example, leading the people along the middle way between excess and deficiency, "the true secret of life."

That Barnes wrote without disapproval of a book put on the Index during the previous pontificate shows how much had changed. While Benedict XV did not become the Papa Angelico of Roger Bacon or the liberal pope desired by Fogazzaro, he was to be for the men of Ward's generation the pope of peace, who desired nothing but peace within the Church and among warring nations.

79. J. S. Barnes, "Benedict XV: An Impression," *Dublin Review* (Oct. 1914): 373–74. For Pope Benedict's life, see Henry Rope, *Benedict XV: The Pope of Peace* (London: Catholic Book Club, 1940); Walter H. Peters, *The Life of Benedict XV* (Milwaukee: Bruce Publ., 1959); and John E. Pollard, *The Unknown Pope: Benedict XV (1914–1922) and the Pursuit of Peace* (London: Geoffrey Chapman, 1999).

80. The climax of Fogazzaro's novel comes when Benedetto, the "saint" of the title, meets with the pope (who is unnamed) and, inspired by the Holy Spirit, condemns the four evil spirits that have entered the Church (the spirits of falsehood, avarice, domination of the clergy, and immobility) and pleads with the pope to renew it. Benedetto dies at the novel's end after a long peroration on the evangelical life. The novel does not prophesy about a liberal Pope Benedict, though there were some who thought that Pope Benedict XV took that name partially because of the hero of the novel.

4 POLITICS

Wilfrid Ward was greatly interested in politics and strongly believed that Catholics should be involved in the affairs of the nation. While the majority of English Catholics supported the Liberals, he was a strong Conservative.[1] He had friends all across the political spectrum, but his closest friends in the political world included such major figures within the Conservative Party as Arthur Balfour, Lord Hugh Cecil, and George Wyndham. He was a Conservative by conviction and temperament; he was a Conservative because he was a conservative. But he was not an inflexible one. As Father Cuthbert said of him after his death, "He could hardly have been a liberal in thought even had he tried, any more than he could be a democrat in politics. By temperament he was essentially conservative: it required the full weight of his intellectual ability to make him an open-minded conservative, that is to say, a conservative who believes the world has a future as well as a past."[2] Despite that, he admitted articles contrary to his own beliefs because it was his stated policy that on issues of national importance all sides should be heard. It was the *Dublin*'s articles on

1. For Catholic involvement in English politics, see Dermot Quinn, *Patronage and Piety: The Politics of English Roman Catholicism, 1850–1900* (Stanford: Stanford University Press, 1993).

2. Cuthbert [Hess], "Wilfrid Ward (I.)," 1. Fr. Cuthbert (1866–1939) was ordained for the Capuchins in 1889, was superior of the House of Studies at Oxford from 1911 to 1930 and provincial for England from 1922 to 1925.

national politics, particularly Ward's own, that attracted the most attention from the press.[3]

Contemplating the English political scene in the early months of 1906, after the January parliamentary elections, could not have been a pleasant experience for Ward. In December 1905 Balfour had resigned as prime minister and a Liberal government headed by Sir Henry Campbell-Bannerman had taken charge. If Balfour had hoped that the Liberals would tear themselves apart once in office and set the stage for a Unionist victory in the expected election, then he was sorely disappointed.[4] In fact, the Unionists (the alliance of Conservatives and Liberal Unionists, those Liberals opposed to Irish Home Rule) suffered one of the greatest defeats in British history. They lost 214 seats, leaving the new Parliament with 401 Liberals (of whom 24 were Lib-Labs), 132 Conservatives, 83 Irish Nationalists, 29 Labourites, and 25 Liberal Unionists. The Irish Nationalists and Labour (who had formed an electoral pact with the Liberals) were allied with the Liberals, though with a majority of 273 over the Unionists the Liberals were not dependent on them. Even the Unionist leadership suffered devastating losses: Balfour and all but four of his colleagues in the cabinet from the Commons lost their seats. While the Unionists were demolished in the Commons, in the House of Lords they held an overwhelming advantage: the Liberals could count on only 88 peers while the Unionists could count on 479 (124 Liberal Unionists and 355 Conservatives). After years of political exile, and with such an enormous majority, the Liberals were in a position to effect numerous changes in the nation.

One of the most immediate results of the Liberal victory of 1906 was the Education Bill (Birrell Bill) introduced by the Liberal government that very April, which would have abolished the voluntary or denominational school system in England.[5] Catholics had always stressed the primary rights of par-

3. *Wilfrid Wards* 2:210.

4. For the 1906 election, see A. K. Russell, *Liberal Landslide: The General Election of 1906* (Newton Abbot: David & Charles, 1973). For a good survey of this final Liberal administration, see Peter Rowland, *The Last Liberal Governments: The Promised Land, 1905–1910* (London: Macmillan, 1968) and *The Last Liberal Governments: Unfinished Business, 1911–1914* (London: Barrie & Jenkins, 1971).

5. For a discussion of the education question, see Marjorie Cruickshank, *Church and State in English Education, 1870 to the Present Day* (New York: St. Martin's Press, 1963); Benjamin Sacks, *The Religious Issue in the State Schools of England and Wales, 1902–1914* (Albuquerque: University of New Mexico Press, 1961); James Murphy, *Church, State and Schools in Britain, 1800–1970* (London: Routledge and Kegan Paul, 1971); and W. F. Brown, "The Education Bill of 1906," *Dublin Review* (Jan. 1907): 128–38.

ents over their children, especially in education, and the need to have children raised where the Catholic ethos could be inculcated, and so were strong defenders of denominational schools.[6] Despite their relative poverty English Catholics had created an extensive system of schools, though this system was growing ever more difficult to maintain, especially when compared with the board schools financed by the local rates. While they received some government aid, it was not until the Education Act of 1902 (Balfour Act), passed by Balfour's Unionist government, that they received something like the kind of financing they thought their due. The provision and repair of school buildings was paid for by the denomination, while the cost of maintenance and teachers' salaries were paid by the local rates. Unfortunately, the Balfour Act caused enormous resentment among the Nonconformists, who saw it as unduly favoring Anglican and Catholic schools, and, to their horror, putting "Rome on the rates."[7] But it was not the Nonconformists alone who disliked it. Many Liberals did not care for denominational education and would have much preferred to take education out of the hands of the churches altogether. Ward strongly opposed this bill in an early article (dated June 11, 1906), both in its principles and in its particulars.[8]

Ward acknowledged that in the public mind (a mind influenced by liberalism) denominational education represented superstition and reaction and encouraged provincialism and sectarianism. And while he agreed that these things were not good, he did not think that such a view of things was either practical or true to human nature. "Thus the full, living, breathing, acting man is almost inevitably a denominational animal." While the goal was to curb excess, the end would be to uproot religious belief and destroy the springs of human action that religious belief very largely supplied.

If a boy's religion is to hold and influence him and make him eventually a strong man, it must be definite, perhaps must even have something in its exclusive dominion over him which in a man would be called bigotry. Tennyson used to say, "We must choose between bigotry and flabbiness." The practical alternative in early youth to a

6. See George Fonsegrive, "La Famille, l'Etat, l'Eglise, l'Ecole et l'Enfant," *Dublin Review* (Oct. 1912): 300–329.

7. This phrase, coined by the famous Baptist minister John Clifford (1836–1923) and used with great effectiveness by the opponents of the Balfour Act, was quite deceiving, as Cruickshank points out (*Church and State in English Education,* 81), for the really great beneficiaries of the act were the Anglicans, who had ten times the number of schools.

8. [Wilfrid Ward], "Denominationalism and the Educational Bill," *Dublin Review* (July 1906): 155–80.

certain narrowness of view is a want of depth and strength. It is just this strength of religion and its depth as a principle of action which is so important to instill early. Greater width of view and the comprehension of different standpoints may be gained later by those who are fitted to think on such subjects. Introduced earlier they may kill religion as a principle of action.[9]

Ward believed that one always lived from a foundation, from "a fixed standpoint and fixed line of orientation." To maintain a bland neutrality was ultimately to refuse to think at all, to be anything at all. "To live and act is indeed inevitably to take sides."[10] It was this rootedness that gave people depth and a capacity to understand and profit from a larger world. Nor did he consider it a good idea to create this neutrality by reducing religious instruction to only those things that all denominations agreed upon, "simple Bible teaching," which was called "our common Christianity." Such instruction still suffered from the deficiency already discussed, being contrary to life by its abstractiveness, but it also meant that that the instruction would be basically Protestant since it would ignore those very things which made Catholicism different. The best guarantee against the narrowness of provincialism and sectarianism, Ward stressed, was not neutrality between the denominations but good denominational education: education by really educated people who both professed the same religion as their students and whose own culture had given them a breadth of view.

After discussing the philosophical issues of the bill, he moved on to its technical difficulties as it now stood after the second reading. While all elementary schools receiving public funds would be under the local authority, which would pay for their upkeep with an agreed rent to the denomination, extended facilities might, as a concession to the denominations, be allowed to them to give denominational education every school day if four-fifths of the children's parents asked for it. But this concession excluded denominational schools in urban areas with a population of fewer than five thousand. He stated that there were some 243 Catholic schools that fell into this category. (Brown, the Vicar General of Westminster and a leading figure in Catholic education, thought nearly half of Catholic schools would fall into this category.)[11] For them, "at the option of the local authority," there might be three days a week of "simple Bible teaching" given at public expense, while Catho-

9. Ibid., 156–58.
10. Ibid., 157.
11. Brown, "Education Bill of 1906," 136.

lic teaching might be given only twice a week, at the expense of the Catholic Church and not by a member of the school staff. (In none of the schools would the local authority pay for denominational teaching.) For at least 23 percent of Catholic schools, therefore, the Catholic character would be lost, and the souls of some twenty-three thousand children would be endangered. Ward also stressed that for none of the schools was there any guarantee in the bill that religious instruction would be given by practicing Catholics or by regular teachers, the only kind that would really do. Since all teachers were appointed at the discretion of the local authority, and since under the bill teachers were not required as a condition of their employment "to subscribe to any religious creed, or to attend or abstain from attending any place of religious worship," anything was possible, including the exclusion of religious (nuns, priests, brothers) because they were religious. Ward did not believe that these were imaginary fears; experience suggested otherwise. Also, if the essence of these schools, as portrayed by the bill, was that religious education should play in them the same important role that it played in real voluntary schools, then religious education should be obligatory. According to the bill, students were only obliged to attend secular instruction. To those who defended the student's right to forego the school's religious instruction as a protection for Catholics in the council schools, he pointed out that there was already a conscience clause that protected this right. Nor was he optimistic that the average Catholic parent could be relied upon fully to send his child to school in time to hear the religious lesson. Ward was critical of other parts of the bill as well, particularly its failure to deal intelligently with schools created after the Balfour Act had come into force. If the bill were not amended, he believed that it should be rejected, even if that meant much economic hardship.

In the article Ward lavishly praised the Irish members for putting their principles and religion above their party interests, but in the end the Irish members, with the support of the English hierarchy and after gaining some concessions, supported it, to the surprise and consternation of the Catholic peers who had worked in the House of Lords to amend it significantly.[12] After the government withdrew the bill on December 20, 1906, various attempts

12. For a discussion of the bill and the controversy around it, see John Cashman, "The Education Bill: Catholic Peers and Irish Nationalists," *Recusant History* 18 (Oct. 1987): 422–39; and Vincent Alan McClelland, "Bourne, Norfolk, and the Irish Parliamentarians: Roman Catholics and the Education Bill of 1906," *Recusant History* 23 (Oct. 1996): 228–56.

were made to pass an education bill. In 1907 and early 1908 an education bill was introduced and failed (first and second McKenna Bills), and in late 1908 the Liberals made one last attempt (the Runciman Bill), which also failed. Only this last garnered any attention from the *Dublin,* which sang a *Te Deum* over its demise.[13] It was not until 1944 (the Butler Act) that the educational system was significantly revised.

In September 1908 the International Eucharistic Congress was to be held in London, and its closing highlight was to be a procession of the Blessed Sacrament through the streets of London.[14] Unfortunately, this technically contravened section 26 of the Catholic Relief Act of 1829, which forbade Catholic ceremonies and the wearing of vestments outside churches and private houses. While Catholics proclaimed that the law was a dead letter (as were many other anti-Catholic laws), the government intervened, fearing violence from ultra-Protestants. The procession was held, but without the Blessed Sacrament and without vestments. One result of all this controversy was the resignation of Lord Ripon (1827–1909), the only Catholic member of the cabinet, over the government's handling of the affair. Another was the introduction, in 1909, by John Redmond of the Catholic Disabilities Bill, which among other things would legalize religious processions and the existence of monasteries, and would alter the sovereign's declaration against transubstantiation. By law, under the Bill of Rights of 1689, the new ruler was obliged when addressing Parliament for the first time to assert that "the invocation or adoration of the Virgin Mary or any other saint and the sacrifice of the Mass as they are now used in the Church of Rome are superstitious and idolatrous." This declaration was to be made "without any evasion, equivocation or mental reservation whatever, and without any dispensation past or future or possibility of it from the Pope or any other authority." King Edward VII, who regarded the words as offensive to his Catholic subjects, tried to get out of saying them, but since only an act of Parliament could rectify this, he said them in a lowered voice. From that point on he tried to revise the declaration.

In the October 1909 number of the *Dublin,* Herbert Thurston, tracing the

13. "Mr Runciman's Bill," *Dublin Review* (Jan. 1909): 173–81.

14. W. S. Lilly, "The Coming Eucharistic Congress," ibid. (July 1908): 51–57; G. I. T. Machin, "The Liberal Government and the Eucharistic Procession of 1908," *Journal of Ecclesiastical History* 34 (Oct. 1983): 559–83. See also Thomas Horwood, "Public Opinion and the 1908 Eucharistic Congress," *Recusant History* 25 (May 2000): 120–32.

history of the anti-Catholic tests and reviewing the Catholic Disabilities Bill and its debates, came to this conclusion: "Reduced to its simplest terms, the opposition to the Bill amounted to this, that it was a good thing that Catholics should understand that they enjoyed their political rights only on sufferance and that they were, and always would be, objects of suspicion to their fellow citizens."[15] The underlying point behind the Catholic protest against this treatment was simple:

> Why should a slur be affixed to the creed of Catholics by special denunciations and disabilities such as are applied to no other religion or sect in the Empire? . . . They are to bear in mind that, amongst anarchists and socialists, atheists, idolaters and heathens, their opinions, and their opinions alone, are proscribed by name and subjected to penalties. No doubt the whip, which is the emblem of their bondage, is not intended to be used, but it is to be hung up in full view of all, that they may not for a moment suppose that they have been admitted to share the benefits of the British Constitution on terms of equality; and, lest, even thus, familiarity should induce complete oblivion, once at least, at the beginning of every reign, the whip is to be taken down and solemnly cracked in the presence of the representatives of Church and State. By such generous treatment will the young Catholics of Ireland and our Colonies learn to appreciate the benefits of British rule, to renounce all dreams of independence and avert their eyes from the temptation to seek religious freedom under another flag.[16]

Catholics had no secret agenda to overthrow the Protestant succession, to gain the throne for one of their coreligionists. Simple justice demanded that these insults to the Catholic faith be removed. He thought it curious that among the people most intent on keeping this Protestant declaration were Nonconformist divines "who cannot endure the thought of any religious pledge being exacted from teachers." Thurston disagreed that only explicit anti-Catholicism could exclude Catholics from the throne. There were a number of ways that the Protestantism of the ruler could be preserved without insulting Catholics, such as different wording or the reception of the Protestant Sacrament—something no Catholic could do. Finally, Thurston suggested that perhaps it was not so much against Catholicism that this opposition was directed, but, as Lord Edmund Talbot, the brother of the Duke of Norfolk and a Conservative MP, had suggested in a speech, against the Anglo-Catholicism of the High Church party in the Church of England. In any case, he believed, a better way could be found.

15. Herbert Thurston, "The Catholic Disabilities Bill," *Dublin Review* (Oct. 1909): 225.
16. Ibid., 226–27.

Only three months after King Edward's death a bill was passed that changed the declaration. It became: "I do solemnly and sincerely in the presence of God profess, testify, and declare that I am a faithful Protestant, and that I will, according to the true intent of the enactments to secure the Protestant succession to the Throne of My Realm, uphold and maintain such enactments to the best of my power." However, the other parts of the bill were not passed, and only in 1926 were more disabilities removed, though some remain to this day.

One of the great issues of this period was tariff reform, and few issues aroused such passions, caused such bitterness and division, and played such havoc with the political system.[17] When Joseph Chamberlain opened his campaign for tariff reform in a speech at Birmingham on May 15, 1903, he unleashed forces that would leave the Unionists the party of protection, and out of power. While the idea was not new (there had been the fair trade movement among the Conservatives in the 1880s), it went against the long-standing tradition of free trade that had dominated British thought since the repeal of the Corn Laws in 1846. It united the Liberals and divided the Unionists, and made the stunning defeat of 1906 far more likely. Balfour attempted to keep the party together by maintaining a balance between the extremes of those who wanted free trade ("Free Fooders") and those who wanted the protection of tariff reform ("Whole Hoggers"). While he managed to keep his government in power till late 1905, this only made things worse in the end. His great ingenuity and political dexterity could not reconcile the irreconcilable, and by February 14, 1906, in the so-called "Valentine letters," he had committed himself to some sort of protection, though the degree of commitment was sometimes difficult to judge. The more extreme protectionists, who came to dominate the party and purge it of their opponents, never completely trusted him. While Ward had written on tariff reform a year earlier, defending Balfour's adroit statesmanship in this bitter conflict, the first article on it in his *Dublin* was by Hilaire Belloc.[18]

17. See Alan Sykes, *Tariff Reform in British Politics, 1903–1913* (Oxford: Clarendon Press, 1979); and Richard A. Rempel, *Unionists Divided: Arthur Balfour, Joseph Chamberlain and the Unionist Free Traders* (Newton Abbot: David & Charles, 1972).

18. Wilfrid Ward, "A Political Fabius Maximus," *Nineteenth Century* 58 (June 1905): 877–97, reprinted with a postscript in *Ten Personal Studies*, 1–47. This article was written at the instigation of Balfour and the proofs were gone over by Balfour's private secretary, Jack Sandars. See Rempel, *Unionists Divided*, 131–32. Hilaire Belloc, "The Fiscal Question," *Dublin Review* (Oct. 1906): 277–99.

Belloc (1870–1953), then a Liberal MP, might have seemed at first glance an odd choice for Ward's *Dublin,* as he certainly belonged to the Radical wing of the Liberal Party.[19] Even at Oxford he had been obsessed with politics, forming the Republican Club with his good friends John Phillimore and F. Y. Eccles, with whom he contributed to a political manifesto, *Essays in Liberalism* (1897), by "Six Oxford Men." With his love of the French Revolution, which Ward detested, and his iconoclastic liberalism, which conflicted with Ward's deferential conservatism, he would seem an unlikely contributor, but his intense Catholicism, his historical sensibility, and his underlying love for "the old things" made his collaboration with Ward possible.[20] Also, like Ward, he feared both socialism and an excessively intrusive state that would limit personal liberty. Elected from South Salford in 1906, he grew disillusioned with the Liberal Party and retired in 1910. It was at this time that he published his most important political works, his attack on the political parties, *The Party System* (1911), written with Cecil Chesterton, Gilbert's brother, and his critique of capitalist collectivism, *The Servile State* (1912). Despite their significance, neither book was really discussed or reviewed in the *Dublin.*[21]

In his article, Belloc pointed out that the tariff reformers gave varied arguments for their program. "The change which Tariff Reformers urge upon us is represented now as a means of benefiting the colonies, and making more complete the homogeneity of the Empire at some expense to our purses, now as a means of increasing the wealth of this country by stimulating its energies; now as imperial, now (in contradiction) as a domestic policy; now as political, and now as an economic idea."[22] He did not see how it could be all these simultaneously. You could not, for example, stimulate the energies of English agriculture by giving preference to Canadian agricultural imports. If the goal was to give an advantage to the colonies, there were less revolutionary ways of doing it. The reformers' main claim seemed to be economic, namely, that protection would make England richer because it would stimulate energies within the country; and this ran through all their appeals to the electorate.

19. For Belloc's life, see Robert Speaight, *The Life of Hilaire Belloc* (London: Hollis and Carter, 1957). For a discussion of Belloc's political and economic views, see John P. McCarthy, *Hilaire Belloc: Edwardian Radical* (Indianapolis: Liberty Press, 1978).

20. See A. N. Wilson, *Hilaire Belloc* (New York: Atheneum, 1984), 150–53.

21. However, in a footnote in an article by J. Keating, S.J., "Civil Liberty in Peace and War," *Dublin Review* (April 1916), the reader was advised to consult *The Party System* for "a detailed and acute, but almost wholly destructive, criticism of the 'Party System'" (355).

22. Belloc, "The Fiscal Question," 280.

The free traders believed that if left to themselves, each following his individual benefit, merchants and producers would produce a maximum of general wealth, and in this they were wrong, Belloc believed, and the tariff reformers right. There were some conditions in which the maximum of wealth would not be produced by free trade, where protection was good economic policy. "All such fancied arguments, as that protection 'taxes the foreigner' or 'provides the money to buy the dearer loaf,' are of about as much value as the opposing propositions that Free Trade alone is consonant with Christianity, or that it is a peculiarly English product and therefore to be revered."[23] If England were to tax all foreign goods, it would be a revolution and a disaster; but a slight tariff on certain noncolonial goods, so small that the increase would not greatly inconvenience the English consumer but would significantly benefit the colonies, might be possible. But, he asked, why should England impoverish herself for the profit of the colonies (who were chiefly valuable to her as payers of interest on the money lent them) when they were flourishing and when England bore the greater part of their defense? Nor was the impoverishment of England the claim of the tariff reformers. Belloc believed that the strongest argument for tariff reform was that it would stimulate industries currently absent or weak, and historically it had been remarkably successful in doing so when used intelligently. Another strong argument for it, he believed, was that a flexible tariff could be very useful as a political weapon, in bringing pressure on other countries or even on the colonies. But neither of these last two cases was sufficiently strong, since England depended too extensively upon her imports (some half her wealth) for her to tamper with free trade.

Belloc's great fear, however, was that the need for revenue, particularly revenue for social reform, would beguile people into certain types of protection, since they would not immediately affect the poorer classes. Belloc believed that England had reached the limits of direct taxation and so some new form of revenue could become attractive. England's "oligarchic system" and the people's contentment with "government by the rich" meant that the well-to-do would pay no more ("the wealthy governing class will not impoverish itself"), while the lower middle class could certainly not pay any more. There was a "tacit understanding" between the governing and the working classes that "it is impossible to lay a burden upon those millions who consent to the

23. Ibid., 284.

lack of security and of property under the condition that, so long as they do not disturb the stability of the State, their 'individual liberty,' as it is called, shall not be interfered with." He did not think it "conceivable" that there could be a further increase in indirect taxation on their beer, tobacco, or tea, or upon those necessities hitherto untaxed. He feared that when protection came to pass, then England's international credit would suffer and she would lose her commercial hegemony.

In a footnote, Ward stated that he did not accept all the views contained in this "able" article; and while he promised to supplement them with other viewpoints, it was three years before tariff reform was mentioned again, and then only in relation to defending the right of Unionists to dissent from the new dogma of protectionism.[24] This article by Ward was a commentary on an article just preceding it by his old friend Lord Hugh Cecil, who had discussed the need for a certain flexibility among party ranks in Parliament, as long as fundamentals were preserved, if Parliament were to function truly and well.[25] While Cecil did not bring up the issue of tariff reform, that was certainly what he had in mind, as Cecil was known as a leading free-trade Unionist—one whose career the tariff reformers had vowed to end.[26] Ward defended Cecil, including his position on tariff reform.

> Unless Tariff Reform is the be-all and end-all of the party, unless the present Unionist coalition is to be avowedly a Tariff Reform party, the exclusion of members on the ground that, on this one point, they cannot agree with the leaders is, he argues, a very extreme measure. It places Tariff Reform in a very unique position. . . . Is such dissent from the Government programme on one point—in the case of Tariff Reform but in that of no other measure—to neutralise agreement on everything else? Does not such a course—I may add, for it is suggested by the personality of the man who is pleading his cause—tend to purge the Unionist party of its men of first-rate ability? For thinking men cannot be made to run in droves with the same ease as unthinking

24. Wilfrid Ward, "Edmund Burke and Party Action," *Dublin Review* (July 1909): 14–36.

25. Lord Hugh Cecil, "The Diseases of the House of Commons," ibid., 25–35. This article began as a speech given at Ward's instigation before the Westminster Catholic Dining Society.

26. For Lord Hugh Cecil, see Kenneth Rose, *The Later Cecils* (New York: Harper & Row, 1975), 230–93, and Richard A. Rempel, "Lord Hugh Cecil's Parliamentary Career, 1900–1914: Promise Unfulfilled," *Journal of British Studies* 11 (May 1972): 104–30. Lord Hugh Cecil (1869–1956), the fifth and youngest son of Lord Salisbury, entered Parliament in 1895, but his rigid Anglicanism and often vitriolic conservatism diminished his influence. In the 1906 election the tariff reformers put up their own candidate, which certainly cost Cecil the election; and after his defeat they made clear that they would do all they could to prevent his return to the Commons.

partisans. We often have complaints as to the lack of first-class ability in the party. Is not this want likely to be increased by a policy which exalts unthinking obedience, in a very complex and difficult issue, as the best qualification for a seat in Parliament . . . ?[27]

Ward noted that the Whole Hoggers looked upon their position with all the blind fanaticism and absolutism of religious dogma: one that supplied them with an optimistic faith, a cry for the elections, and a party watchword; and that made anyone who was less than wholehearted "half a heretic." "Obviously, if the primary object of the party is to picture Tariff Reform to the people in such a way as to make it promise a millennium,—as a faith warranting the expectation of its bringing an earthly paradise; and so to gain their votes by hopes, irrespective of their probability of realization; the men who do this best are either credulous and one-sided men, or blind partisans, or men without knowledge, or unscrupulous men who wish to stand well at the moment with the party, and do not hesitate to win votes by saying what they suspect to be untrue." Ward cited Edmund Burke, who, while believing in parties and in principles and having contempt for those that had none, allowed dissent where it did not infringe upon party principles and expressed the principles of the individual. "The intelligent party man who is at once loyal to his party and yet true to himself is clearly Burke's ideal of an efficient statesman."[28]

Ward thought that Balfour (whom he praised extravagantly in the article) could even be helped by the existence of these Unionist free-trade MPs since, while being too few to prevent tariff reform, they could by their criticism counterbalance the extreme tariff reformers and so make a better result. Ward claimed for himself the position of a moderate tariff reformer:

The present writer can at least claim to speak with no bias whatever on the subject. He is in the position of that large number of electors who form a judgement on the question, based only on the economic knowledge common to most educated men, and on certain maxims which appear to him the best guide in the absence of a specialist's knowledge. The class to which he belongs are in a certain restricted sense Tariff Reformers. They believe the shibboleths of Cobdenism to be artificial, as applied to the existing condition of things in which foreign countries are protectionist. They regard Mr Chamberlain's original representation, in 1903, of a commercial crisis in the country which urgently called for a large measure of Tariff Reform, as having been

27. Ward, "Edmund Burke and Party Action," 37.
28. Ibid., 53, 44.

very exaggerated and inaccurate. But they would wish that any proposed fiscal changes should be fairly and favourably considered on their own merits—on the ground of expediency and unhampered by rigid *a priori* maxims on either side. The wisdom, and even occasional necessity, of retaliation is to them evident. They cannot see that Continental experience bears out the necessity of an absolute rule against the taxation of food, and they agree with those who think that Lord St Aldwyn's old tax on corn, which hurt nobody, was a successful experiment which might be tried on a larger scale.[29]

It was the extremism of the Whole Hoggers, particularly of the Confederates (a secret society of tariff reformers who aimed at purging the party of all dissidents) that Ward found so objectionable. Since national policies must claim broader support, have a certain stability and permanence, and not be open to radical change when a new government came in, the existence of a few free-fooders in the party should not be a problem. If it were, then "a wise statesman's conclusion will be that such a scheme ought not to pass." "Common sense says at least this much—if many of the ablest and most practical men find the path of Fiscal Reform to be beset with difficulties and dangers we should tread it warily. That very attitude, again, which is the *raison d'être* of Conservatism—the sense that drastic change is in itself an evil, and that any change should be undertaken only in virtue of unquestionable evils and on behalf of a gain which is clear—is indisputably against the policy of the 'whole-hoggers.'"[30]

After the election of January 1910 Lord Hugh Cecil was the only free-trade Unionist left in Parliament, and he had become a very passive one, representing a safe Oxford University seat. All the others had either retired, been defeated, changed their opinions, or crossed over to the Liberals, as Winston Churchill did in 1904. While tariff reform did not disappear from the political firmament, for it lay behind many of the actions of these years, it was eclipsed by other issues of a constitutional nature, something far more frightening to a man of conservative temperament.

These constitutional crises, which would undermine the whole ancestral order, were founded on the profound imbalance of the two chambers of Parliament: while the Unionists were weak in the Commons they were strong in the Lords. In the 1890s the Unionists had used the House of Lords to defeat Liberal legislation. It had worked because of the very weakness of the Liberal

29. Ibid., 48–49.
30. Ibid., 50.

majority in the Commons and because there was no issue popular enough to create a broadly based resentment of the noble peers for their obstinacy. In the new Parliament Balfour aimed to do the same, but the Lords had to be very selective in their rejections if the plan was to succeed. They allowed legislation through that was broadly popular, especially if it was favorable to working-class interests, but defeated bills that could not command such support and were antithetical to Unionist interests. Thus in 1906 it passed a Workmen's Compensation Act and the Trade Disputes Act (a favorite of Labour that restored the nonliability of unions for damages incurred in labor disputes); in 1907 it passed a Factory and Workshops Act that was aimed at providing the health and safety of workers; in 1908 it passed the Coal Mines Regulation Act, which secured an eight-hour workday for miners and was the first bill of this sort not aimed at women and children; and, finally, in 1908 it passed the Old Age Pensions Act. But others were rejected: the Education Bill (1906), the Plural Voting Bill (1906), two Scottish land bills (1908), and the Licensing Bill (1908). By the winter of 1908–1909 the Liberal government, its legislative program emasculated, was exhausted and dispirited, with a string of by-election defeats pointing to a Unionist victory in the next election. It was at this time that Lloyd George made the apt comment, "The House of Lords has long ceased to be the watchdog of the Constitution. It has become Mr. Balfour's poodle. It barks for him. It fetches and carries for him. It bites anybody that he sets it on to."[31]

All of this changed with the budget of 1909–1910 ("The People's Budget") introduced by the chancellor of the exchequer, David Lloyd George (who replaced Asquith when he became prime minister in April 1908), in a four-hour speech on April 29, 1909.[32] The budget served a number of purposes. By this time free-trade finance had clearly reached a crisis unless something drastic

31. Quoted in Sydney Zebel, *Balfour: A Political Biography* (Cambridge: Cambridge University Press, 1973), 152.

32. See Bruce K. Murray, *The People's Budget 1909/10: Lloyd George and Liberal Politics* (Oxford: Clarendon Press, 1980). In a later article by J. G. Snead-Cox, "The Budget," *Dublin Review* (July 1914): 170–81, the 1914–15 budget, which placed all the new burdens entirely on the well-to-do, was severely taken to task for many of the same reasons that the "People's Budget" had been taken to task earlier by Conservatives. The 1914 budget was seen as "marking an epoch," as "the beginning of the Revolution," and had now become "the most potent weapon not only for effecting a redistribution of national wealth, but also for the prevention of those inequalities of fortune which have accompanied the growth of our own and every other civilization." Snead-Cox believed that it could not fail to be popular with the general electorate, who would reap its benefits without suffering any of its disabilities.

were done. (We have already seen the belief of Belloc that England had reached the limits of its ability to tax, and that protection might come in for that reason.) The expense of the naval building program with the construction of eight dreadnoughts ("we want eight and we won't wait"), the cost of the old-age pensions, and the lower expected revenue caused by the economic slowdown, meant that vast new sums would be needed. The tariff reformers (and many of their free-trade opponents) believed that protection had now become inevitable, as heavy direct taxes would be politically unacceptable. But in this they were wrong. Lloyd George proved that free-trade finance was viable and showed the way such finance could go. In his budget seven new taxes were introduced and, except for much higher taxes on liquor and tobacco, these really only affected the wealthy. Not only were direct taxes on income increased (which only affected the well-to-do) but a super-tax on the very wealthy was created. What particularly frightened the Unionists was not so much the new land taxes but that a land valuation was inserted into this finance bill. A new Domesday Book was in the making and many Unionists feared what the future would hold. As the Liberal statesman Morley said, "to talk about land to the House of Lords was like talking to a butcher about Lent."[33] Lloyd George's budget was as much political as financial, its purpose as much to revive the fortunes of the Liberal Party as to gather the revenue needed, as much to get legislation that had failed (such as against the liquor trade) through the front door passed through the back door, and to prove the viability of free-trade finance over tariff-reform finance. And in all this it succeeded magnificently. On November 30, by 350 votes to 75, the Lords rejected the budget, bringing on a constitutional crisis and an election.

The election of January 1910 caused great excitement, and an extraordinary number of registered voters (some 87 percent) went to the polls, the largest number ever. Despite an increase in the Unionist vote and their recapture of a great many seats, the Unionists (fighting primarily on tariff reform) fell short of a majority, the new Parliament having 275 Liberals, 273 Unionists, 82 Irish Nationalists, and 40 Labourites. The Irish, while not keen on the budget, knew that only by a Liberal victory could the Lords' veto be removed and Home Rule become a real possibility. Having failed to achieve a victory at the polls the Lords had no option but to pass the budget, but now Asquith had

33. Quoted in Neal Blewett, *The Peers and the People: The General Elections of 1910* (London: Macmillan, 1972), 70.

the issue with which to break the power of the Lords. He introduced legislation that would make the Commons the clear arbiter of government, leaving the Lords only a suspensive veto that would delay legislation but not kill it, and a new election was called for December 1910 to decide the Lords' fate.[34] It was by this assault on the Lords that Ward was particularly incensed.

The destruction of the veto power of the House of Lords was a watershed in British politics. While the franchise had been extended dramatically in the nineteenth century, Britain was still not a democracy. The landed aristocracy was wealthy and powerful, wielding great influence both directly and indirectly; and not more than 60 percent of the adult male population had the vote.[35] Except for money bills, which by long custom the Lords could not impede, their veto power was absolute, part of the unwritten constitution, the glory and genius of the nation. For a man like Ward the attack on the Lords was an attack on the Constitution itself, a radical and dangerous thing. It was an important issue, to which the *Dublin* devoted much attention. In the April 1910 issue there was a symposium on reforming the House of Lords, with two Unionists, Lord Halifax and James Fitzalan Hope, a Conservative MP and Wilfrid's brother-in-law, and an unnamed Liberal.[36]

In the first article Lord Halifax stated that "all sensible and moderate men" wanted to maintain a strong upper chamber but that it had to be done in accordance with the whole history of the House so as not to lose the strengths it possessed at present. He believed that the changes should not impair the continuity of the Lords, should not create a "new body," and should only make it "more efficient in popular estimation." Since the Lords had first been created by the king's calling upon those who were most able to help him carry on the affairs of the country, it would be perfectly in line with that tradition if those now called were those most likely to promote the welfare of the Empire. There were many outside the ranks of the Lords, Halifax believed, for whom such a call would be appropriate, just as there were many peers who had little

34. For a discussion of the fight over the Lords, see Roy Jenkins, *Mr. Balfour's Poodle: An Account of the Struggle between the House of Lords and the Government of Mr. Asquith* (London: Heinemann, 1954).

35. See David Cannadine, *The Decline and Fall of the British Aristocracy* (New Haven: Yale University Press, 1990); and Neal Blewett, "The Franchise in the United Kingdom: 1885–1918," *Past and Present* 32 (Dec. 1965): 27–56.

36. "Reform of the House of Lords," *Dublin Review* (April 1910): 233–49. Sir Charles Lindley Wood, 2nd Viscount Halifax (1839–1934), educated at Eton and Christ Church, Oxford, was the president of the English Church Union (1868–1919, 1927–1934) and leader of English Anglo-

to justify their presence. Certain peers by their personal conduct or indifference to public affairs could be disqualified, but the body should be one of continuity and independence of opinion.[37]

Hope also believed that the House of Lords was too important, as a representative of the permanent, as distinguished from the transient, opinion of the nation, to be radically changed. The Lords served an important purpose in delaying legislation until popular opinion was quite clear about any particular measure, the Home Rule Bill of 1893 being the perfect example of this. While the plan suggested by the select committee of the House for a reform that entailed a House partially elected by its peers and partially selected because of distinguished service was a good one, it suffered from the drawback that it would still be the same body, only smaller and more efficient, that already existed and was the object of displeasure. Whatever was done, it should certainly not be by popular election; otherwise the Lords would be affected by electoral considerations and lose their freedom of judgment. The safest plan, he thought, would be for the Crown to choose a certain number, say 150, of those currently in the Lords and to add to that number no more than 100 life peers. It would thus maintain the best element of the present system and infuse into the Lords new life.

The Liberal contributor to the symposium, not surprisingly, believed that the Lords had no one to blame but themselves for the trouble they were in, not just because of their rejection of the budget but also because of their persistent obstruction of the program for which the Liberals had been elected. Their immoderate behavior had made the continuance of the unrestricted veto of the unreformed House of Lords impossible. He believed that the least possible change was best, so as to maintain the sense of precedence and the continuity of the Constitution. He rejected the more complicated schemes for the reform of the Lords that had been bandied about and endorsed the

Catholicism for many years. He is best remembered for his attempts at Anglican-Catholic reunion, particularly for the Malines Conferences of the 1920s. James Fitzalan Hope (1870–1949), Josephine Ward's brother, was an MP (1900–1906, 1908–1929), deputy speaker (1921–1924, 1924–1929), and a member of the Privy Council (1922). In 1932 he was raised to the peerage as 1st Baron Rankeillour.

37. Halifax also believed that the hereditary principle should be kept because of its importance in the people's imagination, and that the two estates of the Lords Temporal and the Lords Spiritual should be maintained. Except for the old historical peerages (which were not many) and the sees of bishops from before the accession of Henry VIII, from the rest of the hereditary peerage, he thought, representatives should only be elected from among themselves. The unelected peers would then become eligible for election to the Commons.

simple suspensive veto. It would ensure the government a success in carrying out its program but would leave the Lords the ability to amend, revise, and delay legislation so that only those bills that had great popular appeal could be enacted. The proposed scheme could delay a bill for as long as two years, for it would allow the Lords two rejections of a bill, but on its third passage in the Commons it would become law. It would give "perfect security against precipitate and unconsidered change" and force the government to compromise on controversial legislation. Social stability, he believed, rested on instinct and tradition, and it was not the Liberal ideal to destroy what could be modified but to preserve what was best in English society, while righting the wrongs that changing conditions produced. He believed a suspensive veto would do all that.

Ward made very clear in a footnote attached to the Liberal's article that while he was open to some sort of reconstruction of the upper chamber, he thought the suspensive veto no veto at all, and that the removal of the Lords' veto would be revolutionary, government by a single chamber. Ward was no democrat—at least by modern standards—as he made very clear in another article, "The People and the Populace."[38] He believed that the cry of the French Revolution for liberty and equality was both erroneous and dangerous, issuing in Robespierre and the guillotine, and made tyranny inevitable. He did not believe that liberty was a right. While liberty was necessary for men to reach the highest virtue—personal growth only being possible where choice was possible—yet being imperfect beings, and in consequence of our fallen nature, we had to be educated in the proper use of our liberty by the use of restraint. We had to be trained, he believed, to love the highest and best, and we needed the external aid of restraint to do that, just as we trained the young boy gradually, increasing his freedom in proportion as he could handle it. To his mind, equally pernicious was the idea of equality. People were inherently unequal, in every sort of way. It was this absurd idea of equality that had led to the idea that the "will of the people" was a simple counting of heads, and that it should decide all matters. A "sound and safe democracy" must be founded on this principle: "that only those should have political power who are sufficiently educated to meet the test of Socrates; who know on occasion that they do not know and trust those who do."[39] Since expert

38. See Wilfrid Ward, "The People and the Populace," *Dublin Review* (April 1910): 371–82.
39. Ibid., 378.

knowledge could not be expected of all (though the knowledge of our limitations was achievable), and since it was divided among different persons, we should defer, he thought, to those who have such knowledge. Equally we should defer to those with the greatest experience and wisdom. Otherwise democracy becomes "anarchical"; and the real aim of democracy, popular welfare, would be defeated by its false counterpart, "the popular whim, miscalled the will of the people." "Here we have the rationale of political education and of a second chamber as safeguarding the sound root-principle of democracy, namely that the *real* will of the people, when they know the relevant facts, should prevail."[40] While the principles of French democracy were an artificial creation formed by abstract theorizing, those of English democracy were empirical, organic, "a growth according to Nature." "It is based, not on an abstract principle of equal rights for all, but on a right for all, in so far as they show themselves to be fitted by education, to be admitted to some useful part in legislation—not to an equal part, but a part proportioned to their capacity."[41] Ward contrasted the "people," led by their natural leaders, to the "populace," those led by their emotions, whims, and self-interest. In fact, Ward believed that French principles had already "somewhat tainted" English democracy and that power already had been given to those who were not as yet educated to wield it safely, but he hoped that there was still time to educate people according to true principles.

Ward called to his support the unlikely figure of John Stuart Mill, the patron saint of English rationalism and the exponent of classic liberalism.[42] This "devotee of the people, this hater of aristocratic privilege" was not a supporter of the idea that sheer numbers should decide a thing, that the mere counting of heads, "the mandate of the people," should outweigh the opinions of educated people as a determining factor in government. He was acutely aware of the perils of democracy and of the ease with which demagogues (in Mill's words, "a class of base adventurers in the character of professional politicians") could manipulate the uneducated voter by flattery or an appeal to self-interest. His ultimate ideal was a government by the "ablest intellects" chosen by the whole community for the common good, but completely free to make their own decisions, not being bound at all by their constituents' expressed

40. Ibid.
41. Ibid., 379.
42. Wilfrid Ward, "John Stuart Mill and the Mandate of the People," ibid. (July 1910): 85–96.

wishes or pressures. What the people wanted was not as important as what was best for the people, and when Mill himself was asked to stand for Parliament he ran on such an unbending platform and was elected.

In a later article, "The Democracy and the Political Crisis," written before the second election of 1910 held in December, taking his cue from a speech of Balfour's attacking demagogues as the enemies of true democracy (he was certainly thinking of David Lloyd George here), he elaborated his own views on the matter and the crisis that was now enveloping English democracy.[43] The Lords rejected the budget, rightly in his view, because they saw it as an attack on the property of a certain class and not as a genuine financial measure, the Liberals putting partisan and political needs above the financial needs of the country. While the Liberals had been returned to office, it was not really with a majority in favor of the budget, since the Irish, who generally did not favor the budget, only voted for it so as to obtain Home Rule for Ireland. "But the hue and cry against the Lords has been raised with such success by vulgar appeals to envy and class prejudice that it was quite impossible for the Lords even to consider this weighty argument in favour of rejecting the Bill a second time." False democracy, he believed, had compelled the Lords to yield. The prime minister then moved "against a fundamental principle of the Constitution" with his suspensive veto, again appealing to "popular passion," to false democracy, instead of asking the real question of whether the Lords had done their job properly. "No one expects an Upper House to be as friendly to a Radical Government as to a Conservative Government. It is intended to be a Conservative force in the Constitution. It is intended to create difficulties for an unprincipled demagogue and revolutionist if he attains power."[44]

Ward also saw the agents of false democracy in the proposals for the reform of the Lords, though no strong reasons had been made for the urgent necessity of any such reform. To his mind the debates heard in the Lords were certainly as good as if not better than those heard in the Commons, and the working members of the upper house were well equipped to do their work. "The House of Lords has all the weight and stability of an historic institution on its side. To tamper with the Constitution is always dangerous. A certain improvement in the personnel of the Lords, a certain shifting of the chaff, is (it may be argued) a very small gain to set against the diminution of security

43. Wilfrid Ward, "The Democracy and the Political Crisis," ibid. (Jan. 1911): 167–85.

44. Ibid., 168, 170.

and stability caused by unnecessary change in the British Constitution, in deference to the popular cry. It is somewhat like surrendering to the demands of men on strike." But again the outcry might be so great that some change of this sort might well be seen as a practical necessity. "The demagogues might easily work their dupes into a frenzy. And an angry mob is a monster which must be appeased by sacrifice."[45]

He mentioned two other examples of false democracy. One was the inability of the militant tariff reformers to put aside their prejudiced opinions so as to form a united front in this moment of constitutional crisis, a moment on which so much depended. The second was the election itself, where the discussions seemed to be indifferent to the great issues themselves and focused on trivialities or political jockeying. "Motives of self-interest, some of them warranted, more of them based on the false hopes held out by demagogues, constitute, perhaps, the main arguments which actually determine the votes of half the electorate in many constituencies." Greater political education would certainly help, and the true democrat would certainly aim for that, but something more would be needed. "He has to bring home to the people the importance, in their own interests, that they should accept constitutional checks which should prevent evil effects following on their own hasty impulses; and that they should, formally or informally, delegate some of their powers to sincere well-wishers who are better able than they to judge of the probable effect on their welfare of actual legislation."[46]

If the English were to be true to the ideals that created their democracy, they had to protect themselves from popular whim and the appeal of the demagogue. America, "the country which has most emphatically abolished aristocratic privilege" did this by putting in their Constitution various safeguards. They retained powerful legislatures within each state, created a powerful Senate to balance a more popular House, made it difficult to amend their Constitution, separated the powers of government, and gave the president veto power over legislation. The American Constitution was framed by practical men who were aware of the danger of popular impulses. Ward found shocking the ease with which England was willing fundamentally to change her Constitution with the abolition of the veto of the House of Lords and with Irish Home Rule. While he believed that the evil had already gone far and that violent cures tended to be fatal, he believed that it was still possible

45. Ibid., 171.

46. Ibid., 173, 175.

to save English democracy. The best that could be done at the moment, besides trying to educate the people, was to secure and strengthen that one remaining check on hasty change, the House of Lords. While he did not believe that it was practicable for the English to follow the American system, he did believe that the referendum could be useful. It at least secured a vote on a specific topic, canceled the overrepresentation of Ireland, and overrode the current party system, in which independence was becoming more and more difficult. He believed that even a referendum decided by a majority of those actually voting would act as a comparatively conservative force, though he did not think that anyone could seriously believe that the majority of voters could give a reliable verdict on issues demanding expert judgment. "Yet, as things are, the common-sense of the electorate is likely to revolt from extremes from which individual Radical leaders will not shrink, and which their followers in the House of Commons will carry out." The use of the referendum, he believed, could help educate voters because they would be voting on specific issues; and it would remove "the element of truth" in Asquith's complaint that the Lords were too partisan by allowing some sort of appeal from the Lords to the people. "Such a provision would preserve the principles of the Constitution intact, and remove even the most superficial justification that could be alleged for the revolutionary proposal of advising the King to create five hundred Liberal peers." In lieu of the suspensive veto suggested by Asquith, Ward suggested that the Lords might be given the power of delaying legislation two years with an ultimate appeal to the referendum. Whatever was done, it was essential that the fundamental principle of democracy, the benefit of the people, be defended and the dangers of false democracy be avoided.[47]

D. C. Lathbury, in an article reviewing the political situation, while more moderate in tone, agreed with Ward's interpretation.[48] He considered Americans "well advised" for "surrounding the amendment of their Constitution with the safeguards of a complicated machinery" and wished the English had been equally aware. He found the indifference of the populace to the whole question and the radical quality both of Asquith's proposal and of Lord Lansdowne's (the Unionist leader in the Lords) quite surprising. "To all appear-

47. Ibid., 183.

48. D. C. Lathbury, "The Political Situation," ibid. (April 1911): 356–80. Lathbury (1831–1922), educated at King's College, London, was editor of the *Guardian* from 1883 to 1899 and of the *Pilot* from 1900 to 1904. An Anglican and a journalist, he was also the author of five books, including biographies of Gladstone and Dean Church.

ance Englishmen do not care enough about the Constitution to vote either for or against it in any greater numbers than usual. It was once their boast that the form of government under which they lived had so strong a hold on their affections that there was no need to interpose special difficulties in the way of its destruction. . . . The statesmen who have made England believed themselves equally well acquainted with the character of their countrymen and relying on this knowledge they had thought it needless to take precautions against a constitutional revolution."[49] But the recent events had made perfectly clear that Britain needed a written Constitution.

King Edward VII died on May 6, 1910, succeeded by his son George V (1910–1936). An unsigned article, probably by Ward, appeared discussing the historical Catholic loyalty to the Crown and sharing in the national mourning for the late king, who was praised for his friendship toward Catholics.[50] The failure of a constitutional conference between the two parties to settle the issue of the Lords led to the dissolution of Parliament and new elections. Balfour played down tariff reform, but the December election changed little in the balance of power: there were 272 seats each for Liberals and Unionists, 42 for Labour, and 84 for the Irish Nationalists. Under the threat that Asquith would create as many as five hundred new peers—a promise he had wrung out of the king if he won the election—the Unionist leaders decided to pass the Parliament Bill with its suspensive veto rather than to suffer a permanent Liberal majority in the Lords. A great many Unionists violently opposed such a capitulation, and it was only with the greatest effort that these "diehards," as they were called, were overcome and the House of Lords, on August 10, 1911, by a vote of 131 to 114 accepted its diminution of power.

As Phillips has pointed out in his study of the diehards, these men were very different from the crowd of obscure, moss-backed "backwoodsmen" that they have generally been depicted as.[51] In fact, taken as a group, they were

49. Ibid., 359.

50. "Edward VII," ibid. (July 1910): 1–5. The author believed that Edward's reign (1902–1910) marked the "culminating point" in the great change in the national mind toward Catholic beliefs and devotions, and even toward Catholics themselves. While this change was, to a certain extent, caused by the growth of indifferentism, it was also due to the spread of Catholic ideas in the Church of England.

51. Gregory D. Phillips, *The Diehards: Aristocratic Society and Politics in Edwardian England* (Cambridge: Harvard University Press, 1979). See also Ronan Fanning, "'Rats' versus 'Ditchers': The Die-hard Revolt and the Parliament Bill of 1911," in *Parliament and Community*, ed. Art Cosgrove and J. I. McGuire (Belfast: Appletree, 1983), 191–210.

more politically active than the rest of the House of Lords, more active in their attendance, and more prone to speak and be involved in the work of the House. They also included a very large number of men prominent in public affairs, including Privy Councilors, former members of the Commons and cabinet, and men who had served the Empire both at home and abroad. Ward was a diehard, but not being a peer or an MP, he could not vote against the Parliament Bill. Some of his closest friends, the Duke of Norfolk in the Lords and George Wyndham and Lord Hugh Cecil in the Commons, were also diehards. In his own response to the passage of the bill, signed simply "a Unionist view," one sees the almost apocalyptic view of the situation taken by so many diehards.[52]

Ward saw the passage of the Parliament Bill as the "first decisive step in our English revolution" and compared it with King Louis XVI's flight from the Tuileries, which triggered the radicalization of the French Revolution. While admitting great differences between the two, he also saw great similarities. "In both cases the existing order and ancient constitution have been broken up by a violent party professing to represent the will of the people, and the axiom assumed as indisputable in either instance is that the vote of the people, counted by heads, is a court of final appeal, which has given its verdict. In both cases the nobility has been panic stricken and has given up its privileges *en bloc*—in England political privileges, in France mainly fiscal. Again, the first stages are in either instance no measure of the inevitable consequences."[53] The danger was not great and immediate at present because popular opinion seemed to show no great interest, but Ward already saw "ominous signs" that "both the spirit and the principles of revolution are in the air." (He was thinking particularly of the waves of strikes that were just beginning to engulf England and would continue until the Great War.) He believed that from the first it should have been obvious to the Unionist leadership (as it was obvious to others) that Asquith's threat to overwhelm the Lords with a large creation of peers was not a bluff. Their sudden and panic-filled shift of policy showed a timidity that lost the cause its moral strength and made defeat inevitable. Nor was the spectacle of the Unionist leaders working for the passage of the Parliament Bill both passively (by abstaining) and actively (some thirty Unionists voted for it) particularly edifying. "The general impression given to

52. [Wilfrid Ward], "The Passing of the Parliament Bill: A Unionist View," *Dublin Review* (Oct. 1911): 217–34.

53. Ibid., 217.

the public is that the peers who voted for the Bill think more of the damage done to an aristocratic club than to the country or Constitution, and this irrevocably seals the position of the Lords as no better than a club they would defend. They have kept what they care for; they have lost what they failed to value. They retain a remnant (rather a poor one) of social exclusiveness. They have lost political honour and moral influence with the country."[54] He considered it all "pathetic" and "tragic," with the very feebleness of the leadership's response making any reaction against the bill unlikely. Once changes of this sort were made there was little chance that they would be rectified later. Despite his personal admiration for Balfour and Lord Lansdowne, he found it hard to understand their inconsistency in the struggle and their sudden *volte face;* and he could only attribute it to something behind the scenes that was as yet secret. "Probably the true history of what has appeared to the world at large so inexplicable, will not be known in detail for many years to come. Something happened which the leaders had not counted on; something did not happen on which they had counted."[55] What he was certain of was that the final argument used to help sway the vote of the peers—that the creation of new peers would be unpleasant to the new king and that the Unionists should extricate him from such an unpleasant necessity—was both extremely specious and highly effective. Despite the enormous pressure put on the Unionist peers, many rallied splendidly and their words and actions were of such sincerity, deep conviction, and public spirit that they "saved the House of Lords from an ineffable blot on what may prove to be the last page of its history." Ward's disappointment with Balfour over the Parliament Bill featured prominently even in his generally eulogistic farewell to him after Balfour's resignation of the Unionist leadership (November 7, 1911).[56]

Fulfilling his policy of allowing different viewpoints on such issues, Ward allowed a Liberal to give his views of the passing of the Parliament Bill, and again, not surprisingly, it was quite different.[57] The Liberal believed it was the natural and inevitable result of the Lords' rejection of the budget and the vindication of the Constitution against the "revolutionary aggression" of the upper house. While he could understand the anger of the peers over their loss of privilege, he could not understand the intense anger and the sense among so many Unionists ("intelligent men") that they had somehow been deceived or

54. Ibid., 224.
55. Ibid., 230.
56. Wilfrid Ward, "Mr Balfour's Farewell," ibid. (Jan. 1912): 1–11.
57. "The Parliament Bill: A Liberal View," ibid. (Oct. 1911): 235–46.

tricked in it all. Either the defeat was expected and their "outcry about treachery is the mere petulance of a defeated party" or, more charitably, "the claim of the Lords to far-seeing statesmanship collapses at the first test." In two elections the principle of the bill had been before the electors, and in two elections the Liberals had won. While the position of the diehards, the conception of the will of the people as being controlled or expressed through the privileged class, was "neither illogical or indefensible" and in fact "ranks as an intelligent theory of the State that may again be adopted by this or some other highly civilized country," it did not happen to be the "law and custom of the United Kingdom." The Lords should acquiesce in the clearly expressed decisions of the electorate, and that clearly expressed decision was that the Lords should not have the veto. He also attacked the exaggerated passion and violence of the diehards. Lord Hugh Cecil shouting down the prime minister in the Commons had set an evil example that could only lower the reputation and impair the efficiency of the Commons, as well as give comfort to those more radical. Moderate men were glad that the "sanity" of the Unionist leaders prevailed over the "passion" of the diehards. He believed that the Unionists would be wise "to dissociate themselves from the revolutionary propaganda of the hot heads," with their calls to armed resistance, calls that could only lead to "the whole fabric of society being torn into shreds." "Even more astonishing and alarming is this reckless talk of civil war. Nothing could show more clearly how completely many Unionists have lost touch with democratic feeling than such language."[58]

> The events of the first week of August show that the great rising of labour is not inconceivable. But the ideal will not be the restoration of the House of Lords, or the preservation of the Established Church, or the preservation of property. If ever the golden thread of law is snapped and authority lies broken and trampled, the spoils will not go to Lord Hugh Cecil but to Mr Keir Hardie [a leading figure of the Labour Party]. Already the advocacy of resistance to law by Tory speakers in the House of Commons has been quoted with raucous approval from the lorries of strike leaders. If ever the tumbrils rattle over the stones of Tower Hill they will carry not the Liberal cabinet, but the capitalist peers. The danger, through present, is neither pressing nor formidable. One folly and one alone could bring it to a head. If men of education, of wealth, and of position deliberately defy the law, then weakened authority might break beneath the strain.[59]

58. Ibid., 245–46.

59. Ibid., 246. For the Tory revolt, see Phillips, *Diehards,* 142–58; and G. R. Searle, "Critics of

In reviewing Lord Hugh Cecil's *Conservatism* (1912) for the October 1912 number, which Ward had reviewed favorably earlier, G. K. Chesterton criticized modern Conservatism for its excessive reverence for preservation and slow change when dramatic action, even rebellion, was called for.[60] Such Conservatism, he believed, was antithetical to true conservatism, which reverenced an ideal and not just a mode of action. "It is unphilosophical to praise the age of wine that has turned to vinegar, or to preserve pheasants till they have all died of old age or to be proud of an aristocracy that has largely ceased to be even a gentry."[61] While Ward was a man of principle and could appreciate Chesterton's comments, he did not indulge in the rhetoric of rebellion of many Conservatives—either on this issue or on Home Rule. He had no respect for lawlessness, and it did not appear in the *Dublin.* Ward remained a believer in man's natural inequality, and in one of his last numbers, published in the middle of the First World War, another defense for aristocracy and the Lords appeared in an article, "Aristocracy," by Bernard Holland.[62]

Holland maintained that it was to aristocratic rule, "backed by middle-class energy," that the British Empire owed its growth. He admitted that the British aristocracy's decline in influence and power was partially its own fault, having failed in certain essentials and lost its hold upon popular respect. But this could be remedied by self-reform, with the present war acting as an aid "by sweeping away phantoms and teaching a truer scale of values." Real aristocracy needed religion, and Catholicism was its true school. "It teaches with a weight of authority which no merely National Church can possibly possess that reverence for things above, around, and below which Goethe thought so essential to real education."[63] There were disadvantages to an aristocratic class, but Holland believed that its advantages outweighed them. While he did not expect or desire the reestablishment of an aristocratic regime, he hoped that

Edwardian Society: The Case of the Radical Right," in *The Edwardian Age: Conflict and Stability, 1900–1914,* ed. Alan O'Day (Hamden, Conn.: Archon Books, 1979), 79–96.

60. G. K. Chesterton, "What Is a Conservative?" *Dublin Review* (Oct. 1912): 349–56. W. W. [Wilfrid Ward], "Some Recent Books," ibid. (July 1912): 181–82, gave Lord Hugh Cecil's book a very positive review.

61. Chesterton, "What Is a Conservative?" 355.

62. Bernard Holland, "Aristocracy," *Dublin Review* (Jan. 1916): 67–83. Holland (1856–1926), educated at Eton and Trinity College, Cambridge, had been secretary to the Duke of Devonshire (whose biography he wrote), private secretary to the secretaries of state for colonies from 1903 to 1908, and an alderman on the London County Council from 1910 to 1921. He was made a Companion of the Bath in 1904 and received into the Church in 1915.

63. Ibid., 78.

the aristocratic element that remained would not be diminished. Ideally the House of Lords should be reformed and restored to the position it held before the removal of its veto.

One issue that figures prominently in histories of England before the Great War, particularly in George Dangerfield's classic, *The Strange Death of Liberal England* (1935), is that of the suffragettes, whose acts of arson, window breaking, and disruption of public meetings created such a great ruckus.[64] In 1869 women ratepayers gained the municipal franchise, and over time they expanded their opportunities to other local government bodies, rural and district councils, borough and county councils, school boards and Poor Law boards. By 1900 more than a million women could vote in local elections, and from 1907 women could vote and be elected to all local governmental bodies.[65] Only the parliamentary vote eluded them.[66] While the women's movement was primarily middle class, even upper class, and Protestant, it spread among Catholics also, and in 1906 there was formed the nonpolitical Catholic Women's League (CWL), which included such *Dublin* contributors as Mrs. Josephine Ward (Wilfrid's wife) and Mrs. Virginia Crawford. Its aim was to organize women both for their own development and for the educational and social work of the Church.[67] In 1911 the Catholic Women's Suffrage Society (CWSS) was formed, and its goal was directly political, to push for the parliamentary vote for women. It was, however, nonmilitant. It included such *Dublin* contributors as Mrs. Alice Meynell and Mrs. Crawford.[68] The argu-

64. For Dangerfield and his thesis, see C. W. White, "*The Strange Death of Liberal England* in Its Time," *Albion* 17 (1985): 425–47; and J. A. Thompson, "The Historians and the Decline of the Liberal Party," *Albion* 22 (1990): 65–83. A more reasonable thesis is presented in G. R. Searle, *The Liberal Party: Triumph and Disintegration, 1886–1929* (New York: St. Martin's Press, 1992). For the suffragettes, see Brian Harrison, "The Act of Militancy: Violence and the Suffragettes, 1904–1914," in his *Peaceable Kingdom: Stability and Change in Modern Britain* (Oxford: Clarendon Press, 1982), 26–81.

65. See Patricia Hollis, *Ladies Elect: Women in English Local Government, 1865–1914* (Oxford: Clarendon Press, 1987).

66. See David Morgan, *Suffragists and Liberals: The Politics of Woman Suffrage in England* (Totowa, N.J.: Rowman & Littlefield, 1975).

67. See Paula Kane, "'The Willing Captive of Home?' The English Catholic Women's League, 1906–1920," *Church History* 60 (Sept. 1991): 331–55.

68. Francis M. Mason, "The Newer Eve: The Catholic Women's Suffrage Society in England. 1911–1923," *Catholic Historical Review* 72 (Oct. 1986): 620–38. The CWSS became the St. Joan's Alliance in 1923 and Mrs. Crawford was its chairman from 1920 to 1928. See also Elaine Clark, "Catholics and the Campaign for Women's Suffrage in England," *Church History* 73 (Sept. 2004): 635–65.

ments against women's suffrage were varied, some stressing their physical or intellectual incapacity for it, others the unique sphere they inhabited.[69] The *Dublin* devoted just a single article to this topic, G. K. Chesterton's "The Modern Surrender of Women."[70]

Chesterton lamented the tendency to equate progress with an ever-increasing accumulation of what was already happening. The goal, therefore, was to have more of the same. The strong and bold thinker, however, "does not go forward with the flood, but back to the fountain." He follows the thought back to its logical root. It seemed obvious to him that the conflict over the function of the two sexes, "which has lately disturbed a section of our wealthier classes," was due to "this habit of pursuing a thing to its conclusion when we have not tracked it to its origin." Many of the women who seek the vote do so just because men already have it. "They say, 'Men have votes; why shouldn't women have votes?' I have met many able and admirable ladies who were full of reasons why women should have votes. But when I asked them why men should have votes they did not know."[71] For Chesterton, voting involved two primary principles: the coercive idea, the power of using the policeman, and the collective idea, government by public quarrel and public unanimity. These were not the whole of life but merely half of it, the masculine half. This was not feminism but "masculinism," and it made for the surrender of women, for it ignored the feminine point of view, "which was against mere force, but even more against mere argument." It was this "strong feminine position" that had "kept the race healthy for hundreds of centuries" and kept men from taking themselves and their business too seriously. For Chesterton, the female suffrage movement made politics far too important, exaggerating it far out of proportion to the rest of life, thereby endangering what was most important in life, those things for which laws and government were least suited to managing.

Can anyone tell me two things more vital to the race than these; what man shall marry what woman, and what shall be the first things taught to their first child? Yet no one has ever been so made as to suggest that either of these godlike and gigantic tasks should be conducted by law. They are matters of emotional management; of persua-

69. For the anti-suffragists, see Brian Harrison, *Separate Spheres: The Opposition to Women's Suffrage in Britain* (New York: Holmes & Meier, 1978).

70. G. K. Chesterton, "The Modern Surrender of Women," *Dublin Review* (July 1909): 128–37.

71. Ibid., 129.

sion and dissuasion; of discouraging a guest or encouraging a governess. This is the first great argument for the old female point of view, and we could never deny that it had force. The old-fashioned woman really said this: "What can be the use of all your politics and policemen? The moment you come to a really vital question you dare not use them. For a foolish marriage, or a bad education, for a broken heart or a spoilt child, for things that really matter, your courts of justice can do nothing at all. When one live woman is being neglected by a man, or one live child by a mother, we can do more by our meanest feminine dodges than you can do by the whole apparatus of the British Constitution. A snub from a duchess or a slanging from a fishwife is more likely to put things right than all the votes in the world." That has always been the woman's great case against mere legalist machinery. It is only one half of the truth; but I am sorry to see women abandon it.[72]

Women's suffrage would have to wait till the Representation of the People Act (1918), which created universal adult male suffrage and the vote for women over thirty. According to the five-year limit, which was part of the Parliament Act that stripped the Lords of their veto, the next parliamentary election was to be in 1915; the Great War, however, intervened. A coalition government was created in May 1915, in which the Liberals held the main portfolios but which included Conservatives such as Balfour, and even a member of Labour. Much would happen in these war years and before the next election in 1918.

72. Ibid., 132. One is reminded of Chesterton's line about a women's suffrage march: "Ten thousand women marched through the streets of London saying, 'We will not be dictated to,' and then went off to become stenographers."

5 SOCIETY

Ward's interest in politics was an extension of his interest in society.[1] He believed that it was time for Catholics to leave their ghetto and take on the duties of citizenship. His organic view of life was the result both of his religious beliefs and of his old-fashioned, paternalistic Toryism. Ward was a Conservative, and the Conservative Party, far from being opposed to social amelioration, had in fact had done its fair share of it. As Lord Hugh Cecil remarked in a *Dublin* article discussing Lord Randolph Churchill: "But that it is possible to unite a general Conservative policy with some important measures of reform was the opinion not only of Lord Randolph but of many both before and after his time. Indeed, the Conservative Party has always claimed that its hands are free to undertake social reforms, and that it is actually more efficient for such purposes than the Liberal Party because its energies are not diverted in the direction of fundamental or revolutionary change. The Factory Acts, the Conspiracy Act, the Workmen's Compensation Act are illustrations of achievements of no slight importance in the region of social reform."[2] Ward recognized that "the 'right to opportunity' among the many who do not belong to the privileged class-

1. For a good social history of the time, see Jose Harris, *Private Lives, Public Spirit: A Social History of Britain, 1870–1914* (Oxford: Oxford University Press, 1993). For a good survey of social relations of the time, see Alastair J. Reid, *Social Classes and Social Relations in Britain, 1850–1914* (Basingstoke: Macmillan Education, 1992).

2. Hugh Cecil, "Lord Rosebery's 'Randolph Churchill,'" *Dublin Review* (Jan. 1907): 146–47.

es is a sacred one which the developments brought about by time have now made urgent; that rigorous 'social justice' is a solemn duty on the part of the State."[3] Ward looked on with horror, however, at the abstract ideals of the French Revolution, which he believed ignored man's natural inequalities and his embodiment in a particular historical context and tradition; he eschewed all ideologies, whether of the right or of the left. His conservatism was not so much an ideology as a cast of mind. He did not have an ideology, but he did have a religion. His Catholicism supplied him with an all-embracing explanation of man, his rights, his duties, and his destiny. Catholicism also supplied him with a view of the state that recognized that many things fell validly within its domain. While there were elements in him of nineteenth-century liberalism, with its laissez-faire individualism, as Chesterton once remarked, he had no love for liberalism, nor did the Church.[4] Neither did they have any love for the growing ideology of socialism.

With the transformation of the West caused by the Industrial Revolution, the traditional agrarian cultures of pre-industrial Europe went into decline. With that change came the beginning of the "social question" and also the beginning of a systematic Catholic social teaching. In the late Victorian period the social question came to the fore, and ideas of "socialism" began to become so commonplace that even the Liberal politician Sir William Harcourt could remark, "We are all Socialists now."[5] But, as Gertrude Himmelfarb has pointed out, if this was true it was only because the word itself had come to be used of almost any social reform, any act of state intervention, any degree of collectivism, and even any concern with the social problem.[6] There were "Christian

3. W. W. [Wilfrid Ward], "Some Recent Books," ibid. (April 1913): 420. He was reviewing a new book on modern Toryism entitled *National Revival* by [A. Boultwood] (London: Herbert Jenkins, 1913).

4. "In politics he was Conservative in a sense beyond the party label, which, nevertheless, he maintained with some seriousness. I cannot convey the particular tint of his traditionalism in this respect without employing the paradox that he was a Tory who seemed to be more ancestral and historical for having many of the characteristics of the old radicalism. His admiration for Mill was something more than a taste in literature or even a scientific relish for lucidity. He was really at home in the strong simplicities of Individualism. In this he was more like Lord Hugh Cecil, and quite unlike Wyndham, whose Toryism was shot with a sort of adventurous Socialism." G. K. Chesterton, "Wilfrid Ward (II.)," *Dublin Review* (July 1916): 30–31. For a good description in the *Dublin* of the Catholic view of the state and its proper domain, see J. Keating, S.J., "Civil Liberty in Peace and War," ibid. (April 1916): 353–78.

5. Quoted in Gertrude Himmelfarb, *Poverty and Compassion: The Moral Imagination of the Late Victorians* (New York: Knopf, 1991), 309.

6. Ibid.

Socialists" who emphasized the social nature of the gospel.[7] To a certain extent, even liberalism began, by the late Victorian period, to adapt itself to the times. While the Manchester School Liberalism of Cobden and Bright, which was antithetical to the new focus on society and the common good, continued to inspire many Liberals, others, the "New Liberals," realized that freedom was meaningless without the means to use it, that property rights were not an absolute but had a social dimension as well, and that the state could usefully intervene so as to help attain social harmony.[8] British socialism was much more gradualist, reformist, and focused on economics than was continental socialism. Besides the socialism of the working classes and the labor unions, there were also the more upscale Fabian Socialists, whose goal was to educate and influence those in power, to "permeate" institutions and guide policies, and by a slow process to effect a transfer of power and property from individuals to the state.[9]

If the term "socialism" was used so freely and so often in a positive sense, for a great many it was still a bogey, a term of abuse that could disqualify one from the support of decent, law-abiding people. Certainly, in its stricter meanings it was widely feared, both as the enemy of all property and as an enemy of all religion. Socialism had been condemned by the Church many times. At the very beginning of his pontificate, Pope Leo XIII devoted a whole encyclical, *Quod Apostolici Muneris* (1878), to attacking socialism in no uncertain terms. He believed that socialism would lead to "the overthrow of all civil society whatsoever." It was a "plague," "an evil growth," and an "abominable sect" that ignored the natural inequality of men, debased marriage, dishonored all authority (both natural and supernatural), and assailed "the right of property sanctioned by natural law." "And by a scheme of horri-

7. See Edward R. Norman, *The Victorian Christian Socialists* (Cambridge: Cambridge University Press, 1987); Peter d'A. Jones, *The Christian Socialist Revival, 1877–1914: Religion, Class, and Social Conscience in Late-Victorian England* (Princeton: Princeton University Press, 1968); and Himmelfarb, *Poverty and Compassion*, 335–49. Pope Leo XIII, in his 1901 encyclical *Graves de Communi*, remarked that the name of Christian Socialism for the movement of those who followed Catholic social teaching was "very properly allowed to fall into disuse."

8. For the New Liberalism, see Michael Freeden, *The New Liberalism: An Ideology of Social Reform* (Oxford: Clarendon Press, 1978); Peter Clarke, *Liberals and Social Democrats* (Cambridge: Cambridge University Press, 1978); and Peter Weiler, *The New Liberalism: Liberal Social Theory in Great Britain, 1889–1914* (New York: Garland, 1982).

9. See A. M. McBriar, *Fabian Socialism and English Politics, 1884–1918* (Cambridge: Cambridge University Press, 1962); N. I. MacKenzie, *The Fabians* (New York: Simon and Schuster, 1977); and Lisanne Radice, *Beatrice and Sidney Webb: Fabian Socialists* (New York: St. Martin's Press, 1984).

ble wickedness, while they seem desirous of caring for the needs and satisfying the desires of all men, they strive to seize and hold in common whatever has been acquired either by title of lawful inheritance, or by labor of brain and hands, or by thrift in one's mode of life."[10] In later encyclicals such as *Rerum Novarum* (1891) and *Graves de Communi* (1901), Pope Leo XIII reiterated the Church's opposition to socialism. On the Continent socialism was one of the great enemies of the Church (along with liberalism), drawing many Catholic workers away from the faith and propagating an antireligious materialism. Since English Catholics were overwhelmingly from the lower classes, primarily poor Irish laborers, it posed a great danger in England as well. Such was the attraction that some tried to reconcile Catholicism and socialism, and groups of Catholic Socialists were formed. Among the more significant of these were the union organizers James Connolly (1870–1916) and James Larkin (1874–1947), and John Wheatley (1869–1930), who founded the Catholic Socialist Society in Glasgow (1906), later serving as a Labour MP and as minister of health in the 1924 Labour government.[11] Ward's *Dublin* devoted a great deal of space to the subject of socialism therefore, beginning with an article by C. S. Devas, an early leader among Catholics on social issues, in the October 1906 number.[12]

Devas began his discussion of socialism (by which he meant common ownership of property) by noting that an opinion could not be dealt with effectually if one had not first treated it sympathetically, felt its attraction, and distilled from it the soul of goodness it contained. He admitted that the spread of socialism among Catholic workers had caused grave anxiety to the clergy, that much of the criticism against it by popular authors was often weak, that merely negative criticism would not be enough, and that the arguments in its favor were much stronger than many of its opponents supposed.

10. Carlen, *Papal Encyclicals,* 11–12.

11. For Connolly, see C. Desmond Greaves, *The Life and Times of James Connolly* (London: Lawrence & Wishart, 1972); and David Howell, *A Lost Left: Three Studies in Socialism and Nationalism* (Chicago: University of Chicago Press, 1986), 17–139. For Larkin, who was born in 1874, not 1876, see Emmet Larkin, *James Larkin: Irish Labour Leader, 1876–1947* (Cambridge: Cambridge University Press, 1965). For Wheatley, see Howell, *A Lost Left,* 229–80, and Sheridan Gilley, "Catholics and Socialists in Scotland, 1900–30," in *The Irish in Britain, 1815–1939,* ed. Roger Swift and Sheridan Gilley (Savage, Md.: Barnes and Noble, 1989), 212–38.

12. C. S. Devas, "Is Socialism Right After All?" *Dublin Review* (Oct. 1906): 321–38. Charles Stanton Devas (1848–1906), a convert educated at Eton and Oxford, wrote extensively on political economy and social issues. For his life, see Georgiana Putnam McEntee, *The Social Catholic Movement in Great Britain* (New York: Macmillan, 1927), 102–6.

After all, while the crude, violent, and instantaneous schemes for socialism might not work, could that be said of the gradual and orderly Fabian variety? And while socialism was charged with being irreligious and immoral, destructive of the family and the Church, was there any direct connection between collective organization and control and these destructive forces? In Germany socialism now seemed more neutral to religion, seeing it as a personal concern, and there was no reason why it could not move in a more religious direction. Certainly, looking at French politics, the antisocialist Clemenceau was a more rabid atheist than the socialist Jaurès. Could not one say that it was not really scientific socialism that Pope Leo XIII had condemned but the abuses of violence and communism? "Indeed, that by their efforts to universalize private property, to endow the present mill-hand and farm-hand and slum-dweller with their own house and home, goods and garden, to put an end to usury, monopoly and the ruthless warfare of rival traders, the socialists are the true pupils of Leo XIII, and that his true opponents are the receivers—many perhaps unwittingly, but still receivers—through the manifold channels of rent and interest, of profits flowing from sweated labour, from slum dwellings, from extortionate prices, from foul wares, from fouler drink-shops and houses of debauchery."[13]

Having said that, however, he made clear that he did not believe that socialism was the answer to the social problem. Christianity was the answer both to the social question and to socialism itself. Nor did he mean by "Christianity" those heretical sects throughout Christianity's history that had held socialistic doctrines, such as the Fraticelli, or their modern counterparts among the "Christian Socialists." Devas argued that though the Church and her saints had always opposed injustice, avarice, and the abuse of the poor, she had never promoted social revolution and the disappearance of social and economic distinctions. The greatest weakness of socialism, he thought, was its unhistorical character, its failure to understand man and his history. In all civilizations, and by that he meant *civilizations,* not "the Scythians in the time of Herodotus, or the Gauls in the time of Caesar, or the Germans in the time of Tacitus," there was private ownership and service, and great gradations of wealth. To those who considered civilization "artificial" he would reply, referring to Edmund Burke's opinion that art was man's nature and that where his reasonable nature was most cultivated he was most natural, that "conditions

13. Devas, "Is Socialism Right After All?" 322.

of rude simplicity would not be natural, but artificial." The socialist view of history was progressive and evolutionary, man's history an automatic upward movement from his bestial origins until he reached the crown of collectivism. Devas believed that this view was inconsistent with the detailed facts of history, which showed that man really hadn't changed much in all that time and that progress was far from automatic. There were many examples of civilizations that had decayed, or had even reverted to barbarism. While man had the capacity for growth, he also had the ability to regress. Nor could one see in the appalling conditions of the great cities of present-day Europe and America the evolution that one would expect from the socialist evolutionary theory.

Devas believed that if one accepted the Christian view of human nature, there would be no need to distort the facts of history toward either pessimism or optimism, and one would have a criterion with which to judge the constant and the variable in human history so as to remove what is genuinely removable "without plucking up civilization by the roots." "Then we would understand that private capital is inextricably intertwined with civilization; that to equalize for every one the opportunity of gaining wealth and power is to weaken energy, because limiting to the individual the prospect of advancement, and removing the motive to strive for the permanent advancement of family and friends."[14] Moral frailty was not caused by indigence, nor could it be cured by affluence. It was rooted in man's passions and would be at work whatever the social and political conditions. Socialist theory, therefore, was not humane and historical but unreal and doctrinaire.

Devas believed that its doctrinaire quality was shown in its treatment of family life, though present-day capitalism hardly qualified as conducive to family life, either. Christians though, unless they themselves labored for the cause of social reform, could hardly speak against socialism. And certainly those who had waged war against the family by "spreading the pestilential evils of Malthusianism [birth control] and divorce," which led to "lawless passion, transitory households, sterile unions," were also without credibility. Our slackness had been the cause of socialism's growth, and it would destroy not merely the Christian home but the family life of all healthy nations, including pagan ones, the natural good "being preparatory for the gospel and a substratum for grace."

14. Ibid., 329.

For if the collective providence is substituted for the paternal; if the official, not the father, becomes the provider; the community, not the family, the unit of income; then the very well-spring of energy and of self-control is dried up, namely, the desire to provide for wife and children, to shelter them from evil, to raise them to better conditions, to be their earthly Providence. And where the father and husband is stripped of the duties that are his salvation, his children in their turn are stripped of their filial duties to their parents, of their fraternal duties to one another; whether they dwell together in unity or not becomes of no account; the delicate attention to sick and weakly members, the very field where man is seen at his best, is no longer needed; the old maxim, 'Blood is thicker than water,' becomes meaningless; ancestral renown and the honour of the family will be no longer words to conjure with; the salt that kept domestic relations from corruption will have lost its savour; and the socialist community for all its protestations will have assumed the forbidding shape of a gigantic foundling-house.[15]

While this attack on the natural good of the family was the "fatal blot on the socialist escutcheon," its cosmopolitanism, which ignored the inherent nationalism of mankind, was also unreal and destructive. Socialism presupposed the very social virtues and organized society that it would afterward destroy. The very notion of organism implied permanent inequalities of function, power, and dignity incompatible with socialism. The brotherhood of man, the philanthropy and altruism that socialism presupposed in its adherents, were only reasonable on the base of a common fatherhood of God, and a common need and fact of redemption. There was, however, a middle way between the two extremes of individualism and socialism that was manifest in the many laws regulating factories and work, in programs of workmen's insurance (including compensation and old-age pensions), in the growth of workmen's associations, including unions and cooperatives of various sorts, and in the growth of welfare institutions. "To say, then, that if we reject socialism we have no alternative but individualism is contrary to fact; and to say that every step towards social reform is a step towards socialism is to confuse antidote with poison."[16] The problem was to secure the advantages of the capitalist administration of industry without its disintegrating effects on the state, on families, and on the individual. One should not long for a past that was gone. Rather one must welcome the advances that the age has brought in its wake. The days of paternalism, of men depending on the goodwill of others, were

15. Ibid., 331–32.
16. Ibid., 334.

over, Devas believed. Workers needed to be united in associations and protected by factory laws and insurance if they were to have any chance to share in the "growing refinements of the age and the benefits of civilization" that were their due. It was an age of democracy, and the decision would be whether it would be an anti-Christian or a Christian democracy. Neither anti-Christian democracy nor modern skeptical philosophy could be of any help in this fight against socialism. Only the Church had the key with which to understand the situation and to solve it—even for those outside the household of faith. "The natural cannot suffice without the supernatural; or, put in another way, the natural divorced from the supernatural ceases itself to be natural. . . . When, therefore, the foundations of natural civilization begin to totter, the supernatural Church supports them, fulfilling the function of the guardian of humanism and of the religion of humanity."[17] This was why the socialists pursued the Church with such implacable hatred, seeing in her the greatest obstacle to their success.

In an article appearing in the *Tablet* (January 3, 1914), the well-known Dominican Vincent McNabb defended the position that a priest could no more deny absolution to a Catholic Socialist than he could to a supporter of the other parties, since the evils decried in socialism were already present in a society that the other parties had brought about, or at least had upheld.[18] In the ensuing controversy McNabb admitted that certain forms of socialism were compatible with Catholicism, and this controversy was one of the causes for an article in the July 1914 number of the *Dublin* by a former Catholic Socialist, "H" (from the biographical information given in the article, almost certainly Henry Somerville), on their utter incompatibility.[19] In this personal narrative, Somerville (b. 1889), the second of twelve children of a toy-factory foreman in Leeds, described how he had become a Catholic Socialist and formed the Catholic Socialist Society of Leeds. A child of working-class parents who himself worked in a factory from the age of thirteen, he had gotten involved in socialism not because of any intrinsic interest in it but because he was interested in why the Church was so strongly opposed to socialism and

17. Ibid., 338.

18. See Ferdinand Valentine, *Father Vincent McNabb, O.P.* (Westminster: Newman Press, 1955), 135–38. The article can be found as an appendix in Valentine's book, 400–404.

19. H., "The Confessions of a Catholic Socialist," *Dublin Review* (July 1914): 101–15. For Somerville, see J. M. Cleary, *Catholic Social Action in Britain, 1909–1959: A History of the Catholic Social Guild* (Oxford: Catholic Social Guild, 1961), 56–57 and 81–82.

why socialism was opposed to the faith. He became convinced that there was no incompatibility between the two, because the socialism the pope condemned was not the same as that advocated in England, and because there was no logical connection between irreligion and socialist principles. He believed that socialism did not deny private property but only one kind of it, the private ownership of the means of production, distribution, and exchange. As he saw socialism advance, he knew that it would attract more and more Catholics who would then be alienated by the Church's strong condemnation of it. Just as the Church had put herself on the wrong side of progress with her condemnation of Galileo, so she would put herself on the wrong side of progress by her condemnation of socialism. Solely out of zeal for the Church, for he thought socialism's spread inevitable, he formed the first "Catholic Socialist Society" in England. After his bishop condemned it, he began to see that property was a natural right necessary for human flourishing, that without the right to property man would be absolutely dependent on the state for everything, and that individual liberty would be lost. He believed that the "socialism-means-atheism-and-free-love" type of argument that he heard so often was weak and that socialism's threat to liberty should be the main ground of opposition.

W. H. Mallock (1849–1923), perhaps best known for his brilliant *roman à clef The New Republic* (1877), was a writer of serious philosophical and religious books; he also was a frequent lecturer and writer against socialism.[20] Devas had criticized him by name in the previous article for the weakness of his arguments, but he wrote a very able piece for the *Dublin* reviewing the many attempts (about seventy-five) to create socialistic societies or utopian communities in America.[21] His conclusion was that the only ones that had any degree of success were strongly religious—for example, the Shakers, whose beliefs were anything but permissive. Their lives were arranged more along the authoritarian lines of celibate Catholic monastic communities, with

20. For Mallock, see his *Memoirs of Life and Literature* (London: Chapman and Hall, 1920). See also D. J. Ford, "W. H. Mallock and Socialism in England, 1880–1918," in *Essays in Anti-Labour History: Reponses to the Rise of Labour in Britain,* ed. Kenneth D. Brown (London: Macmillan, 1974), 317–42; and A. V. Tucker, "W. H. Mallock and Late Victorian Conservatism," *University of Toronto Quarterly* 31 (1962): 223–41.

21. W. H. Mallock, "A Century of Socialistic Experiments," *Dublin Review* (July 1909): 79–106. See Devas, "Is Socialism Right After All?" 323. V. reviewed Mallock's *Critical Examination of Socialism* (1907) in "Some Recent Books" (April 1908): 421, and complained of the insufficiency of his critique.

their focus on sin and salvation rather than worldly concerns. "The first question asked of each postulant is not, 'Do you believe in the rights of labour, and would you if you could, annihilate all capitalists?' It is 'Are you sick of sin, and do you want salvation from it?'"[22] The religious Oneida Community in upstate New York achieved the same dissolution of the private family not by celibacy or a grudging acceptance of sex as a concession to the weak, but by free love. All attempts at creating secular socialistic societies, such as New Harmony and Brook Farm, had ended in failure. After reviewing these cases Mallock came to three conclusions.

> One is that, however socialism in practice may aim at abolishing the category of employer and employed, it has only prospered in proportion as it maintained and accentuated the category of the directors and the directed, and utterly eradicated the principles of self-employment, in the sense of leaving the labourer to work in accordance with his own discretion. Another conclusion is that, in proportion as the individualistic motive is abolished, the exceptional talents are deprived of any corresponding rewards which will raise their possessors above the common lot, nothing will induce such exceptional talents to exert themselves, unless it is that ascetic enthusiasm which religion alone can generate. And behind these two conclusions there remains a third, which is this—that the individualism of the ordinary world—the desire of each to possess in accordance with his own powers of production, and to retain for himself such advantages as his own efforts have gained, has its deepest roots in marriage and the passions of the individual family, and that, therefore, in order to make socialism possible, marriage and the individual family are the ultimate factors which must be eradicated.[23]

In a second article, "A Catholic Critique of Current Social Theories," in the October 1914 number, Mallock, himself an Anglican, praised the Catholic mean between the extremes of individualistic liberalism and collectivist socialism.

The late nineteenth century was also a period when the Church faced the "social question" in a more systematic way. It was the time of Pope Leo XIII and *Rerum Novarum,* of Cardinal Manning and the London Dock Strike of 1889, and the beginning of the movement known as Social Catholicism.[24]

22. Ibid., 97.

23. Ibid., 98.

24. For Social Catholicism in continental Europe, see Paul Misner, *Social Catholicism in Europe: From the Onset of Industrialization to the First World War* (New York: Crossroad, 1991). For the larger context, see Roger Aubert, *Catholic Social Teaching: An Historical Perspective* (Milwaukee: Marquette University Press, 2003).

While one would have expected English Catholics to be at the forefront of this movement, given their heavily working-class composition and the example of Cardinal Manning, in fact they were not. Manning's successor, Cardinal Vaughan, considered Manning's interest in the social question a sign of his senility, and leadership in the movement moved to the Continent. It was only in 1909, when Charles Plater, S.J., formed the Catholic Social Guild, that the Social Catholic movement took solid organizational shape in England.[25] It is not surprising, therefore, that when the *Dublin* turned its attention to this movement it had to look abroad for ideas and inspiration, to France and Germany, where it was far more extensively developed.

In an unsigned article, Charles Plater described the history of the French Social Catholic movement, particularly the ACJF and the *Sillon.*[26] The largest and most important of these groups was the ACJF, the *Association Catholique de la Jeunesse Française,* a Catholic young men's movement founded by Count Albert de Mun in 1886 that now had seventy thousand members. Democratic in structure and republican in tone, the ACJF not only devoted itself to the study of social problems but was also involved in the foundation of cooperative societies, popular libraries, labor bureaus, workmen's gardens, and the like. *Le Sillon,* founded by the charismatic Marc Sangnier in 1899, while much smaller, also had a profound effect in interesting Catholics in social problems and aligning the Church with the people. While Plater noted that it had met with opposition in some quarters because of its "alleged tendency toward religious liberalism and impatience of authoritative advice," it also had the encouragement of the pope, five French cardinals, and many French bishops; and by its clear Catholic piety (such as its all-night vigils before the

25. For English Social Catholicism, see McEntee, *Social Catholic Movement in Britain;* Barbara Wraith, "A Pre-Modern Interpretation of the Modern: The English Catholic Church and the 'Social Question' in the Early Twentieth Century," in *The Church Retrospective,* ed. R. N. Swanson (Woodbridge: Boydell Press, 1997), 529–45; Josef L. Altholz, "Social Catholicism in England in the Age of the Devotional Revolution," in *Piety and Power in Ireland, 1760–1960: Essays in Honour of Emmet Larkin,* ed. Stewart J. Brown and David M. Miller (Notre Dame: University of Notre Dame Press, 2000), 209–19; and Bernard Aspinwall, "Towards an English Catholic Social Conscience, 1829–1920," *Recusant History* 25 (May 2000): 106–19.

26. [Charles Plater], "Catholic Social Effort in France," *Dublin Review* (July 1906): 87–104. Charles Dominic Plater (1875–1921) entered the Jesuits in 1894 and was ordained in 1910. He was instrumental in helping found the Catholic Social Guild and inspired the Catholic Workers' College (now Plater College) at Oxford. For Plater's life, see C. C. Martindale, *Charles Dominic Plater, S.J.* (London: Longmans, Green, 1922); and Peter Doyle, "Charles Plater S.J. and the Origins of the Catholic Social Guild," *Recusant History* 21 (May 1993): 401–17.

Blessed Sacrament at the Basilica of the Sacred Heart at Montmartre) it had shown its religious fidelity. In a work of readjustment, he thought, there was bound to be some friction, especially where "perfervid young men are engaged in battling against gigantic social evils." In a 1913 article reviewing various social movements in France, the Comtesse de Courson put the membership of the ACJF at 120,000 but did not even mention the *Sillon*.[27] In 1910 it had been condemned by Pope Pius X in a letter to the French bishops, *Notre Charge Apostolique* (August 15), for avoiding episcopal direction and, among other things, for its erroneous notions of authority and democracy. Sangnier (1873–1950), showing his absolute loyalty and obedience, immediately dissolved it.

One great difference between the success of German Catholicism and the failure of French Catholicism was that in Germany the working classes had not been entirely lost to the faith. That was due, in great part, to the role that Social Catholicism played in that country. In Germany Catholicism had reached a high degree of organization, politically with the Center Party of Ludwig Windthorst (1812–1891) and socially with the *Volksverein für das katholische Deutschland* (People's League for a Catholic Germany), founded by Windthorst in 1890. In 1908 and 1909 the *Dublin* devoted a series of unsigned articles by Plater to German Social Catholicism, which he later published as a book under his own name.[28] In the first article, he stated that the three greatest dangers to German Catholicism, "three dangers which, in a very striking manner, have their counterpart in this country," were state absolutism, the growth of socialism, and the apathy of wealthier Catholics toward the needs of the working man. It was to the credit of German Catholicism that it had succeeded, he believed, in overcoming these dangers, and in so doing had saved not only the Church but German society itself. He believed that it was owing to the energy and enthusiasm of one man in particular, Wilhelm Emmanuel Baron von Ketteler (1811–1877), Bishop of Mainz, that these dangers had been averted and that German Catholicism was full of life and a

27. Comtesse Barbara de Courson, "Three Catholic Associations in France," *Dublin Review* (April 1913): 357–81.

28. [Charles Plater], "Catholic Social Work in Germany—I. Ketteler, the Precursor," *Dublin Review* (April 1908): 241–61; "Catholic Social Work in Germany—II. 'The Autumn Manoeuvres,'" ibid. (July 1908): 1–24; "Catholic Social Work in Germany—III. Organization and Method," ibid. (Jan. 1909): 67–86; "Catholic Social Work in Germany—IV. German Methods and English Needs," ibid. (April 1909): 299–328.

power in the land. Von Ketteler saw that the social question was the most important issue of the day, an issue that neither laissez-faire liberalism nor socialism could answer but that the Church could. While he founded a great many social and charitable institutions and promoted self-help and cooperative organizations, he realized that the state too had a share in the promotion of social justice and so advocated government interference in the conditions of production and distribution when the workmen's own organizations were insufficient. By the power of his personality, by his writings, and by his influence within the Church, his program became the program of the Church and of the Center Party. Yet, for all that, he was traditional and orthodox in his faith, his social work being the manifestation of his ancestral Catholicism and deep spirituality.

An important element in the spread of Social Catholicism, Plater believed, were the annual Catholic Congresses, what Windthorst once called the "autumn manoeuvres" of the Catholic forces; it was to these that he devoted the second article. Begun in 1848 to defend Catholic liberties, they had grown larger and more encompassing in their interests, bringing enormous numbers of Catholics of every social class together, representing every religious and social institution. In doing so they had helped Catholics create a complete and positive program for the transformation of German life.

> In other countries we are accustomed to find a few discouraged Catholic thinkers and a few over-burdened Catholic workers struggling in a heroic but disorganized fashion to conquer the apathy of the great mass of their co-religionists. But in Germany the stragglers are the exception. Almost every available man is drilled and made part of the fighting force. He is given his post to defend and his work to do, whether in workmen's club or students' union or professional association. He goes to the Congress or he is represented at it. His activities are brought into relation with those of all his fellow Catholics in every state of life. He feels that he is taking a personal part in momentous evolutions upon which the welfare of his Church and his country depends. He is not a mere spectator at a pageant, but a soldier taking part in manoeuvres performed by the whole of a great army.[29]

While these Congresses had led to the development of an elaborate system of social works, they were still frankly religious, and that was the secret of their success. "All social work must be based on some theory of the meaning and value of life; and the better the theory the better *ceteris paribus* will be the

29. [Plater], "Catholic Social Work in Germany—II," 3.

work."[30] The unity and enthusiasm of the Catholic Congresses and their successful social organization were founded not on the desire for higher wages or improved sanitation but on belief in the Catholic doctrine of the communion of saints.

In the third article he continued his discussion of the Catholic Congresses, describing their thorough organization despite their vast numbers (tens of thousands), their primarily lay character, the variety of topics discussed, and their deep religious spirit and Catholic loyalty. He also described in detail the *Volksverein,* whose membership, all adult men, was now (June 1908) at 610,800. Its purpose was to keep in constant touch with all the social movements, to produce Catholic social literature, and to organize lectures and meetings. But since Catholic social principles were not separable from the faith, it also included among its tasks the deepening of the faith by instruction in apologetics. At its heart was a central bureau, with a full-time salaried professional staff of experts, well versed in literature, economics, or apologetics, all having degrees in political economy or theology. Not only could one personally avail oneself of its excellent library, staff, and lectures, but it also would answer any questions sent to it. Besides its magazines, it produced weekly articles for more than four hundred Catholic newspapers, pamphlets, and other publications—about 15 million publications in the course of a year. He was particularly struck by how well adapted these were to their intended audiences, and how free they were of generalization, condescension, pious exaggeration, and vague sentimentality. They were practical, sensible, and to the point.

The *Volksverein* worked with and for all classes, the professional and commercial as well as the working classes. Through it many Catholic workingmen had been given systematic instruction in political economy, social science, and apologetics, since "the workman can only be reached by the workman." Between the Congresses and the *Volksverein* a social sense had been cultivated. "The former provide an annual review of the troops in which the units are made to feel their relation to the whole body. The latter keeps alive the enthusiasm produced by the annual meetings, and translates it into strenuous work during the rest of the year."[31]

In his final article Plater sought to apply the spirit and methods of German

30. Ibid., 4.
31. [Plater], "Catholic Social Work—III," 85.

Social Catholicism to the English situation. He believed that the German situation was very like the English in that English Catholics were oppressed by a hostile government and menaced by socialism, though in both cases much more weakly. While it could not be denied, he thought, that there was discrimination against Catholics in England, there was nothing here similar to the German *Kulturkampf,* with its aggressive persecution of the Church. Nor was socialism so powerful an attraction in England, where far milder forms flourished. He thought the example of Bishop Ketteler was very important for English Catholics, for it made clear that the social question was not one that the bishops, clergy, and laity could ignore (a point since endorsed by Rome herself), and because by his great efforts he overcame the greatest difficulty of all, the apathy or lack of interest in these questions that was so characteristic of German Catholics until then and of English Catholics at the moment. If such enthusiasm could be generated in Germany, he thought, it could be done in England. The material for it already existed in Catholic schools, where much could be done to interest and instruct the young in their social and civic duties; it already existed in the seminaries, which had been urged by Pope Leo XIII to study such questions; it was present among the workman in their clubs and improvement societies; and it was in evidence among the educated laity, who, if appealed to convincingly, could use their knowledge and experience in the service of the Catholic body. This enthusiasm in Germany had been sustained by the Catholic Congresses, and in England there was already a group, the Catholic Truth Society, whose annual conferences had many of the elements of the German Congresses. These annual conferences were general in their scope and attracted fairly good crowds. The difficulty concerning the annual meeting of the Catholic Truth Society was that, unlike the German Congress, it was not truly representative of the English Catholic body. While the bishops were usually out in force, as were a good many devoted clergy and laity, where were the Catholic nobility and politicians, the Catholic merchants, businessmen, and university students? And, most of all, where were the Catholic working men? The sad state of French Catholicism was due, he believed, to the failure of the influential classes to work for social reform, to the apathy of so many wealthy and leisured Catholics. As with the German Congresses, the annual conferences would create greater social unity, make known to a broader audience the tasks and groups available so as to inspire others to join, and inspire the creation of new organizations. English Catholics, though united in their belief, lacked the organization necessary for their good works, and good intentions did not produce the fruit they should. Their societies and clubs operated in a piecemeal and sporadic fashion, so that even the good work done in one area of the country was often unknown, and therefore untried, in another. The federations of diocesan societies, such as the one founded by the Bishop of Salford, were good examples of what could be done to organize Catholics. Once English Catholics had their own congresses, they would soon develop their own *Volksverein* as well.[32]

Plater wanted to transcend two extremes: those who advocated what he called "the ring-fence policy" of complete withdrawal from national interests and popular movements so as to preserve the purity of the faith, and those who, "carried away by the whirl of secular currents," had lost touch with the principles of Catholicism and in their zeal to permeate society, and had forgotten the need to reinforce "their own spiritual strength." The Church had the commission to teach the world, so retreat was not possible, but without the spiritual resources of the faith to push forward "into alien territory" it would be fruitless. To those who claimed that English Catholics were too few, and that it would be better to combine with non-Catholics in these endeavors, especially since there was so much nonsectarian machinery in place already, he replied that while he did advocate greater membership in and cooperation with other non-Catholic bodies, in so far as that was feasible and appropriate (and there should be more of it), the fact was that Catholics had a different vision of society. An indiscriminate intercourse with non-Catholics, he believed, would lead to the loss of this vision. Whatever lack this might entail in material setting or educational efficiency was made up for by the civic benefits derived from religious formation and character building. And while Catholic numbers were relatively small, they were sufficiently large to maintain organizations whose general need was personal interest and service rather than money. The Fabian Society, he pointed out, was small, yet it had a great influence on social affairs, and in so far as Catholics developed their own organizations they also would become involved in the greater world of social reform.

One of the practical ways that this new social sense manifested itself in England was in the development of clubs and settlements. In 1883 the settlement

32. See Peter Doyle, "The Catholic Federation, 1906–1920," in *Studies in Church History* 23, ed. W. J. Sheils and Diana Wood (Oxford: B. Blackwell, 1986), 461–76. The Salford Federation was, as Doyle points out, the most active and popular of these federations, and to many, both inside and outside the movement, *was* the Catholic federation.

movement began with the founding of Toynbee Hall in the notorious London slum of Whitechapel by Samuel Barnett (1844–1913), a Broad Church rector interested in social questions.[33] With the look and feel of an Oxbridge college, its goal was to bridge the social divide by having the well-to-do live among the poor. Many others followed in its wake and even Catholics became involved, with a Catholic Settlements Association being created in 1907, and the foundation of St. Cecilia's House, St. Anthony's Settlement, St. Philip's House, St. Margaret's Settlement (established with the help of Mrs. Wilfrid Ward), and the men's settlement house at Bermondsley. Unlike the college missions, which were primarily religious in aim, Toynbee Hall was primarily social and educational in its purposes and nonreligious in its coloration. Around these settlements and missions all sorts of organizations and clubs developed.

Bertrand Devas, son of C. S. Devas and associate editor of the *Dublin* from 1907, wrote an article for the April 1909 number on the Catholic boys' clubs.[34] He believed that the inability of successive governments to deal with the elementary schools question had forced Catholics to put their resources into their schools so that they had neither the time nor the money to deal adequately with a problem of equal if not greater importance, that of children between fourteen and twenty. Catholics were in a disadvantageous position because their lack of resources meant they had inferior facilities, especially when compared with other groups. While he hoped that public funds could eventually be provided to help in this area, he believed that facilities could never be the defining reality, because for Catholics these clubs could never be merely cultural or educational. Their main goal was religious: to prevent "the spiritual shipwreck of about four-fifths of the rising generation." He believed that the welfare of Catholic girls had already received much attention. He could point to the existence of at least four ladies' settlements in London, with all the organizations that they entailed, as well as girls' clubs in many other parishes. The creation of the Catholic Women's League, with its quarterly journal, the *Crucible,* he thought an encouraging sign. "When the girls and women go home from needlework class, or evening drill, or mothers'

33. For Toynbee Hall, see Standish Meacham, *Toynbee Hall and Social Reform, 1880–1914* (New Haven: Yale University Press, 1987).

34. B. W. Devas, "Catholic Boys' Clubs in London," *Dublin Review* (April 1909): 339–56. Devas (1882–1916), educated at Stonyhurst and Corpus Christi College, Oxford, died in France in the Great War.

meeting, though they pass beyond the doors they do not pass beyond the influence of the settlement. For the ladies who have leisure enough to assist the work. . . . know them as wives and mothers and sweethearts, as factory hands or drapers' assistants, they know them, in fact, as they know their friends, that is to say according to the degree and duration of the friendship, they know more or less of all that is to be known of them."[35]

Unfortunately, Devas lamented, attempts to organize men's settlements and boys' clubs had been much less successful, and yet the creation of these was essential if priests were not to lose touch with these young men. So far (1909) not one men's settlement had been founded successfully, so it was to boys' clubs that he looked. Devas, himself a layman, hoped that many more laymen would apply themselves to this work. He also remarked that the Catholic Settlements Association had more requests for men from priests than it had men to supply. Nonetheless, he believed that the involvement of the priest was necessary for a club's success. While the Catholic Settlements Association found many men willing to help out more or less regularly once a week, it found no one willing to start such clubs or to give several nights in the week to the work. This, he thought, was "regrettable" but not hard to explain: heroism was not a universal virtue and most men did not have the strength of character to make great sacrifices; those who did had generally already entered the priesthood. Someone had to be there consistently, every day, to make sure that the club was open and to give it general supervision, and because of his availability the priest was the ideal person. Devas believed that half a dozen well-organized men, with a priest supplying unity and direction, were all that was needed for a successful club. But not even an exceptional priest could run a club single-handedly, so there was a real need for laymen if this work was to expand as it needed to do.

James Britten reviewed Picht's *Toynbee Hall and the English Settlement Movement* (1914) for the April 1915 number, tracing its history and pointing out its strengths and weaknesses.[36] While he admired the impressive number of able men and women who were associated with Toynbee Hall and the un-

35. Ibid., 341.

36. James Britten, "Toynbee Hall and the Settlement Movement," ibid. (April 1915): 271–87. Britten (1846–1924), a botanist at the British Museum from 1871 to 1909, was converted at twenty-one and was instrumental in the re-founding of the Catholic Truth Society in 1884, remaining its secretary until 1922, and in beginning its annual conferences, which were later merged into the National Catholic Congress.

doubted good work it did, especially in the area of clubs for neighborhood boys and men, compared with the college missions in the same kind of slum areas its direct influence on the poor was limited. Its educational work was largely for men and women teachers and clerks from outside the area, and the personal involvement of the residents of Toynbee Hall in these clubs, organizations, and classes was often minimal or nonexistent. While bridges had been built between the rich and the poor, it was in the area of their actual intimacy with the poor that he believed it had been least successful. Its residents were outsiders and they remained such, living in buildings specially erected for the purpose, in conditions that distanced them from their slum neighbors. Nor had Toynbee Hall been fertile in creating other, more or less independent and self-governing institutions, as most of the other larger settlements had done. Britten believed that the primary cause of the comparative failure of Toynbee Hall was its lack of religious inspiration. Quoting from the book he was reviewing, he wrote that Toynbee Hall represented "a fiasco of humanitarian liberalism" that lacked the spiritual energies to maintain itself or discharge "the highest and most difficult tasks of humanity." He also spoke about the share Catholics had taken in settlement work and particularly praised the good work done by the women of the Catholic Women's League. Women had taken a prominent part in this work and in fact had shown, he believed, a greater aptitude for organization and cooperation than men had in this area, and that they had a greater ease in dealing with the poor.

Despite the *Dublin*'s extensive and very positive coverage of Social Catholicism, both in articles and in smaller reviews, some Catholics were not convinced and saw socialism behind it all. The Catholic Social Guild, despite the tight control it kept on its publications and program, its avoidance of political commitment, and its general caution, had difficulties with its publisher, the Catholic Truth Society, which ceased to be the guild's publisher after 1914. Also, despite the strong antisocialist message in the pulpits and in Catholic periodicals such as the *Dublin,* not all the bishops were as opposed to socialism as it would appear. The rise of Labour among working-class Catholics made a position of accommodation an increasing necessity.[37]

37. See Kester Aspden, *Fortress Church: The English Roman Catholic Bishops and Politics, 1903–63* (Leominster: Gracewing, 2002), 35–63, 131–37.

One of the most significant public policy discussions of the time was on the revision of the Poor Law. On December 4, 1905, the day he resigned, Balfour appointed a royal commission to study unemployment and the Poor Law, which had remained virtually unchanged since 1834. The New Poor Law of 1834 was built on the principles of centralization, uniformity, and deterrence, with outdoor relief (supplementary payments) to be abolished and only indoor relief in the residential workhouse to be allowed. As a deterrent, the workhouse was to be an unappealing place, with living conditions worse than those of the worst-paid wage earner. On entering the workhouse one lost most civil rights, including the franchise, and those who were fit were to be given tedious and punitive tasks. Its goal was to make employment far preferable to the indignities of the workhouse, and however good the workhouse might become, it would never lose the sense of shame that made it hateful to so many. The principles of 1834, however, were never consistently and strictly applied: the Poor Law Commission could not compel local Poor Law unions to build workhouses or end outdoor relief. The number of people receiving outdoor relief (in money or goods) was never less than twice the number in the workhouse, and in years of distress the number was far larger.[38] The Poor Law also dealt with the unemployed, though only in the 1880s was the question of unemployment taken up seriously by English economic theorists and social reformers. It was clear by then that much unemployment was out of people's control, and with its growth, and the strains that this put on the local rates, new ideas began to circulate on how to deal with it.[39]

The Royal Poor Law Commission was a collection of incompatible elements, so it was not surprising that in the end, in 1909, it produced both a minority report (written by the Fabian Socialists Beatrice and Sidney Webb) and a majority report. Also in 1909, William Beveridge published *Unemployment: A Problem of Industry,* the first systematic study of the problem.[40] While

38. M. A. Crowther, *The Workhouse System, 1834–1929: The History of an English Social Institution* (Athens: University of Georgia Press, 1982), 6–7.

39. For a good survey of British social policy since the Industrial Revolution, see Derek Fraser, *The Evolution of the British Welfare State: A History of Social Policy since the Industrial Revolution,* 2d ed. (London: Macmillan, 1984). For the New Poor Law, see Peter Wood, *Poverty and the Workhouse in Victorian Britain* (Wolfeboro Falls, N.H.: Alan Sutton Publ., 1991); Felix Driver, *Power and Pauperism: The Workhouse System 1834–1884* (Cambridge: Cambridge University Press, 1993); and especially Crowther, *Workhouse System.* For unemployment, see Jose Harris, *Unemployment and Politics: A Study of English Social Policy, 1886–1914* (Oxford: Clarendon Press, 1972).

40. William Henry Beveridge (1879–1963) had been sub-warden of Toynbee Hall in the East End, where he studied social conditions. Later he convinced Winston Churchill, the new

a brief review in the "Some Recent Books" section praised Beveridge's book for its penetrating analysis of the cause of unemployment, and particularly for its treatment of the labor reserve and casual labor, it intentionally did not go in depth because the issue was to be treated more thoroughly later with the report of the Poor Law Commission.[41] It was left to Mrs. Virginia Crawford, a founder of the Catholic Social Guild and a Poor Law Guardian, to discuss these issues at much greater length.[42] The reform of the Poor Law was not only of major importance to the nation in general, since it was the main means of social support, but, as Mrs. Crawford pointed out in her articles, it was of particular importance for Catholics, as they made up a disproportionate share of its beneficiaries.

In her first article, "The Failure of the Workhouse," she praised the impartiality and thoroughness of the majority report (some 1,238 pages long) which made clear, as she knew from her own experience as a Poor Law Guardian, the gaping inadequacies of the system.

> Again and again we have understood the hopelessness of trying to infuse a spirit of helpfulness and social service into a system framed for the grudging relief of destitution alone. If, on the one hand, we have nothing but the mixed workhouse to offer to the actually destitute, while realizing in our hearts that residence within its walls habitually served to the manufacture of fresh paupers, on the other, we have seen wholly insufficient doles of out-relief granted to widows, or, perchance, withheld on trivial grounds, while in contiguous parishes relief was being administered on principles largely at variance with our own, so that the poor have never known what to expect and have been demoralized and discouraged by uncertainty. We have grown accus-

president of the Board of Trade, of the importance of labor exchanges, and when a law passed in 1909 to create a national network of labor exchanges Churchill made Beveridge their director. Beveridge is probably most famous for the Beveridge Report, which created the welfare state in Britain after the Second World War. For Beveridge, see Jose Harris, *William Beveridge: A Biography,* 2d ed. (Oxford: Clarendon Press, 1997).

41. L. T., "Some Recent Books," *Dublin Review* (April 1909): 394–97.

42. Mrs. Virginia Crawford (1862–1948) is perhaps more famous for one of the most notorious scandals of the Victorian era—the one that destroyed the career of the rising Liberal politician Sir Charles Dilke (1843–1911). In 1885 Mr. Donald Crawford, Liberal MP for Lanark, filed a petition of divorce against his wife on the grounds of her adultery with Dilke, based on the evidence of his wife. While Dilke denied the accusations and maintained his innocence to the last, his career was irreparably ruined. Under the influence of Cardinal Manning, Mrs. Crawford became a Catholic in 1889. She was a Poor Law Guardian for Marylebone for thirty years, secretary of the Catholic Social Guild from 1912 to 1919, and later joined the Labour Party, being a borough councilor for Marylebone from 1919 to 1931. The *Dublin* praised her *Ideals of Charity* (1908) as a superb practical handbook for women involved in social work. See V., "Some Recent Books," *Dublin Review* (Jan. 1909): 212–13.

tomed to see one of the most difficult departments of public administration entrusted in considerable measure to people who not only have no training for the duties they have voluntarily undertaken, but who have not even grasped that some sort of qualification was essential, or that dealing with destitution and unemployment demanded a higher level of knowledge and judgement than street paving and dustbins.[43]

She considered the Poor Law a failure—which was also the finding of the whole commission—and its failures could be focused on the two main branches of its administration, the workhouse proper and out-relief. The administration of the Poor Law, she thought, was most successful in those institutions that were physically separated from the precincts of the workhouse: in the infirmaries, which had become for all intents public hospitals, in the specialized institutions for various diseases and for the insane, and in the education of Poor Law children, insofar as they were removed from the influence of the workhouse. All of these had been a boon to the poor and left them without the "pauper taint" characteristic of the workhouse. While it was clear that the poor were better served the farther they were removed from the Boards of Guardians and the general mixed workhouse, the irresistible tendency had been to keep the bulk of the destitute altogether under one roof—this being considered cheaper and less trouble. "Even in the best of our London workhouses there are still to be found, side by side, the aged and the able-bodied of both sexes, children up to the age of three, women, married and unmarried, in the lying-in wards, cripples, blind people, epileptics, feeble-minded boys and girls, as well as temporary lunatics, imbeciles, and other afflicted persons waiting, sometimes for months, for admission to suitable homes."[44] And having brought all these people together, nothing was done with them: while some work was involved, it was of a very low standard, and there was no attempt at training the adults so as to give them a fresh start. The larger the house, the less work there was available and the slacker the discipline. The result was that the workhouse was "too good for the bad and too bad for the good," and the respectable poor had a horror of it and would rather starve than go there. The longer one stayed there, she believed, the more hopeless it became to try and help him, as the very atmosphere was demoralizing, creating people who were incapable of independence and self-support.

The second main function of the Poor Law was out-relief, and this was no

43. Virginia Crawford, "The Failure of the Workhouse," ibid. (July 1909): 60–61.
44. Ibid., 64–65.

less unsatisfactory. There had been no consistency among the various local committees in the policy of giving relief. Both the majority and minority reports had unanimously deplored the haphazard manner of out-relief, while the minority report also commented on the insufficiency of the relief given. Crawford was particularly incensed by the gross insufficiency of the allowance given for the maintenance of small children, who were often left undernourished, poorly dressed, and barefoot. Nor were the homes of many of these children physically and morally healthy. The Boards of Guardians were responsible for hundreds of thousands of these children, and they had failed in their duty. The fault lay, she believed, not so much with the people who ran the system as with the system itself, which was created to relieve destitution and which now had had so much more added on to it.

> Not only are Guardians called upon to perform duties as educational, sanitary and hospital experts, for which they possess no qualification, but they are driven to undertake work which is already being done by authorities far better qualified than themselves. The Guardians feed and educate children: so do the Education authorities. They nurse the sick: so do hospitals and the sanitary authorities. They give relief in the homes of the poor: so do innumerable charitable agencies. Thus, one child of a family may be in a reformatory under the Home Office, another in a special school under the County Council, the mother may be in receipt of out-relief and the remaining children of school age may be enjoying free meals at school, the various authorities all acting without co-ordination among themselves and without official knowledge of each other's intervention. The result is the most amazing overlapping and confusion of authorities, causing, it need scarcely be said, much misuse of public funds and a useless squandering of public effort.[45]

She believed that the three ways of meeting extreme want, the workhouse, out-relief, and private charity, had not been successful. While the majority report proposed to modify the workhouse radically, the minority report wanted to abolish it. Both agreed that the spirit of deterrence that had animated the old workhouse should be abandoned and preventative measures should be created entailing some comprehensive scheme that would include the establishment of labor exchanges, training and detention colonies, unemployment insurance, and the curtailment of work for children and married women. The majority report merely wanted an enlarged and reformed Poor Law, more professional and efficient, given a new name; but it would still be a "destitu-

45. Ibid., 70–71.

tion authority." While Crawford believed that the majority report's scheme would appeal to "those more especially who fear democratic institutions and have a genuine belief in the necessity for educated people settling the domestic affairs of the uneducated," she maintained that it was "unsound in principle" and suffered the same weakness as the present system. "Moreover, I must confess to a considerable distrust of the *personnel* of the scheme. There is much to be said for democratic rule, based on popular election, something for bureaucratic, when you can get it uncorrupt, but there is extremely little to be said for administration by a system of semi-private selection and nomination, which would quickly result in the real power falling into the hands of a clique, from whom there would be neither appeal nor escape. The fact that the clique, in this instance, would consist of highly educated, superior persons does not at all reconcile me to the fact of the poor being left wholly in their hands."[46] The proposals of the minority report, which drew up a less detailed scheme of administration and left many points undeveloped, would eliminate the worst abuses of the workhouse by sorting people out to the official bodies to which they naturally belonged.

In discussing unemployment, as Crawford did in her second article, "Unemployment and Its Remedies," where the disagreements between the majority and minority reports were shown at their most profound, her own preference, again, was for the minority report.[47] Both reports agreed that the Poor Law had been inadequate to deal with the problems of distress due to unemployment, and that the relief schemes of private charities and municipalities had not been very effective. In trying to find a comprehensive scheme of reform for unemployment, she turned to William Beveridge, whose arguments and suggestions could be found in both reports. For Beveridge the problem was an economic one of supply and demand. Able-bodied men could not get work because it was unavailable, not because they were lazy. Displacements could be caused by changes in industry, or by seasonal and cyclical fluctuations, and most significantly by the chronic excess of labor due to the lack of industrial organization. He believed that there was not one labor market but an infinite number of small labor markets, and each maintained its own reserve of labor in excess of its actual requirements. The physical and moral evils of underemployment and casual labor, which went hand in hand, were numerous. But what was the remedy?

46. Ibid., 75.

47. Virginia Crawford, "Unemployment and Its Remedies," ibid. (Jan. 1910): 40–62.

Both Beveridge and the entire royal commission believed that the labor market had to be organized "on a business footing" and that this could only be attained by the establishment of "a connected system of Labour Exchanges" over the whole of Great Britain. By creating a single pool of labor from which the employer could recruit, "decasualization" could be achieved and openings made better known. Beveridge did not believe that casual labor would ever be eliminated, but he thought that the worst aspects of it could be relieved. He also suggested that the fluctuations of trade could be met by elasticity of working hours and by some form of contributory insurance against unemployment.

For the semi-employable "squeezed out" by the changes in industrial structure, who Beveridge thought could be left to the Poor Law, Crawford, hoping that the workhouse would disappear altogether, pointed to the success of labor colonies on the Continent. "One of the great arguments for abolishing the mixed workhouse is that as long as it is allowed to survive it will represent in the public mind a species of convenient rubbish heap on which human wreckage may be flung without scruple. . . . It is undeniably in the interests of labour that the lowest grade of incompetent worker should, if possible, be taken off the market altogether, even if those who compose it have to be maintained temporarily at public expense. It is equally desirable that a less hopeless class, crowded out through inefficiency, should be compulsorily detained and trained in suitable labour colonies, until such time as they may compete once more in the open market with some prospect of success."[48] There was, however, an "incalculably large" number of individuals "neither very vicious nor deliberately idle," "of feeble physique and low mental capacity," "more sinned against than sinning," for whom training was of no use. Crawford believed that while nothing could be done to help them out of that state, a thorough reform of education could reduce future numbers. While Beveridge seemed to Crawford somewhat scornful toward those who would account for unemployment by the lack of trade schools and the shortness of elementary education, she believed that organization without a concurrent cutting down of the number of unemployables would have no chance of success. "Born and bred in the slums of our cities, the victims throughout childhood of insufficient food and unhygienic surroundings, our boys and girls receive, at great expense to the nation, a purely literary education up to their fourteenth birthday and then—

48. Ibid., 52.

we wash our hands of them. . . . At eighteen when they begin to ask for a man's wages they are turned away, to find themselves stranded without knowledge of any industry, without habits of regularity or discipline—for their life has been spent largely in the streets—and often without the physical strength to do a hard day's work."[49] She thought that this was confirmed by the statistics of the distress committees, where some 15 to 20 percent of the applications came from those under twenty-five years of age. Unlike many European countries, England gave its youth little obligatory manual or professional training that would fit them for life. Improved education would reduce juvenile crime and casual labor, the least satisfactory kind of work; it would also reduce overspecialization, as the trade school would give students all-round knowledge, making them less liable to be thrown out of work by changes in the manufacturing process. "Finally, it is only manual training that can cut off the supply of unemployables who clog the wheels of the industrial machine and represent a dead weight of unproductive human material that has to be borne by the community at large. If we have to train such men in the end on a farm-colony under every disadvantage, surely it were both cheaper and kinder to train them from the first in a trade-school?"[50] Crawford emphasized that girls should be trained not primarily for the workshop but for the home and should aim at a general efficiency rather than a specialized skill. But even where instruction in feminine trades was provided, it should be only one or two hours a week and given to strictly domestic subjects such as cookery, ironing, and fine darning. She believed that while girls of the working classes must to a great extent go out to work and be self-supporting, and while many trades and occupations were properly filled by them, under normal conditions the working years of most of them would be short, merely filling the gap between adolescence and marriage. While it was notorious that one of the "unhappy features of our industrial chaos" was the extent to which married women had become the breadwinners of the family, this was an effect of the casual and insufficient earnings of their husbands. A decasualization of men's labor would reduce women's work and also, therefore, the level of infant mortality.

Crawford maintained that educational reform had to go hand in hand

49. Ibid., 53.

50. Ibid., 56. In a later article ("Unemployment and Education: A Lesson from Switzerland," *Dublin Review* [July 1910]: 119–36), she described in great detail the system of compulsory education given in the Swiss canton of Fribourg. She also wrote a book on Switzerland and social policy, *Switzerland Today: A Study in Social Progress* (London: Sands & Co., 1911).

with industrial reconstruction (organization) and that together they would inaugurate "a new era of industrial prosperity for England." While neither could increase the amount of employment available, they would ensure that all that was available would be taken advantage of. Only then would we be in a position to know if recourse to "artificial" means of increasing work was necessary. While the majority report abhorred any state-subsidized labor, Beveridge thought that a "judicious policy of industrial organization," with a more systematic distribution of public aid, would prove "a sufficient solution for all existing evils." While it could not ensure that every man would have the certainty of continuous work, it would guarantee that he would not suffer destitution for want of wages. The minority report, however, asserted that a more generous government response would be needed for periodic depressions in trade as well as the provision of "full and honorable maintenance at the public expense" for any surplus labor that might be found to exist. Crawford thought that idea premature, though these alternatives might prove necessary in the future. With such a grievous social evil there was the danger that shortcuts might be attempted to reach the ideal of full employment, which could be reached only by long and laborious processes. She believed that the problem had been elucidated well by the facts gathered by the commission, that Beveridge had supplied a concise theory of cause and effect, and that the old-age pensions and the establishment of labor exchanges in the next year were further stages to the realization of this program.

Maisie Ward saw these articles as written "rather from a Labour angle," but they were signed and, as a point of comparison, very similar in content to the articles of Leslie Toke, also a founder of the Catholic Social Guild, in the *Downside Review,* a journal with many of the same upper-class Catholic connections.[51] In the end, however, very little resulted from the reports; the workhouse system remained basically intact until after the Second World War and the creation of the welfare state. Oddly enough, the Great War "solved" the unemployment problem, at least for a while. The unemployment rate fell below 1 percent by May 1915 and stayed low for the rest of the war, taking care even of the problem of casual unskilled laborers.

51. *Wilfrid Wards* 2:210. Leslie Toke, "Pauperism and the Nation," *Downside Review* 9 (Nov. 1909): 197–216, and 10 (March 1910): 18–48. There are also no contrary articles or disclaimers, a practice Ward used in other cases when he had qualms about an article.

Unemployment was not the only problem in Edwardian Britain. While it is difficult to ascertain the working-class standard of living, varying as it did by region and occupation, it seems clear that while real wages rose in the 1890s they tended to fall after about 1900 (particularly from 1908 to 1913), so that this period was, in general, one of stagnating or declining living standards.[52] In a time of economic growth and conspicuous consumption among the wealthy, the situation for the workers was far more difficult to bear; it is not surprising that the labor movement grew rapidly at this time. In 1868 the Trades Union Congress (TUC) was founded and by the 1890s it had more than a million members. In 1909 2.3 million workers were affiliated with it; by 1914, 4 million. In the years before the Great War waves of strikes spread across Britain: in 1910 there were strikes in cotton, coal, railways, and shipbuilding, in 1911, among seamen, carters, dockers, and again among the railwaymen; in 1912 there was a vast nationwide coal miners' strike and a strike at the Port of London, and in 1913 strikes among textile workers. While in 1909 there were only 422 strikes, there were 521 in 1910, 872 in 1911, 834 in 1912, and 1,459 in 1913. Nor was it just the number of strikes. The strikes were much larger and entailed a greater loss of working days: 2.7 million days in 1909, 9.9 million in 1910, 10.2 million in 1911, 40.9 million in 1912, 9.8 million in 1913, and 9.9 million days in 1914, primarily in the seven months before the outbreak of the war. In the autumn of 1914 a general strike of the "Triple Alliance" of miners, railwaymen, and transport workers threatened. Troops and police fought strikers at Cardiff, Hull, Manchester, and Liverpool. Fear of revolution filled the minds of middle-class Englishmen with the spread of a new radicalism called syndicalism, which advocated the overthrow of the capitalist system and the state by direct action and the establishment of a new social order based on workers organized in production units. The *Dublin* devoted three articles to the strikes: a basically negative 1912 article by Stephen Harding, and two lengthier and more positive ones in 1912 and 1914 by T. M. Kettle, the first professor of national economics of Ireland at University College, Dublin.

Harding compared the strike to a declaration of civil war, and said that as such it could be justified only by strong reasons, very grave abuses, and the absence of other means of redress. While there were justified strikes, there were also those that sought to take advantage of an employer's inability to re-

52. See T. R. Gourvish, "The Standard of Living, 1890–1914," in O'Day, *Edwardian Age*, 13–34.

sist workers' demands and to get as much as they possibly could. Such a strike would be unjust and no better than a monopolizing trust that unduly inflated prices. Looking at the three biggest strikes, the railway workers, the miners, and the transport workers of the Port of London, only among the railwaymen did Harding find many of the grievances to be "real enough." While the life of the miner was hard and often dangerous, it was not the hardest or most dangerous around ("colliers are a very healthy class, being exceptionally free from tubercular disease"), and miners were certainly well compensated. What particularly disturbed Harding about the strikes of the past two years was the frequent demand that all nonunion workers be excluded from the workplace. In fact, the strike at the Port of London was caused by the unions' refusal to allow the continuation of a nonunion worker. He believed that it was an attack on the man's elementary liberty to offer his labor on his own terms. He was also disturbed by trade unions' cavalier attitude to keeping their agreements. Unless sanctions could be imposed so as to preserve the sanctity of contracts, there would be no end of trouble. He believed that the Trade Dispute Act of 1906 only encouraged further irresponsibility and suspected that the strikes were less than popular among the rank and file, who more or less blindly followed their leaders. He believed that it was necessary for Parliament to pass a law against those "irresponsible" men, whether among the masters or among the men, who commanded the breach of a solemnly agreed-upon contract.[53]

Thomas Kettle (1880–1916), son of one of the founders of the Land League and a rising star in the Irish Party, being an MP from East Tyrone from 1906 to 1910, was a leading intellectual among the burgeoning Irish Catholic middle class.[54] In his first article for the *Dublin* he mocked the modern tendency to panic. "Every difficulty, caught up into the enlarging atmosphere of our

53. Stephen Harding, "Some Recent Strikes," *Dublin Review* (July 1912): 141–54. Egerton Stephen Somers Harding was born in 1886, son of the convert Francis Egerton Harding, educated at the Oratory School and King's College, Cambridge, founded and directed the Huts of the Catholic Club in France and Germany, 1915–1925, and was the general secretary of the Catholic Truth Society from 1922 to 1924.

54. Kettle, a year ahead of Joyce at University College, was the darling of his generation in Dublin. Great things were expected of him. An advocate of constitutional nationalism, he joined the British army and died at the Somme. For his life, see J. B. Lyons, *The Enigma of Tom Kettle: Irish Patriot, Essayist, Poet, British Soldier, 1880–1916* (Dublin: Glendale Press, 1983), who calls him "a symbol and victim of Constitutionalism." "Literally, he gave his life for Britain; figuratively, he sacrificed his life's work on altars of British irresolution over Home Rule" (15).

newspapers, becomes forthwith a crisis, every trouble a tragedy, every political blunder a planned betrayal of the nation and posterity. There is not a schoolchild in the land but has already survived at least three or four final cataclysms, and the ends-of-all-things." While this faculty of exaggeration was not characteristically modern, the very complexity of modern economic life had made everything seem that much more endangered. "Let somebody only push a lever, or even press an electric button out of season, or, still worse, decline to push or press them and the whole fabric falls to pieces." While he admitted that he had exaggerated the modern fear, particularly the fear of syndicalism among the propertied class, he did not believe he had done so by much. "It is a recognizable transcript of the talk of the railway train, the club smoke-room, and the golf-links, that is to say of the three foci of middle-class civilization." He did, however, consider this panic extremely important and useful. "It has at least broken up the monstrous apathy of the comfortable, and delivered them from the sin of being at ease in Zion. It may save them from that, as imaginative persons are sometimes saved from drink by the sight of twisted, sinister, and non-existent snakes." None of the strikes justified, he believed, the despair that it was now fashionable to affect. One had only to look around to see the foolishness of such despair. "If he encounters, day by day, red ruin and the breaking up of laws, pale riders on white horses, and apocalyptic dawns, no more is to be said. He belongs to the 'intellectual minority,' the 'remnant,' and those of us, who do not, may wish him joy of his ticket of admission." Life went on as it always had. "People in general are observed to be still enduring the ancient discipline, and exploiting the ancient joys of life. Dedicated to plough, loom, and engine they still seem to keep on grumbling and toiling; making little of much and much of little; homely, loyal, industrious, reckless, impatient; interested in religion, happiness, the prospects of the football season and the Insurance Act. Some of them even reach as high as the crucial Act of Hope—they marry."[55]

This situation was not at all new, as some claimed, but as old as human nature, and its cause was the miserable conditions of so many workers. "Thirty per cent of them, more than twelve million human beings, count themselves fortunate if they are able to hold their places in the dim borderland where destitution merges into mere poverty. They are constantly slipping into the blacker depths, sometimes to recover their hold, sometimes to perish. As we

55. T. M. Kettle, "Labour: War or Peace?" *Dublin Review* (Oct. 1912): 370–72.

go higher in the hierarchy of skill and opportunity, things, no doubt, improve, but we have to go unexpectedly and painfully high before we reach the plane of the genuine living wage." The condition of the poorest was "a poignant and horrible fact," and the believers in individualism (himself included), who had been too fond of lecturing labor, had better drastically remodel the subsidiary features of the present industrial fabric if they wanted to keep it going on its fundamental lines. "Moreover, we had better recognize that, if the desire of labour to make its future better than its past is criminal, then we are all tarred with the same guilty brush. The continuity of family life, and the wise instinct which sets men planting acorns so that their children may enjoy the matured oak, are the best economic bulwarks of the institution of private property. If anybody is to have the inspiration of this hope then everybody must have it." While this desire had led to the "millennial mirage of Socialism" for some, on the whole people's desires had been very modest. "A little more leisure, a little more comfort, a little more security of life, some slight treasure of hope to bequeath to one's children."[56]

These strikes were not something entirely new, Kettle continued, and one did not have to go too far back in time for comparable periods of industrial unrest. After all, the figure of 37 million working days lost in the first six months of 1912 was not too far from the 31.2 million days lost in 1893. Nor did one have to blame the "New Anarchism" of syndicalism for it all. The cause was simple: the mere need to keep one's wages above the cost of living. Pointing to the researches of respected economists, Kettle elaborated on how in the past decade the curve of prices had outdistanced the curve of wages, and how the rising curve of working-class prosperity had been checked or even depressed below its former level. While some promoted syndicalism—and even they were not entirely clear about what they wanted—they were few and far between. As the recent Trades Union Congress proved, where an all-but-unanimous resolution had been passed against syndicalism, the unions were basically conservative and pacific, not inclined to violence and revolution, and as concerned, since they were consumers also, about maintaining their own necessities. The "new strategy" of syndicalism, the general strike, was also not all that new. The strike was an old and familiar weapon, and the passage from the idea of a single strike to a general one was not that difficult.

Kettle warned, however, that all of this should not lull us into a comfort-

56. Ibid., 373–75.

able apathy, for the flaws and distortions of the present industrial system had now been dramatically revealed. The demand of business for some absolute solution and guarantee of peace was utopian, for "no such Economists' Stone is to be found." Compulsory arbitration was an illusion, as the unions would never, and rightly so, he believed, give up the one weapon they had, the strike. Also, the idea of submitting the unions to military discipline and martial law and hanging strikers as deserters, as some had suggested, was preposterous. The lesson to be learned from these strikes was that public opinion decided the result in the end, and that public opinion needed the help of a skilled official tribunal investigating the truth of the matter. The main hope for peace, however, was the continuation of the conservative attitude of the unions. It was clear that they did not like strikes and were inclined to use them only in extreme conditions. The prospect for industrial peace, therefore, was bound up not with the suppression of unions but with their extension. While there was "a glimmer of truth" in the complaint that the unions occupied a position of privilege, even tyranny, the fact was that the unions had to choose between absolute supremacy in their particular trades or ineffectiveness. More important, wherever they were frankly accepted and treated with respect, they tended to become more conservative.

He was not hopeful about the possibility of modifying the wage system by giving the worker an interest in the capital employed, so that labor and capital were no longer in mutually hostile camps. The two most common options were some form of profit sharing and partnership between labor and management. An earlier unsigned article in the October 1910 number had gone on at great length promoting co-partnership as an answer to socialism.[57] While Kettle could cite some successful examples, the very failure of co-partnership to spread pointed to its inherent limitations. Also, any form of profit sharing would compromise the integrity of collective bargaining that was the essence of trade unionism. While it too had its successes—he could point to Lever, the soap manufacturer, with his model factory and village of Port Sunlight—these depended too much on some particular trade in some particular place, or on some exceptional people or traditions: they were a "happy accident." Since the wage system was likely to remain the norm, it had to be amended. First, wages were far too low for social health or stability. Second, wages must

57. "An Answer to Socialism," ibid. (Oct. 1910): 356–75. See Edward Bristow, "Profit-Sharing, Socialism and Labour Unrest," in Brown, *Essays in Anti-Labour History*, 262–89.

be geared to the cost of living. Third, there should be a minimum wage in every industry. Despite what many had said, this was not a revolutionary and socialistic idea but one associated with "the Catholic School of Economics" on the Continent. While this might not be a genuine living wage, it would be a good beginning. Such a minimum wage act would have to be indefinitely flexible, allowing variations from place to place, perhaps using a sliding-scale arrangement, and it had to be able to be adjusted to the varying actualities to which it was applied. While not a panacea, it was promising, especially when added on to the legislation that the state had already passed dealing with sickness, unemployment, and old age. Kettle called for more than legislation, however; he also advocated a "change of spirit" that would recognize the needs of the worker. While he believed that the Catholic Church had an important part to play in the transformation of the social scene, and that there should be courses in economics and the social sciences in the seminaries, he did not believe that the Church should formulate and insist upon "a rigorous and exclusive social programme." That was both futile and dangerous. "It is indeed part of the mission of the Church to safeguard those ethical truths which lie at the basis of all society; but when it comes to discussion of the technical processes of society, economic and political, every man must effect his own synthesis of principle and technique, and he must be free to follow the light of his own conscience and his experience."[58]

Kettle wrote his second article, "Labour and Civilization," after the famous Dublin Lockout of 1913. Dublin, while not an industrial center, was still a large city of about three hundred thousand people, and was marked by horrendous slums, with some 30 percent of its people living in conditions that were nearly subhuman, and a death rate, brought on by high infant mortality and tuberculosis, that was the worst of any city in Europe. Unemployment was high and labor was cheap, especially among unskilled casual laborers. From 1908 to 1913 the Liverpool-born Irishman James Larkin, whose sharp tongue and militancy earned him as many enemies as friends, had managed to organize the bulk of Dublin's unskilled workers into his Irish Transport and General Workers' Union. Larkinism, with its attempt at "one big union," its use of sympathetic strikes, and its desire not merely to get better wages and conditions but to create a new socialist society, was a type of syndicalism. Larkin's *bête noir* was the successful Catholic businessman and former Irish

58. Kettle, "Labour: War or Peace," 393.

Party MP William Martin Murphy (1844–1919), who owned the *Irish Independent,* the *Evening Standard,* and the *Irish Catholic,* as well as the Dublin United Tramway Company, the largest unorganized entity in Dublin along with the brewer Arthur Guinness and Sons. Murphy, who seems to have been a good employer on the whole, was not one to be bullied, and he vowed to destroy Larkinism. In August a strike was called against the tramway company, but Murphy had already organized the employers in a lockout of all workers who refused to pledge not to belong to Larkin's union. By September 1913 some twenty thousand workers were locked out, on whom another eighty thousand depended. In a series of articles in the Irish Nationalist *Freeman's Journal* in September, Kettle condemned both sides for their extremism and intransigence, and formed the Industrial Peace Committee to help settle the strike.[59] Neither its efforts nor those of others, such as Archbishop Walsh of Dublin (who was sympathetic to labor and had been involved in conciliation boards many times before), could end the deadlock, and within six months the workers were forced back to their jobs.[60]

In his article for the *Dublin,* Kettle presented an even-handed description of the poor conditions that led to the spread of Larkin's union and of the events of the lockout.[61] He had good things to say about both Larkin ("picturesque, eloquent, prophetic") and Murphy ("a humane man, known for his personal honour and charity"), but he also pointed out the recklessness and impossibility of Larkin's strategy and the ruthlessness of the employers, who were indifferent to any attempt at compromise or reconciliation. While the employers seemed to have won, and a sort of peace had been restored, it was a "peace of anaemia, not that of a healthy civilization," for the slums, the hunger, and the hopeless outlook that created the situation in the first place remained. The great task of the day, he asserted, was to rally the worker to the actual shape of Western civilization by transforming it so that it could be a fit place for him. One had to approach him not as "a unit in a Board of Trade table, nor yet as a nihilist, a metaphysician, or a prophet" but as a concrete person who preferred peace to war and work to idleness. Workers were not radicals bent on destroying civilization, since they themselves were civilized

59. See Pádraig Yeates, *Lockout: Dublin 1913* (New York: St. Martin's Press, 2000), 178–79, 227–30, 251–52, 295–98.

60. For Walsh's involvement, see Thomas J. Morrissey, *William J. Walsh, Archbishop of Dublin, 1841–1921: No Uncertain Voice* (Dublin: Four Courts Press, 2000), 241–65.

61. T. W. Kettle, "Labour and Civilization," *Dublin Review* (April 1914): 355–71.

men, seeing in our system of private ownership a sort of bedrock fitness and necessity. Only a social philosophy and the practical policy founded on it could truly rally the worker to civilization. The conservative had to realize that great change must happen, even as the extremist must accept that it would be gradual. There would be conflicts and disturbances, and sometimes the choice had to be between bad wages and no wages: one had to be realistic. Every voluntary and state proposal that tended to broaden the basis of property should be welcomed, as should those who shared common goals, regardless of their differing spiritual orientations. In the end, however, it was personality that counted, and the call that came to each individually, as the seminal social encyclicals of Pope Leo XIII had made so clear: to do what one can was the task, remembering that the one thing needful was a return to real Christianity.

Kettle had mentioned "a living wage," and the *Dublin* reviewed very favorably the important book by the American priest John A. Ryan (1865–1945), *A Living Wage: Its Ethical and Economic Aspects* (1906), whose work influenced the New Deal policies of President Franklin Delano Roosevelt.[62] The reviewer praised Ryan's attempts to move away from vague generalities and give clear principles concerning the living wage. "Labour at the present day is certainly in an unsatisfactory position; unlimited bargaining has degraded it and has frequently compelled the workman to accept, from dire necessity, what he feels is inadequate to satisfy his natural needs. Our standard of fixing wages has become debased; we treat our employees as though they were machines, and measure their worth by the amount of their output." The reviewer pointed to the innate dignity of the human person, and the rights that resulted from it—mere subsistence being insufficient. "'A decent and reasonable life' implies the power to exercise one's primary faculties, supply one's essential needs and develop one's personality: it implies, too, that the labourer may, if he wish, enter the married state. His wage should then be such, in definite right, as to enable him to bring up a family in a suitable manner."

Considering the extensive coverage given the social question and the significance of its authors, it is surprising how cavalierly and briefly, barely more

62. E. S. P., "Some Recent Books," ibid. (April 1907): 396–97. For Ryan, see Francis L. Broderick, *Right Reverend New Dealer: John A. Ryan* (New York: Macmillan, 1963), and Robert G. Kennedy et al., *Religion and Public Life: The Legacy of Monsignor John A. Ryan* (Lanham, Md.: University Press of America, 2001).

than a page in the "Some Recent Books" section, the *Dublin* treated one of the most important books written at this time on the topic, C. F. G. Masterman's *The Condition of England* (1909).[63] Masterman (1873–1927) was a Liberal MP, an upcoming junior minister in the government who was to be heavily involved in the creation of the national insurance scheme of Lloyd George, and the first chairman of the National Health Insurance Commission. He was also a friend of G. K. Chesterton and Hilaire Belloc—though Belloc turned against him when he entered the government and seemed to change his positions. The book went through six editions in just over two years and is historically significant. The reviewer ("B") criticized the work for its excessive gloominess and because he sensed that Masterman wrote it more with his eye on posterity than on the present, for it was exactly the kind of book, the reviewer believed, that a historian a hundred years hence would find invaluable as representing the truth, though, he believed, not the whole truth, of the period.

For, in spite of the fact that chapter and verse can be produced for nearly every statement that he makes in reviewing the morals and temperament of the age, the reader has an unpleasant suspicion that similar chapters and verses could be produced for precisely opposite statements. . . . The historian of the future, therefore, will be well advised if, together with this very gloomy picture of twentieth century society, he studies also some, at present unwritten, book, by, let us say, Mr Chesterton, showing that our morals are excellent, our religion firm and unwavering, and our altruism unexceptionable. And, if he adds the two together, he will come to the conclusion that the reign of Edward VII was exceedingly like the reign of Edward VI, and Edward I, and William the Conqueror; and that human nature is always much about the same in all ages and countries.[64]

One of the great anxieties of this period was the fear of physical degeneration, to which the spread of the idea of eugenics was one response.[65] A child of Social Darwinism, eugenics, from the Greek *eugenes,* meaning "good in birth" or "noble in heredity," was coined in 1883 by Francis Galton (1822–1911), Dar-

63. C. F. G. Masterman, *The Condition of England,* ed. J. T. Boulton (London: Methuen, 1960). See B., "Some Recent Books," *Dublin Review* (July 1909): 210–11. For Masterman, see Lucy Masterman, *C. F. G. Masterman: A Biography* (London: Nicholson and Watson, 1939), and Edward David, "The New Liberalism of C. F. G. Masterman, 1873–1927," in Brown, *Essays in Anti-Labour History,* 17–41.

64. B., "Some Recent Books," *Dublin Review* (July 1909): 210.

65. See Greta Jones, *Social Darwinism and English Thought: The Interaction between Biological and Social Theory* (Brighton: Harvester Press, 1980).

win's cousin.[66] Galton believed in the preeminence of heredity and was fearful that the ranks of the gifted were being depleted by their failure to reproduce. (Galton himself, though one of nine, had no children.) He defined eugenics as "the study of agencies under social control that may improve or impair the racial qualities of future generations either physically or mentally."[67] His goal was to improve the human race by selective breeding, and he even suggested that marriage certificates should be issued so that proper eugenic marriages could be made. In addition to advocating the promotion of the fit, later called "positive eugenics," he was opposed to the propagation of the unfit, later called "negative eugenics." His ideas, however, did not attract much attention or support until the late Victorian and, particularly, the Edwardian period, when it became obvious that Britain's general birthrate was in decline.[68] From an average of about six children born per marriage in the 1860s, it had dropped to about four by the end of the century, and the results taken from the *Fertility of Marriage Census* (done as part of the decennial census of 1911) pointed to a number closer to three. Indeed, the decline would continue, with some fluctuations, so that by the Second World War the number was at 2.04.[69] Many saw this as a sign of "race suicide," a calamity threatening both nation and Empire. Even more worrisome than the general decline was the vast socioeconomic differential in the birthrate, which was much higher among the less educated and skilled, the poorer and less fit, than among their "betters."[70] These anxieties flowed into the more general fear, which had become strong in the late Victorian period, that the race itself was physically and mentally deteriorating owing to the insalubrious environment of modern

66. For Galton's life, see Derek W. Forrest, *Francis Galton: The Life and Work of a Victorian Genius* (New York: Taplinger, 1974), and Nicholas Wright Gillham, *A Life of Sir Francis Galton: From African Exploration to the Birth of Eugenics* (Oxford: Oxford University Press, 2001).

67. Francis Galton, "Eugenics: Its Definition, Scope and Aims," *Nature* 70 (1904): 82, quoted in G. R. Searle, *Eugenics and Politics in Britain, 1900–1914* (Leyden: Noordhoff, 1976).

68. Besides Searle, *Eugenics and Politics in Britain,* see Richard Allen Soloway, *Birth Control and the Population Question in England, 1877–1930* (Chapel Hill: University of North Carolina Press, 1982), 3–48, and *Demography and Degeneration: Eugenics and the Declining Birthrate in Twentieth-Century Britain* (Chapel Hill: University of North Carolina Press, 1990), 1–137.

69. Soloway, *Demography and Degeneration,* 9–10.

70. As Soloway points out, though dedicated to "replication," the officers of the Eugenics Education Society contributed on average no more than 2.3 children, with a quarter having no offspring at all, and the members of the National Birth-Rate Commission, whose report, issued in 1914, "singled out the racial dangers inherent in the small family," had an average of only 1.75 children (ibid., 35–36). Of course, both were dominated by the very professional classes whose birthrate decline they so lamented.

urban life. The Boer War only confirmed these fears when it became clear that some 40 percent of those who applied were physically unfit to serve in the military; and if one combined these rejections with those who were found unfit within two years of enlistment, the failure rate was 60 rather than 40 percent.[71] All this led to a great surge in the popularity of eugenics in the Edwardian period. The Eugenics Education Society was not founded until 1907, never having many members, and the *Eugenics Review* was founded only in 1909, with only a small readership. Even so, the idea of eugenics touched a nerve among a great many in the middle and upper classes, transcending normal political categories and profoundly influencing the culture. For some adherents it even took on the aspect of a religion, a new science that would supersede all other realities and transform the world. It melded well with the deep reserves of pessimism that had developed and with the belief that science would solve social problems, which fueled other movements for social reform, such as the movement for national efficiency.[72]

Because of the military unfitness of so many, an interdepartmental committee on physical deterioration was formed. Its report came out strongly against the idea that the race was degenerating and proposed various public health reforms. A month after the report appeared, in August 1904, the government created the Royal Commission on the Care and Control of the Feeble-Minded. While there was no direct connection between the two events (the 1904 report paid little attention to mental deterioration and made no recommendation for setting up such a commission), the general discussion of national deterioration had supplied enough impetus for such an investigation. Also, mental deficiency offered a useful meeting point for many social concerns. "Mental defectives became such a potent subject for concern because they provided a symbol which linked these overlapping anxieties about moral, demographic, and racial decline: because of their mental defect they sank within society to join the residuum; lacking moral restraint they bred unchecked with similarly weak-minded individuals; and their offspring were brought up in such a socially and morally impoverished environment, and inherited such weak mental powers, that they perpetuated the vicious circle of decline, turning to crime or falling on the rates in order to survive."[73] The

71. Ibid., 41.

72. For a discussion of the movement for national efficiency, see G. R. Searle, *The Quest for National Efficiency* (Oxford: B. Blackwell, 1971).

73. Mathew Thomson, *The Problem of Mental Deficiency: Eugenics, Democracy, and Social*

commission's report was published in July 1908 and the results were disturbing. Among other things it revealed that there had been a massive increase in the mentally defective: while the increase between 1881 and 1891 had been only 3.23 percent, the increase between 1891 and 1901 had been 21.44 percent. It also made clear that feeblemindedness was hereditary, noted that the feebleminded had a higher-than-average birthrate, and proposed that certain categories of them be segregated from the larger community.

While Catholics strongly opposed eugenics, in an article in the July 1911 number of the *Dublin,* "The Catholic Church and Race Culture," Fr. Thomas Gerrard tried to argue that if the goal of eugenics was to improve the racial qualities of future generations, then the eugenics movement needed the Catholic Church and its ideals to achieve success.[74] In tracing the movement from Galton, whose predominant aim was the physical fitness of the race, to C. W. Saleeby, his disciple, with his doctrine of maternalism, Gerrard saw a greater movement toward the Catholic ideal. For Saleeby the psychic element in man, not the physical, was the best survival value, that quality which would best "enable the individual to struggle and live against adverse circumstances." This "psychical element" was not merely intelligence but also "love." Saleeby also insisted on the dignity of motherhood and attacked those who favored permitting infant mortality. He believed that once a life had come into being it ought to continue, and that to deny this was both immoral and worked against the eugenic end. Whereas Galton believed that the cardinal prerequisite for a mother was physical health, Saleeby thought that love for her children trumped physical health. Gerrard noted that some eugenists had taken up Nietzsche's catchword, "superman," believing that this supplied a sentimental, artistic element to the cause, since eugenics as a dry science of anthropometric measurement, statistical observation, and human experiments on Mendel's laws was, of itself, insufficient to direct man's will and action in this quest. But, as Gerrard reminded his readers, Nietzsche meant by the term "superman" something other than man, "a lawless being considered to be above

Policy in Britain, c. 1870–1959 (Oxford: Clarendon Press, 1998), 22. Thomson also believes that the concern for social purity, to protect feeble-minded women from sexual abuse, was an important factor behind both this eugenic interest and the Mental Deficiency Act of 1913.

74. T. J. Gerrard, "The Catholic Church and Race Culture," *Dublin Review* (July 1911): 49–68. Thomas John Gerrard (1871–1916), received into the Church at twenty and ordained for Westminster in 1901, was a frequent contributor to Catholic periodicals and the author of a few books, including an exposition and critique of Bergson from a Thomistic point of view.

man simply because it should be lawless." To any sane man the superman must mean "either super-beast or imbecile," and the danger was that any means might be used to arrive at such a figure, all law and convention being ignored. That this Nietzschean idea had been introduced, he thought, proved the need for a higher factor, a religious factor, to promote race culture. For the eugenist, the final end of man was civic usefulness, but, Gerrard believed, man was made for much more than this, for a life that could be reached only by revelation and grace. And while there had been a tendency in the past to use the claims of the other world to the detriment of this end, sound Catholic philosophy had always insisted that the right use of this world was the means to attain the next. "Fine physique, good digestion, clear eye, keen intellect, and indomitable will are gifts of God and are given precisely to enable man, under the influence of grace, to develop his spiritual nature. . . . We have to seek first the kingdom of the spirit, and then all the riches of the psychic and physical kingdom are added unto us to aid us in our quest."[75]

To the danger of the feebleminded, which was one of the most urgent concerns of the eugenists, there were only two basic defenses: segregation or sterilization. Gerrard admitted that the state had the power to force compulsory segregation and surgery (sterilization) if necessary for the good of the community. He thought, however, that sterilization would be both useless and harmful, eliminating one evil only to generate others, especially as it would probably be done against the will of the person. He pointed out that even Saleeby did not promote it, and that there were many successful examples in Britain, America, Belgium, and Bavaria where the feebleminded had been voluntarily segregated and had no need of surgery. He believed that these institutions constituted a strong practical argument for compulsory segregation as long as there were safeguards.

> Feeble-mindedness is so often a cause of poverty, and poverty so often a cause of feeble-mindedness, that there is a danger of confusing one with the other. Catholics, therefore, need to exercise a strong vigilance lest, under pretence of eugenic reform, the rights of the poor are infringed. Poverty is no bar to the sacrament of marriage. The poor, and even the destitute, as such, have every right to the joys and protection of married life. Destitution is largely due to economic causes. In so far as the poor are the victims of these causes and are not subject to racial defects mentioned above, so far they must be protected against the indiscriminate zealot who would deprive them of their most precious rights.[76]

75. Ibid., 56.

76. Ibid., 62.

Besides, there was so much that was unknown about heredity. Karl Pearson, the expert in biometrics, had said that the Eugenics Education Society should "wait half a century before beginning to move, so imperfect is the exact knowledge upon which it has to go."

The difference between the eugenics of Galton and that of the Catholic Church, Gerrard believed, was that the Church was more far-reaching in what it was trying to achieve. It declared that the root of degeneracy was human sin and proposed virtue as the root cause of its healing. He pointed out that even doctors to whom he had spoken admitted the importance of the human will in helping mental disorders: prescribed remedies were generally no good if the patient did not put his will into it. He did not believe that most of the medical profession had anything to offer as a will-stimulus, while the Church's entire sacramental system was ordered to "this quickening of the will-energy": "to put the human will in the right direction and to keep it there."

> Guided by this supernatural principle of selection, aiming solely at the development of spiritual life, the Church is able to carry out her own system of eugenics. She is able in the first place to promote and control the eugenic principle of selection in marriage. Sir Francis Galton need not have gone to such pains to demonstrate that rational selection in marriage is possible. It is obvious that the Church promotes it and controls it perhaps more effectually than any other organization on the earth. . . . As a matter of positive eugenics she teaches that marriage is a sacrament through which is conveyed a divine strength enabling the married pair to perform all the duties of their state. As a matter of negative eugenics she places impediments against undesirable unions.[77]

Many of these impediments pertained directly to animal and psychic well-being, but even the religious ones were of importance, for it was only through the religious sanction that the other impediments were enforced.

The Church's eugenic instinct was also manifested, Gerrard believed, in her treatment of "racial poisons." While the Church encouraged legislation that would protect the workman from unhealthy environments, it aimed at going to the source. "The only real preventative of alcohol poisoning is the cardinal virtue of temperance. The only real preventative of venereal disease is the angelic virtue of purity. The only real preventative of lead poisoning is the rightly trained conscience of the employer."[78] Police regulations were only for

77. Ibid., 64.

78. Ibid., 65.

the degenerate, while the Church's goal was the perfection of man. He was perturbed by the peculiar blindness of Galton, Saleeby, and the dean of St. Paul's, William Inge ("the Gloomy Dean" was one of the most prominent clerical supporters of eugenics), who wished to eliminate the Church's practice of virginity and celibacy, and blamed it for the brutalization of the human race, particularly in the "Dark Ages." "Their assumption all through is that man is primarily and essentially an animal nature and that his betterment is chiefly if not entirely a matter of germ-plasm, milk, fresh air, sentimental art, and illuminated certificates."[79] They ignored the fact that man was essentially a spiritual being and that his betterment was therefore a matter of spiritual forces. Also, while heredity was an important factor, so were environment and education. That being so, the monks and nuns of the Dark Ages did well both for themselves and for the race. By retiring to cloistral solitude they were able to perfect themselves by mastering their appetites, cultivating their moral and spiritual powers, and training themselves in art and literature. The fruits of such accomplishments could then be passed on to others. Gerrard believed that this was equally true today and that these celibates were the force that leavened the whole lump of the Catholic body. A spiritualized and divinely illumined moral force was the prime factor in sound eugenics, and the ideals enunciated by the Church were the surest guide for the Catholic. "His belief in the Communion of the Saints is his guarantee. He knows that in every age in the past his Church has produced the only supermen worthy of the name, the great experts in moral excellence. If the nineteenth century can witness a Curé d'Ars and a Don Bosco, the twentieth and every other century can do likewise."[80]

Playing on the popularity of eugenics, a contributor in 1916, Dr. Alice Vowe Johnson, at the end of her discussion of the causes and remedies for the high infant mortality among the urban poor, pointed out that with the precipitous birthrate decline (from 36.3 per thousand in 1876 to 21.9 per thousand in 1916), and the obvious class differential, it behooved the nation, if it wanted to prevent race deterioration, to see that everyone was well housed, well fed, and well educated, and receiving an adequate wage.[81]

79. Ibid., 66.

80. Ibid., 68.

81. Alice Vowe Johnson, "Infant Mortality and the Population," ibid. (April 1916): 324–35. She also wished to pull down the unsanitary, overcrowded parts of towns, stop the production of luxuries, redistribute the profits of industry more evenly, and attract people back to the land. Johnson,

After the report of the Royal Commission on the Care and the Control of the Feeble-Minded came out in 1908, nothing was done for a number of years, as more important topics such as the Parliament Act, national insurance, and Home Rule for Ireland absorbed Parliament's attention.[82] But in 1912 the government introduced its Mental Deficiency Bill. In a second article, "The Mental Deficiency Bill," Gerrard discussed the proposal, then still in committee. His approach was very different now, for he no longer spoke the language of eugenics or had many kind words for it. He pointed out that, according to the commission's report, out of a population of 32 million for England and Wales (the bill only applied there) there were, apart from certified lunatics, some 149,000 mental defectives; of these, about half (66,509) were in urgent need of care and assistance. While the bill had many good clauses and while there was a crying need for something to be done for these people, Gerrard saw behind the bill a darker purpose. "There is an ulterior purpose, which may be said to be the improvement of the race by the elimination of certain classes which are considered to be worthless to the State. Or, to put the case less pleasantly, the purpose is to enable the Eugenics Society to make experiment in some of its pet theories. The hand of the Eugenist is in evidence throughout the text."[83] He believed that there were too many loopholes in the bill, so that even if the eugenists didn't get legislation exactly to their liking, they could still achieve their purposes. He lamented that in America laws sterilizing the feebleminded had been passed quietly, pushed by a few enthusiasts, while the nation remained apathetic, and it was his intention that this would not happen in Britain. It was good that the government provided funds for the support of the feebleminded, who had often been left without proper care, but he objected to the looseness of the definition of feeblemindedness, the ease with which a person might be certified as such, and the unlimited power given the government to segregate someone. Since the bill included, for the first time, powers of compulsory detention and segregation of the feebleminded, even for life, its extension of state power could be quite dangerous. Gerrard believed that segregation encroached unduly on the

educated at the London School of Medicine for Women and at Vienna, receiving her M.D. at Bruges in 1900, was an assistant medical inspector to the Board of Education of the London County Council.

82. For the Mental Deficiency Act, see Thomson, *Problem of Mental Deficiency,* 36–51, and Searle, *Eugenics and Politics in Britain,* 106–11,

83. T. J. Gerrard, "The Mental Deficiency Bill," *Dublin Review* (Jan. 1913): 21.

natural law concerning marriage and exaggerated the rights of the state. The regulations also had a purely materialistic conception of race betterment and gave too wide a berth to the officials who would administer the law. While the Church believed that in some cases segregation was necessary for the common good, it was much more difficult to determine what degree of feeblemindedness demanded it. The law also prohibited the segregated feebleminded person from marriage, and to this Gerrard objected strongly. If one accepted that feeblemindedness was hereditary (as the law did), one should apply to it, since the Holy Office had given no guidance as of yet on the topic, the same principles that had been applied to another serious disorder believed to be transmissible—leprosy. While the Church allowed for the segregation of lepers, it also allowed them to marry.

He stated that the law had to protect the good of the person as well as the good of society, and while one was clearly protected by this bill, the other was not. Moral theology tended to discourage the marriage of defectives, but unless the chief end of marriage, the procreation and education of children, was precluded, marriage would still be lawful even if not expedient. "If a man, therefore, is unable through mental defect, to keep himself, his wife and family in reasonable and frugal comfort, if he is incapable of attending to the spiritual, mental, and bodily education of his children, then, and only then, in the interests of the community, may the civil power prevent him from marrying."[84] Marriage was also a remedy for concupiscence, and since sin was a far greater evil than defective children, it would be better for defectives to marry than to fall into sin for the lack of it. If sin could be prevented by marriage, then the Church must stand for the right of the individual to marry. If she would not enforce celibacy for lepers then she could not do so for those feebleminded who were not obviously and immediately a danger to the community. That they were not an obvious and immediate danger, Gerrard believed, was proved by Galton's law, that even among the lower stratum there was a tendency to "recover itself and to retrace its steps toward mediocrity." There was no danger, therefore, of the race becoming a race of degenerates. He could point to other authorities who also warned of the anti-eugenic dangers of tampering with marriage. In any case, too much was still unknown to make such radical demands. Also, there seemed to be evidence that for many of the feebleminded marriage could be a kind of remedy. While the bill did

84. Ibid., 33.

not propose sterilization as such, it did provide, Gerrard thought, an opening for it. He repeated his contention from the earlier article that sterilization was wholly unwarranted because equally good results could be reached by segregation, particularly now that more recent results from America had shown the many limitations, and even drawbacks, of the procedure.

One egregious aspect of the bill, he thought, was the assumption throughout that it would apply only to the poor, leaving the rich degenerate free to propagate his kind while the poor one could not. This was something that Catholics particularly had to keep a watch on, because there were those who explicitly wanted to restrict the fertility of the poorer classes, of which Irish Catholics formed a disproportionate share, believing that the higher fertility of the poor would lead to racial degeneracy. In the end, however, Gerrard reminded his readers that a naturalistic view of the problem was not enough—supernatural virtue would be needed if this question was to be handled properly. The reformer with a purely naturalistic view of life would fall short of all that could be done to help the feebleminded, would fall short of the perfect man that he was called to be.

In the end, the bill was passed in 1913 over the opposition of only eleven MPs, the extreme individualists and the extreme traditionalists. And although it was toned down and slight modifications tightened up some of the language—though not enough to secure Gerrard's approval, as he wrote in a postscript to the article—it generally satisfied the eugenists, who had been consulted on the revisions and whose main demands had been met.[85] But eugenists' hopes of further legislation in their favor were forestalled by the onset of the Great War—a war that they could only see as a biological disaster, since it consumed the nation's finest in staggering numbers.[86]

While the social question was primarily concerned with urban life, some attention was also given to the problems of agricultural life, whose quality had declined profoundly, despite occasional improvements, since the 1870s. The *Dublin* reviewed favorably two studies on agrarian life, both now considered classics: *A History of the English Agricultural Labourer* (1908) by Professor Wil-

85. Searle, *Eugenics and Politics in Britain,* 111.

86. For eugenics and the Great War, see Soloway, *Demography and Degeneration,* 138–62, and his "Eugenics and Pronatalism in Wartime Britain," in *The Upheaval of War: Family, Work and Welfare in Europe, 1914–1918,* ed. Richard Wall and Jay Winter (Cambridge: Cambridge University Press, 1988), 369–88.

helm Hasbach, and *The Village Labourer: 1760–1832* (1911) by J. L. and Barbara Hammond.[87] The first book was praised as "a timely volume, with its apt and full quotations, its orderly and accurate statistics," and as "a veritable godsend." It revealed the "dispiriting tale" of English agriculture and the decline of the peasant and small farmer, beginning with the Reformation ("which robbed them of the institutions which had helped them in their time of need"), which led to the destruction of the yeoman, the depressing of small landowners into laborers, as enclosures intensified, and the "nameless horrors suffered by the luckless laborers during the eighteenth and nineteenth centuries, and the end is not yet." The reviewer also believed that the book would supply "abundant matter for thought" by showing that private individual land holdings, and not collectivism, was the way to solve the agricultural problem. The second book was praised as being "brilliantly successful" as social history, based on "material of unimpeachable authority and authenticity," revealing the little-known story of the social and economic degradation of the largest class in the country, the peasantry, and the destruction of England's village communities in the late eighteenth and early nineteenth centuries, "devised by leading politicians, sanctioned by a Church, and carried out by Act of Parliament."

Finally, in the January 1914 number, Bevil Tollemache discussed the Conservative Party's response to the problems of agriculture.[88] He admitted that in the massive enclosures of the late eighteenth and early nineteenth centuries the foundations of village life had been totally displaced, leading eventually to the depopulation of the countryside, and that many small holders and cottagers suffered real distress as the system of agriculture was restructured. But he also admitted the necessity of this transformation: without it there would have been a national disaster, as the old system could not have produced enough food. While for a time agriculture was helped by the greater efficiency, investment, scientific methods, and machinery that had resulted from the reorganization, a series of bad harvests, combined with the easy importation

87. B. O. P., "Some Recent Books," *Dublin Review* (Oct. 1909): 448–50, and H. L. M., "Some Recent Books," ibid. (April 1912): 390–92. See Stewart A. Weaver, *The Hammonds: A Marriage in History* (Stanford: Stanford University Press, 1997); and Victor Feske, *From Belloc to Churchill: Private Scholars, Public Culture, and the Crisis of British Liberalism, 1900–1939* (Chapel Hill: University of North Carolina Press, 1996), 98–136. In 1917 the Hammonds published *The Town Labourer* and in 1919 *The Skilled Labourer.*

88. Bevil Tollemache, "The Conservative Party and Agriculture," *Dublin Review* (Jan. 1914): 125–48.

of cheap foodstuffs from abroad in the late Victorian period, had dealt a final blow to English agriculture. Agricultural prices had improved lately but agriculture had not, as landlords had not only not taken advantage of any price increases but were selling out because of Liberal assaults on property and the fear of further deprecations. The result was greater insecurity among tenants and further agricultural weakness. The only thing that could remove the twin evils of rural depopulation and agricultural insecurity, Tollemache believed, was to have the tenants purchase their holdings with state help, the landlord willing and at a just price.

Tollemache pointed out that the loss of value in land and the Liberal campaign against landlords had led the landlords to start pulling out. Ever since 1909 land had become an obvious area for Liberal assault, and in October 1913 Lloyd George officially began his land campaign.[89] While the Great War would put this campaign into "cold storage," it was clear that land could no longer be considered the bulwark of security, and in the period just before and after the war there occurred a transfer of land the scale of which rivaled that of "the Norman Conquest and the Dissolution of the Monasteries."[90]

89. See H. V. Emy, "The Land Campaign: Lloyd George as Social Reformer, 1909–14," in *Lloyd George: Twelve Essays,* ed. A. J. P. Taylor (New York: Hamilton, 1971), 35–68; and Roy Douglas, *Land, People and Politics: A History of the Land Question in the United Kingdom, 1878–1952* (New York: St. Martin's Press, 1976), 154–68.

90. See Cannadine, *Decline and Fall of the British Aristocracy,* 704. See ibid., 88–138.

6 LITERATURE

All the great quarterlies were literary quarterlies, discussing every genre of writing and reviewing the newest books. The *Dublin* followed that tradition, and while much of its discussion of literature had no particularly Catholic or religious note, its being a Catholic journal did add a new dimension. It not only tried to present the best of Catholic literature and, in its contributors, the best of Catholic literary ability and critical insight, but even when it covered other authors, it could offer a different perspective. In the October 1912 number Ward discussed Newman's 1854 lecture "English Catholic Literature," in which Newman described one of the special objects of a Catholic university as the promotion of a Catholic literature in the English language. It would be a literature, Newman asserted, that would not be polemical or narrowly sectarian in outlook, but would include "all subjects of literature whatever, treated as a Catholic would treat them, and as he only can treat them."[1] While there were some subjects that were not, at least not intrinsically, areas for a Catholic literature, such as the pure sciences—there was no need for a "Catholic Euclid or a Catholic Newton"—there obviously were many areas where Catholics could

1. Wilfrid Ward, "English Catholic Literature," *Dublin Review* (Oct. 1912): 269–76. This was originally a paper read at the Norwich Catholic Congress in August 1912. See John Henry Newman, *The Idea of a University Defined and Illustrated (I. In Nine Discourses Delivered to the Catholics of Dublin; II. In Occasional Lectures and Essays Addressed to the Members of the Catholic University)* (London: Longmans, Green, 1907), 295–330.

contribute something distinctive. Ward agreed with Newman in all this and added that Catholic literature would show its greatest value not when it aimed directly at an argument for religion but proved itself from its power and truthfulness to life. Ward's goal was to make the *Dublin* a Catholic journal in that sense, faithful but not sectarian; and the breadth of his vision is reflected in its discussion of literature.

The range of literature covered, in both articles and shorter reviews, was broad. The giants of the past were given their due. Thus, for example, during the Tennyson centenary there were two articles on him, and two on Thackeray during his centenary. While a great many authors were discussed, Catholic writers not surprisingly received greater attention than would have been normal. Contemporary literature was much more likely to be discussed in the "Some Recent Books" section than in the main section, and among the shorter reviews books of significant literary value could be found side by side with more ephemeral ones. Some of the most successful books of the day, such as Henry de Stacpoole's *The Blue Lagoon* (the best-seller of 1908) were not reviewed at all, and even favored authors did not have all their works considered. The *Dublin*'s concerns were overwhelmingly European, and English literature received much more attention than foreign.

Among the "triumvirate" of great Edwardian writers, Galsworthy, Bennett, and Forster, only the first two received any notice. John Galsworthy (1867–1933), famous for a collection of novels that make up *The Forsyte Saga,* did produce a few major novels at this time but only one, *The Patrician* (1910), was reviewed. The *Dublin* found the gray world revealed there appalling and the book unprofitable reading except for the fact that it might inspire in the reader a desire to be of help to such a needy world.[2] Arnold Bennett (1867–1931), however, was a great favorite. Famous for his novels set in the Potteries of the Midlands, in what he called the Five Towns, his realism had great appeal. *The Old Wives' Tale* (1908) was praised as one of his best novels.[3] "Mr Bennett makes these people act, feel and think only the most ordinary things; he shews us all their little failings, their absurdities and weaknesses, all their good instincts and humdrum virtues. He interests us deeply in their fortunes, and he makes us love his men and women. He is entirely un-morbid. He never sneers at human nature; he is amused at its limitations and also full of ad-

2. S., "Some Recent Books," *Dublin Review* (July 1911): 190–91.

3. C. B., "Some Recent Books," ibid. (July 1909): 196–98.

miration for its courage and goodness."[4] *Helen with the High Hand* (1910) was also set in the Five Towns, but it was a slight work, and in comparison with his earlier novels of this locale was not worth the telling.[5] While *The Old Wives' Tale* had a certain amount of cynicism and ridicule of human weakness, there was no trace of vulgarity or *banalité.* Unfortunately the heroine of this novel was thoroughly vulgar, unscrupulous about money, a liar, selfish, domineering, vain, and ostentatious, and the reviewer was not really sorry to part company with her. He warned that Bennett could not expect his readers "to accept commonplace characters simply because they have a flavour of the Five Towns and are set with that atmosphere," and said that he expected better of him who had done "work of such rare excellence" before this. *Clayhanger* (1910), also set in the Five Towns, was praised for its faithful and minute analysis of character, motive, and circumstance, and for its kindly recognition of the difficulties of human relations and the mixture of nobility and meanness in the human heart. "As in the *Old Wives' Tale,* the narrative is minute and unsparing in detail, and yet not one triviality is out of place. We love Clayhanger, though his creator spares no pains to show us how his actions were always feeble, though his impulses were generous."[6] The reviewer particularly looked forward to the two sequels promised at the end of the book, where the story would be retold, first from the point of view of the old father and then from that of the woman loved and wooed by Edwin Clayhanger. *Hilda Lessways* (1911), the later sequel, was praised as Bennett in his best vein and as being among his best novels, up there with *The Old Wives' Tale* and *Clayhanger,* though the reviewer believed that it should have come before *Clayhanger,* to which it was a sequel.[7] He also lamented that those parts of the story told earlier in *Clayhanger* from Edwin's point of view generally seemed flat when told from Hilda's.

H. G. Wells (1866–1946) had already published his most popular works, among them *The Time Machine* (1895), *The Island of Dr. Moreau* (1896), *The Invisible Man* (1897), and *The War of the Worlds* (1898), and he continued to publish throughout this period. He received more notice than other writers, but it was not always positive. Thus the reviewer, having already read Wells's earlier novel *Kipps* (1905), picked up *Tono-Bungay* (1909) with anticipation but

4. Ibid., 197.
5. C. B., "Some Recent Books," ibid. (July 1910): 210–11.
6. C. B., "Some Recent Books," ibid. (Jan. 1911): 196.
7. C. B., "Some Recent Books," ibid. (Jan. 1912): 204–5.

ended "with a sense of something very disagreeable being over, of having escaped from an unprofitable atmosphere, and a set of very uncongenial persons, in fact, with a feeling of unmitigated relief."[8] The book was written in an "unenviable and wholly unedifying spirit," concerning a man who was "selfish, heartless, sensual and entirely undisciplined." The best that could be said for the novel was that it showed "the ugliness and waste of lives led without the discipline of religion." Original sin was recognized and dissected under a microscope, he continued, not as something to be combated but as a curiosity that could add zest to your life. Not a single character showed any self-discipline or self-restraint, and the only kind of love displayed by the characters, except for one, was base and selfish. Insofar as religion showed itself in the story, its manner of presentation would be blasphemous were it not so ignorant. The "narrowness and dullness of perception of the book" dragged "every element of human life down to its own base level," and its whole spirit was "materialism at its ugliest and basest." Wells's *Anne Veronica* (1909), a novel, notorious in its time, about a sexually liberated woman, was never even reviewed. Nor was the less objectionable *History of Mr. Polly* (1910). *The World Set Free* (1914), a scientific romance set a hundred years in the future, however, was well received.[9] The reviewer remarked on Wells's sense of the supernatural, which flickered beneath his "fertile and creative imagination" and which every once in a while shed a bit of light along humanity's path, but of which he was afraid "as of yet" and which he would hastily extinguish "under a bushel."

While Mrs. Humphry Ward (1851–1920) is best known for works such as *Robert Elsmere* (1888) and *Helbeck of Bannisdale* (1898), she published novels throughout the Edwardian period and into the war. As a recent biographer pointed out, by 1905 she could plausibly claim to be the most famous living novelist in the world.[10] Russian prisoners in the war with Japan asked for her novels above all others, and Tolstoy considered her England's greatest writer of fiction. In this period, however, her reputation began to slide and her novels no longer were such critical and financial successes. *Fenwick's Career* (1906), *Diana Mallory* (1908), *The Case of Richard Meynell* (1911), *Canadian Born* (1910), *The Coryston Family* (1913), and *Delia Blanchflower* (1915) received mixed reviews in the *Dublin*.[11] The reviewer of *The Coryston Family*,

8. C. B., "Some Recent Books," ibid. (April 1909): 426–27.
9. C. B., "Some Recent Books," ibid. (Oct. 1914): 406–07.
10. Sutherland, *Mrs Humphry Ward*, 260.
11. G. B., "Some Recent Books," *Dublin Review* (July 1906): 198–200; S., "Some Recent

however, while lamenting the defects of Mrs. Ward's style, asserted that "in the face of a rising fashion of deprecation," she could not be ignored as a writer because of "her intellectual force and grasp of characters and situations now too often undervalued."

In response to the perception of the weakening of public mores (which accompanied the fears of national decline and threat), the National Social Purity Crusade was begun in 1901 with the goal of raising the general moral tone of the nation. But it was not until 1908, with the creation of the Forward Movement within it (the Forward Movement for Purity), that it took on real vigor, a main focus being the suppression of unwholesome literature.[12] William Barry wrote an article for the January 1909 number describing the spread of pernicious literature and encouraging Catholics to join the Social Purity Crusade.[13] He considered the spread of this evil literature a "national danger" that should be met both by new laws and by personal activity to encourage "that true manliness which is not yet extinct among us." He felt this danger was particularly great for impressionable children. Barry cautioned that abusive epithets would most certainly be thrown at the promoters of this work, but he deeply believed that this crusade was clearly necessary for the survival of the nation.

No State will last long which has thrown the foundation of morals into a debating society composed of its citizens. There must be a social creed, with sanctions binding on the conscience; a religion of honour, purity, courage, self-denial, reverence for that which is venerable, and tenderness for that which deserves pity. You cannot found a Republic on the licence of sex, the aberrations of passion, the freedom of suicide. Luxurious America is rotting before our eyes. England, serious at heart, we will believe, with shining examples of heroism from the past, and guiding voices not yet wholly silenced, is nevertheless becoming to its own children a portent of frivolity. Christian and Pagan, which will it be in another generation? . . . If literature be a symptom, we are destined to struggle for our faith in the furnace seven times heated of a Pagan democracy. If it be a cause, and it surely is one of the greatest, no efforts can be too speedy or too strenuous to prevent its chief instrument of propaganda, romantic fiction, from poisoning the sources of a better life by its atheism and ethical disease.[14]

Books," ibid. (Jan. 1909): 196–98; K., "Some Recent Books," ibid. (July 1910): 199–201; S., "Some Recent Books," ibid. (April 1912): 419–21; S., "Some Recent Books," ibid. (April 1914): 378–80; and O., "Some Recent Books," ibid. (April 1915): 406–8.

12. See Hynes, *Edwardian Turn of Mind,* 254–306.

13. William Barry, "The Censorship of Fiction," *Dublin Review* (Jan. 1909): 111–31.

14. Ibid., 131.

Among the novels attacked at this time was Compton Mackenzie's *Sinister Street,* whose availability some of the main circulating libraries tried to limit. The headmaster of Eton criticized it in a long letter to the *Times,* declaring that "sanity and upright manliness are destroyed, not only by the reading of obscene stuff, but by a premature interest in sex matters, however excited."[15] Published in two volumes, the first in September 1913 and the second in November 1914, this *Catcher in the Rye* of its generation was a popular success and received critical acclaim.[16] C. C. Martindale praised the first volume in the January 1914 number as being uncannily accurate in capturing the way boys really speak and in describing their mentality.[17] Some critics would see this as a condemnation. "The more truly he can describe, they suggest, such a mentality, the less he ought to do so." The protagonist Michael Fane was called a "prig" and "unhealthy-minded," but Martindale believed that all clever boys have a priggish phase that they grow out of and that Michael was "a singularly clean-minded boy" whose instincts were shown to be rather sound when put in certain unwholesome situations. He found much more "unhealthiness" in Arnold Lunn's *Harrovians* (1913), "a cynical and dispiriting book." And if Michael has his moods, what boy has not? "Boyhood and adolescence are generally gusty times, when in the general hurricane a few fixed points, at most, can be held. They are supplied, to a Catholic, by his dogma and his sacramental practice. It is amazing to the unprejudiced eye how conscience, instinct, and unreasoned tradition carry boys through, even unhelped by Catholic privileges." "Anyhow, to have drawn with utter fidelity the swing of emotion, the unreasoning depression, the bursts of misery, ecstasy, brutality, and poetry, plunging upwards through the normal and commonplace, is splendid art."[18]

Martindale also praised the descriptions of Michael's religious phases, particularly his High Church period, for their seriousness. "*Sinister Street* is a religious document of the first quality. It may not be a book for young ladies, but

15. Quoted in Andro Linklater, *Compton Mackenzie: A Life* (New York: B. Blackwell, 1987), 126. See Compton Mackenzie, *My Life and Times: Octave Four, 1907–1915* (London: Chatto and Windus, 1965), 192–202.

16. Walter Allen, "London Letter," *New York Times Book Review,* March 3, 1968, 20, cited in D. J. Dooley, *Compton Mackenzie* (New York: Twayne, 1974), 9. In the United States the first volume was published as *Youth's Encounter* and the second as *Sinister Street.* The novel remained popular throughout the 1920s and 1930s.

17. C. C. Martindale, "Psychology in the Concrete," *Dublin Review* (Jan. 1914): 22–32.

18. Ibid., 27.

it is emphatically a book for priests. Rarely anywhere have I seen attempted this portrayal of the mystical *éclosion* in a boy's soul." He believed Michael to be "incurably spiritual and a frank mystic" and wondered where the boy would end up in volume two. He doubted that it would be High Church Anglicanism. "Be the Roman system right or wrong, the English imitation *is* undoubtedly just an imitation, and no real thing. Michael had a soul which, whatever its destiny, could not put up with imitation work. He might grow to feel, at the end of illusion upon illusion dissipated, that there was no reality; but he would not at the end accept as reality what was no such thing." There was only one place that he could find true liberty and life, Martindale maintained: Rome.[19]

Martindale was remarkably prescient, for in the second volume Michael realizes the incapacity of High Church Anglicanism to convert the real sinner and at the end he quite literally goes to Rome to become a Catholic priest. This volume was reviewed in the April 1915 number, and the reviewer was touched with a "poignant pain" by the "very beautiful" and singularly successful account of Oxford life, now suspended by the war, her colleges emptied, her halls filled with soldiers and her "digs" with refugees.[20] He praised Mackenzie for his "verbal realism" and believed that the first half, the Oxford half, would hold a permanent place in literature. In the second half, however, he did not find Michael's attempts to recover his lost love, Lily, from "the underworld" convincing. If this quest, "full of self-sacrifice, pure and self-effacing," was born of Michael's unconscious priestly vocation, as was suggested, it singularly failed to affect anyone deeply, including Michael. He maintained that if Mackenzie had been at his best when he took him through this "inferno," described "in the most revolting detail, the characters would have come alive and reacted on each other." "There is no one to love and no one to hate in the last part of *Sinister Street.* The sights, the smells, the noises are acutely repulsive, but the personalities to one reader at least seem to be repulsive outlines on a flat service."[21]

Martindale was right to see the profound religious impulse of the novel,

19. Ibid., 28, 31–32.

20. S., "Some Recent Books," ibid. (April 1915): 395–97. Max Beerbohm believed that there was no book on Oxford like it. "It gives you the actual Oxford *experience.* What Mackenzie has miraculously done is to make you feel what each *term* was like." Quoted in Linklater, *Compton Mackenzie,* 132.

21. S., "Some Recent Books," *Dublin Review* (April 1915): 397.

for that was how Mackenzie himself saw it. During the controversy over the book, Mackenzie wrote, "If a boy exists who can possibly read it, he will find himself left at the end with a definite prejudice in favour of the Christian religion."[22] And, in fact, in April 1914 Mackenzie himself entered the Church.

After English literature, French literature received the greatest attention. P. J. Connolly, S.J., wrote on the religious trilogy of Joris Karl Huysmans and Ferdinand Brunetière. Lady Ashburne wrote on Charles Péguy. F. Y. Eccles (b. 1871), an old friend of Belloc from Oxford and like him of mixed French and English parentage, on Maurice Barrès, Anatole France ("The Mantle of Voltaire"), René Bazin, Ronsard, and other French literary topics. There is even an early review of the future Nobel laureate François Mauriac (1885–1970). His *La robe prétexte* was praised for its ability to convey a Catholic sensibility without becoming a religious tract.[23] "Witty, easy, very amusing, poetical only because so well composed and so free from fine writing, almost every chapter is a *poème en prose*—which impression happily lingers after one shuts the book, all the more happily that it has not obtruded itself during the reading of it." The reviewer deplored "the impure habits of thought and speech" that had too often "blurred the French novelist's sense of the finer shades of sentiment." While Mauriac does write "of realities, purity, desire, puberty, piety, friendship, calf-love, Catholic love," neither he nor his heroes "have ever quite abdicated their royal prerogative, their kinship with Our Lord." Unlike "the neurotic striplings of scores of English novels," they did not find themselves "through those experiments in sin which they call experience." He believed that the novel would probably disturb and displease Catholics less than it would scandalize unbelievers. "Did it not shock the reviewer in the *Temps*—because it was neither a panegyric nor an apology, but an examination of conscience?"

The classics were also not ignored, the most distinguished contributions coming from John Swinnerton Phillimore (1873–1926), classical scholar and poet.[24] His articles on Leonidas of Tarentum, Crinagoras of Mitylene, and As-

22. Quoted in Linklater, *Compton Mackenzie,* 126. As Linklater makes clear, "the religious impulse was uppermost" in Mackenzie's mind.

23. "Some Recent Books," *Dublin Review* (Jan. 1915): 201–2.

24. Phillimore was educated at Westminster School (where he first met Reginald Balfour, the assistant editor of Ward's *Dublin,* and F. Y. Eccles) and Oxford, where he gained a first in Classical Moderations (1893) and in *Litterae Humaniores* (1895). While at Oxford he became a friend of Belloc, and later contributed to Belloc's *Essays in Liberalism* (London: Cassell, 1897). He gained the chair of Greek at the University of Glasgow in 1899 (following Gilbert Murray), and transferred to

cepiades, poets from the *Greek Anthology*, were models of their kind: interesting, light, appreciative, and accessible to the lay reader. His interest in the classics and Catholicism (he converted in 1905) was beautifully expressed in his article discussing the literary significance of Thomas More and the baleful effects of his execution on the development of humanism in England.[25]

While non-Catholic and non-English literature was important, the *Dublin* was at its best in its presentation of English Catholic literature, in such authors as Hilaire Belloc, G. K. Chesterton, Francis Thompson, and Robert Hugh Benson. The "Chesterbelloc" is one of the most famous of Edwardian literary figures, a creation of G. B. Shaw in a 1908 controversy over socialism with G. K. Chesterton and Hilaire Belloc in the *New Age*.[26] This strange, mythical, hybrid creature, a "pantomine elephant" whose front legs were Belloc's and whose hind legs were Chesterton's, was meant to show the unnatural union of men who were so different even in their agreement.

Hilaire Belloc (1870–1953) was a major figure in the Edwardian literary world. He was parodied, as was Chesterton, in Max Beerbohm's *A Christmas Garland* (1912) along with the likes of Hardy, Wells, Kipling, James, and Shaw. He was also a frequent contributor to Ward's *Dublin*. As a man of letters he wrote poetry, satires, travel literature, and history.[27] While Belloc was a fine poet, only one of his poems ("Courtesy") graced the *Dublin*. His political satires *Mr Clutterbuck's Election* (1908) and *Pongo and the Bull* (1910) were generally well received, though a certain mercilessness or bitterness of tone and gross exaggeration were deprecated.[28] His travel book *The Pyrenees* (1909) was

the chair of humanity (Latin) in 1906, which he held to his death. See Steuart N. Miller, "John Swinnerton Phillimore: A Memoir," *Dublin Review* (winter 1960–1961): 316–34, and *Wiseman Review* (spring 1961): 23–47.

25. J. S. Phillimore, "Blessed Thomas More and the Arrest of Humanism in England," *Dublin Review* (July 1913): 1–26.

26. G. B. Shaw, "Belloc and Chesterton," *New Age* (Feb. 15, 1908): 309–10. For a more recent evaluation of the Chesterbelloc, see Samuel Hynes, "The Chesterbelloc," in *Edwardian Occasions: Essays on English Writing in the Early Twentieth Century* (New York: Oxford University Press, 1972), 80–90.

27. For an evaluation of Belloc's literary career, see Michael H. Markel, *Hilaire Belloc* (Boston: Twayne, 1982).

28. S., "Some Recent Books," ibid. (Oct. 1908): 401–2, and S., "Some Recent Books," ibid. (April 1911): 393–95. Of *Pogo and the Bull* the reviewer wrote: "Mr Belloc is exposing the futility of our present Parliamentary system, and gives us, under the disguise of wild caricature, an explanation of what he believes to be its secret workings." There was no review of his third political satire, *A Change in the Cabinet* (London: Methuen, 1909).

also reviewed favorably.[29] A collection of his journalism, *On Nothing and Kindred Subjects* (1908), was praised, his essays manifesting a literary solidity and permanence.

The writing is elastic and spontaneous; *dictated* English, one would say, but the instrument well played and with an increased literary faculty which will satisfy Mr Belloc's many admirers that for all his extraordinary copiousness the brew does not grow small. We recognize the satirist of *Emmanuel Burden* in several political skits; the imaginative *chemineau* of *The Path to Rome* and *Hills and the Sea,* in others; and not least, an excellent poet in the anonymous but easily divined author of the verse quotations in an essay entitled *On Coming to an End.* It needs no great insight or foresight to assert that this little ship is rigged and provisioned for a long voyage. Pathos, satiric humour, fancy, right reason that knows how to preach and yet never wear a sad face: if these cannot make a book live, then welcome the next destroyer of libraries. But the modern books are not many which you can pick up for five minutes and be the happier and the riper.[30]

While Belloc's skill covered a number of genres, his special interest was history. He had taken a first in history at Oxford in 1895 and had hoped to gain a fellowship at All Souls from which he could overthrow the Whig view of history from within. His failure to become a don, however, embittered him against academic historians and forced him to live by his pen, often writing far more than was good for him or his reputation. History remained his great interest, and his beliefs concerning the writing of history were manifested both in his larger works and in his articles for the *Dublin.*[31]

His *Marie Antoinette* (1909) received lavish praise as perfectly evoking not only the character of Marie Antoinette, in all her virtues and faults, but the whole sweep of the drama of the events, both politically and in people's lives.[32] His "character-drawing" and descriptive passages were superb. The reviewer also lauded Belloc for being "refreshingly contemptuous of certain kinds of academic arrogance and political feebleness" that existed even at the present day. His collection of historical sketches, *The Eye-witness* (1908), was also generally praised.[33] Other historical works were not reviewed, however, such as

29. B. D., "Some Recent Books," ibid. (Oct. 1909): 453–54.

30. J., "Some Recent Books," ibid. (July 1908): 210–11. Other collections of journalism—*On Everything* (London: Methuen, 1909), *On Anything* (London: Constable, 1910), and *On Something* (London: Methuen, 1910)—were not reviewed.

31. For Belloc's view of history, see Feske, *From Belloc to Churchill,* 15–60.

32. B., "Some Recent Books," *Dublin Review* (Jan. 1910): 193–95.

33. M. W. [Maisie Ward], "Some Recent Books," ibid. (Jan. 1909): 200–202.

his respected volume on the French Revolution from the Home University Library (1911), his volumes on the great military battles at Blenheim (1911), Malplaquet (1911), and Waterloo (1912), and his history of the battles fought on English soil, *Warfare in England* (1912). Belloc did, however, contribute an article on the Battle of Waterloo to the *Dublin.*

Belloc not only wrote history, he wrote about its importance and its presentation in the *Dublin.*[34] Men write history, he maintained, because the life of man is communal and organic; because men are what they are because of what came before them; because the past is paternal and therefore creative. The past is our authority and author, and a knowledge of it is necessary if man were to be man at all. A society whose history was neglected became weak, and a society whose history was false became diseased. "In a word we must have good history as we must have bread."[35] Mere historical chronicle, which gave only the bald facts, was by its very simplicity useless because it assumed in the reader a perfect knowledge of the society described and of the terms in which the description was made. A second and much more useful sort of history attempted to resurrect the distant past in its detail and atmosphere, bringing it to life through a combination of detailed information and an exact ordering of the material. "This second method of writing history is necessary to those fevered and highly differentiated epochs which some would call the summits of political development, which others would call the corrupt last stages in which a State trembles with an intense activity before it dies or goes to sleep. Our own time is one of these." Belloc did not think that, until quite lately, this method had really been pursued, even by the historians of the nineteenth century. "They have held a brief, they have replied to opponents, they have discussed difficulties, they have attempted to establish theories, but they have not raised the dead."[36]

The honest historian confused the general reader with masses of technical discussion, taking for granted technical terms and debates of which the general reader was unaware. The partisan historian, he thought, at least satisfied the reader, because whatever the history's deficiencies as truth, at least it was clear and vivid and took a position. Belloc believed that this new kind of history was possible because of our abundant information for so many historical peri-

34. Hilaire Belloc, "On a Method of Writing History," ibid. (July 1911): 143–55.
35. Ibid., 145.
36. Ibid., 147.

ods, though it was the most difficult and laborious to write because of the need to master so much detail in order to make it true and living.

Catholics, he believed, had an advantage in writing history, particularly European history, because of their sense of continuity.[37] Having lived within the reality of the faith, the Catholic historian began with a much greater understanding of the European past because for him the past was still alive and familiar. He made this point in his review of the first volume of the *Cambridge Mediaeval History.*[38] Until recently, he stated, all the great names in historical science were names of those who hated, or at best rejected, "the unifying principle of our European story which unifying principle is the Faith." Even such an able historian as Lingard, who wrote the only "full, detailed and documented history of political events" in England and wrote it in an apologetic and careful tone, was ignored because he was a Catholic. Because of this, history had "gone off the lines." This type of history, because of its anti-Catholic bias, could not answer many of the questions legitimately put to it, and so history was compelled to look again "down the perspective of European history from its starting point," getting into the clothes, or better the skin, "of all that from which we came." The historian of Europe needn't be Catholic, in Belloc's view, but he did have to know the faith that made Europe possible. "All European historians must now, if they are to have any weight, know their Europe and coincidently know not only the name and the form but the soul of Europe as well."[39]

Reviewing J. B. Bury's *History of Freedom of Thought* (1913) gave Belloc an opportunity to criticize not only modern German scholarship, "which combines a mechanical bondage to text with a fantastic ignorance of men's ordinary motives and of what may be called the 'Commonsense' of history," but also the Cambridge History School of which Bury was the head.[40] A person in that position was not only representative of its teaching but in some sense also spoke officially for the university when he adopted a definite position on any historical topic. To understand Bury, therefore, was to understand the university—and its weaknesses.

37. Hilaire Belloc, "Catholicism and History," ibid. (Oct. 1911): 321–28.
38. Hilaire Belloc, "The Entry into the Dark Ages," ibid. (Oct. 1912): 357–69.
39. Ibid., 361.
40. Hilaire Belloc, "Professor Bury's History of Freedom of Thought," ibid. (Jan. 1914): 149–71.

Well, it is the whole meaning of Professor Bury's book, of the moment in which it appears and of the Chair and University from which it is issued that it reposes upon the conviction, the aspect or rather the Creed diametrically opposed to the Catholic, and that he has put the process of these twenty-five centuries as an argument *against* the excellence of Jesus Christ and of His Church.

The process is presented as one in which the mind enjoyed during the early period of doubt certain privileges of inestimable value, lost them for centuries through the evil blight of Catholicism, has slowly recovered them again as the Church slowly died, and will soon in her complete destruction enjoy them fully.

He tells the story of a great love from the standpoint of a heart decayed, describing the quiet time before its advent with approval, its dominion as an accursed hallucination, its breakdown as a release.[41]

Belloc considered this kind of history a singular example of "that bad history which a fanatical temper will often breed." One could write an attack on the Catholic Church that was also good history, but Bury's book lacked the historical accuracy that good history should have: accuracy in the general atmosphere of the events, accuracy in the statement of motive and direction in action, accuracy in the statement of dates, wording of documents, and all such details. Belloc then devoted many pages to examples of its errors in all of these areas, ending the piece with this line: "In face of that sort of thing no comment is necessary and any emphasis would be a weakness."[42]

The *Dublin,* however, did not completely accept Belloc's version of history. In reviewing his continuation of Lingard's *History of England* (Lingard ended his history at 1688, so Belloc took the story to 1910), the reviewer praised it as a worthy conclusion to Lingard, written in a clear, vigorous, and definite style and without "that languid so-called impartiality which leaves the reader wondering what the writer himself really does think on any question."[43] One of the strengths of the book, he thought, was its treatment of Ireland, of the American Revolution, and of military history generally, and the greatest defect was a lack of references. But he also admitted that Belloc's view of modern England would probably cause controversy and criticism. "He tells that the future of England depends on whether or no the power of the Crown can be revived once more; that Englishmen are divided into a capitalist minority and a proletariat majority; that the whole tendency is for the proletariat to be

41. Ibid., 154–55.
42. Ibid., 171.
43. T. W., "Some Recent Books," ibid. (Jan. 1916): 183–85.

compelled by law to labour for the profit of the few; that, in brief, we are approaching the full effects of the Reformation after four hundred years in the permanent and secure re-establishment of economic conditions, which, by whatever the process may be marked, will be in essence servile."[44] This was the view described in Belloc's *The Servile State* (1912). While never saying whether he agreed with Belloc's views, he admitted that many readers would probably differ with these strong judgments, and doubted that the volume would ever be popular despite its many virtues.

By 1906 G. K. Chesterton (1874–1936) had already begun to make a name for himself as an accomplished writer, particularly in journalism.[45] In 1901 he began writing articles for the *Daily News,* where his Saturday column would make his national reputation, and in 1905 he started his weekly column in the *Illustrated London News,* which would run for the next thirty-one years. He became an institution in Fleet Street, with his flowing cloak, wide-brimmed slouch hat, and sword-stick, with his good humor and abundant good talk. From a prosperous middle-class family of house agents of Broad Church, even Unitarian, views, he had progressed, after a period of doubt and crisis, to a strongly pro-Catholic position.[46] We have already seen how greatly Ward appreciated the apologetics of his *Orthodoxy,* and it was through Ward that he gained entrance into the Synthetic Society.[47] While he was superb as a writer of familiar essays for the newspapers, he also wrote verse, novels, biographies, and literary criticism.

Chesterton's work on Dickens was not only widely read but also very well thought of by such critics as G. B. Shaw (a good friend and sparring partner), T. S. Eliot, and Lionel Trilling. In the October 1907 number of the *Dublin,* Mrs. Wilfrid Ward discussed the "realism" of Dickens and Chesterton's

44. Ibid., 185.

45. For his life, see Maisie Ward, *Gilbert Keith Chesterton* (New York: Sheed and Ward, 1943); Dudley Barker, *G. K. Chesterton: A Biography* (London: Stein and Day, 1973); and Joseph Pearce, *Wisdom and Innocence: A Life of G. K. Chesterton* (London: Hodder & Stoughton, 1996).

46. While strictly speaking only an Anglo-Catholic at this time, his opinions were so High Church and his sympathies so pro-Roman that it is often hard to see that he was not. About a dozen years before his conversion (1922), he spoke to Fr. John O'Connor (the original "Fr. Brown") about converting and, at Chesterton's serious illness in 1914, Fr. O'Connor visited him so as to give the last rites but was sent away by Chesterton's wife, Frances. His greatest concern at his conversion in 1922 was how his wife would take it. Frances, who had been so important in the development of Chesterton's Christianity, was received into the Church in 1926.

47. See G. K. Chesterton, *The Autobiography of G. K. Chesterton* (New York: Sheed and Ward, 1936), 268–70.

Charles Dickens (1906).[48] While praising the book, she denied that Dickens's characters were unrealistic, as Chesterton claimed. She thought that Chesterton, because he could not believe in Dickens's characters as men, made them into gods. "The real difficulty in Mr Chesterton's path is that in his heart he believes the great Dickens folk to be too good to be true to life, while he also believes them to be too good not to be true in a higher metaphysical sense. . . . The fact is that Mr Chesterton cannot bring himself to realize that such great men as Mr Weller ever trod the streets of London, and all those must part company with him who know with the deepest conviction that they did. With the increase of civilization, education, international communications and self-consciousness—and no one ever developed self-consciousness in the uneducated as Dickens did—very individual, strongly marked personalities do tend to disappear. But they are not all gone yet, nor ever will, until mankind goes too; but highly cultivated minds, moving constantly amidst educated people whose occupations are intellectual, are the least likely to discover them."[49]

While none of his collected journalism was reviewed in the *Dublin,* Maisie Ward, Wilfrid's daughter and Chesterton's greatest biographer, reviewed two of Chesterton's novels for the journal. *The Man Who Was Thursday: A Nightmare* (1908) was a "very fine parable," she thought, though she criticized its "carelessness and want of literary restraint." It was quite as good as his novel *The Napoleon of Notting Hill* (1904) in its basic idea and general thought, but inferior in form.[50] She believed that the "nightmare" element was rather too excessive and thought some of the humor "vulgar" and unamusing, lowering the tone of the work. It was a book that demanded and would repay careful thought; while there were some sayings that were a little too paradoxical, there were many that would remain "the permanent and thankworthy possession of the reader." Maisie Ward also reviewed Chesterton's novel *The Ball and the Cross* (1909), which she called an "allegorical romance."[51] She admitted that there was much brilliance in this "strange, exciting story"; still it had a number of defects. It was in parts confused and obscure, as if the author had written it in haste rather than by design, and the religious arguments of the story, which made up quite a bit of it, were better put in his earlier books, particularly in his *Orthodoxy.* Also, its main characters presented situations

48. Mrs Wilfrid Ward, "The Realism of Dickens," *Dublin Review* (Oct. 1907): 285–95.
49. Ibid., 287–88.
50. M. W. [Maisie Ward], "Some Recent Books," ibid. (July 1908), 190–91.
51. M. W. [Maisie Ward], "Some Recent Books," ibid. (July 1910): 186–88.

that were not entirely believable. But these were only details "in the working out of a fine thought," for there was much fantastic description and humor, sudden touches of poetry, admirable pictures of many common and uncommon types, and a noble conception that underlined it all despite these defects. She reviewed as well his epic poem *The Ballad of the White Horse* (1911), which she considered a great poem ("an event in the world of literature") and praised it for its beauty, vividness, and pictorial power of narration.[52]

One can see all of Chesterton's strengths and weaknesses in his *Victorian Age in Literature* (1912), which some consider the best short volume on Victorian literature and which was given a very positive review in the July 1913 number.[53] Quoting copiously from the book, the reviewer called it "extraordinarily brilliant" and full of "wonderfully true sayings." It was not without its flaws, however. "Mr Chesterton never stops to explain or defend: he hurries on without drawing breath and is in the midst of a fresh and suggestive passage almost before we are ready with an objection to the last remark but one."[54] In a longer work such defects "might be seriously vexing" but, considering its brevity, the reviewer thought that one should be grateful for so much that was "brilliant, thoughtful and true," remembering that one was listening "to talk, the best we ever heard since Dr Johnson's."

Alice Meynell (1847–1922) was also a major contributor to Ward's *Dublin,* with three poems and five essays on various literary figures (Swinburne, Dickens, Thompson, Tennyson, and the Brontës). A well-known poet, essayist, and journalist around whom a literary coterie of some distinction gathered, Meynell came from a well-to-do family of artistic tastes and converted to Catholicism in 1872.[55] She published her first volume of poetry (*Preludes*) in 1875 and was thereafter an accomplished and prolific author, her essays and poems appearing in leading British and American journals such as the *Pall Mall Gazette,* the *Spectator,* and the *Atlantic Monthly.* She married Wilfrid Meynell, another convert, in 1877 and bore eight children while helping him write and edit the *Weekly Register* (1881–1898) and *Merry England* (1883–1895).

52. M. W. [Maisie Ward], "Some Recent Books," ibid. (Jan. 1912): 193–95.

53. A. de H., "Some Recent Books," ibid. (July 1913): 178–81. Hynes considers this to be so and believes that Chesterton was such an excellent critic of the Victorians because he saw the world as they did, as a moral battlefield. See Hynes, "Chesterbelloc," 85.

54. Ibid., 179.

55. See Viola Meynell, *Alice Meynell, A Memoir* (London: J. Cape, 1929); Anne Kimball Tuell, *Mrs. Meynell and Her Literary Generation* (New York: E. P. Dutton, 1925); and June Badeni, *The Slender Tree: A Life of Alice Meynell* (Padstow: Tabb House, 1981).

Her poems for the *Dublin* were intensely religious, but the literary essays she contributed, while able and well written, could have appeared in any secular publication. Her *Ceres' Runaway* (a 1909 collection of essays), her collected *Poems* (1909), and *Essays* (1914) were all given very positive reviews.[56] While her contributions certainly added to the prestige of the journal, the work of a member of her circle, Francis Thompson, was more significant.

Francis Thompson (1859–1907) was a child of devout convert parents in the industrial north of England (first Preston, then Ashton-under-Lyne, near Manchester in Lancashire), where his father was a physician.[57] At eleven he entered Ushaw to study for the priesthood but, on being found unsuitable for the life owing to "a natural *indolence*" and a "strong, nervous timidity," he began the study of medicine in 1877 at Owens Medical College in Manchester. After six years of study and three failed examinations, he left the study of medicine and tried various things until leaving for London in 1885—a move that was made easier by his beloved mother's death and his father's remarriage. Already addicted to laudanum before he went to London, he soon showed the same inability to find steady work and after a while became a derelict living in the streets and in shelters, making pennies by selling matches or calling cabs. Saved from destitution by Wilfrid Meynell, who had published some of his poems in his literary monthly *Merry England,* he became a fixture in the Meynell household and literary circle, producing volumes of poetry, his poem *The Hound of Heaven* (1890) being his most famous. He wrote approximately three hundred poems and more than four hundred reviews and essays. Seven poems and his famous essay on Shelley appeared in Ward's *Dublin,* all but one (the ode to the English martyrs in Ward's second number) published posthu-

56. S., "Some Recent Books," *Dublin Review* (Jan. 1910): 197–99; C. C. M. [C. C. Martindale], "Some Recent Books," ibid. (Oct. 1913): 386–88; and R. W., "Some Recent Books," ibid. (Oct. 1914): 418–20.

57. There are numerous biographical studies of Thompson. The first major one is Everard Meynell's *Life of Francis Thompson* (New York: Burns & Oates, 1913). Meynell knew Thompson well and was one of Thompson's favorites among the Meynell children. His biography, while essential and excellently written, is very restrained in discussing the less edifying aspects of Thompson's life. His sister, Viola Meynell, has a written a fine study, *Francis Thompson and Wilfrid Meynell* (London: Hollis and Carter, 1952), which fills out the description. Among more recent biographies that give a much more complete view, see Brigid M. Boardman, *Between Heaven and Charing Cross: A Life of Francis Thompson* (New Haven: Yale University Press, 1988), and John Walsh, *Strange Harp, Strange Symphony: The Life of Francis Thompson* (New York: Hawthorn Books, 1967). For recent critical work on Thompson, see Beverly Taylor, *Francis Thompson* (Boston: Twayne, 1987).

mously by his literary executor, Wilfrid Meynell, who was also Ward's publisher.

Thompson's essay on Shelley, written in 1889 and originally rejected by the *Dublin* when Moyes was editor, was the most successful piece it ever published. For the first time in the journal's history, it went into a second edition, and then the article was printed separately in a small volume with an introduction by George Wyndham (which was originally a letter he wrote to Ward on the article) and notes by Wilfrid Meynell.[58] Its excellence was even noted by other journals, as this article from the *Observer* (August 1908) shows:

> No literary event for years has been so amazing an instance of buried jewels brought to light as the posthumous article by the late Francis Thompson. *The Dublin Review*, even under the admirable editorship of Mr Wilfrid Ward, had remained a comparatively cloistered publication. It has now leaped into a second edition with a memorable masterpiece of English prose. Brilliant, joyous, poignant are these pages of interpretation, as sensitive and magical as the mind of one poet ever lent to the genius of another. Yet when we turn from the subject to think of the author, the thing is as mournful as splendid. As for Francis Thompson, whose existence was as fantastic in the true sense as De Quincey's, and far more sorrowful, it is as though fate, even after death, pursued him with paradoxes. In this part of his fame he has no share, and his finest piece of prose—and much of his prose, though unknown to the world, was notable—sets London ringing in a way that reminds us of music never played until found among the papers of a dead composer. There are doubtless many who still ask "Who was Francis Thompson?" There are probably many more who, mistaking knowledge of a poet for familiarity with his name, who do well to ask "Who was Shelley?" The Essay answers both questions equally. As in all the highest work of that kind, its author divines the secrets of another nature by the certainty that his own was akin to it; and sympathy, inspiring true vision, reveals the seer as well as the seen. That the Essay should appear at last, instinct with the first freshness of life—that the expression of the inward glory of a man's youth should become his own rich epitaph—this is perhaps worth all the years of oblivion out of which a masterpiece has been redeemed.[59]

The beginning of Thompson's essay was a discussion of the Catholic Church's relationship to poetry, and its views paralleled very well Ward's belief in the universality of the Catholic faith and its capacity to inform and perfect every aspect of culture. It also paralleled Ward's belief that Catholics had neglected their responsibility to the larger culture, much to the loss of both:

58. Francis Thompson, "Shelley," *Dublin Review* (July 1908): 25–49.

59. As quoted in Francis Thompson, *Shelley*, with an introduction by George Wyndham and notes by W. M. [Wilfrid Meynell] (London: Burns & Oates, 1911), 81–82.

> The Church, which was once the mother of poets no less than of saints, during the last two centuries has relinquished to aliens the chief glories of poetry, if the chief glories of holiness she has preserved for her own. The palm and the laurel, Dominic and Dante, sanctity and song, grew together in her soil: she retained the palm, but forgone the laurel. And for this if song is itself responsible, we Catholics are not irresponsible. Poetry in its widest sense, and when not professedly irreligious, has been too much and too long among many Catholics either misprized or distrusted; too much and too generally the feeling has been that it is at best superfluous, at worst pernicious, most often dangerous. Once poetry was, as she should be, the lesser sister and helpmate of the Church; the minister to the mind, as the Church to the soul. But poetry sinned, poetry fell; and in place of lovingly reclaiming her, Catholicism cast her from the door to follow the feet of her pagan seducer. The separation has been ill for poetry; it has not been well for religion.[60]

English Catholics in particular, with their puritanical bent, had shown themselves little open to poetry, lacking "the traditionally Catholic joyous openness." It was not as if poetry had nowhere else to go, for if there was no place for her "beneath the wings of the Holy One, there was a place for her beneath the web of the Evil One." It would be far better to bring her under the "rafter" of the faith, where she could be fed, guided, and disciplined, to "tame her, fondle her, cherish her," but certainly not to distrust and despise her. Thompson asked for a greater interest not merely in Catholic poetry but in poetry in general, for "the bird gives glory to God though it sings only of its innocent loves," and whatever is great and good for the non-Catholic is equally so for the Catholic. While the article was full of praise for Shelley, it was not unaware of his "evil side." He had committed grave sins and even one cruel crime, and his views on free love were abhorrent. If his religion was a pantheistic hymn to humanity, it was still better than the atheism of his boyhood; and he was struggling, "blindly, weakly, stumblingly but still struggling towards higher things." Thompson doubted that any Christian had had his faith shaken through reading Shelley alone.

The most significant of Thompson's poems in the *Dublin* was "To the English Martyrs" ("Ode to the English Martyrs"), one of his last occasional poems and one Ward specifically commissioned for the journal. Written in five months at the Capuchins at Crawley, where he'd been sent to deal with his laudanum habit, in bad health and in the midst of much other writing (he wrote at least ten reviews at this time), it shows Thompson's remarkable ener-

60. Thompson, "Shelley," 25.

gy and resilience. It is, however, not a great poem. As one modern critic put it: "The ode measures how much Thompson's poetic fire had subsided by the last two years of his life."[61] Thompson admitted that it was not his best effort: "Shouldn't dream of publishing it (in a book, I mean). If any poetry *has* got into it, it is a pity; I intended best silver-gilt, & *that* is wasteful—brass much cheaper, & preferred for commercial purposes."[62] Still he thought that the *Dublin* had not been stiffed: "One quite certain thing is, the *Dublin* might go further & fare a great deal worse. Even in my ashes, I think there lives a little more fire than in any other Catholic versifier of whom I know."[63]

The theme of the work was the martyrs of Tyburn, who had given their life for the old faith, a theme as congenial to Thompson as it would be to the readers of the *Dublin.* It begins darkly with the image of the blood-soaked tree of Tyburn ("Rain, rain on Tyburn tree, / red rain a-falling; / Dew, dew on Tyburn tree, / Red dew on Tyburn tree, And the swart bird a-calling"), which casts a dark shadow even over the present: "The shadow lies on England now / Of the deathly-fruited bough, / Cold and black with malison / Lies between land and sun; / Putting out the sun, the bough / Shades England now!" The tone would have been even darker had Wilfrid Meynell not removed forty-seven lines before he sent it off to the *Dublin.*[64] While the broader vision of a world under judgment is lost, there remains a condemnation of an England whose denial of freedom ("her so bragged freedom") to the martyrs and to others will lead to her overthrow, and an understanding in what true freedom consists: "Till she shall know / This lesson in her overthrow: / Hardest servitude has he / That's gaoled in arrogant liberty; / And freedom, spacious and unflawed, / Who is walled about with God." Thompson praises the manner and the inner freedom of the martyrs, especially Thomas More ("Dear Jester in the Courts of God!"), and contrasts this with the horror of their treatment ("Chains, rack, hunger, solitude").

61. Taylor, *Francis Thompson,* 94.

62. Francis Thompson, *The Letters of Francis Thompson,* ed. John Walsh (New York: Hawthorn Books, 1969), 259, quoted in Taylor, *Francis Thompson,* 94.

63. Thompson, *Letters of Francis Thompson,* 257, quoted in Boardman, *Between Heaven and Charing Cross,* 340.

64. The darkness of these lines can see be seen in this excerpt: "We watch the avenging wrath / Drawn downward on its unavoided path / Of the malignant Sun. / Our world is venomed at the flaming heart, / That from its burning systole / Spurts a poisoned life-blood. See / The gathered contagion thence / Such influence / Shed on the seasons, and on men / Madness of nations, plague, and famine stern, / Earthquake, and flood, and all disastrous birth, / Change, war, and streaming pestilence." Quoted in Boardman, *Between Heaven and Charing Cross,* 338–39.

After Thompson's death a number of appreciative articles appeared about him. Alice Meynell's reminiscences in the *Dublin* recounted much of his life (including how she met him) and attempted to clear up untrue stories that had sprung up about him.[65] She particularly wanted to correct the impression that he had committed great misdeeds earlier in life for which the rest of his life was one long expiation, that he was profoundly unhappy and that his poetry was the result of his drug use. Rather, he was "one of the most innocent of men" with "natural good spirits, and was more mirthful than many a man of cheerful, of social, or even of humorous reputation." In any case, whatever darkness and oppression of spirit he underwent had ended some fifteen years before he died. Also, she claimed, none of his poetry, except perhaps "Dream Tryst" (an inferior poem), was written with the help of opium.

Albert A. Cock also contributed an appreciation of his work.[66] He praised Thompson, despite his occasional prosiness and bathos, for his "intuitive and experiential grasp of the spiritual significance of Nature and the Child with which we associate the name of Wordsworth; the ecstasy of Shelley with the constructive synthesis which was Shelley's lack; Tennyson's melodies with richer harmonies, Tennyson's feeling for contemporary problems and aspirations with a power of interpretation rarely reached by the late Laureate; all the virility of Browning without his obstinate involutions of thought and lacunae of argument." He found Thompson's spiritual realization more profound and satisfying than Browning's psychological penetration because it was more vital to the man himself. But his success was preeminently spiritual.

All that mystical longing for "infinite power of soul" which wrung from Richard Jefferies the anguished "Story of My Heart" is, in Francis Thompson, accompanied and followed by a satisfaction (and knowledge of the means of satisfaction) which Jefferies never obtained, for he was not of that Church. Where Newman wins by logic vitalized by the passion of faith, Thompson masters and conquers by the poetry of faith. He is not to be studied as a formal treatise in direction and casuistry, but the director of souls will find in him many secrets and phenomena laid bare as few have done or can do.

65. Mrs. Meynell, "Some Memories of Francis Thompson," *Dublin Review* (Jan. 1908): 160–72.

66. Albert A. Cock, "Francis Thompson," ibid. (Oct. 1911): 247–77. Rev. Albert A. Cock (1883–1953) was educated at King's College, London, where he was a lecturer in education and philosophy from 1906 to 1919, a special lecturer at St. Mary's College, Hammersmith, from 1909 to 1919, and a professor of education and philosophy at the University College, Southampton, from 1919 to 1939. He was ordained in 1939 and was principal of St. John's Diocesan Training College, York, from 1939 to 1945.

Who, knowing the "Hound of Heaven," will assert that the Catholic Church no longer voices the spiritual yearnings of the age? Who, with the "Mistress of Vision" before him, will say that the contemplative, ascetic and mystical ideals of the Church are effete and hopelessly outgrown? Who, knowing the "Making of Viola" and "Ex Ore Infantium," can lament that simplicity and innocence are no longer her attributes, fostered by her creed? Francis Thompson is, in some respects, the greatest achievement of Catholicism in the nineteenth century. His poetry is resident in the man. It is the repetition of the centuries.[67]

It was particularly, Cock thought, as a poet of childhood that Thompson excelled, though he considered "The Hound of Heaven," which he discussed at some length, Thompson's finest poem. Thompson's life and works were "penetrated, suffused, saturated and substantiated by a consciousness of the supernatural, of the symbolic mystery of life, of the secret affinities between stone and star which are not to be lightly defined but rather felt, lived and realized." For Thompson "the world and human life are crammed with Heaven and aflame with God."

Besides poetry Thompson wrote a life of St. Ignatius Loyola (1913), which Canon William Barry compared very favorably with other descriptions of the Spanish saint by Carlyle and Macaulay.[68] "It is an Elizabethan work, this new Life, in its unflagging energy of presentment, its wealth and colour of speech, its solid concrete handling, its freedom from conventions reckoned sacrosanct in the literature to which its subject invites us."[69] It was a portrait from life that only an inspired pen could have written, a pearl of price that dropped from Thompson's dying hand, "written in choicest English, by a master of prose, by a seer and son of the Renaissance, born out of due time."

Short and appreciative reviews of Thompson's poems also appeared in the recent-books section: his *Selected Poems* (1908) and the three volumes of his collected works, *The Works of Francis Thompson* (1913), edited by Wilfrid Meynell.[70] C. C. Martindale wrote a very positive review of the *Life of Francis Thompson* (1913) by Everard Meynell, Wilfrid's son.[71] Despite the difficulties of the task, for Thompson was made to be misunderstood, Martindale praised

67. Ibid., 248, 249.

68. Canon Barry, "Francis Thompson's Ignatius Loyola," ibid. (July 1910): 56–84.

69. Ibid., 56.

70. A. M., "Some Recent Books," ibid. (Jan. 1909): 184–87, and F. G., "Some Recent Books," ibid. (Oct. 1913): 395–97.

71. C. C. M. [C. C. Martindale], "Some Recent Books," ibid. (Jan. 1914): 172–74.

Meynell for doing a superb job in putting Thompson's personality before the world with vividness, dignity, and suppleness of expression.

A number of significant minor figures contributed to the *Dublin.* Louise Imogen Guiney (1861–1920), an Irish American who lived in England from 1889 to 1891 and from 1901 until her death, a poet, editor, biographer, and essayist important in the resurrection of forgotten literary figures and Recusant literature, contributed two articles.[72] Two of the more interesting contributors were Wilfrid Scawen Blunt (1840–1922) and Mrs. Bellamy (Maria Longworth) Storer (1840–1932).[73] Blunt, a cousin of George Wyndham, is far better known today as a diarist and for his political and personal exploits, but he was respected as a poet in his day. He contributed a single poem, "The Dance of Death," to the October 1906 number. Mrs. Bellamy Storer, from a wealthy Cincinnati family and a convert to Catholicism in 1892, is better known for her involvement in American politics. She contributed three poems, including one on the sinking of the *Titanic,* which, if not a great poem, at least had the virtue of being mercifully short.

An important English writer of his day, and a major contributor to the *Dublin,* was Mgr. Robert Hugh Benson (1871–1914). Son of Edward White Benson, Archbishop of Canterbury from 1883 to 1896, and brother of the two well-known authors A. C. Benson and E. F. Benson (of Lucia and Mapp fame), he was an accomplished and successful novelist, preacher, and spiritual director who converted to Catholicism in 1903.[74] His eleven years as a Catholic were also his most fruitful literary years, and almost all of his works come from that period. From the beginning the *Dublin* took notice of his work, and in Ward's very first number his first two novels, *By What Authority* (1904) and *The King's Achievement* (1905), were praised as brilliant historical novels

72. See Alice Brown, *Louise Imogen Guiney: Her Life and Her Works, 1861–1920* (New York: Macmillan, 1921); E. M. Tenison, *Louise Imogen Guiney* (London: Longmans, Green, 1923); and M. A. Hart, *Soul Ordained to Fail* (New York: Pageant Press, 1962).

73. For Blunt, see Elizabeth Longford, *A Pilgrimage of Passion: The Life of Wilfrid Scawen Blunt* (New York: Knopf, 1980). Mrs. Storer was an old friend of William McKinley and played a significant role in gaining Theodore Roosevelt his appointment as assistant secretary of the navy. Mr. Storer, who had served in the House of Representatives from 1891 to 1895 and converted in 1896, was made ambassador to Belgium (1897–1899), to Spain (1899–1902), and then to Austria-Hungary (1902–1906). He was removed from the ambassadorship to Austria-Hungary over the Storers' attempts to have Archbishop Ireland of St. Paul made a cardinal.

74. See C. C. Martindale, *The Life of Monsignor Robert Hugh Benson* (London: Longmans, Green, 1916), and Janet Grayson, *Robert Hugh Benson: Life and Works* (Lanham, Md.: University Press of America, 1998).

whose analytic insight and aesthetic sensitivity captured so well the chaotic and complex Tudor period.[75] While Benson was praised for his use of symbolism, his vivid color and imagery, he was also criticized for his too-great facility, his dependence on externals to convey spiritual impressions, his use of different angles to describe history, and the occasional confusion caused in the readers' minds of the symbolic and aesthetic by his external descriptions. The reviewer made "an earnest and serious request," considering "the wonderful combination of the aesthetic and symbolic view of life, the subtle brilliant sense of historic complexity, the sympathetic pathos and the spiritual clearness, nobility, and sweetness" of *By What Authority,* that Benson "wait patiently a year or more to give him time to live with his characters." Otherwise the very brilliance of his work would obscure the personalities he wished to present. The review of *Richard Raynal: Solitary,* set in medieval England, was equally effusive.[76] The novel was a "spiritual idyll with an exquisite setting" that captured the rich tapestry of the medieval court in its peace and brutality, in the spiritual and the grotesque. "It is also a very delicate and subtle study of the medieval mind with its curious revulsions from the moods of a brutal child to the musings of a mystic." He believed that it should be read, if possible, in one sitting, "in some quiet chamber of an old house invaded by the lights and scents of early spring." "Like a piece of music it should come and go without interruption." The reviewer's only criticism was that in its description of mysticism stronger types could have been used. "They lack the robust sanity, the clearness of judgement, the trumpet-note of triumph, the calm mastery over others that distinguished St Catherine of Siena or St Teresa. They are exquisite figures, spiritual and intensely pathetic, but it would not have detracted from their pathos to have borne in mind that there are greater types than these of humanity made strong to deal with the visible by its intercourse with the unseen."

In praising Benson's ability to make the past live, with his eye for minute detail and "his rich and flowing vein of fancy," the reviewer also criticized his description of Mary Tudor in *The Queen's Tragedy* as being unhistorical, much to Mary's detriment.[77] Maisie Ward reviewed his novel, set in Elizabethan times, *Come Rack! Come Rope!* (1912) in the January 1913 number and was so

75. S., "Some Recent Books," *Dublin Review* (Jan. 1906): 197–99.
76. S., "Some Recent Books," ibid. (July 1906): 197.
77. J. M. S., "Some Recent Books," ibid. (Oct. 1906): 421–25.

impressed by his sympathetic historical imagination that she wished he would write nothing but historical novels. Many great novelists, she wrote, such as George Eliot, had not this gift. She thought his contemporary novels, "clever though they are," weakened his serious purpose and limited the range of good he could do.[78] In its notice of *Oddsfish* (1914), his last historical novel, set in the time of Charles II and the popish plot, the *Dublin* reviewer described well the strengths and the weaknesses of Benson's style.[79] He believed it to be written "with a more even and mature facility" than any of his other historical novels ("This curious chronicle is curiously spontaneous and unfettered by the rich mass of historical detail it is made to carry") and with the same painterly style that showed in all his work.

The success of his method is largely due to his manipulation of detail. Unlike Balzac, who crowds upon his canvas a mass of details, often without much selection, Monsignor Benson fastens the imagination of his readers on some salient detail which is suggestive of many others. The danger of this method is that, having found the bit of material description that can give an extraordinarily vivid impression of a personality, there is the temptation to press it too hard. Thus, while in the earlier scenes the thin, brown hand of the King is extraordinarily suggestive of the rest of the figure, before the end of the book it has become so prominent as to have the fatiguing effect of any literary mannerism. This kind of defect seems, in Monsignor Benson's case, to have been simply the result of the haste that went with much of his most brilliant artistic achievement. Probably he could not have done so well had he gone more slowly.[80]

While his historical fiction was perhaps his most popular and memorable work, Benson's contemporary novels were also well received and praised for the same attention to suggestive and realistic detail that characterized his historical fiction. *A Mirror of Shalott* (1907) was similar to his first work of fiction, *The Light Invisible* (1903), in its form, structure, and subject, being a loose collection of stories about "the mysterious spirit world" (ghosts, demonic possession, and the like).[81] *The Necromancers* (1909) was praised for its powerful description of the dangers of spiritualism—on which he was an expert, writing a series of articles on it in the *Dublin*.[82] *None Other Gods* (1911), a

78. M. W. [Maisie Ward], "Some Recent Books," ibid. (Jan. 1913): 182–84. There was also a positive review of Benson's historical play *The Cost of a Crown*, set at the same time. See "Some Recent Books," ibid. (Jan. 1911): 204–05.

79. S., "Some Recent Books," ibid. (Jan. 1915): 183–86.

80. Ibid., 185–86.

81. W. H. K., "Some Recent Books," ibid. (Oct. 1907): 412–13.

82. C. B., "Some Recent Books," ibid. (Jan. 1910): 210–11. Benson had a lifelong interest in the

modern pilgrim's progress, was favorably reviewed despite its sometimes exaggerated use of suggestive detail, as was *Initiation* (1914), which dealt with the mystery of suffering.[83] *The Coward* (1912) was a "striking psychological study," "full of vivid and often painful description."[84] *An Average Man* (1913) was full of wit and a superb account of the powerful tragedy of a soul unfaithful to its vocation, in spite of its ineffectual priest and often too-impressionistic character.[85] His last novel, *Loneliness* (1914), was also a contemporary story of spiritual struggle, though successful only in its second half.[86] But the novel that probably has the greatest readership now is neither one of his historical novels nor one of his contemporary ones, but his futuristic and apocalyptic novel, *The Lord of the World* (1907). It is set 150 years in the future, when the Church is just a faithful remnant and the Antichrist an apostle of humanity. Oddly enough, the *Dublin*'s review of this work was surprisingly negative and the reviewer experienced "discomfort" (despite frequent moments of admiration) in the "unshrinking definiteness" of Benson's treatment.

A boy's fancy, a man's thought, an artist's perception, a mystic's vision, all these were necessary for the production of *The Lord of the World*. . . . But it is impossible not to feel that all these powers have run wild, and from sheer want of discipline have missed their mark. The boy's fancy has luxuriated in flights of "volors," in magic sunlight, in schemes of organized suicide, the artist's perceptions have presented a series of very highly-coloured pictures, the man's thought on the deeper tendencies of our civilization has foretold too easily the sweep of one great movement of humanitarian philosophy, while the mystic's has been almost the most unbridled of all these elements, and is positively self-indulgent in a facile analysis of the moods of the soul. Things material, things spiritual, both divine and devilish, are crowded on the canvas until the mind is confused and wearied; and it must be steadied by a firm effort before we recognize in this strange book much of what we have always loved in Father Benson's work.[87]

"uncanny and occult," as his biographer Martindale put it, and his contemporary novels abound with it. His interest in spiritualism and related phenomena found expression in a series of articles for the *Dublin:* "A Modern Theory of Human Personality" (July 1907): 78–96; "Spiritualism" (Oct. 1909): 406–21; and "Phantasms of the Dead" (Jan. 1912): 43–63. See Martindale, *Life of Monsignor Robert Hugh Benson,* 2:279–305, and Paschal Scotti, "Necromancy and Monsignor Benson," *Downside Review* 121 (April 2003): 135–49.

83. S., "Some Recent Books," *Dublin Review* (April 1911): 402–4, and N. K., "Some Recent Books," ibid. (April 1914): 398–400.

84. O., "Some Recent Books," ibid. (April 1912): 417.

85. S., "Some Recent Books," ibid. (Oct. 1913): 389–90.

86. S., "Some Recent Books," ibid. (July 1915): 191–93.

87. S., "Some Recent Books," ibid. (Jan. 1908): 189–90.

Benson died on October 19, 1914, after preaching a mission in Salford. In the January 1915 number Mrs. Warre Cornish, who had known him since he was a boy at Eton, where her husband was a teacher, recounted his death and remembered his home life and personality.[88] While Benson was a Catholic for only eleven years, she wrote, they were dazzling ones. She praised Benson the preacher, whose eloquence "owed nothing to the common-places of the day." His historical novels conquered the *Times* and his contemporary novels made "many a man in society" say "This is me" and direct their lives afresh. Above all, however, she called Benson a "mystic," but a mystic who strongly valued dogma and outward forms, and who remained a "John Bull" all his life. He was a mystic whose contemplative nature was nurtured by his mother (the sister of Henry Sidgwick), and whose creative mind needed the combination of inward grace and outward object (in this case, the Church) to be fruitful. She commented that in *None Other Gods* we had the mature expression of Benson's individual beliefs: "First, in the silent inward revelation; secondly, in supernatural influences veiled by, though latent in, Nature; finally, in the power of the forms of the Church to bring not aesthetes but sinners and sufferers to freedom, because they are divinely instituted."[89]

While Mrs. Warre Cornish intentionally set her remembrance of Benson against the backdrop of the death and the darkness of the Great War being waged at the time—the better, perhaps, to show the poignancy of his early and unexpected death—a truer description of his art appeared in a review of A. C. Benson's memorial of his brother, *Hugh: Memoirs of a Brother.*

For Monsignor Benson many problems which usually haunt the modern man of letters seem hardly to have existed. It was not his business nor his vocation to decide any general problems concerning social evils or modern criticism, neither had he with all his sympathies any touch of sentimentality. He hardly knew, it seems, what was meant by the pains and joys of memory. He was set with his face forward doing the work that he was convinced had been set for him with eagerness and enjoyment, despising the incidental suffering and strain of the weakness of the body. Alive to everything in the external world, missing no beauty of shadow on the grass, or movement of animal life, or the dignity and the language of old habitations, his art dealt rather with the light of the morning, with the splash and lightness of water in the early sunshine than with the tender hues of evening. The "happy autumn fields" for him

88. Mrs. Blanche Warre Cornish, "The Death of Monsignor Benson," ibid. (Jan. 1915): 122–39.

89. Ibid., 134.

would not have been associated with "the days that are no more" but with the glory of the present harvest.[90]

Another major interest of the *Dublin* was Irish literature, both in English and in Gaelic. The 1890s saw the beginning of the Irish Literary Revival and the Gaelic League.[91] The Gaelic League was founded by Douglas Hyde and Eóin MacNéill in 1893 to "de-Anglicize Ireland" by reviving the Irish language and restoring its literature. W. H. Kent, himself of highland Scottish and Irish descent, defended in the January 1907 number the revival of Gaelic against those who thought it useless, backward, or trivial.[92] While Kent admitted that in studying Gaelic one certainly reaped the kind of benefits that come from the study of any language (even so-called dead ones such as Greek and Latin), there was a far more important benefit in studying Gaelic, for it put its student "in touch with the literary and historical traditions of his own race and country." The aim of the Gaelic League was not just the preservation of the Irish language, or even the preservation of existing Irish literature, but the creation of a modern Irish literature. Irish might seem the language of illiterate peasants who have no need for a literature at all, much less a modern one, but Kent pointed out the extensive oral literary tradition of all the Celtic peoples. "In most other lands old national legends and poetry are buried in books, and a knowledge of them is generally confined to a comparatively small class of scholars or men of literary culture. It has been far otherwise with the Gaels,

90. S., "Some Recent Books," ibid. (July 1915): 187.

91. See P. J. Mathews, *Revival: The Abbey Theatre, Sinn Féin, the Gaelic League, and the Co-operative Movement* (Notre Dame: University of Notre Dame Press, 2003). Hyde, son of a Church of Ireland clergyman, wished the movement to be nonsectarian and nonpartisan, but nothing in Ireland at this time could be devoid of a political and religious dimension, and over time it became a Catholic and nationalist organization. See David W. Miller, *Church, State and Nation in Ireland: 1898–1921* (Pittsburgh: University of Pittsburgh Press, 1973), 34–43. Many Irishmen, including the Catholic leadership, believed that English was the only means by which the Irish could achieve greater influence and power, and while they were generally supportive of the Gaelic League and its ideals as reflective of the nation, they did not think that true de-Anglicization was either feasible or desirable.

92. W. H. Kent, "The Gaelic Revival," *Dublin Review* (Jan. 1907): 98–112. Kent (1857–1935) joined Manning's Oblates of St. Charles in 1876 and was ordained a priest by him in 1881. A frequent contributor to Catholic periodicals, he was entrusted in 1906 with Cardinal Manning's papers and given the task of writing a new biography to counter Purcell's slanders. The book was written, and while still at press part of it was used in "Manning and Gladstone: The Destroyed Letters," ibid. (Jan. 1906): 41–58, but it was never published and has since disappeared. The article discusses some other parts of Kent's book as well.

among whom a large body of literature in prose and verse has been handed down by oral tradition. And it will sometimes happen that a wide knowledge of this ancient literature is possessed by men who are without the mechanical acquirements of reading and writing, and for this reason are absurdly supposed to be illiterates."[93] Such was the vitality of this old Gaelic literature that even today there were a great many "illiterate" peasants who still had a familiarity with it; and with the Gaelic Revival, he believed, this "living literature" would not die out in Ireland as it was dying out in so many other places, destroyed most often by the very schools that were created to educate the common people. Kent lambasted the English national prejudice that everyone should speak English and attacked the philistinism that lay behind it.

> Let us suppose that fortune had favoured the arms of Asia, and Athens had become a petty province in the Persian Empire. Or to take a more modern case we may imagine for the moment that England, in the early sixteenth century, had been absorbed in the vast dominions of the Spanish sovereign. In these cases, a candid critic would say, on the same principles, that if Sophocles has anything worth saying he must say it in Persian, and if Shakespeare has anything that the world would care to hear he should write in Spanish. It is surely no disparagement to Spanish and Persian poetry to say that this would have been an irreparable loss to the world's literature. For it is obvious that there is much in Sophocles that could have been written in no tongue but the Greek, and much in Shakespeare that could only be uttered in English. These are, of course, extreme cases; but they serve to illustrate a general principle, to wit, that each language has a distinctive quality or capacity of its own, and that its function in literature cannot be fulfilled by another.[94]

Gaelic literature was given much attention: Alfred Perceval Graves wrote three articles on Gaelic poetry for the *Dublin*.[95] Irish literature in English, not surprisingly, was given far more. Among those writing in English, the most popular Irish writers discussed were contemporary novelists such as Canon Patrick Augustine Sheehan (1852–1913) and George A. Birmingham, the pen name of the Anglican Canon James Owen Hannay (1865–1950). Both novelists, despite their religious differences, were nationalists, and both wrote, at this time, almost exclusively on Irish themes. Sheehan's nationalism was mod-

93. Ibid., 103–4.

94. Ibid., 109.

95. Graves (1846–1931), son of the Anglican bishop of Limerick, educated at Trinity College, Dublin, served for many years as an inspector of schools and was a leading figure in the London Irish Literary Society. He was a Gaelic scholar, poet and songwriter. His fourth son was the novelist Robert Graves.

erate and generally nonpolitical. A supporter of Home Rule and of William O'Brien's All-for-Ireland League (1910), whose nationalism tried to conciliate the more moderate Irish Protestants, he got along well with some of the Anglo-Irish aristocracy he knew, rather liked the English, having worked in England early in his priesthood, and was somewhat irenic. Ultimately, however, his concern was spiritual and religious. The Catholic Church in Ireland was the center both of his own worldview and of his view of Ireland. Birmingham too was a moderate nationalist, a supporter of the Gaelic League (for a while he was even on their central council) who hoped for the reconciliation of the Anglo-Irish aristocracy with Irish nationalism before the Anglo-Irish aristocracy was pushed aside and it was too late.

Canon Sheehan, parish priest of Doneraile in County Cork and best known for his *My New Curate* (serialized in the American *Ecclesiastical Review* in 1898–1899 and published as a book in 1900), published many novels dealing with contemporary Irish rural life and the clergy.[96] By the time of his death a hundred thousand copies of his books had been sold and he had been translated into eight languages. In commenting on his *Lisheen* (1907), the *Dublin* reviewer praised him for his sympathetic understanding of the sufferings and sorrows of Irish peasant life, for his "genius to enthrall the ordinary reader by his most wonderful presentments of living human beings," and for his ability to describe the simple and homely lives of the Irish poor in all their joys and sorrows, which the reviewer wished Sheehan would do more of.[97] But he criticized Sheehan's unconvincing upper-class melodrama and, most particularly, his belief that landlordism was the "one evil power" that accounted for all of the suffering of the Irish people. The same reviewer praised the artistry of *The Blindness of Dr. Gray* (1909), considering it the "strongest" of his novels, and proclaimed it "one of those books in which history is written."[98] He also commented on the controversy it had engendered (without discussing the nature of that controversy) and the criticism made by its main character, Dr. Gray, a stern priest of the old school, that the Irish had lost

96. For Canon Sheehan, see Michael Barry, *By Pen and Pulpit: The Life and Times of the Author Canon Sheehan* (Fermoy, Ireland: Saturn Books, 1990); Catherine Candy, *Priestly Fictions: Popular Irish Novelists of the Early 20th Century* (Dublin: Wolfhound Press, 1995); and Ruth Fleischmann, *Catholic Nationalism in the Irish Revival: A Study of Canon Sheehan, 1852–1913* (New York: St. Martin's Press, 1997). See also Lawrence W. McBride, "Imagining the Nation in Irish Historical Fiction, c. 1870–c. 1925," in Brown and Miller, *Piety and Power in Ireland,* 81–107.

97. S., "Some Recent Books," *Dublin Review* (Jan. 1908): 185–87.

98. S., "Some Recent Books," ibid. (July 1910): 183–86.

their patriotism and become materialistic now that they have gained possession of the land.

Birmingham was a clergyman of the Church of Ireland and rector of Westport in Connaught at this time.[99] While he is perhaps best known for his humorous novels, his early novels were much more serious, touching upon political and social issues, particularly the revitalization of Ireland and the nature of her identity. The *Dublin* praised two of these "Irish novels," *Hyacinth* (1906) and *The Seething Pot* (1905), as "very thoughtful and interesting."[100] The reviewer singled out Birmingham's characterizations, his humor, his comments on contemporary Irish national life, and, most particularly, his "atmosphere of poetry and mysticism." "In one sense the book [*Hyacinth*] is a study of what the author regards as the three religions of Ireland, Catholicism, Protestantism and Patriotism. With a rare breath of vision, the inner life of each, the current of 'mystic devotion,' is presented. Perhaps in England we hardly understand patriotism as a quasi-religious sentiment. Who can regard the 'weary Titan' and her 'Atlantean load' with the enthusiasm, the burning pity and love, that the true Irishman feels towards Ireland?"[101] He chided Birmingham, however, for his lack of appreciation for all those English who had stood by Ireland through thick and thin. The same reviewer wrote appreciatively of another nationalist novel, *Benedict Kavanagh* (1907), noteworthy for its rare appreciation for the virtues of Protestant Ulster, the "more valuable since the author's sympathies are clearly with Connaught and the West."[102] Its hero becomes a devotee of the religion of patriotism when he becomes a worker on the land and an active member of the Gaelic League, much to the reviewer's approval. "The Gaelic League, 'educational, non-political and non-sectarian,' is uniquely fitted to cope with those terrible hindrances to national life which Mr Birmingham so well describes: the profound cleavage between the two Churches, mutual party hatred and distrust, acute class distinction, long-fostered lack of initiative in dealing with practical difficulties, and worst of all, cowardice and time-serving in the electorate."[103]

99. For his life, see Brian Taylor, *The Life and Writings of James Owen Hannay (George Birmingham), 1865–1950* (Lewiston, N.Y.: E. Mellen Press, 1995).

100. R. C. T., "Some Recent Books," *Dublin Review* (April 1906): 432–34. Strangely enough, the reviewer made no mention of passages that offended many Catholics in Ireland.

101. Ibid., 433.

102. R. C. T., "Some Recent Books," ibid. (April 1907): 425–28.

103. Ibid., 427.

In *The Northern Iron* (1907), a story of the Irish Rebellion at the time of the French Revolution, Birmingham frankly showed his sympathy for the United Irishmen who were in rebellion, but he was also aware that the loyalists cared equally for Ireland, achieving an admirable balance, in the reviewer's opinion.[104] *The Red Hand of Ulster* (1912), which Birmingham's biographer called "a bizarre combination of a Gilbert and Sullivan comic opera and a work of astute political prophecy," dealt with a revolt against the British by a Protestant Ulster opposed to Home Rule. The reviewer found the novel extremely funny, and was unsure whether it was meant to be taken seriously.[105] Eventually Birmingham's humor at Irish expense got him into serious trouble. Rioting occurred in 1914 at Westport over his play *General John Regan,* which was accused of insulting the Catholic priesthood, Irish maidenhood, and western Irish life.

While Sheehan and Birmingham were popular writers, the writers of the Irish Literary Revival gained the most critical attention and lasting fame.[106] Katherine Tynan (1861–1931), a Catholic, an important figure of the Revival, and a close friend of William Butler Yeats, contributed to the *Dublin* two poems and an essay on the poet Lionel Johnson, another member of the group.[107] The two most significant figures in this movement, however, Yeats (1865–1939) and John Millington Synge (1871–1909), were both from Protestant stock, though not supporters of the Protestant ascendancy. In discussing *The Dublin Book of Irish Verse* in the July 1910 number, the reviewer ("D. McC.") remarked that there was a certain truth in the cynic's jibe about the "Celtic Renaissance": "that the literary movement thus designated is not Celtic and is not a Renaissance."

> Writers like Yeats and "A.E.," Lionel Johnson and Norah Hopper, can hardly be said to represent all the racial tendencies of the Celt, nor is their wistful and haunting mu-

104. G. F. G., "Some Recent Books," ibid. (April 1908): 394–95.

105. M. W. [Maisie Ward], "Some Recent Books," ibid. (Oct. 1912): 400–402. See Taylor, *James Owen Hannay,* 117.

106. A good introduction is Ulick O'Conner, *Celtic Dawn: A Portrait of the Irish Literary Renaissance* (London: Hamish Hamilton, 1984).

107. Yeats's most recent biographer describes the later career of Tynan as that of "a high-class hack-writer of relentless facility." See R. F. Foster, *W. B. Yeats: A Life,* vol. 1, *The Apprentice Mage* (Oxford: Oxford University Press, 1997), 55. Tynan wrote more than two hundred major pieces (including novels, plays, anthologies, reminiscences, and books of poetry) and a vast amount of lesser journalism. See Ann Connerton Fallon, *Katherine Tynan* (Boston: Twayne, 1979). Her essay on Johnson was "A Catholic Poet," *Dublin Review* (Oct. 1907): 327–44.

sic an echo from any strain of older days. It sounds with no clangour of far-off strife; the ambitions, tribal rivalries, keen loves and hates, heroisms and sins of unsubdued humanity, find there no expression, nor is the devotion that of the ages of faith. Fond as are all these poets of using the names of Ireland's saints and legendary heroes, they give us neither the spirit of Patrick and Columba, nor that of Cuchullain, car-borne through the battle. The wild old stories of passionate battles, and love as passionate, are by them softened to symbols, treated much as Maeterlinck treats his Arthurian nomenclature. The beauty of their work is not a revival, it is a creation, and one characteristic of the modern idealist,—dreamer, and doubter of his dreams. It is a beauty best felt in certain half disembodied moods of reverie; a poetry of woven winds, twilit distances, and desire so tremulously sweet, that it shrinks from the fulfilment of desire.[108]

Both Yeats and Synge used Irish traditions and characters, and although their work had great artistic merit and received enormous support, a great many Irish Catholics, both at home and abroad, disliked it intensely. Thus, in its first week on stage Synge's *Playboy of the Western World* (1907) was shouted down by indignant Irish nationalists, and it met with protests in Ireland and the United States by those who believed that it denigrated Ireland. Perhaps the greatest creation of the Irish Literary Revival, especially when one considers that Ireland had no tradition of national drama, was the Abbey Theatre, which opened in Dublin on December 27, 1904, and for which Yeats, Synge, Lady Gregory, and others supplied plays.

In the January 1913 number of the *Dublin* Charles Bewley tried to explain why so many Irish had difficulties with the Abbey Theatre's productions.[109] The English and the Americans had been captivated by these plays, seeing them as classic and perfect representations of Irish peasant life. The Irish, by contrast, both in Ireland and in America, tended to see them as a "parody and a perversion of Irish peasant life, a libel on the national character, immoral both in language and in plot." Unfortunately, thought Bewley, much of this criticism was unintelligent and indiscriminate—which was a shame, because

108. D. McC., "Some Recent Books," *Dublin Review* (July 1910): 198. One should add that he did like Yeats's poetry.

109. Charles Bewley, "The Irish National Theatre," ibid. (Jan. 1913): 132–44. Bewley (1888–1969), educated at Winchester and Oxford and a convert (1911), was an Irish lawyer and served the Irish Free State in a number of diplomatic missions: in Berlin in an unofficial capacity from 1921 to 1923, as Irish minister to the Holy See from 1929 to 1933, and as Irish minister to Germany from 1933 to 1939. For his life, see Charles Bewley, *Memoirs of a Wild Goose* (Dublin: Lilliput Press, 1989).

there was much in the plays genuinely deserving of criticism. The playwrights were certainly Irish, Bewley wrote, "But there is an Ireland which is not to be found in the geography books, which is bounded not by four seas, but by history, religion and tradition; and of this Ireland I doubt whether Yeats, Synge or Robinson ever received the citizenship. They may be familiar with every glen in Wicklow and every island off the Galway coast, but I do not think they have ever penetrated into the recesses of the Irish mind." It was not that these people were part of "England's faithful garrison" in Ireland, since their sympathies were probably with the Irish people. "But there is a great difference between being 'with the people' and 'of the people,' and the man who would interpret the people's soul must be both. He must know them from the inside as well as from the outside if he would arrive at complete comprehension. Mr Yeats and his fellows know them well from the outside: to the deeper and more intimate knowledge they have never attained."[110]

While there existed a great gulf between rich and poor, governors and governed, in every country, this was even truer in Ireland, Bewley believed, because of its history, religion, and tradition. The Irish peasant was at a far greater remove from the Irish Protestant landowner than the English peasant was from the English landowner. Despite this, he maintained, no man better understood the Irish peasant than Dr. Douglas Hyde, the son a Protestant clergyman and president of the Gaelic League. Hyde was able to bridge that gap because he approached the task humbly and carefully, without preconceived ideas, and with sympathy. This was not true, however, of the modern school of Irish drama, whose ideas and technique came from abroad. And while Bewley had no objection to the adaptation of technical methods from other places, it was absurd to put Parisian literary ideas in the mouth of an Irish peasant. Yeats and Synge thought that opposition to the bourgeoisie was the common ground of both peasant and artist. But their glorification of the pagan past, in all its primitive savagery and contempt for Christianity, could only alienate the peasant and show the artist's distance from him. Thus, for example, in Yeats's *Crucifixion of the Outcast,* an old Irish bard, having come to the door of a Christian monastery for shelter, is treated badly by the brothers, who finally crucify him. On the way to his death, carrying his cross, he stops and sings them "the story of White-Breasted Deidre," for which they beat him "for waking forgotten longings in their hearts." The "old pagan

110. Bewley, "Irish National Theatre," 134.

land, mother of mystery and magic, of poetry and song," is contrasted with Christianity, "preoccupied with souls rather than art, ruthless toward her enemies," a Christianity that "brings to an end the old world of joy and laughter." While Bewley admitted that there were traces of the primitive pagan past among the Irish peasantry, it was hardly their primary characteristic. "And it is by this pagan element that modern Irish dramatists have been chiefly attracted—by the superstitions that the Church has not been able to crush, by the outbursts of primeval savagery that take place in the least savage of races. The ancient paganism of the wandering man, of the hunter, of the tiller of the soil, has been rediscovered, dragged into the light, and claimed as sister by the neo-paganism of the literary decadent."[111] He particularly objected to the displacement of reason by uncontrolled passion. "No wonder that their types are not universally recognized as true to life, when they have selected from the Irishman's complex personality those few attributes to which they feel themselves most akin, and have labeled them 'Ireland.' No wonder that Ireland and Irish-America refuse to acknowledge as Irish, characters devoid of those particular qualities which have distinguished Ireland in the eyes of the world."[112]

To have no sympathy for the profoundly Catholic character of Irish peasant life, thought Bewley, was to fail to understand it. "The Catholic religion, according to him [Yeats], consists of a number of beliefs, more or less picturesque, which the Irish peasant holds together with a number of other beliefs relative to fairies, pookas, sowlths and other supernatural beings."[113] Yeats depicted the Christian God as alien, his rites as powerless, his religion as one based on fear, his priests as mercenary, and his adherents as "weak-minded."

To the predictable response that dramatists are not compelled exclusively to treat the typical or the normal in their works, Bewley responded that if these Irish dramatists wanted to portray the abnormal, they should portray it as abnormal, not as normal. "It is here that the distinction lies between *Macbeth* and *The Playboy of the Western World.* In the former play there are indications of a sane and healthy public opinion: the average Scot is horrified at Duncan's murder: Shakespeare's indictment is against an individual, not

111. Ibid., 138. Yeats recounts this line of Lady Gregory: "'I have longed,' she said once 'to turn Catholic, that I might be nearer to the people, but you have taught me that paganism brings me nearer still.'" W. B. Yeats, *Autobiographies* (London: Macmillan, 1955), 400.

112. Bewley, "Irish National Theatre," 139.

113. Ibid., 140.

against a nation. In Synge's hands the story would have taken a very different shape: Macbeth would openly exult in his murder, and Banquo and Macduff vie with one another in an ecstasy of enthusiastic loyalty to the murderer: retribution would only follow when it was discovered that Duncan was not dead after all."[114]

If the plays failed because they depicted peasants without religion, Bewley thought, they failed equally because they showed them as devoid of patriotic sentiment. While Yeats had given some expression to this sentiment, the majority of the productions of the Abbey Theatre had not. Only one of the Abbey Theatre dramatists did Bewley really approve of, pointing to William Boyle's *The Building Fund* as a truer presentation of the Irish countryman than anything in Synge and Yeats. Those who entertained hopes of a native Irish school of drama had been disappointed, he believed, but there was still the opportunity for the younger members of that school to "lift the movement out of the groove" and to "search for material, not in the dramas of Synge, but in the living realities of Irish life."

There was much truth in these criticisms. There can be no doubt of the profound influences on Yeats of "the literary coteries of London and Paris."[115] In his case, certainly, the Celtic Renaissance was something new, not a revival of something old, a new creation influenced by foreign (non-Irish) literary movements such as aestheticism and symbolism. Yeats's antipathy to Catholicism was part of his family's rejection of Christianity in general (his father, son of a Church of Ireland clergyman, was a freethinker) and his personal belief in the occult. His contempt for the Irish Catholic middle class, which he considered philistine, was part of the aesthete's disdain for middle-class "materialism" and his glorification of the artist. His dislike, even hatred, of the English meant that he would be a nationalist, but he opposed mainstream Irish nationalism, with its conventional pieties, and refused to subordinate art to politics. "More generally, it can be said that while Yeats was trying to establish a new priesthood for a new Ireland, mainstream Irish nationalism already had a religion—the church of Rome."[116] Conor Cruise O'Brien reminds us that Yeats's nationalism was of the O'Leary school, which did not endorse parliamentary action, disliked agrarian agitation, and strongly opposed acts of

114. Ibid., 143.

115. See Thomas William Heyck, "The Genealogy of Irish Modernism: The Case of W. B. Yeats," in Brown and Miller, *Piety and Power in Ireland,* 220–51.

116. Ibid., 247.

terrorism—the only means by which Ireland received a hearing and redress in the nineteenth century.[117] From 1903 to 1916 Yeats was particularly uninvolved with practical political matters. Finally, while Yeats did not support the Unionist politics of the Protestant governing class, he still shared its sense of caste superiority over its Catholic neighbors. His sensibility, therefore, was opposed to that of the Irish Catholic majority on many levels.

117. See Conor Cruise O'Brien, "Passion and Cunning: An Essay on the Politics of W. B. Yeats," in his *Passion and Cunning and Other Essays* (London: Weidenfeld and Nicolson, 1988), 8–61.

7 IRELAND

The Irish Question, "the damnable question," was a thorn in England's flesh during the whole of the nineteenth century and into the twentieth, but its roots went back deep into history.[1] Though Ireland was formally united to England only in 1801 by the Act of Union, England had been involved in Irish affairs since the days of the Normans, and in the modern period Ireland was in a subordinate position and under the English Crown—at least in name. Very much John Bull's other island, every phase of English history had its Irish counterpart, each phase diminishing further Gaelic ("mere Irish") control and, from the Reformation, Catholic control. As in England, Church property in Ireland was expropriated; a Protestant Established Church (Church of Ireland) was created; and the same kinds of penal laws seen in England were imposed in Ireland. William of Orange's defeat of King James II at the Battle of the Boyne (1690) and the defeat of James's supporters at Aughrim and their surrender at Limerick (1691) had shattered the forces of Catholic Ireland, many of whom left for the Continent. The majority of the population remained Catholic, subjected to a ruling class of Protestant landlords, the Protestant ascendancy, and forced to support an alien religion, the Church of Ire-

1. Two good surveys of the Irish Question are Nicholas Mansergh, *The Irish Question, 1840–1921* (London: Allen and Unwin, 1965); and George Dangerfield, *The Damnable Question: A Study in Anglo-Irish Relations* (Boston: Little, Brown, 1976).

land, with their tithes. Between confiscation and apostasy, Catholic ownership of the land declined from about 59 percent in 1641 to about 22 percent in 1688, about 14 percent in 1703, and scarcely 5 percent in 1778—though these figures pertain only to outright ownership and do not take into account the various strategies Catholics used to maintain control of property.[2] Despite appearances, Catholicism was not broken, and the eighteenth century even saw its revival. The penal laws could never be implemented fully, and in 1778, 1782, and 1792 a great many of the disabilities were removed. In 1793 Catholics gained the vote on the same limited franchise as Protestants, though they could not be elected to the Irish Parliament. Pitt had virtually promised the complete emancipation of the Catholic body when he carried the union of Ireland and Britain, but it was not until 1829 and the mass politics of Daniel O'Connell that this came about.[3] Having achieved Catholic emancipation, O'Connell began a movement for the repeal of the Union, but he died in 1847 without having succeeded. The Great Famine of 1845–1849 left little room for politics but proved a seedbed for more revolutionary ideas. While the Young Ireland rising of 1848 proved a complete failure, the Irish Republican Brotherhood, the Fenians, were far more successful. Founded in 1858, this secret society had only one aim, Irish independence, and believing that Britain would never give in without physical force it prepared itself for an armed uprising when the time was right. Thousands of Irish joined despite the disapproval of the Church, but the attempted rising in 1867 proved a failure also. The rising did, however, awaken Gladstone to the need for justice for Ireland and a program for the solution of her problems. The failure of the Fenians and the successes of the constitutional nationalists, the Irish Party, weakened support for revolutionary action.

If the problems of Ireland were to be redressed, it would be through the Parliament at Westminster, and the Irish MPs often disrupted the flow of parliamentary business to make this point. In 1869 Gladstone's disestablishment of the Church of Ireland removed one cause of dissatisfaction, and beginning in 1870 various attempts were made to remove the others.[4] The extension of

2. See Thomas Barlett, *The Fall and Rise of the Irish Nation: The Catholic Question, 1690–1830* (Dublin: Gill and Macmillan, 1992), 47–48.

3. See Fergus O'Ferrall, *Catholic Emancipation: Daniel O'Connell and the Birth of Irish Democracy, 1820–1830* (Dublin: Gill and Macmillan, 1985).

4. See P. M. H. Bell, *Disestablishment in Ireland and Wales* (London: S.P.C.K., 1969), 1–157; and Donald Harmon Akenson, *The Church of Ireland: Ecclesiastical Reform and Revolution, 1800–1885*

the franchise throughout the nineteenth century helped, since it shifted political power ever more toward the Catholics: the 1884 Reform Bill more than tripled the number of Irish voters, including not only the better-off classes but also many of the cottiers and agricultural laborers. The Home Rule movement grew in strength, and in the 1885 election the Irish Nationalists achieved a near-sweep of the constituencies outside Ulster, gaining some eighty-six seats at Westminster. It was at this time that Gladstone introduced his first Home Rule bill (1886) which led to the splitting of the Liberal Party and the beginning of the Conservative (Unionist) hegemony, which lasted, excepting an interlude from 1892 to 1895, until 1905. It was during this brief period of Liberal control that the second Home Rule bill was defeated in 1893. During the years of Conservative control things had quieted down somewhat. In Westminster this was due to a number of things: the controversy and fragmentation of the Irish Party over Parnell's involvement with Kitty O'Shea, and her divorce; the development and use of new procedures to cut off obstructive tactics in Parliament; and the enormous Conservative majorities, which made the votes of the Nationalists superfluous. In Ireland this was due to the combined Conservative policy of coercion and conciliation.

Arthur Balfour had a profound influence on Irish policy, first as chief secretary for Ireland (1887–1891) in his uncle's government, then as leader of the Conservatives in the House of Commons, and then as prime minister.[5] Under Balfour the Unionists began a two-pronged effort to pacify Ireland through a policy of a repression of "lawlessness" by coercion laws (it was at this time that he gained the name of "Bloody Balfour") and by a program of constructive reform ("killing Home Rule by kindness").[6] This program of "constructive Unionism" included the 1892 creation of the Congested Districts Board to re-

(New Haven: Yale University Press, 1971), 226–74. In 1838, to end the "tithe wars" of the 1830s, the tithe (the annual charge on the land to support the Church of Ireland) was moved to the landowners (though the Catholic tenants still paid it indirectly through their rents), and with disestablishment tithes were kept but were to be used for social welfare programs.

5. See Catherine Shannon, *Arthur Balfour and Ireland, 1874–1922* (Washington, D.C.: Catholic University of America Press, 1988). The Balfour influence was even stronger in that his brother, Gerald, was chief secretary from 1895 to 1900, and that Gerald's successor, George Wyndham, had been Balfour's private secretary (1881–1891) and protégé.

6. For the Unionist program in Ireland, see Lewis Perry Curtis Jr., *Coercion and Conciliation in Ireland, 1880–1892: A Study in Conservative Unionism* (Princeton: Princeton University Press, 1963); Andrew Gailey, *Ireland and the Death of Kindness: The Experience of Constructive Unionism, 1890–1905* (Cork: Cork University Press, 1987); and William R. Ferrell, *George Wyndham at the Irish Office, 1900–1905* (master's thesis, University of South Carolina, 1974).

generate rural life in the West of Ireland and undertake other economic projects, and culminated in the Irish Land Act of 1903 pushed by George Wyndham, the chief secretary from 1900.[7]

One of the major areas of concern for the Irish was ownership of the land.[8] Primarily an agricultural nation, Ireland in the later nineteenth century had been filled with agrarian unrest and violence, particularly during the depression of the mid-1870s and early 1880s. Agricultural prices had declined owing to the importation of cheaper foreign produce, and the depression in English agriculture and the beginnings of farm mechanization there reduced the opportunities for the poorer peasants to supplement their wages as migrant workers in England. Then, in 1879, Ireland suffered the worst potato failure since the Great Famine. While the worst was averted, the economic losses were severe, and many tenants were in debt and liable for eviction. The Land League was formed in 1879 to protect these tenants from eviction, and an elaborate system of resistance was developed so as to foil eviction attempts. Acts of violence and boycotts against landlords and their agents were common and effective. Gladstone's second Irish land bill (1880–1881; the first was in 1870) tried to give sanction to the "three F's": fixity of tenure, fair rent, and free sale. When the Conservatives came to power they enacted the Ashbourne Act (1885), which helped the peasants purchase their land. The Land League and the Land War (1879–1882) were followed by the National League and the Plan of Campaign (1886–1889). Perhaps the most significant land measure in Irish history was Wyndham's Land Act (1903), and while it did not completely end agricultural unrest it significantly mollified it and set the stage for its future direction.

T. W. Russell (1841–1920), a Presbyterian Ulster MP (Liberal Unionist 1886–1910, Irish Nationalist 1911–1918) who, representing the Protestant

7. George Wyndham (1871–1913), a Conservative MP from 1889 to 1913, was chief secretary from 1900 to 1905. For Wyndham's life, see John William Mackail and Guy Wyndham, *The Life and Letters of George Wyndham,* 2 vols. (London: Hutchinson, 1925); and Max Egremont, *The Cousins: The Friendship, Opinions and Activities of Wilfrid Scawen Blunt and George Wyndham* (London: Collins, 1977).

8. See John E. Pomfret, *The Struggle for Land in Ireland 1800–1923* (Princeton: Princeton University Press, 1930); Barbara Solow, *The Land Question and the Irish Economy* (Cambridge: Harvard University Press, 1971); Michael J. Winstanley, *Ireland and the Land Question, 1800–1922* (London: Routledge, 1984); Sally Warwick-Haller, *William O'Brien and the Irish Land War* (Dublin: Irish Academic Press, 1990); and Philip J. Bull, *Land, Politics and Nationalism: A Study of the Irish Land Question* (New York: St. Martin's Press, 1996). For the land question in the context of the whole of Great Britain, see Douglas, *Land, People and Politics.*

farmer interest, had long pressed for land reform and had been deeply involved with Wyndham's Land Act, wrote an article for the January 1907 number of the *Dublin* on the "agrarian revolution" that Wyndham's work had accomplished.[9] He attacked the old system of land tenure (landlord and tenant) as being "forced upon Ireland by conquest and confiscation" and said it "worked little else but ruin and havoc in the country." The tenant equipped the farm, constructed its buildings, and developed the land, while the landlord did little but collect his rent. He "reaped where he had not sown," and as the competition for land increased, he increased the rents until it sometimes became impossible for tenants to remain. Russell believed that Gladstone's Irish Land Act of 1870 should have given tenants some fixity of tenure and allowed for compensation for improvements if they were evicted, but the landlords undermined it. The agitation of the Irish Land League, however, led to Gladstone's Irish Land Act of 1881, which created a Fair Rent Court, gave greater protection from eviction, and allowed the tenant, subject to certain restrictions, to sell his interest on the open market. This measure, he thought, particularly sobered the landlords, who discovered that "they were no longer lords of the soil," and could no longer raise rents or evict tenants as they pleased. The country "somehow or another" would have to get back to the people who worked it. The growth of this feeling led to the first Land Purchase Act in 1885, an act of the Tory government that placed 5 million pounds at the disposal of the tenants to acquire ownership of their holdings. The success of this measure led to further sums being allotted for the task, subject to long-term payment, again, he thought, with great success. However, many landlords would not sell the land to their tenants, nor would Parliament "as then constituted" adopt the principle of compulsion despite the great agitation for it in Ireland. Eventually, though, through a conference led by Lord Dunraven (4th Earl of Dunraven, 1855–1939, prominent southern Irish landlord and Unionist) with representatives of both the landlords and tenants in December 1902, it was concluded that dual ownership of the land was "prejudicial to the interests of both landlord and tenant" and that single ownership should be brought about by a scheme of universal purchase. The government under Wyndham took up and developed the conclusions and agreements of this conference, and the Irish Land Act of 1903, which placed 100 million pounds at the disposal of the tenants for the purchase of their land, became a reality.

9. T. W. Russell, "The Story of an Agrarian Revolution," *Dublin Review* (Jan. 1907): 20–25.

Russell pointed out the great success of these land purchase acts since 1885. They had been financially successful, as the tenants had been good about repaying the money lent them; and, as the government itself had shown, the condition of the holdings had improved after purchase and compared most favorably with land still under rent. Some 180,000 holdings had been bought, bringing greater agrarian peace to Ireland. Indeed, Russell predicted that within seven years the agrarian difficulty in Ireland would be at an end. "I have heard this great change called a bloodless revolution. In one, and a very true, sense it deserves this title. . . . It in reality brings to a close a cruel and desolating war—a war in which more blood has been spilt than on the greatest battlefields—a war which desolated Ireland—which drove people in millions from her soil—which laid the basis of hatred and strife all over the land."[10] While the Wyndham Act was far from perfect, for it tended to benefit the better-off tenants and it failed to solve the problems of the congested districts (the particularly impoverished parts of the west of Ireland), it did basically end landlordism and create a nation of peasant proprietors.[11]

Unlike many English Conservatives (and not just Conservatives), including Balfour, Wyndham seemed not to suffer from anti-Irish or anti-Catholic prejudice.[12] His mother was born in Ireland and was a descendant of Lord Edward Fitzgerald, a leader in the rebellion against the English in 1798. He mixed freely among the Irish and was interested in their happiness. He appointed as his undersecretary Sir Anthony MacDonnell, a Catholic and an

10. Ibid., 25. As an incentive to sell, the landlords received a 12 percent bonus on the selling price, to be paid out of Irish revenues for each sale (some £12 million was appropriated for this), and they were granted the right to sell their demesnes, the portion of their estate reserved for their private use, to the estates commissioners for a sum up to £20,000 and could repurchase these on the same terms offered to tenants. They were also paid in cash, not stock (which had been true since 1891), for any land bought by their tenants.

11. For a critique of Wyndham's act, see Douglas, *Land, People and Politics,* 136–37. Later, when it was clear that the Wyndham Act had been too successful and was impossible to continue in its entirety, the Liberal government passed the Irish Land Act of 1909, which made more funds available, but the sellers were now paid in stock, not cash, and the 12 percent bonus was replaced by a sliding scale.

12. See Shannon, *Arthur Balfour and Ireland,* 19–20, 69–70, and 77–81. Balfour once told Lord Salisbury: "I have never made up my mind whether I dislike the Orangemen, the Extreme Ritualists, the political disputers, or the R.C.s the most. On the whole, the last, but they are all odious" (ibid., 79). Nor would he have disagreed, on the whole, with Lord Salisbury's infamous comment that the Irish were no more capable of self-government than African Hottentots. See also Lewis Perry Curtis Jr., *Anglo-Saxons and Celts: A Study of Anti-Irish Prejudice in Victorian England* (Bridgeport, Conn.: University of Bridgeport, 1968), and *Apes and Angels: The Irishman in Victorian Caricature* (Washington, D.C.: Smithsonian Institution Press, 1971).

Irishman, who had distinguished himself in the Indian service. He also appointed Bertram Windle, then dean of the medical faculty at Birmingham University, a Catholic convert and a supporter of Home Rule, the Gaelic League, and the Land League, to be president of Queen's College, Cork. He was full of good intentions and applied himself with great energy to the situation before him, but he was too optimistic considering the tangled and embittered history of that much-disputed land. At Wyndham's death in 1913 Ward wrote a short eulogy of his friend in the *Dublin,* and it was his work in Ireland that he most particularly commended.[13]

When he was made Chief Secretary for Ireland his moment seemed to have arrived. He took up his task not as a party politician with a conventional programme, but as a philosophic statesman and an observer of men. He made a profound study of the country, of its social and economic conditions, and also its history and of the racial peculiarities of its people. The drama of Irish history and of his own position and work appealed to him. "I feel like a Ghibelline Duke in the land of the Guelphs," he said to the present writer. He had great schemes for Ireland founded on the views he had rapidly formed of the requirements of the country. He carried through the first part of the program, showing a power and grasp of a complicated situation which was new to him which made an experienced Irish land agent say to the present writer, "If he had lived all his life in Ireland he could not have worked out the details of his scheme with closer practical knowledge or greater perfection." Circumstances cut short his Irish career; and his great schemes for the country, the fruit of so much thought and study, were never executed or even made known to the public. The blow dealt him by this check can only be appreciated by those who realize how infinitely beyond the purview of the normal Chief Secretary his studies and his schemes had extended. He had equipped himself for a ten years' campaign. He had to be satisfied with three.[14]

But "constructive Unionism" could only go so far, and the failure of a moderate attempt at devolution in 1904 led to Wyndham's resignation and the abrupt end of attempts at reconciliation. In 1900 the Irish Nationalists were reunited under John Redmond (1852–1918), who had stayed loyal to Parnell after the Kitty O'Shea scandal had shattered the party.[15] In 1905 Arthur Griffith founded Sinn Féin ("we ourselves") as a separatist party, but it had little support as long as Redmond's constitutional nationalism remained rele-

13. Wilfrid Ward, "George Wyndham," *Dublin Review* (July 1913): 160–65. Ward also wrote a more extensive essay, "George Wyndham: Some Impressions by a Friend," *Quarterly Review* 219 (July 1913): 291–314, which was reprinted in *Men and Matters,* 70–104.

14. Ward, "George Wyndham," 161.

15. See F. S. L. Lyons, *The Irish Parliamentary Party, 1890–1910* (London: Faber and Faber, 1951).

vant. With the overwhelming victory of the Liberals in 1906, the two political issues of most concern for Ireland, higher education (the universities) and Home Rule, now seemed open to solution. The university question, being easier to deal with, came up immediately. Except for the remnant of Newman's failed Catholic University at St. Stephen's Green, Dublin (which did not have a charter and could not give degrees), and those institutions for the training of the clergy, such as Maynooth, the only other institutions of higher learning were Trinity College, Dublin, founded by Queen Elizabeth in 1591, the sole college of the University of Dublin, and the three Queen's Colleges at Cork, Galway, and Belfast, created in 1845 and forming what was called the Queen's University. Catholics had been able to take degrees at Trinity since 1793, though they were excluded from fellowships until 1873, when all religious tests were abolished. While there had been Catholic students at Trinity, which had the great attraction for socially aspiring Irish Catholics that Oxford and Cambridge had for English Catholics, and although a Catholic was elected a fellow in 1880, it remained a bastion of the Protestant ascendancy.[16] In the Queen's Colleges Catholic influence had been excluded, and at the Synod of Thurles (1850) the Irish bishops had condemned the nondenominational Queen's Colleges as "godless colleges" dangerous to faith and morals. It was for this reason that they called on John Henry Newman in 1854 to create a Catholic University for Ireland; and it was for this institution that he wrote his classic *The Idea of a University.* After much frustration and lack of support, Newman resigned in 1858, though the institution limped on. Gladstone made an attempt to pass an Irish university bill in 1873. The plan entailed only one university for Ireland, the University of Dublin, with Trinity College, its theological department, as a separate institution, along with the Queen's Colleges of Cork and Belfast, Magee Presbyterian College of Theology in Derry, the Catholic University in Dublin, and any other colleges that fulfilled the requirements. It met with objections from all sides, and after every real concession to the Catholic Irish had been withdrawn, even the Irish members voted against it, and it lost by three votes in the Commons. In 1879 Disraeli's Conservative government created the Royal University, which was given the power to award degrees to anyone who passed its examinations. The Queen's Uni-

16. It also remained a bastion of Unionism. The first Catholic fellow, Thomas Maguire, was an aggressive Unionist. He not only wrote pamphlets against Home Rule but was involved in the attempt to discredit Parnell through the Pigott forgeries.

versity was abolished but the Queen's Colleges remained. As a kind of indirect subsidy for Catholic university education, fifteen of the Royal University's twenty-eight fellowships were given to the Catholic University College, Dublin. While this was meant to be only a temporary measure, the political situation made it impossible to create a final solution. The Liberals supported the undenominational principle, strongly so when it came to education, and the Conservatives worried about opposition within their ranks from Scotland, Lancashire, and Ireland (particularly Ulster). Irish Catholics, some 74 percent of the population, wanted a university of their own, in harmony with their principles, traditions, and national sentiments, and pointed to the fact that while Queen's College, Belfast, and Trinity College were "officially" undenominational, they were in fact strongly Protestant. Nor did the Queen's Colleges in Cork and Galway, which had been meant for the overwhelmingly local Catholic population, have many Catholic faculty members.

Ward was very interested in the Irish universities question. He was an examiner in mental and moral science at the Royal University of Ireland in 1891–1892 (the Royal University was just an examining board), and had been on the Robertson Commission (1901–1903), which investigated the question of Irish university education excluding Trinity College.[17] The conclusions of the Robertson Commission were that the Royal University should be made a teaching university, with the Queen's Colleges at Belfast, Galway, and Cork as constituent colleges, and a Catholic college should be created in Dublin, endowed and equipped on a scale required of a first-rate institution. In 1903 Wyndham and Lord Dunraven proposed a national university consisting of Trinity College, Queen's College, Belfast, and a college acceptable to Catholics, all on an equal footing. But nothing came of either the Robertson Commission conclusions or the Dunraven-Wyndham scheme, and Wyndham's failure to bring in any bill on the Irish university question permanently destroyed his support among Irish Catholics. Another commission, under Sir Edward Fry (the Fry Commission), was appointed by the Liberal government on June 1, 1906, and on January 12, 1907, it issued its report. While all the members of the commission were agreed on the need for a college acceptable to Catholics, they disagreed on the means to achieve it. The Catholic bishops themselves disagreed about what should be done. While Archbishop Walsh strongly desired a Catholic college with Trinity College as part of the Univer-

17. For Ward and the Robertson Commission, see *Wilfrid Wards* 2:50–79.

sity of Dublin, the rest preferred a Catholic university or a Catholic college within the Royal University.

The first notice of this question in Ward's *Dublin* was an article by Bishop Edward O'Dwyer of Limerick in the April 1906 number. O'Dwyer, a member of the senate of the Royal University, had long been involved in the university question, which he put before all else, and had given an impressive performance as a witness before the Robertson Commission.[18] After lambasting the Conservatives who had formed the first commission, promising legislation at its conclusion, he bemoaned the state of Catholic Ireland's dearth of higher studies: "Ireland is poor, and for many years has been sinking into deeper poverty; its population has been decreasing at a rate which is a source of national anxiety; every phase of life is exhibiting symptoms of failure and decay; yet the brain-power of its people, the one element of strength and health which the country possess, and by which, if properly developed, everything might be regained, lies a neglected and wasted force which, for some inscrutable reason, no English Government will bring into play."[19] He complained that instead of a true teaching university there was only an examination board that had proved barren of results and that the commission itself had criticized. He argued that it was now up to the Liberals to make good this deficiency. Despite their antipathy toward "religious education other than that of the Nonconformist type," their appeal to Home Rule principles "necessarily would include the settlement of our own educational claims." He did not think that English religious prejudices should determine the nature of the laws of Ireland, and he considered Lord Dudley's famous dictum, "to govern Ireland according to Irish ideas," valid for both Whigs and Tories, any other conception of government being little different from tyranny. University reform, he opined, "is covered and included by the concession of Home Rule," and to delay dealing with the education problem until Home Rule is a reality "is not, as the Americans say, 'good enough.'" He suggested that if the Liberals were seeking a buffer between themselves and endowing any institution that might be serviceable to Catholics, the already existing senate of the Royal University was ideal. It was diverse in its constituents, representative of the religious bodies of Ireland, and, as a whole, had worked out well. Let them put university reform into its hands and let it settle it.

18. See Morrissey, *Bishop O'Dwyer,* 56–74, 253–300.
19. Edward O'Dwyer, "Irish University Education," *Dublin Review* (April 1906); 343–44.

They know, because they have touched with their hands, all the conditions of the problem to be solved; the materials and resources on which they can count; the possibilities of the case; the shoals and quicksands to be avoided. In a word, being Irishmen who have been administering for many years a very imperfect but at the same time influential and widespread institution, they know its shortcomings and the way to remedy them, and they understand the undercurrents of Irish intellectual, social and religious life which have to be allowed for in any satisfactory solution of the case.[20]

After the Fry Commission had finished its work Bishop O'Dwyer wrote another article, in the April 1907 number, defending its report and recommendations.[21] The main recommendation had been that since Trinity College, by its strong Protestant Episcopalianism, was not serviceable to Catholics, the creation of a Catholic college in Dublin was necessary. While the Irish bishops would have preferred a Catholic University, they could accept a new college in the University of Dublin or in the Royal University. While O'Dwyer would have preferred a Royal University solution rather than a University of Dublin one, the intention of the government was clearly to create a Catholic college with Trinity within the University of Dublin. The federation of the Queen's Colleges in a national university with Trinity would be an immense improvement over the current situation; and while he gratefully recognized the work the Jesuits had done at University College, "their little college, which has kept the lamp of learning so splendidly alight these years," it had to be replaced "by an institution more truly national in its constitution and government." Trinity College, grown rich and satisfied in her monopoly, would find this change difficult, he thought, but it only stood to gain, since it had cut itself off from the rest of the nation, which for the most part now preferred the English universities. He thought that Trinity could remain basically the same, safe in its academics and endowments, but by its inclusion could again be the teacher of the Irish nation as part of a reformed University of Dublin, perhaps leading to an intellectual activity such as they had never known. To those who complained that this new college would be denominational, he pointed out that Trinity, with its Divinity School and its chapel, all endowed by public funds, was no less denominational. Nor should one fear that this plan would weaken the university, which would now become the

20. Ibid., 351. Morrissey called the article "impressive," and it won the praise of Wyndham as well. See Morrissey, *Bishop O'Dywer*, 299.

21. Edward O'Dwyer, "Irish University Education," *Dublin Review* (April 1907): 225–45.

place for Catholics to get their degrees and so would rapidly grow in quality. One great fear was that the two colleges in Dublin would monopolize education and drain off the students from the Queen's Colleges, though he sensed that there seemed to be some idea in the government that they might themselves eventually grow large enough to gain university charters.

Bertram Windle, the president of Queen's College, Cork, wrote the final two articles on the topic of Irish university education, perhaps because of Ward's conflicts with O'Dwyer over the *Pascendi* article, or perhaps because of his extremely strong criticisms of the bill when it was introduced by the Liberals at the end of March 1908. The first article, in the July 1908 number, written while the bill was still moving through Parliament, reviewed the situation of the Irish colleges and discussed its salient points.[22] On the universities question there were three possible options. The one-university scheme, which would create one national university from all the various colleges, Windle thought "a hopeless dream" that would sterilize education and be ultimately unworkable. The two-university scheme would create a Catholic college with Trinity College to form the University of Dublin, with the other Queen's Colleges being joined into a revived Queen's University. This option was destroyed by the opposition of Trinity. Finally there was the three-university scheme, which, because it had the least opposition, was the one most likely to pass Parliament. Under this scheme Trinity College would be left to itself, Queen's College, Belfast (dominated by the Ulster Presbyterians) would become a separate university, and the former Queen's Colleges at Cork and Galway would be united with a new college in Dublin to form a common federal university. Windle wrote his second article after the bill's final passage and the three-university-scheme had been accepted.[23] While pleased that Mr. Augustine Birrell, the chief secretary of the Irish Office, had successfully shepherded the bill through Parliament and achieved what others had failed to do over many decades, he had a number of complaints. First, that Trinity College (of which he was an alumnus), by its strict adherence to the Protestant Episcopal Church "of which it has been so long the faithful ally" and its exclusion from the new national university, was condemning itself to decline: it had cut itself off from Catholic Ireland, and the groups from which it had previously drawn its students were either declining (the land agents, the smaller landlords, and

22. Bertram Windle, "The Irish Universities Bill, 1908," ibid. (July 1908): 147–59.

23. Bertram Windle, "The Future Universities of Ireland," ibid. (Oct. 1908): 310–20.

the Episcopal clergy) or were sending their young men to Oxford and Cambridge instead. Second, that a federated university was a weaker sort of institution. This criticism was softened, though, by the fact that the bill made sure to give each constituent college a great deal of freedom and autonomy. Third, that the absence of funds for student housing weakened them as true teaching institutions. Fourth, so as to assure the bill's passage, a number of clauses had been added that were clearly aimed at the Catholic Church. One clause specified that professors of theology could only be set up by private funds and that these academics could never be members of the board of studies of the university, or of the academic councils of the colleges or of any faculty except that of theology. Another clause stated that the colleges could not erect chapels within their precincts, even with private funds. While he found these points annoying and even humiliating to all Catholics, he admitted that "we must be thankful for such mercies as are vouchsafed to us, and must in common fairness admit that the Nonconformist members of Parliament have conceded points to Irish and Catholic opinion which, from their particular angle of vision, must certainly have seemed to be very great and very important."[24] The final result could be criticized on many points, but it was a result that the Irish bishops could live with and that had given them most of what they wanted.[25] The new national university was officially nondenominational; still, it could be adapted to the needs of Catholic Ireland.

With the settlement of the university question only one political question remained unsolved, that of Home Rule. And with the removal of the absolute veto of the House of Lords, it became a real possibility. Twice before the Liberals under Gladstone had attempted to pass Home Rule for Ireland only to see it defeated:[26] the first time in 1886, when it was defeated in the House of Commons at its second reading, and the second time in 1893, when it passed

24. Ibid., 318. The Jesuits cut their ties with the Catholic University, and its buildings were taken over by the new Dublin college.

25. For the Church and the Irish universities bill, see Miller, *Church, State and Nation in Ireland,* 189–204, and Senia Paesta, "The Catholic Hierarchy and the Irish University Question, 1880–1908," *History* 85 (April 2000): 268–84. In 1910, when Gaelic was made compulsory for admission to the newly created national university, the bishops, fearing that this would supply a pretext for Catholics to go to Trinity College, were successful in their push for allowing a period of transition. See Miller, *Church, State and Nation in Ireland,* 234–42.

26. For Irish Home Rule, see Alan O'Day, *Irish Home Rule, 1867–1921* (Manchester: Manchester University Press, 1998); and John Kendle, *Ireland and the Federal Solution: The Debate over the United Kingdom Constitution, 1870–1921* (Montreal: McGill-Queen's University Press, 1989).

in the Commons (by 32 votes) only to be defeated in the Lords (419 to 41). The third Home Rule bill was introduced on April 11, 1912, by Asquith's government. The *Dublin Review* devoted three articles to Home Rule. The earliest merely discussed the economics of it, declaring that if Home Rule were to become a reality, Ireland should be fitted to a colonial settlement with the greatest freedom of taxation and spending, since Britain's ambitious taxation and policies were unsuited to Ireland's prosperity and were very likely to become more so with time.[27] The other two were of a more political nature: one for Home Rule and one against, though published in different numbers. What is interesting, and indicative of the *Dublin*'s readership under Ward, is that, although he attached a disclaimer to the pro–Home Rule article stating the *Dublin*'s policy of allowing varying viewpoints on such national issues, he felt no need to put a disclaimer on the anti–Home Rule article, as if he expected the first to be somewhat objectionable to his readers.

While there were Catholic Unionists in Ireland, they were a distinct minority among Irish Catholics and were easily outnumbered by their Protestant brethren.[28] The Unionists in the south, though economically and socially powerful, were politically weak.[29] In the north, however, they were numerically strong, and in northeastern Ulster they were a majority.[30] Gaelic Catholic Ulster had been a center of opposition to the English, and under James I it saw the most successful of the "plantations" to pacify the rebellious Irish. Settled by English and Scottish Protestants, eastern Ulster had a Protestant majority and was a center of an often rabid anti-Catholicism.[31] Ulster Orangeism (after William of Orange) was organized to maintain the Protestant supremacy, and the Unionists appealed to it repeatedly as Home Rule became a real possibility. For many, Home Rule meant "Rome Rule." Visiting Ulster

27. Frank MacDermot, "The Fiscal Powers of an Irish Parliament," *Dublin Review* (Oct. 1911): 290–303. See also Patricia Jalland, "Irish Home-Rule Finance: A Neglected Dimension of the Irish Question, 1910–1914," *Irish Historical Studies* 23 (May 1983): 233–53.

28. For Irish Catholic Unionism, see John Biggs-Davison and George Chowdharay-Best, *The Cross of St Patrick: The Catholic Unionist Tradition in Ireland* (Abbotsbrook: Kensal Press, 1984).

29. For southern Unionism, see Patrick Buckland, *Irish Unionism One: The Anglo-Irish and the New Ireland, 1885–1922* (Dublin: Gill and Macmillan, 1972). "Between 1885 and 1914, unionists were regularly returned only for Trinity College and Dublin Co. South, though they were successful in the St Stephen's Green division of Dublin on occasion and in Galway City in 1900" (21).

30. For northern or Ulster Unionism, see Patrick Buckland, *Irish Unionism Two: Ulster Unionism and the Origins of Northern Ireland, 1886–1922* (Dublin: Gill and Macmillan, 1973).

31. See Oliver Rafferty, *Catholicism in Ulster, 1603–1983: An Interpretative History* (Columbia: University of South Carolina Press, 1994).

in 1886, Lord Randolph Churchill played "the Orange card," asserting that "Ulster will fight and Ulster will be right." On February 2, 1910, Sir Edward Carson (1854–1935), a southern Unionist barrister, British solicitor general from 1900 to 1905, and an MP for Trinity College, took charge of the Ulster Unionists with the goal of using Ulster intransigence to destroy Home Rule for all Ireland.

Ward was a Unionist, as were many upper-class English Catholics, including the Duke of Norfolk, who often acted as a go-between with the Vatican for the British government over Irish affairs, much to the chagrin of Irish nationalists. The article opposing Home Rule appeared in the April 1912 number and was written by the Catholic Conservative MP, James Fitzalan Hope, Wilfrid's brother-in-law.[32] Hope believed that of all political topics this one had been the least considered on its merits and the most influenced by every sort of popular passion and crude bigotry. So it was important for English Catholics to get beyond the "ravings of Orange extremists" (from which he excluded Sir Edward Carson) and their followers in England and to examine the case impartially. The case against Home Rule, he said, would hold just as well if it were applied to Scotland or Wales, or whether the whole island were Catholic or Protestant, "or had been wholly perverted to Shintoism or Theosophy." He believed national sentiment was a good thing and that the British Empire freely and generously recognized the principle of nationality, though in different ways. "Scotland gratifies her national spirit by the maintenance of her ancient institutions; Wales hers, by the general, and even official use of her own language and separate educational system. Ireland, however, has no ancient laws to cherish; and the Irish language is, for the most part, an exotic, the grammar of which is laboriously acquired by a few ultra-patriots."[33] Since the Irish had a natural taste for politics, Hope maintained, they must be satisfied in their political ambitions—and he believed that they were. Irish representation, proportionally, "in the government of the greatest Empire the world has ever seen," was far in excess of the other constituent parts of the United Kingdom, and by her sizable numbers in Parliament she was a force in legislation and could gain comparable benefits. He did not think the complaints about the lack of self-government were, in one sense, true. He believed that Ireland, because of her political influence, was often treated differently

32. James Fitzalan Hope, "Home Rule for Ireland," *Dublin Review* (April 1912): 353–69.
33. Ibid., 356.

from the rest of the realm, and much according to her desires. The Liberal education bills were never even considered for Ireland, for example, because it was known that the Irish did not want them; and in Lloyd George's budget, which had to apply to the whole kingdom, there was a different and more favorable scale of duties for licensed houses (pubs), which applied only in Ireland. He believed that Ireland already enjoyed self-government "to a remarkable degree," though it was exercised not in Dublin but at Westminster.

Stripped of patriotic sentiment and looking at the business of ordering the functions of government efficiently, he saw two major points against Home Rule. First, since Parliaments, especially the modern sort, seemed insatiable in their desires to do more, interfere more, and demand more taxes, Ireland would be better off without one. He did not believe that the average Irishman desired the kind of state intervention that seemed "to have mildly captivated many Englishmen." He did not think the Irish would like the restrictions of freedom and the greater taxation that would certainly follow the creation of an Irish Parliament. Second, Home Rule would be a disaster financially because Ireland could not herself afford the programs from which she was presently benefiting. And it would be "monstrous" for England to pay Ireland's bill.

> England at present pays, out of money raised from taxation of Englishmen, to keep Ireland going; her defence, her State social benefits, and so forth, are provided to a considerable amount out of English money. And of course, England looks to have control. It is now proposed that Ireland should be free from that control, and yet that England should still go on paying! . . . It is a proposal, in effect, for making Great Britain a tributary of Ireland . . . We have heard a lot about injustices to Ireland—in the past they undoubtedly existed; but we are now in the presence of an amazing attempt to commit an injustice upon England . . . So England is to pay the piper, while Ireland calls the tune.[34]

Hope did not doubt that some extension of local self-government could be arranged, or that things such as the referendum could be used for particularly Irish issues. All in all, his arguments were very similar to the standard Unionist arguments.[35] Only in his failure to play the "Orange card" of Protestant Ulster ("Ulsteria") did he differ—and that is not surprising, since as a devout Catholic he could only have found the Ulster Orangemen's anti-Catholicism

34. Ibid., 362–64.
35. See Shannon, *Arthur Balfour and Ireland*, 165–70.

repugnant. Like most Unionists he believed a number of things: that much of the desire for Home Rule was "the artificial product of persistent propagandism and organization" and without real depth, and was due to a silly sentimentalism "for the sake of the memories of ancient wrongs"; that the Irish politicians were moved more by a desire for new sources of patronage for themselves and their followers than by a love for Ireland; and that things had gotten so much better in Ireland that there was no need for such a radical measure. "It is not as if England were levying tribute from Ireland: Ireland would then be right in struggling for independence; but the boot is on the other leg. It is not as though England to-day were a hard taskmaster, denying liberty to Ireland: Ireland would then be justified in striving for freedom, even at the heavy risk to her financial stability. But it is not so. Ireland is as free as England, and the administration of Dublin Castle, though it doubtless has its defects, is not to-day the tyranny which it sometimes appears to patriotic minds."[36]

An Irishman thinking of the coercion laws (which were a permanent part of the Irish legal code) might question Hope's contention that Ireland was as free as other parts of the United Kingdom. The main fault of the Unionist point of view, though, was pointed out very well in the article in the October 1913 number discussing what would happen if Home Rule were defeated:

> The great fault of English politicians has always been that they have ignored what Professor Kettle has called "the open secret of Ireland," her craving for the recognition of her nationality. They have persisted in prescribing material panaceas for a spiritual need and in asking her whether she is not really cured at last. Such remedies as Land Acts can never be accepted as a substitute for self-government. As Mr Winston Churchill well said, Ireland will never barter her soul for a tax on imported butter . . . There is no Irishman who would not prefer peace to hostility, provided only it be peace with honour. There is no district where the Nationalist would not live in complete harmony with his Unionist neighbours, once his inextinguishable craving for self-government is satisfied. But until that satisfaction is granted, there can never be permanent peace. Ireland is not, and does not seem likely to become, West Britain.[37]

The author, Bewley, pointed out that if the Home Rule bill should fail, especially after Ireland had already made political and economic sacrifices to gain it, the Irish Party under Redmond would lose all credibility and the more

36. Hope, "Home Rule for Ireland," 364–65.

37. Charles Bewley, "If Home Rule Is Defeated," *Dublin Review* (Oct. 1913): 263.

extreme forces (the Sinn Féin party in particular) would benefit. Anti-English feeling, which had been dying down since the Boer War, would be intensified.

Irish Nationalists recognize that it was not so much the English people as the House of Lords that was responsible for many of Ireland's grievances during the nineteenth century. Now, the Irish democracy looks to English democratic feeling as its natural friend and ally. It believes, rightly or wrongly, that the people of England are in favour of permitting Ireland to manage her own affairs. It is willing to let bygones be bygones, and by accepting the present Bill to turn its eyes from memories of the dead past. It recognizes that England is freely offering compensation for injustices which she committed more through ignorance than through malice, and as freely proclaims its acceptance of her terms. . . . And though Irish nationalists are willing to-day to take their places in that Empire in all loyalty and affection as citizens of a self-governing Ireland, it does not follow that they will be equally ready to do so on a future occasion. When confidence has once been betrayed it can never be restored in full, and a measure extorted by years of unremitting agitation can never carry with it the same power of healing old wounds as if it had been a free gift. England has an opportunity to-day which may never present itself a second time: it is for her to decide whether she will let it slip as she has let slip so many opportunities in the past. But, before she commits herself irrevocably, she should remember that, though the passionate desire of more than a century may not proclaim itself in violent acts, yet it is not easily extinguished, and that, though Ireland is wrapt in profound peace, it is not the peace of apathy, but the anxious silence of expectation.[38]

One book on Home Rule that the *Dublin* considered of "first-class importance which a thoughtful man, whatever his opinions," would read again and again "with increasing admiration and delight" was Erskine Childers's *The Framework of Home Rule.*[39] This "judicious book," by an Englishman, an ardent imperialist, and a well-known writer on military subjects, approached the problem historically, comparing the history of Ireland with that of other parts of the Empire. Childers believed that Ireland was essentially a colonial problem and that it should be solved according to the same pattern—which is to say, it should receive autonomy. He also believed that Ireland should be given complete powers to raise revenue and set expenditures.

38. Ibid., 264–65.

39. F. M., "Some Recent Books," ibid. (April 1912): 392–95. Childers (1870–1922), who wrote *The Riddle of the Sands* (London: Nelson, 1903), the best of the invasion novels from before the Great War, was a gun runner for the Irish Volunteers in 1914, fought for the British in the First World War, represented the Irish cause at Versailles, and, as a member of the Irish Republican Army, was executed for his opposition to the Irish Free State.

The Home Rule bill Asquith introduced on April 11, 1912, gave extensive control to the Imperial Parliament at Westminster, especially in the areas of finance and taxation, the Dublin Parliament possessing limited powers of raising revenue or varying customs and excise duties or on new taxes passed by the Imperial Parliament. It was to have a bicameral subordinate legislature, having "power to make laws for the peace, order, and good government of Ireland," but with supreme power to reside in the Imperial Parliament. The lord lieutenant was kept, though the position was now open to Catholics, and given substantial power, being appointed by the Crown for a six-year term. There would be a House of Commons of 164 members elected by the existing constituencies; and an upper chamber, or Senate, would have 40 members, initially appointed by the lord lieutenant, "subject to any instructions given by His Majesty in respect of the nomination," and then elected in separate constituencies according to the principle of proportional representation by the same electors as those of the Imperial Parliament.[40] When the two houses disagreed on a bill, they would all sit together, and a majority would be decisive. The Irish Parliament had no jurisdiction over matters affecting the Crown, war and peace, the army and navy, treaties, dignities, treason, general taxation, "reserved services" (land purchase, old age pensions, national insurance, the Royal Irish Constabulary for the next six years, the post office savings bank, public loans, and the collection of taxes), and it was forbidden to endow any sect or infringe on religious liberty. Also, an imperial-dominated Privy Council was created and given the power to determine the validity of any Irish-made law. Irish representation at Westminster, always a sticking point since by now Ireland was overrepresented there, was to be reduced to 42 seats (although the population of Ireland really entitled them to 64): 34 county seats and 8 borough seats (Belfast 4, Dublin 3, Cork 1).

Despite the extreme limitations on this Irish Parliament, the Unionists strongly opposed the bill. It passed, however, its first reading by the Commons on July 7, 1913, by a vote of 352 to 243. It was defeated by the House of Lords on July 15; but following the Parliament Act of 1911, if it passed the House of Commons in three successive sessions it would become law, and on May 25, 1914, the Home Rule bill passed its third reading in the House of

40. The Irish House of Commons would consist of 164 members: 59 for Ulster, 41 for Leinster, 37 for Munster, 25 for Connaught, and 2 university seats; or 128 county MPs, 34 borough MPs, and 2 university MPs.

Commons. It looked very likely that civil war might just begin in Ulster.[41] On September 28, 1912, almost three-quarters of all Ulster Protestants over the age of fifteen signed the Solemn League and Covenant, which promised to use "all means which may be found necessary to defeat the present conspiracy to set up a Home Rule Parliament in Ireland" and "to refuse to recognize its authority." The violent language of Ulster found support among major Conservative politicians in England. Ever since the Parliament Act and Balfour's retirement from the leadership, a "new style" had appeared among Conservatives, violent, confrontational, and highly irresponsible. Bonar Law, Balfour's successor, was himself of Ulster Presbyterian descent and publicly supported rebellion, most notably at a rally before more than thirteen thousand supporters at Blenheim Palace on July 27, 1912, when he gave a speech declaring that "there are things stronger than parliamentary majorities" and that he could imagine no lengths of resistance to which Ulster could go in which he would not support her.[42] Among those attending was the Duke of Norfolk.[43] Much more dangerous was the formation of an Ulster Volunteer Force some eighty thousand strong, including many ex-servicemen, in January 1913. These forces were strengthened when, on April 24, 1914, with no military or police hindrance, some thirty-five thousand service rifles, each with a hundred rounds of ammunition, were imported and distributed. Just weeks earlier some fifty-eight army officers at Curragh Camp near Dublin had threatened resignation unless they were assured that they would be exempt from acting against Ulster. The activity in Ulster inspired a reaction on the Catholic side. By May 1914 some seventy-five thousand recruits had been collected into the Irish Volunteers, but when they brought in arms on July 26 they were hindered by British troops, who fired on rock-throwing civilians on their way back to barracks, killing three and wounding thirty-eight. One will never know if civil war would have broken out had not the invasion of Belgium by Germany and the declaration of war on August 4 changed the dynamics of the situation. Home Rule was suspended for the duration of the war.

41. See Patricia Jalland, *The Liberals and Ireland: The Ulster Question in British Politics to 1914* (New York: St. Martin's Press, 1980).

42. Nor was Balfour, who retained great influence, any less irresponsible or belligerent. For Balfour, see Shannon, *Arthur Balfour and Ireland,* 164–210.

43. While Norfolk attended the rally, the story that he presented "a golden sword" to Carson in appreciation of his resistance to Home Rule does not seem to be true. See Ian Colvin, *Carson: The Statesman* (New York: Macmillan, 1935), 129–30.

Redmond threw his support behind the war effort, hoping it would prove Irish loyalty and help gain English respect, but by the end of 1915 there was much disillusionment with Britain and with the Irish Party. Not only had Home Rule been suspended but it had been significantly modified, for even before the declaration of war an amending bill had been introduced that would allow counties to exclude themselves temporarily. As Home Rule was put "in storage," it was clear that something less than the entire nation would be included in it; and it was highly likely that it would not be temporary. Also, to the consternation of nationalists, the 1915 coalition government included not only Unionists but the *bête noir* of Home Rule advocates, Carson himself, who was made attorney general. On Easter Monday, April 24, 1916, the tragic Easter Rising took place in Dublin. It failed, and while the rebellion had very little popular support (the arrested rebels were greeted by jeers and rotten fruit and vegetables from the crowd as they were marched to prison), the executions and reprisals that followed swung opinion strongly against England and compromise. Things would never be the same again.

8 FOREIGN AFFAIRS

As a member of a universal church and a citizen of the greatest of world empires it was impossible for Ward not to be interested in foreign affairs, and his journal reflected that. Ward reveled in the Church's universality and was at pains to show off her accomplishments in other parts of the world. Also, since she was under attack in a number of countries at this time, Ward took the opportunity to present her case before an often uncomprehending British public. While many of the *Dublin*'s foreign affairs articles touched upon Catholicism, particularly in its political or social dimension, a great many were secular in nature. Not surprisingly, as a believer in the British Empire, then covering one-sixth of the world's land area and a quarter of its population, many of the articles dealt with parts of the Empire or foreign affairs as seen from an imperial perspective. A periodic column, "Foreign Politics of the Day," by Lancelot Lawton, began to appear in the *Dublin* in 1911 for the purpose of addressing foreign affairs both more systematically and more from the position of *realpolitik*.[1]

The country that attracted the most frequent attention from the

1. Despite the fact that Lawton was such a significant contributor to the *Dublin* and the author of four large books (three on Soviet Russia), it was impossible to find anything on him in the usual biographical sources. Owing to the efforts of Dr. M. N. E. Tiffany—whom I thank profusely for her help—we now know that he was born in 1880 in Liverpool (son of a journalist) and died in Cambridge in 1947. His death certificate states that he was "an Author, Historian and Economist." He attended Catholic schools, so it is likely that he was a Catholic.

Dublin was France, and this was almost exclusively for religious reasons.[2] France, center of so much of the Church's missionary and intellectual life, had, since the Enlightenment and the Revolution, become also a center of anticlericalism and anti-Christian *laïcisme.* While Napoleon's Concordat (1801) had restored the Church to a favored position after the savage depredations of the Revolution, it had not restored her with the same rights and freedoms that had prevailed before. Still despoiled of her properties, she had become a dependent of the state, under the thumb of the Ministry of Cults, which paid her salaries and watched her every move. While Catholicism revived in the nineteenth century and the position of the Church seemed to grow stronger, still she was not free, nor did she regain her primacy in the culture. Her religious orders remained circumscribed and her ability to influence future generations through education was limited. The Falloux Law (1850) allowed the Church to expand in secondary education, but with the fall of the Second Empire of Louis Napoleon and the coming of the Third Republic, things began to change. The strongly monarchical and Catholic government that took over after the fall of Louis Napoleon and the Franco-Prussian War reinforced the link between the Church and the political right in the minds of the people, and made any shift toward real republicanism a shift also against the power of the Church and the clergy. To the republicans, clericalism was the enemy. Imbued with a purely secular and positivistic view of the world, they saw the Church as retrogressive and superstitious, the enemy of reason. France would be renewed by a new republican and secularist ethos, and this was to be inculcated through the schools. To ensure this result, the government centralized primary education and made it obligatory and free, and attempted to eliminate any Church influence in public education. In the 1880s new laws removed religious instruction from all state primary schools, replacing it with *instruction morale et civique,* and began the exclusion of all religious from teaching in them.[3] To limit Church influence in secondary educa-

2. For France, see Maurice Larkin, *Church and State after the Dreyfus Affair: The Separation Issue in France* (London: Macmillan, 1974); Malcolm O. Partin, *Waldeck-Rousseau, Combes, and the Church: The Politics of Anticlericalism, 1899–1905* (Durham: Duke University Press, 1969); John McManners, *Church and State in France, 1870–1914* (London: S.P.C.K., 1972); and the first two chapters of Harry W. Paul, *The Second Ralliement: The Rapprochement between Church and State in France in the Twentieth Century* (Washington, D.C.: Catholic University of America Press, 1967). The only secular article on French politics is a comparison of the two politicians, the Socialist Jaurès and the Republican Clémenceau.

3. For a discussion of the failure of the French *morale laïque,* see Michael Maher, "Some Factors in Moral Education," *Dublin Review* (April 1909): 281–84.

tion, the Jesuits and some three hundred unauthorized orders were dissolved and expelled, and secondary state education was created for girls. The government also reinstated civil divorce and military service for seminarians; state ceremonies became completely secular, and the posts of military and hospital chaplains were abolished. In the 1890s Pope Leo XIII tried to move Catholics away from their monarchism and toward the Republic (the *Ralliement*), but without success. The Republic's anticlericalism and corruption were just too much for French Catholics to swallow. In any case, the Dreyfus Affair destroyed any hope of reconciliation between the Church and the more moderate republicans, as the old alliances reasserted themselves. Nationalists, monarchists, and many Catholics supported the honor of the army (one of the few places where Catholics could still serve their nation without hindrance) and so denied Dreyfus's innocence, while the defenders of Dreyfus and the Republic stood on the other side. The vast majority of Catholic clergy remained aloof from the whole affair, but the virulence of others, such as the Assumptionists, made up for that. The Dreyfus Affair poisoned politics in France and led to a ministry of "Republican defense" under Waldeck-Rousseau. His attempt to limit the influence of the religious orders led to the Associations Law of 1901. But the moderate bill he intended was extensively changed, and under his successor, the ex-seminarian and rabidly anticlerical Émile Combes, almost all the unauthorized religious orders were abolished and their property expropriated, and even the institutions of the authorized orders suffered. In a country that contained some 3,216 different orders (of which only 914 had been previously authorized), with nearly two hundred thousand members, this was devastating, especially for Catholic schools. In July 1904 diplomatic relations with the Holy See were broken off and a law was passed excluding religious from all teaching within ten years. In December 1905 France unilaterally abrogated the Concordat with the Separation Law, the law taking effect one year later. No longer would the state pay clergy salaries, and all Church property was to be given to *associations cultuelles* to be administered, failing which it would be forfeited to the government.

The Law of Separation was passed just before Ward's first number, and in that number there was an article by the Abbé Dimnet discussing the advantages and disadvantages of the law.[4] One obvious advantage, Dimnet wrote,

4. Ernest Dimnet, "The Church in France: Its Present Position," ibid. (Jan. 1906): 176–85. Abbé Dimnet (1866–1954) was a frequent writer on English culture. For his life, see his autobio-

would be the freedom of the Church from state control, which was quite extensive and often petty. Most important, no longer would the bishops and the higher clergy be government appointees. Another clear advantage would be that the Church was now free to reorganize her pastoral care so as to adjust to the demographic changes that the Concordat had not taken into consideration. Many major centers of population had too few priests, while many rural areas had far more than they needed. The obvious drawback of the Law of Separation would be the loss of clerical salaries, which the Concordat assured, though Dimnet thought that this loss could, in a very great many cases, be rectified, especially if money were collected in some general fund. "It would then appear, at first sight, that liberty has been bought cheap enough for the Church of France. The Pope's power to name the Bishops, the Bishop's power to appoint priests of his choice to the *cures* they choose, the liberty to go in and out, to form associations, to speak one's mind on all questions, in short, to try the methods made popular by the admirers of the American clergy—all this surely is worth forty wretched millions of francs."[5] But that was only the theory. In reality, the Separation Law hampered the Church in all sorts of ways.

A socialist association can hold meetings at the Labour Exchange, in which every possible method for subverting the constitution of the State may be discussed, and anarchists are at perfect liberty to hear in the room they hire a Russian prince explain his formulas—not social but chemical and explosive; but a priest is not free to say what he pleases to the congregation which supports him; he has not even the right to lock the door of the church if he thinks it advisable. He cannot use the church for other than purposes of worship. If he dare directly to blame the acts of Government, he is liable to a heavy fine. In short, a special interpretation is constantly given to the Law of Associations when the Association happens to be religious. . . . To sum up, it is plain that the liberty provided by the new law is not everybody's liberty, but a poor semblance of it which is all that the State will mete out to a spiritual community.[6]

Dimnet reminded his readers that it was the method of the anticlerical party to acclimatize the public to an idea or measure before developing its more stringent aspects. The Associations Law began in a progressive spirit and was intended by Waldeck-Rousseau as a "charter of liberty and stability, a sort of

graphical *My Old World* (New York: Simon and Schuster, 1935) and *My New World* (New York: Simon and Schuster, 1937).

5. Dimnet, "Church in France," 179.

6. Ibid., 180–81.

Concordat for the orders," but it became in the end a tool not merely against the unauthorized religious orders but against all religious orders. "This lesson has not been forgotten, and French Catholics will long feel shy of the *dona ferentes* Freemasons." Another cause for alarm was that the *associations cultuelles* could be the source of local schisms, because there was no direct reference to the Catholic hierarchy in the law. That so many of those involved in its passage had praised the law's schismatic possibilities did not make him feel any better about it. Yet, despite these fears and the lack of freedom, he believed it probable that the Holy See would now accept the law. In the absence of any great popular opposition, the Church would be wise to do so for the moment, but "the watchword has almost uniformly been, 'Wait until the Sovereign Pontiff speaks.'"[7]

Eventually the "Sovereign Pontiff" did speak, and in an encyclical of that February, *Vehementer Nos,* he formally condemned the separation and the *associations cultuelles.* While the French bishops also condemned these, they were aware that the Church would be left almost penniless if it rejected the law and would not legally be able to possess anything in the future, and they were willing to make the best of a bad situation. The pope disagreed, and in a second encyclical the following August, *Gravissimo,* he condemned any compromise with the law. Later that year, Ward wrote an unsigned article in which he laid out the risks in either accepting or rejecting the Separation Law.[8] While admitting that the matter had now been decided by the pope, and that Catholics were loyally obeying his injunctions ("however Catholics may differ as to the best means of securing the vitality of their religion in these difficult times"), still it was important, he thought, to discuss what was happening in France, because the English press had so overlooked or misunderstood the real situation, obsequiously accepting deceitful abstractions, showing far too much respect for party labels, and not caring "to explain the false associations by which the Church and the democracy have been thrown into apparent opposition."

The encyclical *Gravissimo,* he wrote, was not an injunction to *disobey* the law "but to refuse the precarious advantages, burdened with vexatious conditions, which it offers." By the proposed associations for public worship, the *associations cultuelles,* the state would regain the control it had given up by the

7. Ibid., 181, 185.

8. [Wilfrid Ward], "The Church of France and the French People," ibid. (Oct. 1906): 400–411.

abrogation of the Concordat. By disestablishment all Catholic institutions had lost their legal status, and to retain their property, they had to submit to many vexatious restrictions from which other associations were free. The men who created the law "have openly and repeatedly declared their purpose to 'uncatholicize France'; and they have explicitly confessed that they regard the Act only as a provisional measure in the accomplishment of that end." And although the text of the law was less illiberal than it could be, there was every reason to suspect, "as Danaan gifts," these temporary concessions and precarious privileges.

Ward made himself the devil's advocate and forcefully stated the case of those who would accept the law: that it did not exclude the hierarchical nature and organization of the Church and even supposed it; that it allowed associations to be organized into groups, in which, by the introduction of uniform statutes, episcopal authority and discipline could be maintained; and that the expropriation of Church property, the closing or possible sacrilegious use of churches, a persecuted and homeless clergy, and possible civil conflict were not worth the fight. "Why not attempt to make the best of it? Why prefer certain destitution along with an autonomy which can never be complete, to a partial subjection which time and the ingenuity of jurists may mitigate, and which leaves Catholics, at least for the present, in possession of their patrimony? Why anticipate calamities which are only contingent, and voluntarily abandon, from the first, the parish churches and all they contain, the seminaries, the houses of bishops and priests—because sooner or later they may be forfeited?"[9]

But the pope, he wrote, had finally rejected these arguments, since neither the letter nor the spirit of the law provided absolutely any security against the danger of indiscipline and schism. The Holy See feared that since nothing prevented an individual association from changing its statutes, it would be impossible to control it if its members were sufficiently agitated, and the fact that disputes affecting associations were referred to the council of state was no comfort, since that body was the creature of the government. Ward also thought that the pope's decision might not be based on what was expedient but was, rather, an appeal to the French people. Ward was aware of the apparent apathy of the French toward the separation, and he downplayed the clear victory of the government in recent elections. There were other factors in the

9. Ibid., 404.

race, he wrote, and since the Separation Law was a fait accompli, and since the more obnoxious of its acts, such as the attempt to inventory all Church property, had been temporarily suspended because of the disturbances they had caused, there did not seem much the people could do. He also believed that the government had succeeded in exploiting the traditional fear of monarchism and clericalism. "Among the 38,000,000 of French Catholics—the largest number assembled under one flag—very many, no doubt, are indifferent . . . it is a more pertinent fact that nearly all of them are Republicans—easily alarmed by the bogey of monarchical conspiracy, always jealous of ecclesiastical encroachments."[10] The government was thus able to hide its real aim, the destruction of Christianity, which it held "for a mischievous superstition." Ward hoped that the shock of the pope's verdict on the *associations cultuelles* and the real results of the law, once it took effect, would jolt the French out of their lethargy.

Ward ended his piece with one major worry. He saw that the monarchists, "the faithful friends of proscribed dynasties," already had disproportionate power and patronage in the French Church, and he feared that the Separation Law would throw the Church even more into the hands of "the pious hospitality of the rich." The French clergy, then, would "rapidly lose contact with the people and compromise the Church still further in the eyes of its enemies by a yet more intimate dependency on persons who are believed to dislike the form of government which France has chosen for herself."[11]

Many other articles appeared concerning the French Church. In an unsigned article, a longtime English Protestant resident of Paris wrote on the importance of French Freemasonry, whose aggressive atheism and political involvement, unlike the British variety, had been such a factor in recent events.[12] Count Albert de Mun, one of the French Church's most influential political and social figures, gave a thorough discussion of the situation from his perspective, "sur cette question si grave, si complexe et si difficilement intelligible pour les étrangers." He defended the pope's actions (admitting that he was merely summarizing the very complete arguments that Ward had made in the *Nineteenth Century* that January), giving a fuller history of the campaign that

10. Ibid., 409.

11. Ibid., 411.

12. "Anti-Clericalism in France," ibid. (April 1907): 351–70. In 1908 there were about thirty-two thousand Freemasons in France. For French Freemasonry, see Mildred J. Headings, *French Freemasonry under the Third Republic* (Baltimore: Johns Hopkins University Press, 1948).

the state had waged against religion in the Third Republic, and speaking with the authority of someone intimately involved in it all.[13] The issue resurfaced periodically in the pages of the *Dublin,* right up to the changed situation of the Great War, the last and longest of these articles appearing in 1913, by George Fonsegrive, author and editor of *La Quinzaine,* who described the situation now that the law had been in operation for seven years.[14] The good news, he wrote, was that the massive drop among seminarians that had followed the separation had stabilized and that there had even been an upturn, though he doubted that the numbers would ever be as high as they had been before. Confidence in the security of the diocesan priesthood had been regained when it became clear that the loss of all state income would not leave priests destitute. He did not mean to imply that things were fine, he said, given that priestly income was only two-thirds of the already meager salary of before. Nor had the faithful been everywhere as generous as they should have been, their generosity often declining over time. "They see the Church still alive, and influenced by the spirit of economy they begin to think that in order to live she does not really need all they had at first intended to put on one side for her."[15] He reminded his readers that if the clergy had had a hostile press during the time of the Concordat as money loving, their rejection of the *associations cultuelles* had lost them not just their churches, rectories, seminaries, and episcopal palaces, it also lost them more than 400 million francs in various endowments, funds, and pensions. Yet they did not complain. "They see the prejudice against them diminishing. They feel that the people are getting nearer to them. . . . The priest is no longer an official, he has more freedom of movement, he excites less envy, less jealousy. He does his military service like every one else. He is nearer to the people and people draw nearer to him."[16] Nor did the Church entirely lose her churches, for when it was

13. Albert de Mun, "La Question Religieuse en France," *Dublin Review* (July 1907): 155–85. For de Mun, see Benjamin F. Martin, *Count Albert de Mun: Paladin of the Third Republic* (Chapel Hill: University of North Carolina Press, 1978). For Ward's article, see "The Pope and France," *Nineteenth Century* (Jan. 1907): 27–41.

14. George Fonsegrive, "The Present Religious Situation in France," *Dublin Review* (Oct. 1913): 300–331. Fonsegrive (1852–1917) was such a promoter of Christian democracy that some considered him a "social Modernist." Other articles were Marquise de Chambrun, "The French Bishops and the Education Problem" (Jan. 1910): 182–92; Eugène Tavernier, "The Elections in France" (July 1910): 162–76; and Marquise de Chambrun, "Church and State in France" (April 1911): 253–68.

15. Fonsegrive, "Present Religious Situation in France," 306.

16. Ibid., 307.

clear that she would not accept the Separation Law and its *associations cultuelles,* the government nevertheless left them in the hands of the Catholic clergy and even acted against any attempt by schismatic groups to gain them for themselves. While the Church had no legal ownership and many points remained undecided, at least there were places for divine worship. Under the Concordat it had been difficult to create new churches and parishes, and with the massive population shifts of the recent period many people had been left without pastoral care. Now free of the Concordat, Fonsegrive wrote, the Church had rectified that situation. For example, in seven years, nine more parishes had been created in Paris, and in its suburbs some fifteen parishes and twenty-four chapels of ease, with more to come. He could point to many other successes, particularly in the area of Catholic societies and associations. Catholicism in France, he believed, had passed through a crisis "strengthened and rejuvenated." It was not the separation itself that had caused this, however, but the devotion of the faithful in union with their priests and bishops, and in union with Rome.

> The religious life is everywhere increasing in depth and intensity. . . . The unpopularity of the priest in the towns is growing less; cultivated young men welcome him and even seek him out of their own free will. The human mind has found the limits of science and has felt that they are narrow and hard, all men of culture recognize to-day that our whole life is, as it were, bathed in mystery. Faith is no longer a suspect but a friend. Those who have it not are seeking it, and those who have found it treasure it. Those even who despair of finding it respect it. And all, or nearly all, recognize that truth can only be where she declares herself, where she is supplied with all she needs to make her accessible to man—that is to say, in Catholicism, and finally in Rome.[17]

Anticlerical legislation was also a topic of concern in Portugal and Spain. The *Dublin* devoted four articles to Portugal, where a revolution overthrew the monarchy in 1910 and began an aggressive assault against the Church, and three articles on Spain, where the attacks on the Church were much less serious.[18] As with France, the British press had shown no appreciation for or understanding of the Catholic position. "The enlightenment, we are told, has

17. Ibid., 330–31.

18. Three articles by Francis McCullagh, "The Portuguese Revolution" (Jan. 1911): 85–110, "The Portuguese Separation Law" (July 1911): 126–42, and "The Portuguese Republic and the Press" (April 1913): 314–29; and one by Camillo Torrend, S.J., "Anti-clerical Policy in Portugal" (Jan. 1912), 128–51. See R. A. H. Robinson, "The Religious Question and the Catholic Revival in Portugal, 1900–1930," *Journal of Contemporary History* 12 (April 1977): 345–62.

crossed the Pyrenees, and another Latin race is chafing under the restrictions of an obscurantist Papacy."[19] In Portugal the religious orders had been dissolved, the Church disestablished, and an antireligious program without equal in recent memory begun. The Church-state conflict in Spain was over an attempt by the left wing of the Liberals to destroy the religious orders by an associations law similar to the one in France. In 1907 the *Dublin* devoted two unsigned articles to the issue, and in 1910 one signed one.[20] The first and the third were substantial and fairly objective descriptions of the troubled recent history of Spain, of the history of relations between the Church and the state, and of the contours of Spanish politics. The second article, written nine months after the first, the Liberal ministry having collapsed and the Conservatives victorious under Antonio Maura, revealed very well the moderately conservative, moderately Catholic viewpoint of the *Dublin.* It praised Maura as a man of integrity and a good Catholic who had no desire to alienate the Holy See or infringe upon the rights of the Church, and who would pass responsible reform. It also criticized those intransigent Catholics (particularly the Carlists) who, "however admirable in private life and in generous devotion to their cause, can suggest no remedy for modern evils save the return to an order of things which has passed away forever." Such intransigence was not the policy of the Holy See, under either Pope Leo XIII or Pope Pius X, the article hastened to add. The writer also revealed a certain romantic attitude toward traditional Catholic peasant cultures that was characteristic of much of Catholic thought of the time.[21]

In all our judgements about Spain we must remember this. The people of the country districts are poor and illiterate. They seldom taste flesh meat, and their education is of a kind that dispenses with books. But they are intensely religious, they are high-minded, and they are remarkably happy. A German politician has recently been scolding them for not making money. But at least they have ideals, for which money would

19. "Church and State in Spain," *Dublin Review* (Jan. 1907): 33.

20. Ibid., 33–41; "The Reaction in Spain," ibid. (Oct. 1907): 272–84; and Mgr. Bidwell, "Spain and the Church," ibid. (Oct. 1910): 376–96. For the Spanish Church-state conflicts, see William J. Callahan, *The Catholic Church in Spain, 1875–1998* (Washington, D.C.: Catholic University of America, 2000), 57–93.

21. This should not be surprising considering the deep-seated traditionalism of Catholicism and its residual strength in the more rural areas of Europe. In Great Britain, this mentality was particularly strong among the distributists, influenced by G. K. Chesterton and Hilaire Belloc, in men like Eric Gill and Vincent McNabb, and among the Irish clergy who believed that urban life would corrupt the simple piety of the faithful and tried to preserve Ireland's agrarian nature. See Miller, *Church, State and Nation in Ireland,* 70–75, 249–50, 270–76.

> appear to be rather a poor substitute. They derive a keen pleasure from fine actions. To give hospitality, to help the needy, to defend the weak—these things afford them sensations quite beyond the possibilities of the municipal tram. Contact with nature and a living participation in Catholic ideals give a deep spiritual significance to their obscure and patient lives. People such as these are not so plentiful that we can afford to crush them in our economic mills. There is much room for wise social reform, but it must not be applied without reference to the national character.[22]

In praising Maura, the author connected him to another traditional peasant culture, that of the Irish: "In some respects it is Señor Maura who stands for the Celtic spirit. His faith in religious traditions and his protests against an all-absorbing commercialism remind us of what Cardinal Newman discerned so clearly—that the strength of the Irish people lies in their spiritual mission, and that the modern spirit of Liberalism is endeavouring to put out the ancient lights of the world."[23]

A major controversy in Spain, and internationally, concerned the case of Francisco Ferrer and the so-called "Tragic Week" in Barcelona.[24] Ferrer, a Freemason, an anarchist, and a strong anticlerical, had created an experimental school on rationalist, antiauthoritarian, anticlerical lines in Barcelona in 1901, and from that had become a promoter of secular education in general. In 1906 one of his associates had tried to assassinate King Alfonso XIII. Ferrer was arrested but eventually released owing to the lack of evidence and the intense international pressure created by sympathetic organizations of the left. In 1909 a general strike and violent antigovernment rioting broke out in Barcelona over the government's war in Morocco. The strike and rioting then became a rebellion and took on a strongly anti-Catholic coloration, culminating in the destruction and looting of many Catholic churches, convents, and monasteries as well as Catholic schools and welfare institutions. After it was crushed Ferrer was arrested and executed for his alleged part in it, and that execution led to another massive international protest. While Ferrer was not the paragon his defenders portrayed him as, and while he certainly was not the chief organizer of the rebellion, as the military claimed, neither was he an innocent bystander in *la semana trágica.* Catholics, on the whole, believed him guilty; and Hilaire Belloc devoted two articles in the *Dublin* to the Ferrer

22. "Reaction in Spain," 283–84.

23. Ibid., 283.

24. For Ferrer and the "Tragic Week," see Joan Connelly Ullman, *The Tragic Week: A Study of Anticlericalism in Spain, 1875–1912* (Cambridge: Harvard University Press, 1968).

case, arguing that the truth of the case was generally unknown in England because of poor reporting and that the very uproar about it suggested something significant.[25] In the first article he gave a history of the cause of the riots, of Ferrer's life, of the destruction in Barcelona, including the exclusive attack on Catholic institutions, and of Ferrer's trial. He noted Ferrer's involvement with revolutionary activity, his high membership in the anti-Catholic Freemasons, and the clear evidence against him from the trial. In the second article he examined the agitation that Ferrer's execution caused and commented on certain of its characteristics. He noted that it was directed against the Catholic Church and seemed to be synchronized, that it occurred only in large cities, principally in capitals, with priority given to those in which Catholicism governed the popular mind, and that its agency was the press, which distorted the truth of the case, asserting falsehoods by suggestion, that is, by excitement of mind and not by reason. While the English press was far more temperate, he believed, it too lacked the facts of the case and so spread falsehoods about it. However, it was the breadth and lack of spontaneity in the agitation that led Belloc to call the organization behind it "the International." It was neither some highly organized Masonic plot (as Belloc's fictional Frenchman might think), nor something purely spontaneous (as Belloc's fictional Englishman was inclined to think). But of the two, the former was much closer to the truth, for there was certainly some real organization behind the agitation. In any case, something else had to be taken into consideration: that this "motive force" would be powerless were it not for "the hunger and thirst for social justice" among the populace of the great cities, a populace that the Church had lost hold of at the beginning of the Industrial Revolution.

One case where the *Dublin*'s desire to defend the Church and respect for traditional authority did it no credit was its treatment of the Congo Free State. In the scramble for Africa in the second half of the nineteenth century, even Belgium, or rather, King Leopold II (1835–1909), had gained a share. The Congo Free State, in the very center of the continent, had been acquired by Leopold by the use of cunning and under the guise of philanthropy, and had become his personal property. He ruthlessly exploited it economically, first for

25. Hilaire Belloc, "The International. I. The Ferrer Case," *Dublin Review* (Jan. 1910): 167–81, and "The International. II. The Motive Force," ibid. (April 1910): 396–411. Belloc's association in the article of Judaism with usurious capitalism and anti-Christian Freemasonry, while characteristic of Belloc, was highly uncharacteristic of Ward's *Dublin.*

ivory and then for rubber, causing the deaths of millions.[26] While publicly forbidding the slave trade, his Congo regime used forced labor on a pharaohic scale. By the turn of the century stories of atrocities and the use of inhuman methods had become too numerous to discount. In May 1903 the House of Commons unanimously passed a resolution urging the humane treatment of the Congo natives, and that same month the Foreign Office asked its consul in the Congo, Roger Casement, to investigate. His damning report was published in early 1904. Hoping to deflect criticism, and aware that a similar technique had worked in the 1890s, Leopold created a commission of inquiry to go to the Congo and investigate. But when its report came out in 1905, it left no doubt of the scope of abuses there. The Congo became a *cause célèbre* in Britain, and condemnation of Leopold's regime there was almost universal. It drew the attention of the *Dublin* because of its importance to the British public and because the criticism of Leopold also involved criticism of the Catholic missionaries in the Congo, whose great patron Leopold was.

The *Dublin* article, written by John de Courcy MacDonnell, an Irishman living in Belgium, defended both King Leopold and the Catholic missions.[27] He chided those well-intentioned defenders of the Catholic missions who said that the missionaries were not aware of what was happening around them. It was, rather, their intimate knowledge of the situation that explained their support of King Leopold and his Congo government. Although there were many evils in the Congo Free State, the missionaries were also aware of all the good Leopold had done. The evils described in the reports were not inherent in the system of government but rather the remnants of that condition of barbarous and savage cruelty that the system was created to stamp out—and that it was stamping out. If things had been as bad as the enemies of the Congo Free State claimed, he explained, then the Catholic missionaries would have denounced them long ago. Certainly they had not been hesitant to denounce offenders, or to report evil or harsh practices.

MacDonnell praised the heroic actions of the missionaries and pointed out that they shared the same goal as the government. "In the Congo two armies

26. See Adam Hochschild, *King Leopold's Ghost: A Story of Greed, Terror, and Heroism in Colonial Africa* (New York: Houghton Mifflin, 1998).

27. John de Courcy MacDonnell, "The Catholic Missions in the Congo Free State," *Dublin Review* (Oct. 1906): 362–82. MacDonnell (1869–1915) was at one time the editor of the *Pan-Celtic Quarterly* and a leading figure in the "Celtic Renaissance" in Europe. Born in Ireland and educated at Clongowes Wood College, he wrote a number of books, including one on Leopold II (1905).

are fighting, united, for two united causes: the armies of the Church and State are fighting for Christianity and civilization." The natives, however, could be led into the higher paths only if they were forced to work. "If the native is not employed in regular, that is constant, labour, contact with civilization will still further debase him and accelerate his destruction." MacDonnell even quoted a letter from a bishop in the French Congo stating that the natives ("blacks") would only be civilized in spite of themselves and would only work if they were forced. MacDonnell considered the "labour-tax" the most equitable way to civilize them and make them work: "for any other system would inevitably result in the strong and the powerful forcing weak women and domestic slaves to do the labour, while they (unemployed even, as formerly, in warfare or in the chase) wallowed in idleness and sank lower in bestiality."[28] He also defended the Church's recruitment of children, particularly orphans, for their school colonies, as the agricultural and technical schools were called. Many of these children, he claimed, were sent freely by their families and chiefs. While he admitted that according to their native culture, with its much greater sense of extended family, many children really weren't orphans, he saw these schools as the only way to keep these children from "domestic slavery," from vice, and, for the weakest, from being abandoned to die of starvation or exposure. MacDonnell blamed the negative reports on biased evidence reported to the commissioners, who themselves had no sympathy for the Church and who ignored the good work the missionaries had done. He also attacked the continental Liberals and their press, whose hatred for the Church and the religious orders was the cause of the calumnies they spread.

King Leopold attempted to win British Catholic support by portraying himself as the Catholic victim of Protestant hostility. While he did win the advocacy of the *Catholic Herald* and the *Tablet,* his attempts were generally a failure, for the Congo reformers had been very careful to avoid anything that might incite religious conflict. By 1906 even the Belgian Catholics, King Leopold's strongest supporters, had begun to turn against him. In 1906 a respected Jesuit professor at Louvain, Arthur Vermeersch, published *La Question Congolaise,* which severely criticized the Congo system and called for radical reform.[29] No other article appeared in the *Dublin* despite Belgium's annexa-

28. Ibid., 364, 365.

29. See S. J. S. Cookey, *Britain and the Congo Question, 1885–1913* (New York: Humanities Press, 1968), 139–40, 154–55.

tion of the Congo in 1908, the death of King Leopold in 1909, and the continuation of the controversy for some years longer.

If France was the eldest daughter who had lost her way, Germany was the poor stepchild who had struck it rich. In the late nineteenth and early twentieth centuries the German Church was often seen as a model of what the modern Church could be. While French Catholicism was divided politically and had shown herself unable to defend the rights of the Church, in Germany not only had Catholicism survived the attempts of Bismarck to break it through his *Kulturkampf* of the 1870s and 1880s, but a powerful Catholic party, the Center Party, had arisen.[30] Under Windthorst it withstood the onslaught of Bismarck, and after the fall of Bismarck it became a power in the Reichstag, an important player in the passage of legislation and a consistent supporter of successive governments. Despite this, Catholics remained profoundly discriminated against, and all their attempts at acceptance brought them little result. This was made very clear when the Reich chancellor, Prince Bernhard von Bülow, formed a coalition of all the major parties, "the Bülow Bloc," against the Socialists and the Center, and called an election for 1907. It was the triumph of the Center Party in the 1907 elections, an election that almost matched the *Kulturkampf* in its violent anti-Catholicism, that first captured the attention of Ward's *Dublin.*[31] Despite the resolute opposition of the Liberal-Conservative-Progressive government on the one hand and the Socialists on the other, the Center had managed not only not to lose seats but to gain them, making it the largest party in the Reichstag. The article praised the party for its unity (despite the differences between its conservative and democratic wings), its continued support for moderate social reform, and its principled protest against the abuse of the natives prevalent in the German colonies. It was the last that particularly had earned it the hatred of the government.

30. For the *Kulturkampf,* see Ronald Ross, *The Failure of Bismarck's Kulturkampf: Catholics and State Power in Imperial Germany, 1871–1887* (Washington, D.C.: Catholic University of America Press, 1998); and Margaret Lavinia Anderson, "Kulturkampf and the Course of German History," *Central European History* 19 (1986): 82–115. For the Center Party, see Margaret Lavinia Anderson, *Windthorst: A Political Biography* (Oxford: Clarendon Press, 1981); Ellen Lovell Evans, *The German Center Party, 1870–1933: A Study in Political Catholicism* (Carbondale: Southern Illinois University Press, 1981); Ronald Ross, *Beleaguered Tower: The Dilemma of Political Catholicism in Wilhelmine Germany* (Notre Dame: University of Notre Dame Press, 1976); David Blackbourn, *Class, Religion and Local Politics in Wilhelmine Germany: The Centre Party in Württemberg* (New Haven: Yale University Press, 1980); and John K. Zeender, *The German Center Party, 1890–1906* (Philadelphia: American Philosophical Society, 1976).

31. "The Victory of the German Centre Party," *Dublin Review* (April 1907): 371–81.

While the article acknowledged that the Center was now ideally placed, since future legislation, whether of the right or of the left, needed its support for success, it gave greater acknowledgment to the very unity of the Catholic body that the Center symbolized. "At a time when Catholics in other lands have shown indifference and even acquiescence in the tyranny and persecution of hostile Governments, the Catholics of Germany have stood side by side united into one powerful organization, exerting their full influence upon their Imperial Parliament. They have neither strayed to the right nor to the left, but have brought together the most discordant elements under one common banner. Radicals and Conservatives have alike sacrificed their party prejudices for the common good, and they are now at the dawn of the twentieth century able to show to the world a noble example of Catholic unity and of Catholic strength."[32]

The article also defended the Center against the charges that it was an antinational clerical party, pointing out its historical independence from the Catholic hierarchy (it even ignored the pope on occasion), and referring to all the government measures it had supported in the past, including an expansionist colonial policy ("in the interests of Christianity and civilization") and successive navy and army bills (though the article did not give much emphasis to that). The Center, unlike the Socialists, who refused to accept useful reforms because they did not go far enough, had shown responsibility and practical good sense, and had a record of progressive social legislation on sickness, old age, and disability insurance to its credit.

Other articles pointed to the success of political Catholicism. The former Belgian minister of justice wrote of the Catholic party's triumph in the 1912 Belgian elections, in which it won an even greater majority against the anticlerical alliance of Liberals and Socialists.[33] A year later another article described the failure of a Socialist-led strike to revise the constitution and praised the Belgian Catholic party as a model for British Catholics of how to thrive in a modern industrial country.[34] Lady Dorothy Acton described the

32. Ibid., 383.

33. Leon de Lantsheere, "The Belgian Elections of 1912," ibid. (July 1912): 60–177. See Carl Strikwerda, "The Divided Class: Catholics vs. Socialists in Belgium, 1880–1914," *Comparative Studies in Society and History* 30 (April 1988): 333–59, and *A House Divided: Catholics, Socialists, and Flemish Nationalists in Nineteenth-Century Belgium* (Lanham, Md.: Rowman & Littlefield, 1997).

34. Francis McCullagh, "The Belgian Strike," *Dublin Review* (July 1913): 127–47.

success of the Catholic party in the Netherlands, where, despite its social and numerical inferiority, it had achieved great political influence (and saved its schools) by an alliance with the Calvinist Anti-Revolutionary Party as a Christian block of "theocratic principles" against the Liberals and Socialists.[35] As in Germany, there was a strong social Catholic element to its program, and it promoted such things as national insurance against sickness, accidents, and old age.

There was also an unsigned article about Karl Lueger (1844–1910), the mayor of Vienna from 1897 to 1910 and the leader of the Christian Socialists, the largest party in Austria.[36] By defending the "little man" from the laissez-faire capitalism of the doctrinaire Liberals, which was dominated by "Jewish financiers," and by promoting city control over all public enterprises (gas, electric, water, and transport) in combination with other civic improvements such as parks, hospitals, schools, baths, and municipal savings banks, Lueger had transformed the city into one of the great capitals of Europe. While the Christian Socialists were not avowedly a Catholic party (unlike the Clerical Conservatives), under Lueger they had moved closer to the Church, defended its interests (particularly in education), and desired to renew society on a Christian basis. While the author admitted that Lueger was a demagogue and agitator ("a type to which we have not yet grown accustomed in England") and deplored the inflammatory quality of some of his speeches, he defended the proposition that in the end no one was a greater supporter of property, social order, and the Habsburg dynasty. Lueger, speaking the language of the people, had done what no one else could have: he won the sympathy of the lower classes, leading them away from a far more dangerous socialism. "Genial and impulsive natures can alone hope to win them: and impulsiveness under stress of great excitement becomes violence."[37] He also defended Lueger's anti-Semitism by pointing out that Lueger was opposed to any sort of violence toward Jews (and was shocked by the idea), that his open-handed charity had helped Jew and Christian alike, and that his anti-Semitism should

35. Lady Dorothy Acton, "The Catholic Party in the Netherlands," ibid. (April 1913): 232–53.

36. "A Great Burgomaster and His Work," ibid. (Oct. 1908): 321–45. See John W. Boyer, *Political Radicalism in Late Imperial Vienna: Origins of the Christian Social Movement, 1848–1897* (Chicago: University of Chicago Press, 1985), and *Culture and Political Crisis in Vienna: Christian Socialism in Power, 1897–1918* (Chicago: University of Chicago Press, 1995); and Richard S. Geehr, *Karl Lueger: Mayor of Fin de Siècle Vienna* (Detroit: Wayne State University Press, 1990).

37. "A Great Burgomaster," 342.

be seen as political and economic, not personal or racial, as an attack on the capitalist money-power that oppressed ordinary working people.[38]

The United States and the Church there were of particular interest to English Catholics. Ward was well known in American Catholic circles, the *Dublin Review* was read there, and both Ward and Abbot (later Cardinal) Aidan Gasquet visited America and wrote articles in the *Dublin* about it. Both were highly impressed by its dynamism and optimism, wealth and openness to men of ability and drive, and the flourishing nature of the Church there.

Ward's first number included a highly impressionistic travelogue by Gasquet.[39] Gasquet was stunned by the remarkable vigor and success of the Church in America, by the spread of schools, churches, and other institutions, by the full seminaries, the thriving religious orders, and the proliferation of Catholic societies. He was also impressed that all of this was achieved without any state aid and was paid for by the zeal of the faithful. He was especially impressed by the great energy and desire for self-improvement that seemed so characteristic of America.

> It is hardly possible to over-estimate the evidences of energy and life which I saw in all the educational establishments I visited whilst in the United States. Something of this, no doubt, is due to the tonic effect of the wonderful air of the American continent, which acts as a stimulant on the nerves and quickens the pulse with a feeling of life such as have rarely experienced in Europe. . . . But the quality of the air is not sufficient to account for everything in the way of energy. There has grown up in the youth of the great American nation a determination to succeed in what they take up, which is both honourable and laudable. They manifest an inflexible will to seize every opportunity by which success can be achieved. Nothing is left to chance, and as far as may be every risk of failure is guarded against. . . . We in Europe, who have a great

38. Boyer, in *Political Radicalism in Late Imperial Vienna* (206) and *Culture and Political Crisis in Vienna* (26–28), points to the essentially rhetorical, political, and nonracial quality of Lueger's anti-Semitism. While this practice was dreadful, it did no great harm to the Jewish community, though it created bad models for men more literal-minded than Lueger. Lueger did not intend the "systematic de-legalization" of the Viennese Jews (contra Geehr, *Karl Lueger,* 171–207). See also Bruce F. Pauley, *From Prejudice to Persecution: A History of Austrian Anti-Semitism* (Chapel Hill: University of North Carolina Press, 1992).

39. Abbot Gasquet, "Impressions of Catholic America," *Dublin Review* (Jan. 1906): 79–98. Francis Neil Aidan Gasquet (1846–1929) entered Downside Abbey in 1866, was ordained in 1874, elected president of the English Benedictine Congregation in 1900, and made a cardinal in 1914. A historian of English monasticism, he was put in charge of the Commission for the Revision of the Vulgate. For his life, see Shane Leslie, *Cardinal Gasquet* (London: Burns & Oates, 1953).

past, with all that this implies, with all that antiquities and traditions, historic monuments and manuscript records mean, have a great advantage, but in the long run energy and determination will make up for these. Energy and dogged determination to make the best of any and every opportunity are the qualities of young America to-day. Their "go" and "life" are delightful to witness, and compared with them we in England are very little better than asleep, as the Prince of Wales impressed on us four years ago.[40]

Gasquet was surprised by the number of young men working their way through college as waiters and stewards during the summers—and by the number of doctors and lawyers he met who had done just that. On one of his trips he even met a train conductor who spent all of his free time on the job educating himself by reading.

While Gasquet was taken with American life in general, he was more impressed by how successfully the Church had affected the life of the nation. He was astonished that he could get Friday abstinence fare on the train, Catholics being so numerous and demanding on the subject. He thought the Church the most potent religious force on the continent, particularly through her schools, which, unlike the "godless" state schools, proclaimed "the paramount importance" of religious education as "the only basis of true training and morality."

Ward lectured in America in late 1913 and early 1914 (and again in 1915) and his two-part article was also highly impressionistic and extremely enthusiastic.[41] He too was impressed by the great vigor and success of Catholicism in America, and by the energetic nature and wealth of American life. He was also impressed by the powerful and growing influence of Catholics in public

40. Gasquet, "Impressions of Catholic America," 89.

41. Wilfrid Ward, "A Visit to America," *Dublin Review* (April 1914): 209–36, and (July 1914): 1–18. See *Wilfrid Wards* 2:441–49. After the wildly eulogistic articles by Gasquet and Ward on the United States, the 1915 article by the former dean of Harvard and future diplomat William Richards Castle (1878–1963) seems oddly discordant. It was as pessimistic and bleak as the two Englishmen's had been optimistic and joyful. Castle wrote that the twin American ideals of democracy and progress had been corrupted. Progress, he believed, had come to mean social revolution and a hatred of the wealthy, and democracy had come to mean the leveling of all distinctions, whether natural or artificial, and the distrust of wealth, intellect, and men of qualifications. A flood of radicalism had been let loose upon the land, he thought, wiping away old landmarks in the name of the common good and of progress, and those who had the least stake in the nation were the ones who dominated. Their class legislation and their mania for new laws had circumscribed personal liberty and endangered private property. See W. R. Castle, "Some American Problems," *Dublin Review* (Oct. 1915): 309–23.

life (something of a recent phenomenon, he was told), meeting Catholic governors and the Catholic chief justice of the Supreme Court, Edward White, as well as prelates, monsignors, and wealthy laymen. The great ethnic and linguistic diversity of the Catholic body was new to him, as was the ritual diversity, for many followed the Eastern rites. While he lectured before many Catholic institutions and groups, meeting the cream of American Catholic life, he also addressed a great many secular groups and institutions, giving talks at Cornell, Columbia, and Harvard and meeting some of the most influential men in the nation. He was impressed by how many Americans seemed open to the faith and how well the Church had adapted to American life, and he particularly praised the Paulist Fathers, whose ability to address outsiders with sympathy and understanding he admired greatly. After a second lecture tour of America, in 1915, he wrote another article devoted to the University of Notre Dame, a university of more than a thousand students, where he had spent "two happy weeks."[42] He gave a detailed history of the university as the creation of French heroism and American energy and practicality. It was a university so thoroughly American that "no one dreams of the French accent in speaking of Notre Dame or the founders of the University," for all were pronounced "as though they were English." He also wrote that he hoped to devote another article to the "actual working of an institution of which the origin has in it so much of religious romance."

The other great entity to which Ward belonged was the British Empire, and the *Dublin* reflected his belief in it. In reviewing Monypenny's biography of Disraeli, Ward lauded Disraeli's "Imperial idea," even accepting the jingoism that accompanied it as necessary.[43] Whatever its origins, the Empire was justified by its intrinsic qualities and the benefits it offered. "The English Empire was not pursued at the dictates of a philosophical imperative; it grew up out of the genius and generosities of an adventurous people, its justification in the past—so far as it can be justified—being in relation to irreflective impulses, its justification in the present, its organic life, its majestic exhibition to the world of the principles of good government, in a word, of independence."[44] While there were no articles on Britain's territories in Africa, a review of a new biography of Cecil Rhodes did call him a "great man" and praised his vision

42. Wilfrid Ward, "An American University," *Dublin Review* (Oct. 1915): 284–94.

43. Wilfrid Ward, "Disraeli," ibid. (Jan. 1913): 1–21, and (April 1913): 217–31.

44. B. de S., "Some Recent Books," ibid. (Oct. 1914): 402.

for South Africa, including his attempts to absorb the Boer republics.[45] The greatest of the British possessions, India, by the late nineteenth century had begun to experience greater unrest and desire for self-rule, with the Indian National Congress being formed in 1885 to help achieve that ideal. Lord Curzon, British viceroy from 1899 to 1905, was an able if imperious administrator, but his partition of the province of Bengal in 1905 had led to massive unrest. Mass meetings, protest marches, and the boycotting of British products followed, spreading from Bengal to the rest of India and leading to terrorist bombings and assassinations. The Indian Councils Act of 1909 (commonly called the Minto-Morley reforms after the British viceroy and the Indian chief secretary), which introduced a democratic element into the government, helped, but it did not satisfy the more radical nationalists and it angered many conservatives, both in India and in Great Britain, who believed that India's safety and integrity could only be maintained by strong British rule.[46]

In addition to a few religious articles concerning India, two articles on Indian politics appeared in the *Dublin.* The first of these, in early 1911, "From Talk to Trouble in India," was a violent and mocking assault on the Indian politicians (and their British allies) who promoted self-rule, whom the author called dangerous "babblers."[47] These mock parliamentarians of the Indian National Congress ("the parliament of talkers"), he believed, took advantage of Britain's freedom of speech and liberality in India to sow sedition. While such freedoms were permissible in England ("we are prepared to listen to Mr Bepin Chandal Pal with the same amused tolerance with which we hear ranters in the Park, or report without agitation enthusiasm for the Jacobite cause"), they were dangerous in India, where they had led to violence and the murder of British subjects. Such "blind" and "ridiculous" desires for self-government, the author wrote, would entail the wholesale evacuation of the British from India and would lead to its fragmentation ("the Afgans would have started from the other end of India to see what the Nepalis had left that had not already been annexed by the native princes"); and after a welter of confusion India would again be under a European power, "perhaps with a mailed fist instead of a velvet glove." Nor did the author see how the domi-

45. P. H. K., "Some Recent Books," ibid. (Jan. 1911): 191–94.

46. See Lawrence James, *Raj: The Making and Unmaking of British India* (New York: St. Martin's Press, 1997), esp. 301–436, and Syed Razi Wasti, *Lord Minto and the Indian Nationalist Movement, 1905 to 1910* (Oxford: Clarendon Press, 1964).

47. "From Talk to Trouble in India," *Dublin Review* (April 1911): 297–323.

nance by this group of high-caste Hindus, whose main aim was "the rehabilitation of the Hindu system and the supremacy of Brahmanism," could be good for India. "Brahmanism is responsible for the condemnation of some fifty millions, out of the three hundred millions in India, to a life of unspeakable degradation."[48] The author believed that Britain had been too indulgent ("untrained visionaries in England interfering with the work of the man on the spot") and that with the help of some among the British ("friends amongst the garrison") "many of the best talents and energies of educated India" were being removed from the more difficult field of social reform to the more popular field of political agitation. A large share of the blame for this, the author thought, was due to giving the Indians a Western education that placed certain ideas before a people that had not gone through the necessary steps to develop them. Only by a strong hand, and by assuring that the services in India had an irreducible minimum of Europeans, he believed, could India be maintained.

> Finally, we must for ever remember that we only obtained sway over India because we were strong, and that we shall only remain in India if we are strong, strong not only to govern the strong, but strong enough to prevent our weakness in dealing with Bengalis from earning us the contempt of the strong. . . . Tact and skill in managing men are needed, but in the end the ultimate arbiter of destinies is the sword, and that must never be lost sight of. We took India by the sword from swordsmen, and not by the tongue from talkers, and if we give it up to the talkers it is not they who will retain it.[49]

The second article, a year later, "The Changes in India and After," was as calm and matter-of-fact as the other was agitated and opinionated.[50] It announced the "epoch-making changes" in the Indian administration, which had moved the capital of British India from Calcutta to Delhi and reunited Bengal. It was the partition of Bengal that, as "an open sore," had led to the unrest of these years, and by its nullification it removed "a potent weapon from the hands of the irreconcilables." But as a quid pro quo Bengal would no longer be the center of administration (Calcutta was in Bengal), the ancient capital of Delhi being far better situated as well as having far greater historical associations for both Hindu and Mohammedan. This was all the more

48. Ibid., 314.
49. Ibid., 322–23.
50. "The Changes in India and After," ibid. (April 1912): 287–306.

appropriate, the author believed, because in the Liberal government's policy of devolution (the Morley-Minto reforms) greater power was to be given to the provincial legislative councils, though limited power since India was not "ripe for representative government." Only those from the small class of the wealthy and educated were to have the vote, a group unrepresentative of the great mass of the people. It was "unthinkable," the author continued, that the British parliamentary franchise should be given to the masses, since they were overwhelmingly illiterate, apathetic toward public affairs, and without leaders and organization of their own. The article ended on a triumphant note, describing the recent king-emperor's visit to India, which had "turned the whole current of native feeling from unrest and discontent to peace and loyalty."

In reviewing a book on contemporary India, *The Real India* by J. D. Rees, in the January 1909 number, the Oxford don Francis Urquhart (F.F.U.) agreed with the author that the main cause of Indian disaffection was the European education given to the natives.[51] The greatest danger of this European education was that it destroyed old beliefs and principles without putting anything in their place. While Urquhart considered the present educational system in India full of faults (the schemes of study were too ambitious and the attainments too low, and it had a terrible examination system), he disagreed with Rees that the British could or should have excluded Indians from a European education, or that India should be run on more completely Oriental lines. Urquhart believed that the intermingling of the two cultures was inevitable once Britain overtook the administration of India. Being a Westerner, he did not believe that the British should defend their presence by asking the Indians ("our fellow subjects") always to look backward, remembering the misgovernment and anarchy before British rule, but also to look forward. The educational system was the window to that future. That, however, was just part of a larger problem, "becoming every year more critical," of trying to combine "Eastern and Western ideals and methods in the Western Government of Eastern nations." While Urquhart supported the Empire, he could still see the oddity of it. "Though the English position in India is justified by the past, by the deep divisions amongst the many peoples under one rule, and by their desire to profit by the material civilization of Europe, still it cannot

51. F. F. U. [Francis Urquhart], "Some Recent Books," ibid. (Jan. 1909): 208–10. Francis Fortesque ("Sligger") Urquhart (1868–1934) was a well-known and devoutly Catholic history don at Balliol College, Oxford. See Cyril Bailey, *Francis Urquhart: A Memoir* (London: Macmillan, 1936).

but be abnormal that a population of 300,000,000 should be governed by some 1,500 officials of an entirely alien race. Mr Rees is, perhaps, inclined to overlook that difficulty."[52] Urquhart thought that Rees's long residence in India and his active participation in its government had accustomed him to see this as normal when in fact it was rather strange. In any case, the British administration was already mainly Oriental in that it was based on authority from the top down. Of one thing he had no doubt, though, and this was that the greatest tact, patience, and wisdom, both in Britain and in the Indian administration, would be needed.

Despite its size, the British Empire could no longer live in "splendid isolation," and the opening years of the twentieth century were marked by a series of "foreign entanglements": a military alliance with Japan (1902), an understanding if not an alliance with France (1904), the *Entente Cordiale,* and with Russia (1907). Despite its fragility and strains, over time a clear Triple Entente of Great Britain, France, and Russia came into being; and if not formally created as a counter to the Triple Alliance of Germany, Austria-Hungary, and Italy, it became one. The Liberal government, dominated by Liberal Imperialists, continued this policy of alliances and thus maintained the balance of power. The strengthening of the entente, which did commit Britain militarily, owed a great deal to the clumsiness of German foreign policy, for in the 1890s Britain had been inclined to an alliance with Germany over her traditional enemies France and Russia (now allies). The massive German naval buildup in the 1900s, which threatened British naval supremacy, the blustering attempts by Germany to humiliate France over Morocco in 1905 and 1911 (the Moroccan Crises at Algeciras and Agadir), and the generally aggressive German stance in world affairs made the entente a reality. Beyond the Great Power alliances and the danger of a European war, the Far East, Turkish Empire and the Middle East, and the Balkans were the areas of contention.

The first area of conflict was the Far East, particularly China and Japan. When Commodore Perry sailed into the Bay of Yedo in July 1853 he set in motion a chain of events that transformed Japan from an isolated agrarian feudal society into a rapidly industrializing, highly centralized modern powerhouse.[53] The wisdom of Japan's adoption of Western ways, and with it her en-

52. F. F. U., "Some Recent Books," 209.

53. For Japan, see James L. McClain, *Japan: A Modern History* (New York: W. W. Norton, 2002), 119–356; and Donald Keene, *Emperor of Japan: Meiji and His World, 1852–1912* (New York: Columbia University Press, 2002).

trance as a world power, was confirmed by her defeat of China in 1894–1895 and particularly by her defeat of Russia in the Russo-Japanese War (1904–1905), which surprised a West that had grown used to Oriental weakness before European arms. But Japan's success came at a price, and no country, to British eyes, had risen so high and fallen so low in estimation as Japan. Stephen Harding, reviewing Lancelot Lawton's book on the Far East, *Empires of the Far East* (1912), put it well.

Japan was held up as a marvel of progress; in forty years she had risen from a state of barbaric seclusion, to one of enlightened culture and civilization. Her people were a lovable and chivalrous race, and to their innate courtesy and philosophical cheerfulness they were believed to join a keen business acumen and a large-minded statesmanship. Their patriotism and stoical endurance of suffering were magnificent, and in the war against Russia the Japanese soldier was as great a hero as his leader was a military genius. So also the country was rich and fertile, and under an admirably constituted government it was destined to a glorious future. Then with many people a reaction set in. The Japanese were nothing remarkable. They had displayed a wonderful power of mimicry and that was all. Their civilization was but superficial and their boasted high qualities illusory. The natural resources of the country were small, her government unsound, and her greatness would prove but transient.[54]

The reason for this shift in British opinion was Japanese behavior in China and Korea after Japan's successes in the Russo-Japanese War. As Lancelot Lawton wrote of it later, in his foreign affairs column:

Japan has now risen to a position of dominating superiority in the Far East. The whole of Asia with breathless interest witnessed her struggle, marked clearly her methods, and rejoiced with her in the victory obtained over the military forces of Russia and over the diplomatic forces of the rest of the world—a victory, in short, over the whole of Western Civilization. . . . Again and again she declared that her only object in waging war was to preserve the integrity of China and of Korea; and, in so far as killing and wounding can be conducted on humane principles, the behaviour of her forces in the field was exemplary. Once, however, peace was declared in her favour, the methods she proceeded to employ in order to gain a foothold on the Continent of Asia merited no other description than that they were atrocious. The Open Door was slammed in the face of the Powers. Korea was subjugated with fire and sword, and annexation quickly followed. Thus, without a murmur of protest, Christianity surrendered, to the persecution of a heathen race, one of the fairest fields for missionary effort in the whole world, a field where the amount of real good accomplished was far

54. Stephen Harding, "The Position in Japan," *Dublin Review* (April 1913): 326.

in excess of anything achieved elsewhere in the Far East. In Southern Manchuria, too, the Japanese oppressed the natives, bullied the Chinese officials into acquiescence with their extortionate demands, and persistently hampered foreign trade. To-day, the powers they have usurped in this region are tantamount to those which are usually attached to a legitimate Protectorate.[55]

Harding agreed with Lawton's assessment (which was the same in his book as in his later column) that Japan's behavior in China and Korea was atrocious, but he disagreed with Lawton on a number of points. He disliked Lawton's negative view of Japanese ethics, particularly in reference to women. He thought that Lawton, by his constant criticism of women's low social status in Japan and of Japanese culture's frank acceptance of prostitution (and even of parents' selling their children into "a life of shame"), was applying European standards to an Oriental culture, ignoring the fact that the transformation of moral principles takes much longer. "On the whole, therefore, while we may be justified in saying that a nation with such a code of morality as the Japanese cannot claim to be civilized in the accepted sense of the word, we have no right to lay this to their charge as a fault."[56] In this, and in many other ways, Harding thought the Japanese was "still rather a savage." Yet, commenting on the death of a high Japanese official in Korea who had committed hara-kiri as a protest against official corruption, he believed that this showed that "if Japan had not yet acquired all the essentials of civilization, neither has she lost her ancient virtues, and that in some at least of her sons the spirit of *Bushido* [Japanese chivalry] still lives." He remarked that Christianity had failed to have a significant impact because of its contrast with the Oriental character and because of the "widespread agnosticism" of the people, but also because of its loss of face due to Japan's defeat of Christian Russia. He believed that despite her resources, given her increased population and the fact that only a few industries were open to further expansion, and with the Western nations closed to further immigration, Japan's future would have to be in her colonies. But the costs of developing her empire, he believed, with its large standing army and powerful fleet, had exhausted her treasury and led to the present political crisis, a crisis only made worse by the extra-constitutional power of the military and the *Genro* (the elder statesmen who created modern Japan). Indeed, Harding doubted that the belief in the divinity of the emper-

55. Lancelot Lawton, "Foreign Politics of the Day," ibid. (Oct. 1911): 376–77.
56. Harding, "Position in Japan," 329.

or could continue undiminished as the crushing costs of the military and the oppressive conditions of labor led to unrest, strikes, and the growth of socialism. But if Japan could stay solvent till her colonies began to pay, it seemed likely that she could overcome her severe financial difficulties, especially considering what she had already achieved. "She has been in worse positions in the past and has come out of them successfully."[57]

Lawton, in his foreign affairs column, was not so sanguine; and his concerns were more geopolitical. He believed that Japan, in her "lust for armaments" and desire to dominate the Pacific, had exhausted her treasury and become corrupt: "Everywhere beneath the lacquer rottenness was exposed."[58] While he admitted that Britain's alliance with Japan had not served the interests of Western civilization very well, still, he believed, Britain should not be criticized, for if she had not allied herself with Japan, some other great power ("a Power, moreover, antagonistic to Great Britain") would have done so. The revision of her treaty with Japan now prevented any danger to Britain's relationship to the United States ("our sisterland") and to the British colonies in the Pacific. Japan's conquests and military buildup, although it did not bode well for peace, had forced Britain's white colonies (Australia, New Zealand, and Canada) into greater military preparedness and greater unity with Britain.[59]

Lawton also believed that the interests of Russia, the United States, and the British Empire in the East were identical: self-preservation against the dangers of an aggressive Japan. In a sense, there was a "Yellow Peril" (not in the crude sense, though he did believe that it was reasonable for the West to keep Japanese immigrants out), and whatever the morality of deciding the issue, "expediency will alone decide." Also, he believed that what the Japanese might demand the Chinese would eventually demand as soon as they too became strong militarily. However, there was no danger as yet of Japan and China allying against the West. It was much more likely that China would be the first victim of any Japanese expansion. Britain, therefore, should try to restrain her ally who so desperately needed her finance.[60]

The reviewer ("D.A.L.D") of Frank Fox's *The Problems of the Pacific* (1912) believed that the "Yellow Peril" was not, as yet, a peril for the "White Man"

57. Ibid., 330, 342.

58. Lancelot Lawton, "Foreign Politics of the Day," ibid. (July 1914): 150–52.

59. Lancelot Lawton, "Foreign Politics of the Day," ibid. (Oct. 1911): 370–80.

60. Lancelot Lawton, "Foreign Politics of the Day," ibid. (Oct. 1913): 382–85.

because China was too occupied with internal matters and because Japan, lacking mines, minerals, and other resources, lacked any power of initiative and invention.[61] The Japanese were but "very clever parrots" and their nation was already a waning power, her greatness "a flash in the pan." He asserted that the United States, especially once the Panama Canal was finished, was the only true rival to Great Britain.

If Japan was a worry to the European powers because of her strength, China was a worry because of her weakness. Until the middle of the nineteenth century China had lived in hieratic splendor and self-absorption, a nation of some 400 million needing nothing from the outside and looking upon other powers as inferiors. That changed with the defeats and concessions forced upon her by the Western powers beginning with the Opium War with Britain (1839–1842) and culminating in the international military intervention caused by the Boxer Rebellion of 1900. With a far more ancient and advanced culture than Japan, China found it much more difficult to imitate the West and had not gone through such an extensive modernization. In 1911 the Manchu Ch'ing dynasty had fallen and a republic had been declared, Yüan Shih-k'ai, a leading figure in the previous regime and the creator of the modern Chinese army, being its first president. In an article in the April 1912 number, "The Destiny of China," C. J. L. Gilson was initially hopeful of its future, showing respect for Chinese civilization but admitting that the Chinese and European races were quite out of sympathy with each other.[62] This hopefulness continued in an article in the July 1913 number by Stephen Harding, "The Chinese Republic and Yüan Shih-k'ai."[63] Harding asserted that Yüan had the reputation of being "enlightened and progressive" and friendly to the West, and was widely praised in the English press, but he was also a man who could not be entirely trusted, having earlier betrayed his emperor, Kuang Hsü, to the dowager empress Tzü Hsi when Kuang Hsü attempted reforms. Yet, despite that and despite his ambition, Harding believed, with his obvious ability he was the only chance for China to escape anarchy. It was most likely, though, that he would at some point declare himself emperor, but that would only be

61. D. A. L. D., "Some Recent Books," ibid. (Oct. 1912): 402–6.

62. C. J. L. Gilson, "The Destiny of China," ibid. (April 1912): 325–37. Captain Charles James Louis Gilson (1878–1943) served in the post-Boxer allied army of occupation in China and wrote a number of adventure stories set in China.

63. Stephen Harding, "The Chinese Republic and Yüan Shih-K'ai," ibid. (July 1913): 112–26. For China at this time, see Jonathan Spence, *The Search for Modern China* (New York: W. W. Norton, 1990), 245–99.

the Chinese way. "China has had many revolutions in the past, but she has always had an emperor."[64] In fact, autocratic rule seemed a necessity for China because of the "hopelessly inert and apathetic character of the Chinese race" and because only "a strong central authority ruling *à l'orientale*" could maintain order and peace. The Chinese, he believed, did not desire a social revolution but a "change of directors," and while China's ancient ways and institutions may have had their faults, they had given to China a political longevity greater than any other nation's. Harding was particularly worried about the havoc that might be wrought by revolutionaries who, having returned from England, America, and Japan full of new ideas, were estranged from their own tradition.

Lawton's comments about Yüan were much more positive than Harding's.[65] Yüan's patriotism and personality, he maintained, could not be gainsaid, and while he admitted that Yüan had become far more autocratic than even the emperors had been, and that he had destroyed every single representative institution, Lawton believed that his dictatorial rule was necessitated by the difficulty and lawlessness of the situation. Lawton thought that the West, seeing the material advancement of China, had exaggerated the Chinese capacity for change, something that Yüan ("a Chinaman of Chinamen") had not done. Using Chinese methods, Yüan would lay the foundations of a new China, and Lawton was hopeful that he would not betray his opportunity.

As the history of the twentieth century has proved, the Japanese were much more than "very clever parrots," and Japan's critics were wrong in calling her a decadent or waning power; but they were accurate in their assessment of the danger she posed by her aggression and military buildup. Yüan did in fact become a dictator (even an emperor), but he was a failure, and when he died in 1916 his rule was already collapsing around him.

The other great empire now in decay, the Turkish Empire, still controlled a good part of the Balkans, as well as Asia Minor, Syria, Palestine, Mesopotamia, and much of Arabia, including the holy cities of Mecca and Medina. Sir Mark Sykes (1879–1919), soldier, traveler, and an expert on the Middle East, described from personal experience the polyglot and precarious nature of the Turkish Empire in the January 1909 number.[66] In a eulogy for Sir Nicholas

64. Harding, "Chinese Republic," 120.

65. Lancelot Lawton, "Foreign Politics of the Day," *Dublin Review* (July 1914): 145–50.

66. Mark Sykes, "Modern Turkey," ibid. (Jan. 1909): 144–72. An extremely devout Catholic, Sykes served in the Boer War from 1899 to 1902, was personal secretary to George Wyndham from

O'Conor, the British ambassador to the sultan from 1898 to his death in 1908, Sykes described the situation of Abdul Hamid II (1876–1909), who was sultan until a few weeks after O'Conor's death, when he was overthrown by the Young Turks, and who trusted O'Conor beyond all others.

Surrounded by spies and blackguards of every description, feeling that his failing health and intellectual vigour must sooner or later put a period not only to his policy but perhaps his dynasty and his empire, seeing his authority undermined both from within and without—holding the Powers at arm's length with bribes and concessions, crushing the corrupt bureaucracy which eventually overthrew him by means of espionage, collusion and terrorism—fending off the Balkan States by a hundred subtle turns and devices—keeping the tottering fabric of Asia together by every kind of ridiculous or criminal expedient—this weary, harassed, tragic soul turned in relief to the one personality who, though it represented an odious and fatal policy, yet was direct, honest, sympathetic, and understanding.[67]

Abdul Hamid II managed to maintain his empire's integrity and to keep the Great Powers at bay, playing them off against each other, and despite his autocratic and bloody ways the empire did experience some degree of modernization. In 1908 the Young Turks, using their influence in the army, seized power and repelled an attempted counterrevolution by forces loyal to Abdul Hamid in 1909, described by Francis McCullagh in the October 1909 number.[68] The question was whether Turkey, "the Sick Man of Europe," could be saved. McCullagh believed that Turkey, despite its Mohammedanism, had the capacity to reform itself since the Turks had already ignored or reinterpreted so much of the Koran and Islamic law.[69] The most important act so far of these "Modernists," McCullagh believed, was the "encyclical letter" by the Sheikh-ul-Islam (something of a spiritual leader to Turkish Islam) to all the naïbs, ulemas, muftis, and sheikhs of the empire, urging them as a religious duty to propagandize in favor of constitutional government and the frater-

1904 to 1905, and served as a Conservative MP from 1911. He is perhaps best known for the Sykes-Picot Agreement of 1916, which would have divided the Middle East after the Great War. For his life, see Shane Leslie, *Mark Sykes: His Life and Letters* (London: Cassell, 1923); and Roger Adelson, *Mark Sykes: Portrait of an Amateur* (London: J. Cape, 1975).

67. Mark Sykes, "Sir Nicholas O'Conor," *Dublin Review* (Oct. 1913): 279.

68. Francis McCullagh, "The April Mutiny in Stamboul," ibid. (Oct. 1909): 283–305. Francis McCullagh (1874–1956) was a journalist with extensive experience in the Middle East and Far East, and the author of many books. Francis Urquhart (F. F. U.) reviewed McCullagh's book on the April Mutiny, *The Fall of Abd-ul-Hamid* (London: Methuen, 1910), very favorably in "Some Recent Books" (April 1911): 395–97.

69. Francis McCullagh, "Modernism in Islam," ibid. (April 1910): 272–97.

nization of Moslems with other religious groups. The Young Turks, through the schools and the press, promoted this new Islam, and while their use of the Koran had been very selective (they ignored texts that could be cited in favor of absolutism, bigotry, and obscurantism), it had so far succeeded, experiencing very little opposition. He feared, however, that the Young Turks would go too fast too soon, becoming intolerant of the "Old Turks" and their ways. While many doubted that the Islamic Turks could renew themselves, there was also the question of whether Turkey's neighbors, both great and small, would allow her to renew herself. McCullagh doubted that they would, and pointed to the feverish war preparations going on both in Turkey and in the Balkans, and the fear of an energetic modernist Islam even among the Great Powers.

Edwin De Lisle, in an article entitled "Under the War Cloud" in the January 1912 number, maintained that it would be better to have Turkey speedily dismembered if only to preserve peace.[70] He believed that a European war was a real possibility. First, because of the perpetual conflict between "a moribund and quasi-barbaric Mohammedan civilization" (Turkey) and "the old, yet ever young Christian peoples of the Near East." Second, because the German Empire, full of martial vigor and ready to burst her boundaries, had been denied an empire commensurate with her power and importance. Britain, France, and Russia had their empires, so it was only "fair play" to let Germany have hers, and why not at the expense of the Turks? "Why then should England wish to prevent Germany from acquiring an Asiatic Empire, let us say West of the Persian Gulf, and East of the Mediterranean? It is unfriendly; it is impolitic. In fact, it is impossible. The Turk must wane, the German wax!"[71] The blighted Ottoman Empire, he believed, was doomed to disappear anyway, and in fact was fast doing so. Germany would only be doing what Britain had done for herself much earlier. He believed that Britain and Germany, as Teutonic powers kindred in race, religion, and in their royalty, should be allies. Not only would the downtrodden Christians of the East benefit from the partition of Turkey and German predominance, but Europe herself would be spared a disastrous war.

70. Edwin De Lisle, "Under the War Cloud," ibid. (Jan. 1912): 152–61. De Lisle (1852–1920), educated at Oscott and the Universities of Münster and Innsbruck, was the son of the famous convert Ambrose Phillips de Lisle and a former Unionist MP (1886–1892).

71. Ibid., 153.

The four European emperors, for our king is now an emperor, if they would only join hands, could achieve their glorious consummation almost without bloodshed. Moreover, the shrinkage of the Western birthrate is an ominous feature which must compel us to husband our forces, the flower of the human race, lest the Yellow Peril, as it has been called, become a reality. Infidelity and infecundity, those twin evils of modern thought and higher civilization, have already cast their shadow upon us. The evil which has long been visible in France can now be discerned in Prussia as well as in Great Britain. Europe must pull herself together, or all may yet be lost.[72]

De Lisle also made the unusual claim (unusual at least for an Englishman) that while the late King Edward VII had been given credit as the "peacemaker" of Europe, that title really belonged to Kaiser Wilhelm II. The more common opinion in Britain was that if war came it would be because of, not despite, Kaiser Wilhelm. In late 1911, as a friendly gesture to Germany, the British government considered lowering Britain's battleship ratio with Germany from 2:1 to 16:10. In February 1912 Richard Haldane, just before leaving the War Office for the position of lord chancellor, was sent on an informal mission to Germany to seek some sort of rapprochement. He met with the emperor, the imperial chancellor, the naval minister (Admiral von Tirpitz), and other members of the government. He made clear that England did not want war but that Germany's naval buildup was forcing Britain to respond, that Germany's military buildup was drawing other nations together for their own security, and that in the event of any attack on Belgium or France, Britain would not be neutral. The Germans did not give up their naval expansion, but far more significant was the massive increase in the size of the German army. A "land armaments race" began among the European powers that made war far more likely.[73] October 1912 saw the beginning of the First Balkan War, in which Serbia, Bulgaria, Greece, and Montenegro drove the Turks from most of her European possessions. As a result of the Second Balkan War (begun in June 1913), Bulgaria lost territory to all her enemies (by the Treaty of Bucharest of August 1913), and Serbia made great gains. A powerful Serbia was a threat to Austria-Hungary, whose multinational empire held a great many Serbians, particularly after the annexation of Bosnia-Herzegovinia in 1908.

Lawton, writing in the January 1913 number, praised the Triple Entente as the best means of securing world peace because it maintained the balance of

72. Ibid., 159.

73. See David G. Herrmann, *The Arming of Europe and the Making of the First World War* (Princeton: Princeton University Press, 1999).

power in Europe, Germany being afraid of the combined armies of France and Russia and the combined navies of France, Russia, and Great Britain. While discussing the Balkan Wars he made clear, despite the British press's misunderstanding of the complexity of foreign affairs, that the need of Serbia for an outlet to the sea, because it affected the balance of the great alliances, was worth bringing Britain to the brink of war.[74] Whatever touched upon the power of Britain's ally Russia and her interests, or increased the power of Austria (as part of the Triple Alliance), he believed, would affect Britain as well. For Britain to be lukewarm toward her allies would only encourage the aggression of Germany and her allies, and inevitably bring on war. Britain could not stand alone in "splendid isolation." While there was a serious risk of Great Britain being involved in a vast conflagration "over a cause with which she is not intimately concerned," the combined power of the entente made that possibility, "generally speaking, remote." "For dependent as each member of the group is upon the goodwill of its friends it is unlikely that any two nations will engage in conflict over a trivial cause. It is still more improbable that the whole of Europe will be plunged into a conflagration on account of a matter of relatively small importance. Strength respects strength, and for this, if for no other reason, the two groups into which the powers are divided, will, should occasion require, search long and earnestly for the narrow path that leads to peace rather than plunge headlong into the unknown depths of the abyss of destruction."[75] Lawton did not believe, though, as some did, that the Triple Entente precluded greater friendship with Germany (which was eminently desirable), for its elasticity allowed reciprocal arrangements between individual nations on isolated questions.

In his final article before the war, written just before the assassination of Archduke Franz Ferdinand at Sarajevo (June 28, 1914), Lawton again defended Britain's alliance with Russia over Germany by pointing out that Germany, not Russia, was the greatest threat to the British Empire. First, because Germany by her aggressive military preparedness was far more able to attempt "to determine the destiny of the world," while Russia, being so large, was not so well prepared or developed, and was largely absorbed with internal problems. Second, because Germany's territorial ambitions could not be satisfied without damage to British interests, while an alliance with Russia could only bring

74. Lancelot Lawton, "Foreign Politics of the Day," *Dublin Review* (Jan. 1913): 145–63.
75. Ibid., 149.

security to British interests in the East, particularly to India. He praised the statesmanship of Sir Edward Grey, the foreign secretary, for its realism, for understanding that diplomacy was only another term for compromise and that concessions had to be made on individual points if the general balance of power was to be maintained. Thus, for example, for the greater good of Britain he let Japan have her way with Korea and Russia have her way with Mongolia and northern Persia. Only by such behavior could the Triple Entente (and Britain's useful alliance with Japan) be maintained against the Triple Alliance. It was a scheme, he believed, that pleased no one entirely; but it maintained the peace and it would again, even if it were a strained peace. "No sooner does one nation expand its arrangements for war than another not only follows the evil example but improves upon it. It is this constant overhauling in the mad career of armaments that gives to the world peace among the nations. But what a strange peace! Not the peace of tranquillity, but the stillness of suspense."[76] The fear of "Armageddon" would keep the Great Powers at peace, Lawton thought, and to help keep that peace, lesser nations would have to suffer. "For the time being justice in the strict sense is submerged, and as a consequence isolated questions affecting little States cannot be dealt with according to the dictates of conscience. No accusation of cynicism lies here. In the face of the larger evil the lesser must go uncorrected."[77] Despite his dark words about the possibility of a cataclysmic war, Lawton did not wish to counsel despair, for the very fact that the nations had been able to negotiate with each other separately "again and again" afforded "a hopeful ray of light amid the general gloom that has settled over Europe." As an example of this ability to negotiate, he pointed to the recent progress in bringing about a "comprehensive understanding" between England and Germany.

The "comprehensive understanding" that Lawton referred to was most certainly the arrangements with Germany over its involvement in the Baghdad Railway (June 1914), which, while supporting its construction, protected British supremacy in the Persian Gulf.[78] The assassination of the heir to the Austro-Hungarian throne on June 28, however, put an end to such successes and supplied the pretext for the Armageddon that Lawton had mentioned.

76. Lancelot Lawton, "Foreign Politics of the Day," ibid. (July 1914): 137.

77. Ibid.

78. For British policy in the Middle East, see Roger Adelson, *London and the Invention of the Middle East: Money, Power, and War, 1902–1922* (New Haven: Yale University Press, 1995).

9 THE GREAT WAR

No topic so dominated the *Dublin Review* as that of the Great War. As befitted the first total war of the modern era, almost whole numbers were devoted to it.[1] From the very beginning many people sensed that this war was something larger than its immediate causes, something larger than a fight for honor or territory, or to avenge the assassination of the Austro-Hungarian heir. Rather, it was the manifestation of a great cultural struggle, a struggle for civilization. This idea was first developed by Lancelot Lawton—who for all intents and purposes became the *Dublin*'s war expert—in the first issue after the war began.[2]

While Lawton discussed in some detail the more immediate causes of the war, not ignoring the complex and cumulative nature of incidents and trends, he emphasized the larger historical framework. He laid the start of the war firmly at the feet of Germany, whose aggression was its ultimate cause. He admitted that Germany's historical development and geographical position were a stimulus to her aggression: German unity and power were themselves the result of violence and war, a child of the Prussian victories over Denmark, Austria, and

1. For a short and very readable introduction to the tangled topic of the war's origins, see David Fromkin, *Europe's Last Summer: Who Started the Great War in 1914* (New York: Knopf, 2004).

2. Lancelot Lawton, "The Causes of the War," *Dublin Review* (Oct. 1914): 226–56.

France. Lawton even sympathized with Germany's desire for expansion. But her glorification of power and force, and her willingness to use it, had made Germany "the enemy of civilization." A decade of "academic theories" (from Treitschke, von Bernhardi, Mommsen, Sybil, von Tirpitz, and others) had "poisoned the soul of modern Germany" and persuaded the German people that they were "the Chosen and Elect, endowed with the Heaven-bestowed right to exterminate that they may enlighten." "With Imperial approval, and oftentimes patronage, a host of missionaries—Professors, Generals, Admirals, and swarms of individuals of lesser rank—were enlisted to spread far and wide the Faith of Force. The traditions and the maxims of Frederick the Great and Bismarck and the military philosophy of Clausevitz [*sic*] completely dominated the trend of intellectual movement, and the culture of old Germany was literally swamped amid a torrent of Chauvinism." Education and even the teachings of Christianity had been twisted and misdirected to suit the purposes of the state. The triumph of Germany in this war, therefore, would be the triumph of a rival system of civilization, a triumph of materialism, reaction, tyranny, and barbarism over liberty and progress, of which the burning and sacking of towns and the shooting of women and children were but minor examples. This war was also, in a sense, a religious war, insofar as the very principles of Christian justice and mercy were being trampled upon. Using apocalyptic language ("the coming of the Armageddon" and "struggle to the death"), Lawton compared the war to the crusades of old. "It is indeed a holy war upon which we are engaged, a war for freedom and for Christianity. Our soldiers, fighting with all the dogged tenacity of their race upon the soil of France, are in the truest sense of the term modern crusaders. . . . Because of the fervour of our faith in the righteousness of this cause, a fervour so strong as to be almost spiritual, we believe that the God of Battles will be with us."[3]

Nor did Lawton think that Germany was the only culprit. Austria's desire to crush "the independence of a virile little nationality" (the Serbians) was the immediate cause of the war. But Austria, "a tottering Empire" possessed of "no moral warrant for continued existence," had become "for all practical purposes a vassal of the Kaiser." Its war party, "preying upon the bereaved feelings of the aged Emperor, had succeeded where hitherto, in spite of persistent effort, they had failed." But even here Austria was only part of the gen-

3. Ibid., 228, 231.

eral struggle between pan-Germanic and pan-Slavonic forces whose clash was inevitable. Austria's attempt "to blot out" Serbia could only be compared with Germany's contemptuous disregard for the "scrap of paper" that had guaranteed Belgium's neutrality. England was fighting "for the right of the little nations to exist" and "for the vindication of the public law of Europe," but she was fighting for much more than that.

Ward was a strong supporter of the Allied cause and even helped in its propaganda efforts in the larger Catholic world, where the cause of godless anticlerical France, heretical Protestant England, and schismatic Orthodox Russia could not be very popular. He also attempted to garner public support from among the Catholic hierarchies of England and Ireland.[4] He felt the rightness of the cause, but for him it was essentially the violation of a nation whose neutrality Britain had pledged herself to defend by a signed treaty. While he certainly believed that the war was a conflict of worldviews, he was less sanguine in his views, lacking the quasi-religious fervor of so many. Unlike Lawton, he did not believe in "the march of progress," nor did he so readily see the war as a "holy war" or use religious language to describe it. That way of thinking was more a staple of liberal Protestantism, to which "progress" and "Christianity" had become synonymous, and this view held no attraction for him. He had no illusions about the Great War being "the war to end all wars." In a review of a published sermon, *The Allies of Faith,* by an American professor named Adams Brown, he criticized such Christian utopianism and belief in progress. Initially, Brown had seen in the war the collapse of "millenniums of progress," a descent into barbarism, and the failure of Christianity (which he seemed to associate with the "Fatherhood of God and the Brotherhood of man"). Yet, on further thought, the war had given him hope insofar as it showed the power of ideals and had unlocked the deep reserves of human self-sacrifice that could now be converted to the "imperialism of Christ" and the creation of a future kingdom of peace. With such a view Ward could not concur.

We shall no more succeed in banishing war from human society than we shall banish sin. In both cases, no doubt, we may strive for the ideal aim with might and main, but it will never be realized. Success can only be partial. And complete success is

4. For Ward and the war years, see *Wilfrid Wards* 2:450–71. Ward was very successful in gaining the public support of the English bishops for the war, but among the Irish bishops he generally failed.

perhaps not desirable in the interests of civilization, as war can best cure the very vices which beget war. Undoubtedly to Christianize the world is to starve the sources of war—selfishness, greed, ambition, hate, rivalry. Christianity condemns all these vices, and if every man could be made a perfect Christian we should have no more war. But experience shows that these anti-Christian vices cannot be extinguished though they may be made, from time to time, less widely operative. Thus we see a place for war in the providential scheme. It is more effectual than the best sermon in making men less selfish, greedy, ambitious, vindictive, and envious. But its terrible warning is forgotten in course of time. The vices flourish rankly again and they must issue once again in warfare which is also once again their retribution and their corrective. It is a cycle which, in the nature of things, must recur.[5]

Unlike Adams Brown, when Ward looked at recent history he saw no evidence that civilization had progressed and was progressing. While there had been "a certain growth of sentimental altruism," he believed that there also had been a decline in universal ethical standards, in heroic self-sacrifice and in the sense of duty—the only things that could truly strike at the root causes of war. In fact, progress was most evident in the very sciences that had made modern war horrific in a way that was unimaginable to a simpler, if more warlike, age. Ward found the abstract idealism of men like Adams Brown unreal. The self-sacrifice that war encouraged was not to some vague ideal, nor could it be harnessed to vague ideals:

A man will die in defence of wife and child; he will hardly die in the cause of abstract humanity, though the good of humanity is a higher ideal aim than the life and welfare of his wife and child. He will die for his country; he will not die for the universe; though the well-being of the universe is a greater good. The smaller and closer aim inspires his deeper feelings; the higher and more distant leaves him cold. It is not, I repeat, primarily an ideal aim, but an object of deep affections which brings out the self-sacrifice of war. . . . The early martyrs did live and die for the Christian faith, and what has once been may conceivably be again. But it was not a vague ideal or humanitarian sentiment for which they died; it was the personal love of Christ—loyalty to Him and trust in His promise.[6]

Brown's plea that the self-sacrifice elicited by war be enlisted in the Christian cause might be "inspiring and worth striving for to the utmost," but Ward believed that original sin precluded success except among the limited few.

Moreover, Ward recognized, war could bring out the worst in men as well

5. W. W. [Wilfrid Ward], "Some Recent Books," *Dublin Review* (Jan. 1915): 178–79.
6. Ibid., 180.

as the best. Many stories of German atrocities circulated in England following the invasion of Belgium, and in the January 1915 number he discussed them at length.[7] He recognized that the demonization of the enemy was common in war, and he was perfectly willing to admit that the Germans were not wholly evil. But this did not mean, as some were saying, that they were no worse than others. After careful investigation, and giving many well-founded examples, he was able to assert that terrible atrocities did occur in Belgium. There had been repeated killings of unarmed civilians (men, women, and children), the killing of priests and other notables, the destruction of property and even whole villages, plunder, rape, and much else. These were not exceptional but the average conduct of the German soldiers, bent on victory at all costs. Ward thought that to whitewash the crimes committed in Belgium was unjust both to Belgians' sufferings and to the cause of civilization.

The two main theorists behind the philosophy used to justify German aggression were the soldier Friedrich von Bernhardi (1849–1930), who had served on the German general staff and later commanded the Seventh Army Corps, and the academic Heinrich von Treitschke (1834–1896), a professor of history and political science in Berlin and the official historiographer of Prussia. Bernhardi's *Germany and the Next War* (1912), influenced by Darwinian ideas of "survival of the fittest," elaborated the view that the waging of war was not only a right and a duty but was a "biological necessity of the first importance" without which nations would grow unhealthy and weak, and the race and civilization falter and decay. Germany had to extend her power, to seek a "world empire," or she would die. In reviewing Cramb's *Germany and England* (1914), supposedly a reply to Bernhardi, the reviewer ("B de S") asserted that whatever might have been true in the past, no great empire would in the future be founded by a deliberate policy of aggression and conquest; that wherever there was civilization there was the knowledge that nothing worth deciding was decided by an appeal to force; and that international law was not a phantasm but an ideal worth defending.[8]

Ward wrote an article on Treitschke in the January 1915 number. He be-

7. Wilfrid Ward, "The Conduct of the German Soldiery," ibid. (Jan. 1915): 30–56. While many doubted the truthfulness of these stories after the war, they have now been verified in John Horne and Alan Kramer, *German Atrocities, 1914: A History of Denial* (New Haven: Yale University Press, 2001). See also Larry Zuckerman, *The Rape of Belgium: The Untold Story of World War I* (New York: New York University Press, 2004).

8. B. de S., "Some Recent Books," *Dublin Review* (Oct. 1914): 400–403.

lieved that Treischke's main error was not so much the exaltation of the individual state, as many believed, but his (and even more his disciples') inability "to comprehend the sacredness of a pledge, or what is meant by an obligation in the court of honour."[9] It was true that Treitschke thought permanent international courts of arbitration undermined the sovereignty of the state, but he did accept the idea of international treaties and an international law of war. Yet he considered the pledges made in any treaty to be elastic, with the silent stipulation *rebus sic stantibus,* so that changed conditions might remove any obligation, even of a signed treaty. Also, since the state had the right to declare war whenever it chose, it also had the right to cancel any agreed-upon treaty. While Ward admitted the force of some of this, he also asserted that, since a treaty was a signed compact, when any party no longer found the treaty acceptable such a shift had to be stated. This might lead to a new treaty, but it would certainly make obvious to all the rejection of the old one. To do as the Germans had done with Belgium, however, was completely wrong. By the very treaty that preserved their neutrality the Belgians were prevented from making foreign alliances, leaving them comparatively defenseless. Not only had the Germans given no warning about abrogating the treaty, they had reaffirmed their commitment to it the previous April and again four days before their invasion. Such a cynical application of Treitschke's theory stamped "the German as a cad and a barbarian."

Truthfulness and honor had ceased to be sacred if they conflicted with the cause of national aggrandizement, and this same lack of integrity, Ward believed, could be seen in the manifesto put out by the leading German *savants,* men such as Harnack and Haeckel, denying that the Germans had violated Belgium's neutrality or committed atrocities in Belgium. This manifesto also proclaimed that German militarism stood in no opposition to German culture and in fact was the result and protector of German culture.

But German militarism, or "Prussianism," as many called it, with its glorification of power, was nothing new. Bernhardi, Treitschke, and their ilk were not its only progenitors. Some wanted to go much further back, and Msgr. Barnes (now co-editor of the *Dublin*), in the October 1915 number, linked it to the Teutonic knights, whose last grand master, a Hohenzollern, had secularized his territory, creating the Duchy of Prussia.[10] In the same number

9. Wilfrid Ward, "The Interpretation of Treitschke," ibid. (Jan. 1915): 74–88.

10. A. S. Barnes, "The Teutonic Knights and the Kingdom of Prussia," ibid. (Oct. 1915):

Ward asserted that the German mentality was itself the cause of German militarism.[11] Various people, including Baron von Hügel, had pointed to the immense self-confidence, doggedness, and ruthless determination of the modern German as the antecedent cause of German savagery in the present war.

He [von Hügel] finds them wanting in individual judgment and initiative, in ready understanding of the mentality of an antagonist, in capacity for rapid modification of his plans. But on the other hand he finds him capable of extraordinary intensity and thoroughness and perseverance in organization and concomitantly ever in need of a theory and a system on which he plans and organizes with ruthless logic. Thus, the more delicate and instinctive intellectual gifts he is seriously wanting. Such a mentality is responsible for his strength and his weaknesses alike. It renders him "steady, but also obstinate; virile and brutal; profound and pedantic; comprehensive and rich in outlook, and rationalist and *doctrinaire.*"[12]

It was these very gifts, Ward thought, that encouraged the German belief that the world was theirs to conquer, and that this would benefit the world. Yet these very elements, especially when tied to the unscrupulous military code of Frederick's Prussia, made him unfit to rule an empire and led to his conduct in the war. Ward also believed that the spread of anti-Christian philosophical principles in Berlin had helped dissolve many Christian scruples. While in England such principles might "simmer for a long time without practical effect," German thoroughness and need for explicit theory made the result quite different. The Englishman only half-believed many of the theories he publicly advocated, half-unconsciously mistrusting them as inadequate to the complexity of life, and adopted them more slowly into his practical life. There was one more thing, he thought, that helped explained Prussianism: the genuine human desire for something beyond the individual, for some great cause beyond oneself and one's comforts. The Prussian militarist rightly idealized this innate desire, which took its noblest form in the Christian idea of chivalry, even as he corrupted it with a pagan warrior code and a pagan exaltation of war.

Medieval chivalry gave a rational and Christian satisfaction to the instinct which detects something noble in the heroism of the soldier. It stamped on the civilization of

---

272–83. Arthur Stapylton Barnes (1861–1936) was an Anglican parson received into the Church by Merry del Val in 1895 and ordained in 1898. Author of many articles and books, he was Catholic chaplain at Cambridge from 1902 to 1916 and at Oxford from 1919 to 1926.

11. Wilfrid Ward, "Prussianism, Pacificism and Chivalry," ibid. (Oct. 1915): 209–25.

12. Ibid., 214.

the eleventh and twelfth centuries the ideal of Christian knighthood, which included the idealization of courage and endurance in the battle field, but as part not of a war ideal of human life as a whole, but of a peace ideal. It destroyed the absolute divorce between the nobility manifest in war and the instinct for peace and justice. In place of the pitiless soul of Achilles it held up pity as the very motive force of military courage. Cruelty and treachery which necessarily followed from the pagan warrior's inspiring aim—which was victory at all costs—were the antithesis to the Christian warrior's ideal. His word was his bond: his first duty to defend the weak, to free the oppressed.[13]

The manifesto of the German intellectuals denied that the Germans had behaved brutally in Louvain, but it did admit that "with a heavy heart" they had been "obliged" to bombard a portion of the town "in retaliation for a treacherous attack" on the occupying army by the "raging" townsfolk. No example of the German policy of *Schrecklichkeit* ("frightfulness") so undermined the claims of German "culture," wrote William Barry in the January 1915 number, than the tragic and senseless destruction of much of the ancient university town of Louvain and its priceless university library.[14] It was here too that one saw most clearly the contrast between English freedom, with its inward sense of right and wrong, its conscience, and "German culture armed with cannon shot and petrol." "The disciples of Kant and Goethe join hands with the legions which Bismarck, Treitschke, Bernhardi, have trained to battle, and the insane Nietzsche has maddened for world-dominion."[15]

In the April 1915 number Ward quoted extensively from the Pastoral Letter of Cardinal Mercier, Primate of Belgium, on the conquest and devastation of his native country.[16] He had first read the letter while lecturing in America and was surprised at how deep an impression it made there. While it was certainly patriotic and enumerated the atrocities committed by the Germans, it was not a call to anger and revolt (in fact it called for submission to the German authorities, now that they held control), but a powerful meditation on the mystery of suffering and the Christian's response to it. Yet for this he and his publisher had been temporarily arrested on New Year's Day 1915.[17]

By the time the first war issue of the *Dublin* appeared, the German ad-

13. Ibid., 222.

14. William Barry, "The Lesson of Louvain," ibid. (Jan. 1915): 89–110.

15. Ibid., 110.

16. Wilfrid Ward, "Cardinal Mercier and the Martyrdom of Belgium," ibid. (April 1915): 217–26.

17. "The Arrest of Cardinal Mercier and his Publisher," ibid. (April 1915): 359–72.

vance had been stopped just short of Paris by the first Battle of the Marne; and the unnamed author of the first "Notes on the War" column (probably Lancelot Lawton, who wrote all the others) believed that the German cause was now lost.[18] The entire success of the German plan, a plan that had become public knowledge before the war began, depended, he argued, on the quick defeat of France by an invasion through neutral Belgium and the capture of Paris before the superior forces of the Triple Entente could be rallied against Germany. However, he wrote, Belgian resistance had delayed the Germans, and the successes of the French and British in the Battle of the Marne, which had caused the Germans to lose the initiative and even to retreat, meant that time was no longer on Germany's side. In a signed article, now almost four months into the war, Lawton pursued this argument, claiming that, given their failure to crush France in the opening weeks of the war, Germany was doomed to failure.[19] The Germans were still very far from defeat—they were in possession, after all, of a great deal of foreign territory, and their armed forces were still intact, extensive, and rather successful—and the Allies had won these victories at great cost. Still, he believed, the critical period had passed. Germany had the "mightiest fighting machine of its kind in the world," yet it had failed because it had set for itself an impossible task and imagined with its overweening vanity that it was a nation of supermen. Nor were its subsidiary plans any more successful. Its use of Turkey and attempt to incite an Islamic holy war had failed to arouse the Moslem subjects of the Crown, and had only precipitated events that would help the Allied cause. While economic pressure was useful in bringing the war to an end, and while there were already signs of German exhaustion, the process was too slow. Considering the high levels of popular support for the German government, something much more dramatic, he believed, was needed to shatter the German illusion of invincibility. Only a serious invasion of Germany could do that, and it was through Russia, "whose millions of peasants are the deciding military factor in the whole conflict," that this second and final stage would come about. The west was becoming "a war of field sieges" where progress would be slow, while the eastern front was becoming "the main theatre of hostilities."

18. "Notes on the War," ibid. (Oct. 1914): 378–99. The article was dated Sept. 14.

19. Lancelot Lawton, "Germany's Great Failure," ibid. (Jan. 1915): 1–29, and L. L. [Lancelot Lawton], "Notes on the War" (Jan. 1915): 140–63.

In his next "Notes on the War" (dated March 4, 1915) Lawton explained the difficulties the Russian forces faced and the reason for their failure, in Western eyes at least, to achieve any great success.[20] Russia's lack of military supplies, her deficiency in communications and transport, and the vast extent of the front, with its terrible conditions, all hindered her ability to fight. Yet the Russians had achieved some victories and rendered valuable services to her Western allies. The Russians had pinned down at least a million German soldiers in the east and at critical points had forced Germany to transfer troops from the western to the eastern front. She had also achieved signal successes against the Austrians and helped to pin down the Turks. "Formerly it was said of Russia that she might be thwarted but that never could she be beaten. In every campaign undertaken by them the Russians have been beset by those disabilities which I enumerated earlier. But at the same time always they have had in their favour certain great advantages such as are possessed by no other nation. Russia has illimitable space in which to retire if necessary. From her great population she can select for her armies men who are physically perfect specimens of manhood. The life that these men live in their villages enures them to the rigours of the Russian climate and particularly fits them for the hardships of campaigning."[21] No praise was too high, he believed, for the hardihood and gallantry of the Russians, as well as for the great suffering and heavy losses they had experienced.

Lawton particularly admired the Russian peasants, whom he saw, in almost Tolstoyan fashion, as the most democratic and Christ-like of peoples, and he attacked those who thought of Russia as a semibarbaric Asiatic nation.[22] His defense of the "calm sacrifice" of the peasant soldiers, whom he believed the finest in the world, continued even after it was clear that they were in rapid retreat, losing all of Russian Poland by the end of August 1915.[23] Despite their serious losses in men, material, and territory, despite the destruction of villages, crops, and factories, despite the flood of refugees into Mos-

20. L. L. [Lancelot Lawton], "Notes on the War," ibid. (April 1915): 374–91.

21. Ibid., 389.

22. Lancelot Lawton, "A View of Russia," ibid. (April 1915): 227–56. The article was written in opposition to the article of Maurice Baring, "The Causes of the Failure of the Russian Revolution," ibid. (Oct. 1910): 239–60. Baring criticized the Russian "Intelligenzia," who, though they idolized the people, were also alienated from them by their absorption in dogmatic, foreign, atheistic, and destructive philosophies. He also criticized the peasants for their desire for personal gain and to be free of all laws, "human, moral or divine."

23. Lancelot Lawton, "The Significance of the Russian Retreat," ibid. (Oct. 1915): 337–62.

cow and Petrograd (as St. Petersburg was renamed at the beginning of the war), Lawton believed that Russia's reserves of manpower were inexhaustible and that her heartland was safe. But he underestimated the opposition to the war that had developed in Russia, and he misjudged the causes behind the labor agitation plaguing the country, which he thought was over purely internal issues and directed toward greater efficiency in fighting the Germans.

Eleven months into the war, Lawton's outlook continued to be very positive, and he deprecated the "unhealthy pessimism" heard in some quarters.[24] True, certain "side issues" showed less hopeful signs, but time was on the Allies' side. Although the Germans were dug into strong defensive positions (trench warfare and field sieges having become the norm on the western front), the experts generally agreed that they were now using up their reserves of men and supplies, that they were "playing their last card." They had failed to knock out France in the early months of the war, and then had failed to knock out Russia, so they were faced with a two-front war that they could not win. The Allies only grew stronger, while the Germans had insufficient forces to maintain their position on the western front.

Was the attack on the Gallipoli Peninsula, on the Dardanelles in Turkey, one of the side issues Lawton mentioned? Only when discussing the Russian retreat of the summer did Lawton mention Gallipoli, and then only to show the need of such a campaign to supply the Russians with desperately needed military supplies and to relieve pressure on them from the Turks in the Caucasus. The truth about Gallipoli came out only in September, and A. H. Pollen, in his article on German submarine warfare, did discuss it directly. He castigated the British failure to use troops in their first attack on the Dardanelles in February 1915, instead waiting until April to do so. "What might have been almost a bloodless victory has become probably the bloodiest fight of the war. In spite of a combination of incredible skill and incredible valour resulting in the most remarkable martial performance in history, victory is not yet in sight."[25] Gallipoli was not mentioned again, not surprisingly, considering that the Allies not only failed in their objective and made an ignominious retreat but suffered 265,000 casualties in the process.

Lawton's October report primarily reviewed the Russian retreat but also

24. Lancelot Lawton, "Eleven Months of War," ibid. (July 1915): 146–83.

25. A. H. Pollen, "The Submarine Campaign," ibid. (July 1915): 100. Arthur Joseph Hungerford Pollen (1866–1937), educated at the Oratory School and at Trinity College, Oxford, was a naval expert.

discussed broader issues. He deplored the press's "hysterical campaign" against the English government, which he believed caused confusion both here and abroad and "put heart into our enemies." He also reprimanded the "pessimists" who had expected a short war and were now unhappy that it had become a "war of exhaustion." In fact, he claimed that he had always believed this would be a total war, one that could end only when one side had been exhausted, its male population of military age decimated. He believed that the war would go on for at least another two years (and it might last considerably longer) but that the superiority of the Allies in resources made victory inevitable. It would culminate, he thought, in an invasion of Germany and Austria from all sides. Modern warfare, which was a war of nations, not governments, required a new way of thinking.

This was Lawton's last column on the war. Articles by others still appeared, but there was no longer a running commentary on the actual fighting. It is not clear why this happened. The absence of further articles by Lawton might point to some dissatisfaction with his work. Certainly he tended to be too optimistic concerning the Allies, invariably seeing their actions in the best light possible, even at times distorting what was really happening. Thus, for example, he repeatedly stated that the French knew and had prepared for the major German force to go through Belgium, when it was clear by their actions that this was not so. Nor did Lawton describe the real horror of the fighting. But in all this he was not much different from others. Between government censorship and reporters' desire to support the Allied cause, war news tended to become propaganda.[26] Even the disaster at Gallipoli became known only after strenuous efforts and the intervention of the prime minister. In any case, it was becoming obvious that these commentaries were of little real value: the "Roll of Honour" in the daily newspapers, with their columns of names of the dead, made a mockery of the positive spin. One historian of the Great War has called 1915 "the death of innocence"; the ideals of nobility and courage with which the war began were consumed by the horror to which it gave birth.[27] Nineteen-fifteen not only ended without Allied victory but with the Central Powers in the ascent. Still, Germany had failed to defeat her main en-

26. See Phillip Knightley, *The First Casuality: From the Crimea to Vietnam; The War Correspondent as Hero, Propagandist, and Myth Maker* (New York: Harcourt Brace Jovanovich, 1975), 80–112; and Gerard J. DeGroot, *Blighty: British Society in the Era of the Great War* (New York: Longman, 1996), 180–187.

27. Lyn Macdonald, *1915: The Death of Innocence* (New York: Henry Holt, 1995).

emies or to destroy their capacity for taking the offensive. The British had already lost some 400,000 men in battle by 1916 (conscription was introduced in January 1916) and greater losses were yet to come. Still ahead was the Battle of the Somme (beginning in July 1916 and lasting nearly five months), in which the British suffered more than 400,000 casualties for negligible gains, and Passchendaele (from July 31 to November 10, 1917) where the army of Field Marshal Sir Douglas Haig, the British commander, suffered 70,000 dead and 170,000 wounded, again for negligible gains. By the time Ward died, in April 1916, the war was not even half over. Later in 1916, on December 8, Lloyd George ousted Asquith as prime minister with Conservative support.

The campaign in the British press against the government (now a government of national unity) that Lawton had referred to earlier was discussed more fully in an article that, though unsigned, was extremely like Ward in style and thought.[28] It criticized the exaggerated pessimism of some newspapers and attacked them as being misguided, ignorant, and unrepresentative of the national temper. "There is a good deal to be proud of in John Bull's character and temper. He has little imagination. . . . But he is not at all disposed to ignore in practice the difficulties he has to overcome. His very lack of imagination is a great safeguard not only against panic but against the approaches of panic in time of trial. . . . He is before all things confident and persevering. He is a good fellow and he is thoroughly angry when he is out against a bully or a tyrant."[29] Many newspapers, however, in their "shrieks" of pessimism after only eleven months of war, finding fault with everybody and everything, magnifying every enemy success and belittling every Allied achievement, had presented to "the public gaze a picture of querulous panic which is a libel on the character of John Bull," rejoicing his enemies and making many Englishmen feel ashamed of the figure he cut in public. The attacks on Lord Haldane and Lord Kitchener [the secretary of state for war] were particularly absurd and ignorant, the writer thought.[30] It also praised strongly, and quoted extensively, a speech by Balfour that had soberly outlined the indisputable facts of

28. "The National Temper and the Press," *Dublin Review* (Oct. 1915): 241–51.

29. Ibid., 241.

30. Lord Haldane (1856–1928), whom Ward knew well from his involvement in the Synthetic Society, while secretary of state for war (1905–1912) had been responsible for the prewar reforms of the army. He was forced out of the government entirely in the cabinet reshuffle of May 1915 that created the wartime coalition. See Stephen E. Koss, *Lord Haldane: Scapegoat for Liberalism* (New York: Columbia University Press, 1969).

the case, showing why confidence in victory was not exaggerated. The writer believed that the running of the war should be left to the experts; and while this was not perfect, it was still better than the general paralysis that would follow if the war were conducted by "a leadership of a huge debating society in the Press of which the *personnel* not only does not consist of experts, but is, in spite of conspicuous exceptions, distinctly below the average Englishman in that good sense and practical courage on which so much depends."

In nine cases out of ten the lay critic's suggestions are based on half-knowledge. The long odds are that the first-rate expert—who holds office in virtue of tried reputation—is right, and such a critic is wrong. At all events the expert is pretty sure to be acting on a definite plan, and to hamper him by agitation on behalf of another plan is probably to get neither carried out effectively. It is only when it is clear that important necessities in the actual plan of operations have been overlooked or neglected, and that nothing short of a public outcry will set this right, that such an outcry is warranted, and then it really voices public opinion and the critics will be generally recognized as patriots, and not as wanton pessimists. . . . Public criticism of the authorities that is hostile in its tone should be the very last resource in war-time. Suggestions can very easily be made through the Press in a form which will not tend to discredit our responsible leaders, whom no one supposes to be infallible.[31]

The writer also thought it would be "unfortunate" to muzzle the press because of some reporters' irresponsible love of sensationalism and petty jealousy, and he did not think this would be necessary if the newspapers would only show the same practical common sense and patriotism common among the general public. The suggestion of some journals that the conduct of the war should be entrusted to a small committee of the cabinet was a good example of how the press had played a positive role in the war, as long as they did not then begin to hinder its efficiency with carping criticism. He believed that much could be said for a government by a few strong men, particularly in such times of crisis.

The war introduced new kinds of warfare, and the *Dublin* took notice of two in particular, the airplane and the submarine. Its discussion of the airplane primarily described the rapid development of its use in the fighting, first for reconnaissance and directing artillery fire, and then as a method of bombing.[32] The use of airplanes was remarkably new, but already they had

31. "National Temper and the Press," 248.

32. Eric Stuart Bruce, "The Use of Aircraft in the Present War," *Dublin Review* (Jan. 1916): 84–102.

proved, the author thought, very useful. The airship (Zeppelin) had proved less useful to the Germans than expected because it was a fair-weather machine and the squalls of the North Sea limited its use.

The submarine received more attention, for it offered the Germans a way to get around the superiority of the British navy and to blockade Britain as she was blockading Germany. The Germans had used submarines from the beginning of the war—the first sinking of a merchant vessel without warning occurred on October 26, 1914—but the official submarine war began only on February 18, 1915. The goal of the submarine war was the destruction of all shipping, even neutral ships if they were not recognized as such, coming into or out of British waters.

A. H. Pollen wrote two articles on the subject. In the first, he criticized the extravagant claims being made for the submarine and the exaggerated fears of the damage German submarines could do.[33] First, he wrote, the Germans had only between thirty and sixty submarines. Second, if one looked at the number of ship arrivals and departures to date, only a small fraction, less than 1 percent, of the targets had been attacked. Third, such were the inherent limitations of torpedoes that a ship going at a decent speed or with prompt recognition of a torpedo's coming could generally avoid being hit. Other measures, such as the use of netting, were also useful as protection against submarine attack. The "shadow of menace from this source" seemed "ridiculous."

Pollen returned to this topic in a second article three months later, after some sixty ships had been sunk in the intervening period, including the fastest and most luxurious passenger ship in commission, the *Lusitania*—to which he gave a great deal of space.[34] He admitted that his faith in the protective measures mentioned in his earlier article had been shaken. The Germans had learned from their mistakes and were building far larger boats, which were not as limited as the earlier ones. Barriers were clearly useless and methods of using magnetic or acoustical appliances to detect submarines as yet insufficiently developed. But speed was still useful, and except for the *Lusitania,* whose great length made her as easy to hit at eighteen knots as a proportionately shorter ship would be at fifteen, no ship that could go faster than fifteen knots had been destroyed. It was also clear, he believed, that the *Lusitania* had

33. A. H. Pollen, "The Submarine Myth," ibid. (April 1915): 326–40. For the history and use of the submarine by the Germans against Britain in the early part of the war, see Edwyn Gray, *The Killing Time* (London: Seeley, 1972), 13–115.

34. A. H. Pollen, "The Submarine Campaign," *Dublin Review* (July 1915): 87–102.

been targeted by the Germans and had done nothing to protect herself. A whole slew of ships had been sunk in that zone recently, including one at almost exactly the same spot just a day earlier, yet the *Lusitania* had not chosen a safer route but more or less her normal route through the danger zone. In addition, instead of sailing at her maximum speed of twenty-six knots in the danger zone, she had lowered her speed to eighteen and sailed in broad daylight. Nothing Pollen had seen so far told him anything new about the capabilities of the submarine or convinced him that it was a more serious danger than before. It was well to remember, he continued, that the rate of loss to submarines, a million pounds a month, was negligible when compared with the total cost of the war, that it was less than a quarter of 1 percent of British shipping, and that the use of submarines had not destroyed the essential reality of Britain's control of the sea.

In September 1915 the Germans discontinued their campaign of unrestricted submarine warfare. The promised goal of the campaign (that within six weeks they could bring Britain to her knees) had obviously failed, despite the modest successes. Also, as the outrage in the United States over the sinking of the *Lusitania* (on which 128 Americans had died) made clear, the danger of bringing the United States into the war by the continuation of such a campaign was too great. The resumption of unrestricted submarine warfare early in 1917 created a far more desperate situation for the British, but it was also the main cause of the United States' entrance into the war, tipping the balance to the Allies.

Considering how German Catholicism had been praised in the *Dublin* earlier, the support of German Catholics for the war could only be a disappointment. It was not until the January 1916 number, however, almost a year and a half into the war, that this issue was taken up.[35] The article pointed out that when Germany invaded Catholic Belgium and Catholic Luxemburg, not a single member of the Center Party had raised his voice in protest. To the contrary, the party had openly defended the violation of these neutral nations. The Center had failed in the time of crisis, the article continued, and the evil fruit of this could be seen in the violent and immoral language of Center Party newspapers and among its political figures—men such as

35. "German Catholics and the War," ibid. (Jan. 1916): 13–35. For German Catholics at this time, see John K. Zeender, "The German Center Party during World War I: An Internal Study," *Catholic Historical Review* 42 (Jan. 1957): 441–68, and "German Catholics and the Concept of an Interconfessional Party, 1900–1920," *Journal of Central European Affairs* 23 (1964): 424–39.

Matthias Erzberger, who argued for ruthless and utterly unscrupulous methods of warfare, and, even worse, Martin Spahn, who outdid even Bernhardi in the immorality of his principles and their application to the war.[36]

The article accused the leaders of German political Catholicism (and its press) of being infected by anti-Christian and immoral Germanism, but it excused most German Catholics as being both voiceless and deceived. The writer rejected the thesis of some entente apologists that German Catholicism was in a lamentable state, infected with the subjectivism of Luther and Kant or under the influence of modernism. Nor were German Catholics the first to have fallen into an un-Catholic nationalism; there was the precedent of the Cisalpines in England. It was preposterous to believe, the writer continued, that the average German Catholic had knowingly sold his soul to "Deutschland über Alles." Men could only form their consciences from the material available to them, and German Catholics got their information "through the medium of an enslaved Press." It was a principle of moral theology that those who acted in invincible ignorance, believing their cause just and true, could find grace and merit just as if it were the most pure of sacrifices.

> We can but accept the position as a terrible, yet an inevitable, concomitant of the state of war. But we need not read into it more than it means, or affix to German Catholicism in the mass the stigma certain segments of it have well deserved. Rather we may discern signs of hope, and anticipate with confidence a great and healing mission for our co-religionists of the rank and file in Germany when their opportunity comes and they may again find freedom and a voice. . . . How well many thousands of our German co-religionists have thus died there is abundance of testimony, nor need our appreciation of their sacrifice be the less by reason of our own bounden duty in conscience to go on killing still more thousands of them till the cause of righteousness is vindicated, and the objects entrusted to our arms attained.[37]

The article blamed the collapse of political Catholicism on the Center Party's abandonment of its Catholic identity, and its attempts to transform itself into an interconfessional or nondenominational party. It noted the splitting of the party into two camps: the Berlin faction, which stood for "integral Catholicism," and the Cologne faction, which stood for interconfessionalism.

36. For Erzberger, see Klaus Epstein, *Mathias Erzberger and the Dilemma of German Democracy* (Princeton: Princeton University Press, 1959), which has Erzberger's notorious article, "No Sentimentality," in Appendix 4, 410–12. Erzberger eventually moved away from his extreme positions, though not for moral reasons, and died at the hands of ultranationalist assassins in 1921. Spahn left the Center for the German Nationalists in 1919 and joined the Nazis in 1933.

37. "German Catholics and the War," 33–34.

There were difficulties of personality and faults of temper on both sides, and an abundant crop of extremely disedifying incidents, which it would do no good to revive in these pages. But the broad fact remains that under the influence of Cologne the Centre has become no longer an organization for Catholic defence, but an undenominational political party, and, what is more, the docile instrument of the Berlin Government and of its pan-Germanism in the extremist form. The mischief began when men of the type of Windhorst [*sic*], champions of the rights of nationalities, of creeds, of minorities, upholders pre-eminently of ideals, were succeeded by men like Lieber, above all things "Government men," men of *real-politik,* and when leaders of a powerful opposition were content to range themselves in the train of the King of Prussia and his half-Christianised hordes from the ill-gotten territories of the first apostate Hohenzollern.[38]

The writer argued that the crucial point was the attempt to create nondenominational Christian unions, pointing out that these unions were not like English unions, which confined themselves to secular concerns, but were comparable to the mixed reality of the Catholic school system. Years of bitter contention had been ended only by Pius X's 1912 encyclical *Singulari Quadem,* which tolerated these unions even as it expressed its preference for Catholic ones. After the encyclical, the article continued, things went from bad to worse, as Cologne captured the party, the party caucus finally declaring (February 8, 1914) "that the party is not a Catholic party, but . . . the party to which Catholics ought to belong; that they ought to submit themselves to its politics, and that if their conscience forbids this, it is their duty to keep silence, for the sake of unity and discipline."[39] Because of this subservience of religion to politics, all Catholic defense had ended, and a craven acquiescence followed. The sad thing was that this gained the party nothing, "either for this world or for the next," for having "tied itself to the chariot-wheels of the Protestant ascendancy party," it could be safely ignored.

It must have come as a surprise to many readers of the *Dublin* to hear that the great Center Party had ceased to be Catholic. These conflicts, the *Zentrumsstreit* or "center conflict," and the *Gewerkschaftsstreit* or "trade-union conflict," had been going on in a very public and bitter way since 1906.[40] But

38. Ibid., 19.

39. Ibid., 21.

40. See Ross, *Beleaguered Tower,* 49–131, and Evans, *German Center Party,* 178–202. The most insightful discussion of the *Zentrumsstreit* is Margaret Lavinia Anderson, "Interdenominationalism, Clericalism, Pluralism: The *Zentrumsstreit* and the Dilemma of Catholicism in Wilhelmine Germany," *Central European History* 21 (1988): 350–78.

almost nothing of this had appeared in the journal. When it came to the faith and all that touched upon it, the *Dublin* always tried to stress the positive and edifying, downplaying, or ignoring what was scandalous or unpleasant, and so the editors had avoided the subject. While it was true that the Center Party had never been, strictly speaking, a confessional party, and was not under clerical control, nonetheless without Catholicism it would not have existed. Nor did the Cologne faction want to remove its connection to the Catholic faith completely, because it understood that obvious point. More than anything else, the German Catholic community desired acceptance and parity in the Empire, and the ferocious anti-Catholicism of the 1907 election was certainly a clear reminder to them of how little they had achieved. This would explain their electoral shift to the right after 1907 and their frank acceptance of nationalism. The Socialists became the largest party in the Reichstag after the 1912 election, as the Center lost seats. If the Socialists, who were far more hated and alienated from the government and society than Catholics, could support the war, one could hardly expect Catholics to do any less. But the readers of the *Dublin* were never told of the Center Party's shift toward the government or of its nationalism, or of its losses in the 1912 election—at least not until it became necessary and convenient to tell them.

France and French Catholicism, on the other hand, whose travails the *Dublin* had so sadly chronicled, seemed to experience a rebirth because of the war. In the January 1915 number, F. Y. Eccles, reviewing Abbé Ernest Dimnet's *France Herself Again* (1914), traced the decline in public spirit and national vitality that had beset France from the latter days of the Second Empire.[41] With Dimnet, he believed that the origins of this "distemper" were intellectual, beginning first with the Romantics, who, "under the colours of universal charity," held "the frontiers of country of less account than the differences of condition," and getting much worse under such naturalists as Taine and Renan, "whose common tendency was the destruction of all generous enthusiasm." This "humanitarianism," which deprecated national identity, along with its dread of Caesarism, was common among many of the triumphant republicans who dominated the Third Republic. The Dreyfus Affair (which Eccles saw as part of an international conspiracy against the French army) led to the reign of Combes, whose anticlericalism and lack of patriotism did so much harm to the national spirit and weakened the military. The "unprecedented

41. F. Y. Eccles, "The French Awakening," *Dublin Review* (Jan. 1915): 164–75.

humiliation" of the Tangier incident precipitated a change that the Agadir incident only intensified. Eccles considered this not only a political but also an intellectual change. Naturalism no longer dominated French taste and criticism, and the classical virtues of order, clearness, and precision seemed to take on new life. The rising generation and the growing influence of the Church helped in this regeneration. Anticlericalism, Eccles believed, now seemed a spent force, and unbelievers felt much greater sympathy toward the Church. "The intellectual dilettante had lost its vogue, and internationalism has no longer any prestige with French crowds. Not only experience, but a vigorous instinct—as sure as the sense of idiom which guards languages from corruption—has come to the rescue of minds thrown off their balance by indulgence in the pleasures of irresponsible speculation."[42] While the French Parliament had lagged behind the nation in this regeneration, its election of Poincaré showed that even the parliament had realized what the nation desired.

One of the results of the anti-Catholic laws passed in France was that for the first time in history a large number of priests were actually fighting in the French army, not being exempt from the draft or from fighting units. In an unsigned article a little more than a year into the war, the *Dublin* discussed the effect of this on the French army and on religion in the army in general.[43] While there were about three hundred military chaplains, another twenty thousand priests served as soldiers, a majority in noncombatant roles; but all those under thirty and in good health were actively involved in fighting. For this group the irregularity that they should have incurred for taking part in military operations was suspended for the duration of hostilities. Politicians had created such laws to weaken the Church, the article asserted, but they in fact had given the Church an opportunity, allowing her priests access to soldiers that would have been difficult otherwise and allowing millions of soldiers personal experience of priests, which was eliminating misunderstanding and antipathy and creating a new solidarity between priest and people consecrated by a common danger and a common sacrifice. The dangers of the war itself had led to a revival of piety, and the author gave examples from the

42. Ibid., 173. A perfect example of the nationalist and religious revival among the younger generation before the war was Ernest Psichari (1883–1914), a grandson of Renan and a child of the intellectual elite of the Third Republic, who both became a Catholic and joined the army. See Robert Wohl, *The Generation of 1914* (Cambridge: Harvard University Press, 1979), 5–41.

43. "Religion in the French Army," *Dublin Review* (Oct. 1915): 295–308.

front of the good work and heroism of these soldier-priests, the devoutness of the men they served, and the moments of grace experienced on the battlefield.

Although the French religious revival early in the war was genuine, for there was a quantifiable return to religious observance, and although there were some permanent results, on the whole the revival was temporary, and already by 1915 fervor had begun to slacken.[44] War often produces religious fervor, but it also often produces superstition and credulity; witness the wide acceptance of the story of the "Angels of Mons" who allegedly aided the British retreat from Mons in 1914. In the April 1915 number of the *Dublin,* Herbert Thurston addressed the spread of false prophecies that had circulated in books and the press since the war began.[45] He reviewed many earlier examples of public "prophecy" (even by canonized saints) and put particular emphasis on the "two stout volumes" of *Voix Prophétiques* produced as a result of the Franco-Prussian War, the fifth edition of which had the approval of Mgr. Dechamps, the Archbishop of Malines. All of these prophecies had proved completely false. In Thurston's view, the only advantage of the present "prophetic literature" over the older literature was that there was not so much of it. The dominant feeling about it could only be "the sense of humiliation at having wasted valuable hours over such unprofitable material." The great danger of these false prophecies was that they could encourage elusive hopes and lead people to forget that God helps those who help themselves. Thurston pointed out that Catholicism had no monopoly on such credulity, as the great interest in astrology, palmists, crystal gazers, and, in evangelical circles, commentaries on the Apocalypse showed. War prophecies had attracted comparatively little attention even among Catholics, and Catholics had not demanded their acceptance as a test of orthodoxy.

Thurston's larger book on the topic, *The War and the Prophets* (1915) was reviewed in the April 1916 number, and the reviewer, though he agreed with Thurston on the whole, thought him a little too ruthless with his skepticism. "Our only criticism is that he does the work even too thoroughly and does not allow to some prophecies the credit which is fairly due to them. Indeed,

44. For the French religious response to the war, see Annette Becker, *War and Faith: The Religious Imagination in France, 1914–1930* (New York: Berg, 1998), and Annette Becker, "The Churches and the War," in *The Great War and the French People,* ed. Jean-Jacques Becker (New York: St. Martin's Press, 1986), 161–91.

45. Herbert Thurston, "The Plague of False Prophets," *Dublin Review* (April 1915): 341–58.

so thorough is his scepticism that it comes almost as a surprise to find that there is one prediction in which he is almost inclined to believe."[46]

Throughout the war the Holy See tried to promote a peaceful resolution and maintained a strict neutrality, a position that Bishop Frederick William Keating of Northampton defended in the July 1915 number of the *Dublin.*[47] Keating thought it interesting that while the European press generally saw the correctness of the Church's neutrality, those who had been most anti-Catholic before the war were now most eager to see the pope take sides—and most ready to condemn him when he did not. It would not have been surprising, he wrote, if the Vatican were pro-German, considering that it had been treated far better by the Central Powers countries than by the Allies. Yet, as the "Common Father of Catholics," the pope could hardly take sides, even as he tried to use his influence both to criticize abuses and to gain concessions. His success depended on his clear impartiality and disinterestedness, Bishop Keating wrote, and it was naïve and silly to suggest that the pope's infallibility imposed on him the duty of defining the rights and wrongs of every international quarrel. Still, the papacy was the supreme moral power in the world, and under the present pontiff it had made its views known about unacceptable behavior in the war—both diplomatically and more publicly in guarded though pointed terms—and had tried to gain concessions from the belligerents to mitigate the evils of warfare. The bishop also pointed out the difficulties under which the pope was working. The days when popes were great world powers died with the Middle Ages, as St. Pius V's disastrous bull against Queen Elizabeth showed. Today the pope's power was limited to moral influence, and moral influence did not go very far against the passions of war. Also, at this point any public censure of the Kaiser would be perceived as a partisan act and would gravely endanger the Catholic Church in that land without reaping any corresponding benefit. The temporal losses, though great, would be of little account compared to the spiritual peril in which such an action would place so many German Catholics. Touched by a patriotism

46. "Some Recent Books," ibid. (April 1916): 405. Unfortunately, the review does not tell us which prophecy Thurston was almost inclined to believe.

47. Frederick William Keating, "The Neutrality of the Holy See," ibid. (July 1915): 134–45. See also Rope, *Benedict XV,* 51–202, and Pollard, *Unknown Pope,* 85–162. Keating (1859–1928), Bishop of Northampton from 1908 to 1921 and then Archbishop of Liverpool from 1921 to his death, was known as a keen advocate of Social Catholicism and an early supporter of the Catholic Social Guild. See Kester Aspden, "Archbishop Frederick Keating and the Catholic Social Movement, 1908–1928," *Downside Review* 120 (Jan. 2002): 11–32.

now consecrated by their dead, and dizzy with military successes, they would consider such a censure ridiculous and reject its messenger. The loss of so much of Germany had been the outstanding calamity of the Reformation, and public censure "might easily precipitate another schism more fatal still." "The Catholic Church is the only international system that has survived in the universal upheaval. It alone has survived in virtue of its supernatural unity, the fruit of its Divine Founder's prayer, and the *raison d'être* of the Papacy. Even for purely secular ends, especially the more speedy and the more stable re-establishment of honourable peace, Catholic unity is too precious to be risked."[48]

Also in July 1915, Pope Benedict XV moved from general exhortations and secret diplomacy to a more aggressive and public diplomacy to end the war, when he issued his apostolic exhortation entitled "To the Belligerent Peoples and Their Rulers," an apocalyptic warning of what would follow if a negotiated peace were not sought. The *Dublin,* which, like the English hierarchy and English Catholics generally, remained strongly supportive of the war, made no comment on the pope's peace initiatives. After conscription became law on January 27, 1916, Stanley Morison (1889–1967), who worked at Burns & Oates, and Francis Meynell (1891–1975), Wilfrid Meynell's son, formed the Guild of the Pope's Peace, an association for Catholics that promoted and prayed for the pope's peace activities.[49] Never very large, and gaining little support among the faithful, it was attacked by Bishop Ambrose Burton of Clifton in late April.

Even as the war raged on, there was discussion of what would follow after Germany's certain defeat and the kind of reorganization of Europe that would make another such war impossible. In the April 1915 number's "A Plea for International Law," Francis Urquhart asserted that the old Concert of Europe, based on mutual distrust, was self-condemned, for it had forced even the most inoffensive and peace-loving of countries to imitate the most warlike and expansive, showing that only military power could guarantee freedom.[50] Some permanent "strongly knit inter-State organization" or "Confederation" was needed, he believed; and while some sort of force or policing power was

48. Keating, "Neutrality of the Holy See," 144.

49. See Nicolas Barker, *Stanley Morison* (London: Macmillan, 1972), 62–64, 67–69; and Francis Meynell, *My Lives* (New York: Random House, 1971), 82–103.

50. Francis Urquhart, "A Plea for International Law," *Dublin Review* (April 1915): 312–25.

necessary for such an organization, too many were concentrating on this aspect. Far more important, he thought, was the need to develop a new international "conscience" without which no law could be accepted and enforced. Lacking traditional authority and sanctions, international law needed moral force. The denial of a right and wrong for nation-states and the conviction that national self-interest was the only guide had led to the war in the first place. The growth of nationalism had weakened the idea that mankind belonged to a family of nations, and the idolatry of the state had overridden all law and justice, even the elementary dictates of humanity. Such "patriotism" had caused terrible evils, and Catholics, despite their common membership in the Church, had shown themselves no less prone to it than others. What was needed for international law, especially in the area of war, was some generally accepted basis of moral principle, such as existed in the traditional law of nations as elaborated by the seventeenth- and eighteenth-century legists. The weakness of the old international law, Urquhart believed, was that it was rigid and conservative and only confirmed the status quo. Also, it tended to identify the nation with the government or sovereign. It took a new ideal, that of nationality, to overthrow it, and from the time of the Napoleonic Wars that is what had happened. In domestic politics the state could correct the status quo so as to remove obsolete institutions and foster new energies; but this was not true in international affairs, where there was no common state. The great virtue of the old international law was that it "linked together principles of national conduct with the rules universally accepted in private life," so that the state's behavior was based on moral principle. Urquhart believed that the knowledge of international law had to be revived, revised where necessary, and its principles generally accepted. Without the development of conscience and the spread of that moral force among the peoples of Europe, arbitration would have little weight, and the international policeman, even if he could be found, would only arouse bitter resentment.

Every available force should be brought to bear on this question; the lawyer, the moralist, the theologian. The Church should take the lead. In the past she has been rather shy of interfering in matters of this kind. There was a proposal at the time of the Vatican Council to lay down some principles "de re militari et bello," but the Council did not last long enough for the question to be raised. In general the ecclesiastical authorities have been anxious not to come into conflict with national sentiment, and afraid perhaps of finding themselves in the strange company of anarchists and "sans patrie." But all such fears should be thrown aside. The problem of national sin can no longer be avoided. As guardian of the moral law it would seem to be the Church's first duty in these days of bewildered consciences to state the principles of Catholic tradition on what constitutes lawful war.[51]

Other articles also called upon the Church, and particularly the pope, to be more actively involved in elucidating principles on the international scene. In the January 1916 number, Sir George Sherston Baker, a British judge, traced the history of international law on war from the ancient world onward, and concluded that the present conventions on war were insufficient and that the pope, therefore, as the only one who could, both by his office and by his eminence, should define *ex cathedra* the Christian principles of warfare.[52] In the July 1915 number, Father Cuthbert, seeing Prussian militarism as merely the final result of the egoism that had begun with the Renaissance and Reformation, which had dissolved the supranational Middle Ages and its universalism, asserted that it had been a mistake to exclude the Holy See from recent international agreements, and that the prestige and moral influence of the papacy was needed if the reconstruction of international law was to succeed.[53] Cardinal Gasquet, looking at the beneficial involvement of the papacy in international affairs of the past, also asserted that only the papacy could supply the moral authority necessary for justice between nations.[54] The present war certainly showed the need for the necessary restraints of religious and moral principles, and he believed that the war, for all its horrors and losses, might be a blessing in disguise if it roused people "to the claims of the eternal principles which rule the destinies of individuals and nations."

In the January 1916 number Father Cuthbert wrote that the postwar settlement would have to take into account national sentiment.[55] He understood that many conservatives, seeing how nationalism had undermined the established order, viewed it with distrust and antipathy, and that many Catholics had denounced nationalism as destructive of the unity of Christendom and contrary to Catholic universalism. He also understood that there were many

51. Ibid., 324.

52. George Sherston Baker, "Catholicism and International Law," ibid. (Jan. 1916): 103–18. Baker (1846–1923) was an authority on international law and the author of a number of well-known books on it.

53. Fr. Cuthbert [Hess] O.S.F.C., "War and the Conscience of Nations," ibid. (July 1915): 74–86.

54. Aidan Cardinal Gasquet, "The Guarantees of International Honour," ibid. (Oct. 1915): 363–74.

55. Fr. Cuthbert [Hess] O.S.F.C., "A Plea for Nationalism," ibid. (Jan. 1916): 36–50.

who, though not in principle opposed to nationalism, had been alienated by it because of how badly it had so often turned out. So often the methods used to achieve and continue it were ugly, and so often foreign dominion had merely been replaced by a native military or political caste just as inimical to the real liberty of the people as what it replaced. He believed, however, that these defects of nationalism were not intrinsic but were due to the materialist conception of statecraft that had perverted the state in the modern period. The nationalist ideal as it emerged from history was pacific and bound up with the liberty of the people, while the statecraft of modern Europe from the fifteenth and sixteenth centuries to the French Revolution and even, to a large extent, now was formed on the principle that might makes right, to the subversion of liberty, both in internal affairs and between nations.

No political or social system could endure or have any moral authority which ignores the essential constitution of human nature itself, or takes away the rightful liberties of the human spirit: and national life is undoubtedly one of those liberties. Whatever legists and materialists may say, an ideal for which men, and the better sort of men, are prepared to sacrifice every material advantage, and even to die—which evokes, as few other things can, the noblest emotions—such an ideal must express something deeply sacred in a man's life. . . . A people, therefore, to whom the national ideal of life is sacred cannot part with it except to their own spiritual loss. If there is one lesson history teaches clearly and dogmatically, it is that once a national spirit is awakened it cannot be crushed out except as the people become morally and spiritually devitalized.[56]

The political reconstruction of Europe, therefore, had to give national sentiment its due, "both in the formation of the State and in the organization of any international system," if it was to be successful. The international community, "whether governed by imperial or more universal law," had to be a community of peoples, each "in possession of its own national ideal, and with a legitimate liberty to develop its own national life, and each co-operating with the other with a respect for the other's rightful liberty." The moral sense of Europe had outgrown the moral sanction of force and the old statecraft with it. "The real bond of a nation, as distinct from the mere State, is not its material interests, but its habits of thought, its community of ideas, its common aspirations towards the realisation of some special soul-liberty in which the individuality of each member of the nation finds the widest freedom of

56. Ibid., 39.

development whilst at the same time it is conserved in its fundamental character."[57] The genius of the national spirit was to bring men into touch with the universal life of the human spirit, but by way of some fundamental "soul-quality" from which the distinctive national character sprang. True nationalism lay between a cosmopolitanism "without definite line or colour," in which the individual personality was lost "in a blur of emotions and ideas," and a lack of national interest that lessened one's interests and "confined the free development of mind and character." Only one universalism—the Catholic Church—had ever been successful, and that was because it was of the supernatural and not of the secular order, based on the divine personality of Christ, which was above and encompassed all the developments of human personality. But even the Church had to recognize that people differed dramatically in their thought and temperament, witness the many different schools of religious thought and the variety of religious orders.

Political recognition of nationality was not enough, however, for true nationalism depended on its idealism and moral force. It was created, Father Cuthbert thought, not by logical theories, whose "transparent clearness" was frequently delusive, but by vital instinct and intuition. One must look at a nation's martyrs and confessors, and to its literature, to understand its ideals and spirit. He saw two dangers: excessive conservatism, which cut off a people from any real intellectual or moral intercourse with life beyond their own confines, and a watery internationalism that was alien to the national genius. One led to complacency and dangerous egoism, while the other led to the destruction of a nation's distinctive moral fiber, leaving it prone to "anarchic individualism and a morbid depression of spirit" that sought "an unhealthy sensational excitement." He thought that England had lost this national spirit.

What the loss of its spiritual idealism means to a nation has been but too well exemplified in English national life during the past century. Whether in town or village the prevalent note had become a deep underlying pessimism. There was but little of the real joy in life, and a constantly growing hunger for artificial excitement which follows upon spiritual depression. The mass of the people, to escape from the drab monotony which enveloped their work-a-day life, were driven to the unhealthy stimulant of a sensational music-hall or picture-palace or to the rush of a week-end excursion. Our literature, too, was largely dominated by the same pessimism which had infected our social life.[58]

57. Ibid., 40–41.
58. Ibid., 48.

But Father Cuthbert thought that the war had awakened Britain and that better things lay ahead. The conscience of the nation seemed much more aware of moral and spiritual values, and of the beauty latent in daily life. It was now possible to get rid of the materialist teaching and drab utilitarianism that had befogged people's vision and deprived England's national habits and institutions of that poetic glamour without which life itself was debased. The greatest danger, he feared, was worship of the state, which had been the bane of nationalism for centuries. Only authentic nationalism, true to its spiritual origin and nobler ideals, could bring real comity, liberty, and life.

Hilaire Belloc was far more prescient than any of these writers about what would follow the war. In an article in the October 1914 number on the modern French temper, Belloc remarked that the Germans were so convinced that their enemies had "wickedly plotted the destruction of the German people without provocation" that if they lost the war the result would be an intense legacy of hatred and a whole "cycle of wars in which our civilization will sink from one lower level to another"—"*unless* disarmament be imposed by the victors."[59]

Under the pressures of war Britain did change, with much greater government control and a loosening of social mores.[60] And while Britain *did* win the war, it did so only at a phenomenal cost, so high a cost that one historian has considered Britain's involvement in the war a mistake.[61] There were heavy economic costs, of course, but even more poignant were the heavy human costs: about 723,000 British servicemen died, the social elites bearing a disproportionate share of the losses.[62] Ward's sons survived the war. Herbert served in India and Mesopotamia. Leo, while repeatedly rejected as physically unfit, got a commission in 1917 but was kept on guard duty in England. But many of the children of Ward's friends did not survive the war. The Empire not only

59. Hilaire Belloc, "The Modern French Temper," ibid. (Oct. 1914): 372.

60. See Arthur Marwick, *The Deluge: British Society and the First World War* (Boston: Little, Brown, 1965). Gerard J. DeGroot argues for less social change in *Blighty: British Society in the Era of the Great War.* "The war was not a deluge which swept all before it, but at best a winter storm which swelled the rivers of change. And, just as it (like all wars) provided opportunities for positive change, so too it stimulated conservatism and counter-reaction, rendering progress erratic and limited" (291).

61. See Niall Ferguson, *The Pity of War* (New York: Basic Books, 1999), 458–62.

62. See J. M. Winter, *The Great War and the English People* (Cambridge: Harvard University Press, 1986), 65–99, for a discussion of British war losses, including the disproportionate losses of the social elites.

survived but was increased, though its conviction and strength suffered a great blow. Samuel Hynes considered the war the great political and *imaginative* event of its time, for it altered not merely the ways in which people thought about war but also about how they thought about the world, and about culture and its expressions:

> Even as it was being fought the war was perceived as a force of radical change in society and in consciousness. It brought to an end the life and values of Victorian and Edwardian England; but it did something more fundamental than that: it added a new scale of violence and destruction to what was possible—it changed reality. That change was so vast and so abrupt as to make the years after the war seem discontinuous from the years before, and that discontinuity became a part of English imaginations. Men and women after the war looked back at their own pasts as one might look across a great chasm to a remote, peaceable place on the other side.[63]

63. Samuel Hynes, *A War Imagined: The First World War and English Culture* (New York: Atheneum, 1991), xi. See also Modris Eksteins, *Rites of Spring: The Great War and the Birth of the Modern Age* (Boston: Houghton Mifflin, 1989).

10 CONCLUSION

In early 1915, while lecturing in America, Ward was told that his time as editor of the *Dublin Review* was at an end. The details are not entirely clear because the records of Burns & Oates were destroyed in 1941, during the London Blitz, and we have only Ward's correspondence to go on, but it seems that at least since mid-December 1914, Wilfrid Meynell, the head of Burns & Oates, was working to get rid of him.[1] Already in late December Norfolk was writing to Bourne about his fear over a change of editors and his desire that Ward remain.[2] Ward described the events in a letter to Lord Halifax:

1. In a letter to Ward dated April 19, 1915, A. Perceval Rich refers to a letter of Dec. 15, 1914, from Meynell to Ward, which Meynell seems to have written without consulting the other directors of Burns & Oates. He also states that having looked at all the correspondence and Ward's summary, it seemed to him that Meynell had determined from the first to get rid of him. "To entirely disregard the work you had done on behalf of the Review during your stay in America seems to me most discourteous but the absolute want of recognition of your work as Editor for nine years and the manner in which you raised the subscription list during your Editorship points to personal spite, I think, and the desire to pay off a grudge." WWP VII/248/1.

2. In a letter to Bourne, Dec. 20, 1914, Norfolk wrote: "I hear there is a proposal that Ward should retire from the editorship of the Dublin. I cannot but think that this would be extremely unfortunate and that it would raise very widely felt regrets. I am not quite clear who makes the appointment but I cannot help hoping you may see your way to bring about an interchange of views which may avert what I could only regard as a calamity. I hope your Eminence will not think I am interfering in what does not concern me but I am sure you will feel the matter is one of general Catholic interest." WWP VII/43e (3).

I will tell you a piece of news confidentially. By a most amazing series of manoevres Burns & Oates are getting rid of my editorship of the *Dublin.* They disguised it until the last minute, pretending that a notice I received was only a formality, preliminary to certain readjustments rendered necessary by the fall of American sales produced by the War. But at the eleventh hour this disguise is dropped. I believe the Meynell family want to have the practical direction of the Review (Meynell is manager of Burns & Oates). The duke who has done his very best to arrange matters thinks their behavior absolutely incredible and impossible. Some day you shall see the correspondence, which is really quite extraordinary. Of course, I regret the loss of work which I felt to be useful, though my work in America seems likely to become permanent and lessens my sense of the loss of occupation. As to the way they have behaved I comfort myself by thinking "that the disciple is not better than the Master." It is a curious thing that Newman's biographer should receive at the hands of a Catholic Organization just the kind of treatment which he received, and just the same signs of total want of appreciation or understanding of his work.[3]

Norfolk intervened with Bourne, who promised to try to arrange some sort of consultation when Ward got back from America.[4] Meynell, however, in a letter to Bourne dated April 7, 1915, explained why this was not possible.

A conference would seem to offer no hope, at a time when delay is dangerous to the *Dublin,* and with an Editor who, as such, is in our opinion constitutionally intractable. It is now many months since we were obliged to suggest the necessity of a recurrence to Quarterly types in the articles published in the *Review.* To go into details would be invidious; but anyone who has lately read the *Review* will easily name articles altogether out of place in a Quarterly, and a Catholic Quarterly, maintained, under the best of conditions, only with difficulty.

Your Eminence will appreciate that it has been very hard to all concerned in the *Dublin*'s reconstruction to put aside pressing personal considerations. But, having come to the conclusion that the level of articles must be raised if the *Review* is to recover its status and its subscribers, and that Mr. Ward's co-operation in this task is not to be counted upon, we do not think that a prolonging of the state of tension will serve any useful end.[5]

Norfolk was flabbergasted, and in a letter to Bourne (April 9, 1915) he showed his exasperation: "It is hardly conceivable that people can behave in this way.. To part with an editor when he is in America and to decline, at the

3. Ward to Halifax, April 13, 1915, WWP VI/13 (124). The Ward/Burns & Oates correspondence seems to be lost.

4. Norfolk to Bourne, April 3, 1915, WWP VII/43e (4).

5. WWP VII/43e (6).

request of your Eminence, to wait a few days to discuss the situation with him on his return seems such an extraordinary want of common decency that it is clear there must be something behind it."[6] He was certainly made even angrier because Mrs. Ward had told him that Wilfrid had been distinctly assured when he went to America that no decision would be made about this in his absence.[7] Mgr. Arthur Barnes (who would become Ward's co-editor with the January 1916 number) wrote to Bourne of his fears for the *Dublin* ("To me it seems that a change of Editors *at this moment* would be disastrous and quite possibly kill the Dublin outright") and to say that he was circulating a memorandum to convince Burns & Oates "that their view of W. Ward's editing is shared by practically no one else."[8] The memorandum stated that "we . . . have learnt with distress that a change of Editor is in contemplation" and praised the *Dublin* under Ward, "who had raised it to a position of dignity and influence among non-Catholics as well as Catholics," adding that "in no other hands could its value be so completely maintained."[9] It was signed by more than 150 people, including two archbishops, eleven bishops, leading figures of the Catholic intelligentsia and aristocracy, and many influential non-Catholics, among them the former prime minister, Arthur Balfour, the editor of the *Edinburgh Review,* and the prominent Anglican divines F. C. Burkitt and H. Scott Holland. In the letter to Bourne mentioned above, Barnes stated that he did not expect Bourne to sign the memorandum as he was the owner of the journal.[10] Barnes organized a campaign to restore Ward to the *Dublin,* of which the memorandum was only a part (Ward was left out of this to preserve his dignity), and in this he succeeded.[11] In Maisie Ward's biogra-

6. WWP VII/43e (7). See also Norfolk's letter to Ward, April 12, 1915, in which he attacked the "caddish" behavior of the directors of Burns & Oates and their attempts to hide their desire for control behind a loss of income. WWP VII/222 (129).

7. Norfolk to Bourne, April 3, 1915, WWP VII/43e (4).

8. Barnes to Bourne, April 19, 1915, WWP VII/43e (8).

9. The memorandum was dated May 19, 1915. See Mrs. Wilfrid Ward, ed., *Last Lectures by Wilfrid Ward* (London: Longmans, Green, 1918), 291–95, for the memorandum and its list of signatories.

10. He said that only one person invited to sign the memorandum had declined. One might guess this was Baron von Hügel, who had often suggested that Ward should resign and whose name was noticeable by its absence from the list; but von Hügel wrote to Ward on April 29, 1915, of his shock and unhappiness at the turn of events ("the news . . . was entirely unexpected, and truly unpleasant and repulsive to us"). He pointed to the war as the true cause of the decline in circulation, as it had been for *all* such publications. WWP II/6 (191).

11. Leo Ward (Wilfrid's son) wrote to his father (April 22, 1915), elaborating Barnes's plan in

phy of her father this affair barely registers: "A suggestion was made that the *Dublin* should have a new editor."[12]

In late 1915 Ward's health began to fail. This was partly brought on by the strain caused by the death of his eldest brother, Edmund, in September 1915, and the tangle he had made of his estate.[13] Edmund was eccentric, to say the least. He never married, spending most of his time abroad and playing master of ceremonies at liturgical celebrations (at which he was very good). Edmund had inherited the Ward family property on the Isle of Wight, which under normal circumstances should have continued in the family, but his benefactions would have exhausted the estate and Ward felt obliged to sue if he were to preserve any part of it. The wrangling over the estate and the conflicts with other members of the family over it were highly distasteful to him, and a great drain on his time and energy. Only after Wilfrid's death was a compromise reached and the lawsuit dropped. Within a month of his brother's death, however, the first symptoms of Wilfrid's last illness appeared. After attempts at convalescence had failed it became clear that he had incurable cancer, and he died on April 9, 1916. On his tombstone was carved, "The desire of wisdom bringeth to the Everlasting Kingdom."

Though Ward was barely sixty at his death, he seemed like someone much older. Chesterton once commented that for a man who was remarkably young for his years, and natural and attractive to the young, Ward somehow appeared, rather, to be a contemporary of the great men of his father's generation. Ward was, in many ways, a man born out of due time. In his political and social conservatism, he was born too late, and in his openness to theological and philosophical trends, too early. The Great War had accelerated the trends that would bring an end to the "long garden party" of the Edwardian Age and the relatively traditional world that Ward understood and loved, so it was somehow appropriate that he should not live to see its final disappearance. Chesterton said it best:

> Had he died only a few years ago, our sorrow over so just a critic and so generous a friend might almost have had a touch of sombre thankfulness, that he had not lived

---

detail and the part Wilfrid was to play in it. WWP VII/304/2 (9). See also Herbert Thurston, S.J., to Ward, April 24, 1915, WWP VII/291a (34).

12. *Wilfrid Wards: II,* 473.

13. For Edmund Ward and his will, see Maisie Ward, *Unfinished Business,* 44, 72–75. See also Dana Greene, *The Living of Maisie Ward* (Notre Dame: University of Notre Dame Press, 1997), 46–47, 213n11.

to see what England and the old English institutions which he valued already threatened to become. It is harder to spare him now that the death-pang comes in the midst of birth-pangs so gigantic; and we know, what he would never have doubted, that a Christian nation is not so despicably to die. He remains now like a bridge between a better England and an England that shall again be better; and under that bridge between the two there flowed a foulness that he will never understand.[14]

In retrospect, how can we evaluate Ward and his review? The first object of any journal is to be read, and in this he was very successful. While we do not know its circulation, we do know that the *Dublin* had reached a rather low ebb before he took it over, and that at one point he had even quadrupled its circulation. Not only did he improve its circulation, he also increased it among the right sort of people, the "upper ten thousand" who were the leaders of the nation. Another way of judging the journal is to look at what he wanted to achieve. His daughter Maisie said that her father saw "in the conduct of a great Catholic review, many of the possibilities he has seen in a great Catholic University."[15] The review was to be a school where the full range of Catholic learning and the best of the Catholic mind could be presented. In this, I believe, he was also successful. Most of the leading Catholic scholars and writers of the day, and many who were not Catholic, were among his contributors, and almost every area of human accomplishment in science and art found a place in the pages of the *Dublin.*. While learning and style were essential, Ward also wanted his journal to be orthodox and faithful to the Catholic spirit. In this, I think, he was again successful. Certainly Bishop Hedley thought so, as he wrote after the first number.

To me, it seems to be a great Catholic success. It would not be hard for you and your brilliant fellow workers to make up a striking and popular number of a Quarterly. The difficulty is to do this within the limits, not merely of Catholic orthodoxy, but of Catholic loyalty and sentiment. In the unrestricted play of opinion which marks periodical writing at the present day, we, of course, are heavily handicapped by the salutary claims of our faith and our spirit. Nothing rejoices me so much as to see our best men piously accepting these conditions, and yet arresting the attention of the world.[16]

Ward wanted his journal to be Catholic but not sectarian, to eschew bitter anti-Protestant diatribes and unnecessary controversy, and to foster mutual

14. G. K. Chesterton, "Wilfrid Ward (II)," *Dublin Review* (July 1916): 32.
15. *Wilfrid Wards* 2:206.
16. Quoted ibid., 204.

understanding between Catholics and non-Catholics and cooperation in subjects of common interest. At the same time, he did not wish to encourage intellectual flabbiness or paper over real differences. His desire was to educate Catholics to their responsibilities and potential, to broaden their horizons, and to show the non-Catholic world what it was missing. To a great extent he was successful in this. Non-Catholics certainly read the review, though Ward had no illusions about how much he could achieve. Nor was the Catholic side entirely amenable either, as Ward's troubles with his detractors show. His institutional loyalty and deferential conservatism meant that criticism could go only so far, and led him sometimes to downplay or ignore the failures of the Church or of her members. And while his essentially positive and constructive attitude was a strength, its downside was a tendency to be less than entirely forthright on certain issues where scandal might be involved.

Mrs. Wilfrid Ward ended *Out of Due Time* with a long statement by Paul d'Etranges, the charismatic leader of the reform movement, whose journal George Sutcliffe had edited. When the Holy See had condemned the movement, George had submitted but d'Etranges had not. Now, years later, having submitted himself, d'Etranges recounted his aspirations and confessed his errors. Toward its end he quoted from Newman's *Apologia Pro Vita Sua,* describing how there is a time for everything and that one must not try to outstrip its time, spoiling a cause by ignoring the voice of authority and so ruining the opportunity of those coming after, who may bring the issue to a happy conclusion. Ward's greatest accomplishment was that he realized this. His life's work had been to reconcile the Church and the age. By his loyalty and obedience when authority had shown itself unresponsive to his goal, he was able to maintain a sufficient opening for others to continue his work.

If there was to be an English Catholic intellectual revival following the Great War, it was in no small measure due to the efforts of Wilfrid Ward. After Ward's death Father Cuthbert said much the same thing: "Much has yet to be done before Catholicism will again be in the position it held in the golden period of the Middle Ages as the synthesis of the unchanging Christian Faith and the achievements of the human spirit in philosophy and art, in social life and political ideals. But when that day comes Wilfrid Ward will be given no mean place amongst the prophets of the dawn."[17]

17. Fr. Cuthbert [Hess], "Wilfrid Ward (I.)," 22.

APPENDIX
CONTENTS OF THE *DUBLIN REVIEW*, JANUARY 1906–APRIL 1916

JANUARY 1906

St. Thomas Aquinas and Medieval Thought. [Ward], 1–27.
An Irish Election. Viscount Llandaff, 28–40.
Manning and Gladstone: The "Destroyed" Letters. [Ward], 41–58.
Leonidas of Tarentum: Ivy Berries from the Anthology. Professor J. S. Phillimore, 59–78.
Impressions of Catholic America. Abbot Gasquet, 79–98.
The Functions of Prejudice. [Ward], 99–118.
To the Body. A Poem. Mrs. Meynell, 119.
The Praetorium of Pilate and the Pillar of Scourging. Fr. Herbert Thurston, S.J., 120–42.
The Letters of Catherine of Siena. 143–57.
Anglicanism: Old and New. W. S. Lilly, 158–75.
The Church in France: Its Present Position. Abbé Ernest Dimnet, 176–85.
Some Recent Books. 186–213.
Foreign Catholic Books. 213–19.
The Catholic Record Society. 220–21.
Books Received. 222–32.

APRIL 1906

Cardinal Newman and Creative Theology. [Ward], 233–70.
An Historical Meditation. Rev. R. H. Benson, 271–80.
The Holy Latin Tongue. Rev. W. Barry, D.D., 281–304.
Jaurès and Clémenceau: A Contrast of Temperaments. 305–17.
Weismann and the Germ-Plasm Theory. Professor Windle, F.R.S., 318–42.
Irish University Education. Bishop of Limerick, 343–56.
Experience and Transcendence. Baron Friedrich von Hügel, 357–79.
To the English Martyrs: A Poem. Francis Thompson, 380–85.
Christian Doctrine in an Early Eastern Church. 386–405.
Some Recent Books. 406–40.
Books Received. 440–48.

JULY 1906

Our Latin Bible. Rev. W. Barry, D.D., 1–23.
Some Characteristics of Henry Sidgwick. Wilfrid Ward, 24–37.
Matilda of Tuscany. Viscount Llandaff, 38–71.
In a Library. A Poem. G. W. [George Wyndham], 72–73.
Crinagoras of Mitylene. Professor J. S. Phillimore, 74–86.
Catholic Social Effort in France. [Charles Plater], 87–104.

The Syrian Christians in India. 105–22.
The Plaint of the Kine. Bishop of Salford [L. C. Casartelli], 123–28.
The Condemnation of Pope Honorius. Dom John Chapman, O.S.B., 129–54.
Denominationalism and the Education Bill. [Ward], 155–80.
Some Recent Books. 181–228.
Catholic Reviews, Home and Foreign. 228–32.

OCTOBER 1906

For Truth or for Life. [Ward], 233–51.
The Report of the Ritual Commission. R. H. Benson, 252–66.
Aeneas Sylvius and Nicholas de Cusa: Symbols of the Renaissance. 267–76.
The Fiscal Question. Hilaire Belloc, MP, 277–99.
Fénelon in Exile, 1699–1715. Hon. Mrs. Maxwell Scott, 300–320.
Is Socialism Right After All? C. S. Devas, M.A., 321–38.
Guidford Slingsby and John Morris: Two Servants of Lord Strafford. 339–58.
The Dance of Death. Adapted from Victor Hugo's "Fantômes." Wilfrid Scawen Blunt, 359–61.
The Catholic Missions in the Congo Free State. John de Courcy Macdonnell, 362–82.
Winchester, Mother of Schools. Mgr. Stapelton Barnes, M.A., 383–99.
The Church of France and the French People. [Ward], 400–411.
Some Recent Books. 412–38.
Books Received. 438–48.

JANUARY 1907

Lord Acton and the "Rambler." [Ward], 1–19.
The Story of an Agrarian Revolution. T. W. Russell, MP, 20–25.
Lyra Devota: Poems. Katherine Tynan and others, 26–32.
Church and State in Spain. 33–41.
The Condemnation of Pope Honorius. Dom John Chapman, O.S.B., 42–72.
The Liturgy of Toledo. Rev. William Barry, D.D., 73–97.
The Gaelic Revival. Rev. W. H. Kent, O.S.C., 98–112.
Robert, Earl of Lytton, Statesman and Poet. 113–27.
The Education Bill of 1906. Right Rev. Mgr. Brown, 128–38.
Lord Rosebery's "Randolph Churchill." Lord Hugh Cecil, 139–49.
René Bazin's Apology for French Catholics. Reginald Balfour, 150–65.
The Fame and Failure of Ronsard. F. Y. Eccles, 166–77.
Some Recent Books. 178–218.
Catholic Reviews, Home and Foreign. 218–22.
Publications of the Catholic Truth Society. 223–24.

APRIL 1907

Irish University Education. Bishop of Limerick, 225–45.
The Future of the Free Churches. Rev. Vincent McNabb, O.P., 246–57.
Asclepiades. Professor J. S. Phillimore, 258–70.
For Truth or for Life. [Ward], 271–79.
Buckfast Abbey. Dom Adam Hamilton, O.S.B., 280–88.
Courtesy: A Poem. Hilaire Belloc, MP, 89.
The Précieuses. Viscount St. Cyres, 290–303.

De Vries and the Theory of Mutations. Professor Windle, F.S.A., 304–13.
The Story of a Paris Convent. 314–33.
The Task before the Anti-Vivisectionists. Bertram Collingwood, M.D., 334–50.
Anti-Clericalism in France. 351–70.
The Victory of the German Centre Party. 371–83.
Some Recent Books. 384–432.

JULY 1907

Two Views of Cardinal Newman. Wilfrid Ward, 1–15.
Madame Swetchine. 16–34.
Roma Sacra. Rev. William Barry, D.D., 35–55.
Ferdinand Brunetière as Critic and Man of Letters. P. J. Connolly, S.J., 56–73.
Two Posthumous Poems. Nora Chesson, 1. St. Patrick of the Blessings. 2. Saint Juliet. 74–77.
A Modern Theory of Human Personality. R. H. Benson, 78–96.
St Ninian, a Missionary of the Fifth Century. Margaret Kinloch, 97–114.
The Feast of the Dead. Fr. Herbert Thurston, S.J., 115–30.
Count Lally, of Fontenoy and the Bastille. D. C. B., 131–54.
La Question Religieuse en France. Comte Albert de Mun, 155–85.
Some Recent Books. 186–220.

OCTOBER 1907

The Papal Deposing Power. Rev. Willam Barry, D.D., 221–43.
Caius Maecenas. Francis Holland, 244–54.
The Trilogy of Joris Karl Huysmans. P. J. Connolly, S.J., 255–71.
The Reaction in Spain. 272–84.
The Realism of Dickens. Mrs. Wilfrid Ward, 285–95.
The Excavations at Gezer and the Light They Throw upon the Bible. Hugh Pope, O.P., 296–324.
Martha and Mary. A Poem. 325–26.
A Catholic Poet. Katherine Tynan, 327–44.
Mendel and his Theory of Heredity. Bertram Windle, F.R.S., 345–56.
Dante and the Union of Italy. Rev. P. Haythornthwaite, 357–77.
Reginald Balfour: Some Reminiscences. Rev. R. H. Benson, B. S. Devas, Prof. J. S. Phillimore, and Fr. Cuthbert, O.S.F.C., 378–88.
Some Recent Books. 389–428.

JANUARY 1908

The Encyclical "Pascendi." [Ward], 1–10.
Letters of Queen Victoria, 1837–1861. Rev. R. H. Benson, 11–28.
A French Chesterfield. Viscount St. Cyres, 29–43.
The Religion of Charles II in Relation to the Politics of His Reign. Mgr. Stapelton Barnes, M.A., 44–63.
Father Ignatius Ryder: A Reminiscence. Wilfrid Ward, 64–79.
The Garden of Eden. A Poem. Miss Ethel R. Wheeler, 80–83.
The Roman Church Down to the Neronian Persecution. Rev. F. J. Bacchus, 84–108.
Catholic Records in the Diocese of Chester. Rev. J. Chambers, 109–26.
A Student and Social Worker of the Eighteenth Century. 127–47.

Olden Faiths and New Philosophies. Rev. W. H. Kent, O.S.C., 148–59.
Some Memories of Francis Thompson. Mrs. Meynell, 160–72.
Some Recent Books. 173–215.
Publications of the C.T.S. 215–16.

APRIL 1908

Rome and Democracy. Canon William Barry, D.D., 217–40.
Catholic Social Work in Germany—I. Ketteler, the Precursor. [Charles Plater], 241–61.
The Worldly Wisdom of Thomas A Kempis. Percy Fitzgerald, 262–77.
Personal Memories of James C. Mangan. Late Sir Charles Gavan Duffy, 278–94.
The Garden. A Poem. Katherine Tynan, 295–96.
The Orthodox Eastern Church. W. S. Lilly, 297–314.
The Cause of the Eleven Elizabethan Bishops. Rev. G. E. Phillips, 315–23.
Stonehenge and the Stars. President Windle, F.R.S., 324–37.
Saint Dominic and Saint Francis: A Parallel. 338–50.
The Inflation of Assessment. Hilaire Belloc, MP, 351–62.
Mr Balfour on Decadence. Wifrid Ward, 363–75.
Some Recent Books. 376–422.

JULY 1908

Catholic Social Work in Germany—II. The "Autumn Manoeuvres." [Charles Plater], 1–24.
Shelley. Late Francis Thompson, 25–49.
The Coming Eucharistic Congress. W. S. Lilly, 50–57.
Good Friday's Hoopoe. A Poem. Douglas Ainslie, 58–60.
Christian Science. Rev. R. H. Benson., 61–71.
Arundel Castle and the House of Howard. 72–95.
Anatole France on Joan of Arc. Rev. F. M. Wyndham, 96–109.
Recent Work on the New Testament. Dom John Chapman, O.S.B., 110–26.
The Tombs of Batalha. 127–46.
The Irish Universities Bill, 1908. Bertram C. A. Windle, F.R.S., 147–59.
Three Notable Editors: Delane, Hutton, Knowles. Wilfrid Ward, 160–81.
Some Recent Books. 182–216.

OCTOBER 1908

The Ushaw Centenary and English Catholicism. Wilfrid Ward, 217–43.
Maurice Barrès. F. Y. Eccles, 244–63.
Revising the Vulgate. Abbot Gasquet, O.S.B., 264–73.
Francis Thompson: In Memoriam. Mrs. Wilfrid Ward, 274–77.
The Epistles of Erasmus. 278–99.
Plots and Persons in Fiction. Mrs. Wilfrid Ward, 300–309.
The Future Universities of Ireland. Bertram C. A. Windle, President of Queen's College, Cork, 310–20.
A Great Burgomaster and His Work. 321–45.
The Neronian Persecution. Rev. F. J. Bacchus, 346–59.
Adam Mickiewicz: Poland's National Poet. Miss Mary Monica Gardner, 360–75.
John Keble. An Unpublished Fragment. Cardinal Newman, 376–83.
The Pan-Anglican Congress. Rev. R. H. Benson, 384–97.
Some Recent Books. 398–432.

JANUARY 1909

Mr Chesterton among the Prophets. Wilfrid Ward, 1–32.
The Measure of National Wealth. Hilaire Belloc, MP, 33–52.
English Catholics in the XVIIIth Century. Mgr. Bernard Ward, 53–66.
Catholic Social Work in Germany—III. Organization and Method. [Charles Plater], 67–86.
Sonnet. R. B., 87.
Eugène Fromentin. Professor J. S. Phillimore, 88–110.
The Censorship of Fiction. Canon William Barry, 111–31.
Duchesne's Ancient History of the Church. Dom John Chapman, O.S.B., 132–43.
Modern Turkey. Mark Sykes, 144–72.
Mr Runciman's Bill. 173–81.
Some Recent Books. 182–215.
Publications of the Catholic Truth Society. 215–16.

APRIL 1909

Lollardy and the Reformation. W. S. Lilly, 217–44.
Moral Fiction a Hundred Years Ago. Wilfrid Ward, 245–66.
Some Factors in Moral Education. Rev. Michael Maher, S.J., 267–87.
Catherine of Braganza and Old Hammersmith. 288–97.
The Sisters of Perpetual Adoration. A Poem. E. M. Dennis, 298.
Catholic Social Work in Germany—IV. German Methods and Needs. [Charles Plater], 299–328.
Niccolò Machiavelli. Herbert M. Vaughan, 329–38.
Catholic Boys' Clubs in London. B. W. Devas, 339–56.
The Mantle of Voltaire. F. Y. Eccles, 357–67.
The Needs of Humanity. Cardinal Gibbons, 368–77.
The Export of Capital. Hilaire Belloc, MP, 378–93.
Some Recent Books. 394–440.

JULY 1909

The Literary Aspects of the Old Testament. Canon William Barry, 1–24.
Politics and Party. I. The Diseases of the House of Commons. Lord Hugh Cecil, 25–35.
II. Edmund Burke on Party Action. Wilfrid Ward, 36–58.
The Failure of the Workhouse. Mrs. Virginia M. Crawford, 59–77.
Light at the Evening Time. A Poem. W. G. Hole, 78.
A Century of Socialistic Experiments. W. H. Mallock, 79–106.
St Anselm of Canterbury. Mgr. Moyes, 107–27.
The Modern Surrender of Women. G. K. Chesterton, 128–37.
Lord Curzon and Oxford Reform. F. F. Urquhart, Fellow of Balliol College, Oxford, 138–46.
English Catholics in the Eighteenth Century. 147–71.
Swinburne's Lyrical Poetry. Alice Meynell, 172–83.
Some Recent Books. 184–224.

OCTOBER 1909

The Catholic Disabilities Bill. Rev. Herbert Thurston, S.J., 225–38.
Maria Edgeworth & Etienne Dumont. Rowland Grey, 239–65.
The Taxation of Rent. Hilaire Belloc, 266–81.
London. James Barr, 282.

The April Mutiny in Stamboul. Francis McCullagh, 283–305.
The Tennyson Centenary. Wilfrid Ward, 306–22.
St Anselm of Canterbury (concluded). Canon J. Moyes, 323–52.
Epigenesis and Preformation in Organic Development. Rev. G. A. Elrington, O.P., 353–70.
A Medieval Princess: Madame Loyse de Savoye, 1462–1503. M. M. Maxwell Scott, 371–92.
The Ancients in Racine and in Shakespeare. F. Y. Eccles, 393–405.
Spiritualism. Rev. R. H. Benson, 406–21.
Some Recent Books. 422–64.

JANUARY 1910

Challoner. Canon William Barry, 1–27.
The Ethics of Strong Language. Wilfrid Ward, 28–39.
Unemployment and Its Remedies. Mrs. Virginia Crawford, 40–61.
Tennyson. Alice Meynell, 62–71.
Ecclesiastical Ballads. Francis Thompson, 72–74.
The Oriel Noetics. Wilfrid Wilberforce, 75–90.
New Learning. Rev. C. C. Martindale, S.J., 91–110.
The Martyrs of Cambrai. Comtesse Barbara de Courson, 111–38.
The Liber Sententiarum. Rev. J. de Ghellinck, S.J., of Louvain University, 139–66.
"The International." I. The Ferrer Case. Hilaire Belloc, 167–81.
The French Bishops and the Education Problem. Marquis de Chambrun, 182–92.
Some Recent Books. 193–230.
Publication of the Catholic Truth Society. 231–32.

APRIL 1910

Reform of the House of Lords. I. Viscount Halifax, 233–36.
II. James Fitzalan Hope, MP, 237–40.
III. A Liberal. 240–49.
The Centenary of Alfred de Musset. Rowland Grey, 250–71.
Modernism in Islam. Francis McCullagh (Petersburg correspondence of the *New York Times*), 272–97.
Orison-Tryst. A Poem. Late Francis Thompson, 298–99.
The Gate of Sin. A Poem. Mrs. Bellamy Storer, 300–301.
The Truth about Cromwell's Massacre at Drogheda. J. B. Williams, 302–13.
Roger II and Frederick II—A Study of Kinship. Dora Greenwell McChesney, 314–44.
Anglicanism Sixty Years Ago. James Britten, 345–70.
The People and the Populace. Wilfrid Ward, 371–82.
A Catholic Colony. Rev. R. H. Benson, 383–95.
"The International." II. The Motive Force. Hilaire Belloc., MP, 396–411.
Some Recent Books. 412–37.
Chronicle of Recent New Testament Works. Dom John Chapman, O.S.B., 438–48.

JULY 1910

Edward VII. 1–5.
Cardinal Vaughan. Wilfrid Ward, 6–24.
Pascal and Port Royal. Mrs. Reginald Balfour, 25–50.
Poetry: I. Ad Castitatem. Late Francis Thompson, 51–53.
II. Westminster Cathedral. MCMX, 54–55.

Francis Thompson's Ignatius Loyola. Canon William Barry, 56–84.
John Stuart Mill and the Mandate of the People. Wilfrid Ward, 85–96.
The Origin of the Douay Bible. Rev. Hugh Pope, O.P., 97–118.
Unemployment and Education: A Lesson from Switzerland. Mrs. Crawford, 119–36.
Beaconsfield. J. H. Moffatt, 137–50.
After the Symbolists. F. Y. Eccles, 151–61.
The Elections in France. Eugène Tavernier (Editor of the *Univers*), 162–76.
Some Recent Books. 177–216.

OCTOBER 1910

Cardinal Vaughan (concluded). Wilfrid Ward, 217–38.
The Causes of the Failure of the Russian Revolution. Hon. Maurice Baring, 239–60.
What Is Toleration? G. K. Chesterton, 261–69.
A Note on Comparative Religion. Rev. C. C. Martindale, S.J., 270–84.
Carmen Genesis. A Poem. Late Francis Thompson, 285–87.
St Paulinus of Nola. Prof. J. S. Phillimore, 288–305.
Punch and Pontiffs. Sir F. C. Burnand, 306–21.
The Lay Paradise. 322–45.
A University for Hong Kong. Sir F. Lugard, 346–55.
The Answer to Socialism. 356–75.
Spain and the Church. Mgr. Manuel J. Bidwell, 376–96.
Some Recent Books. 397–432.

JANUARY 1911

Disraeli. Canon William Barry, 1–23.
The Estimate of Elgar. Cecil Barber, 24–35.
The Decay of Fixed Ideals. Meyrick Booth, 36–51.
Christopher Columbus. Rev. Herbert Thurston, S.J., 52–68.
The Economics of "Cheap." Hilaire Belloc, 69–84.
The Portuguese Revolution. Francis McCullagh, 85–105.
University Teaching for the Chinese. Rev. Lord William Gascoyne-Cecil, 106–10.
Poetry. I. The House of Sorrows. Francis Thompson, 111–13.
II. The Kingdom of the Blind. Mrs. Bellamy Storer, 113–14.
Queen Elizabeth and the Foreign Ambassadors. 115–33.
Some Malayan Superstitions. Sir Hugh Clifford, K.C.M.G., 134–54.
Romance. F. Y. Eccles, 155–66.
The Democracy and the Political Crisis. Wilfrid Ward, 167–85.
Some Recent Books. 186–210.
Catholic Truth Publications, 1910. 210–12.

APRIL 1911

Lord Acton and the French Revolution. W. S. Lilly, 213–29.
Charlotte and Emily Brontë. Mrs. Meynell, 230–43.
The Bicentenary of the Piano. [Cecil Barber] Clement Antrobus Harris, 244–52.
Church and State in France. Marquis de Chambrun, 253–68.
Poetry: I. To a Mystic. Isabel Clarke, 269.
II. Speculum Amoris. Late Father Tabb, 270.
Fairies—from Shakespeare to Mr Yeats. H. Grierson, 271–84.

Dr Ryder's Essays. Dom Chapmam, O.S.B., 285–96.
From Talk to Trouble in India. 297–323.
The Decree "Ne Temere." Mgr. Bidwell, 324–35.
Mr Churchill's Prison Policy. 336–55.
The Political Situation. D. C. Lathbury, 356–80.
Some Recent Books. 381–410.
Chronicle of Recent New Testament Works. C. [Chapman], 411–24.

JULY 1911

The Coronation. Rev. Herbert Thurston, S.J., 1–22.
The Saracens in Christian Poetry. William Wistar Comfort, Professor of Oriental and Romance Literature at Cornell University, 23–48.
The Catholic Church and Race Culture. Rev. T. J. Gerrard, 49–68.
Poetry: Fac Me Cruce Inebriari. T. Gavan Duffy, 69–70.
Points of View. R. H. Benson, 71–92.
Totemism and Exogamy. Prof. Windle, F.R.S., 93–106.
Catholicism and the Spirit of the East. Canon William Barry, 107–25.
The Portuguese Separation Law. Francis McCullagh, 126–42.
On a Method of Writing History. Hilaire Belloc, 143–55.
Bishop Hay. Bishop Hedley, 156–79.
Some Recent Books. 180–216.

OCTOBER 1911

The Passing of the Parliament Bill. I. A Unionist View. [Ward], 217–34.
II. A Liberal View. 235–46.
Francis Thompson. Albert A. Cock, 247–77.
Some Modern Martyrs. W. S. Lilly, 278–89.
The Fiscal Powers of an Irish Parliament. Francis McDermot, 290–302.
Poem: A General Communion. Alice Meynell, 303.
St Vincent de Paul and the Highlands of Scotland. Dom Odo Blundell, O.S.B., 304–20.
Catholicism and History. Hilaire Belloc, 321–28.
Fiona Macleod and Celtic Legends. Mrs. Reginald (Charlotte) Balfour, 329–40.
A Great French Bishop. Lady Sophia M. Palmer (Comtesse de Franqueville), 341–62.
Foreign Politics of the Day. Lancelot Lawton, 363–82.
Some Recent Books. 383–424.

JANUARY 1912

Mr Balfour's Farewell. Wilfrid Ward, 1–11.
The Thackeray Centenary.
I. An Impression of Thackeray in His Last Years. Mrs. Warre Cornish, 12–28. II. The Religion of Thackeray. Rev. P. J. Gannon, S.J., 29–42.
Phantasms of the Dead. Mgr. R. H. Benson, 43–63.
Poetry: Pandolfo Collenuccio. Prof. J. S. Phillimore, 64–67.
Tennyson at Freshwater. Wilfrid Ward, 68–85.
The Fortunes of Civilization. Canon William Barry, 86–106.
Early Irish Religious Poetry. Arthur Perceval Graves, 107–27.
Anti-clerical Policy in Portugal. Professor Camillo Torrend, S.J. (editor of the *Broteria*), 128–51.

Under the War Cloud. Edwin de Lisle, 152–61.
An Agnostic Defeat. G. K. Chesterton, 162–72.
Some Recent Books. 173–214.
Catholic Truth Society Publications, 1911. 214–16.

APRIL 1912

Cardinal Newman's Sensitiveness. Wilfrid Ward, 217–29.
Milner and His Age. Canon William Barry, 230–55.
English Cardinals since the Reformation. Rev. Edwin Burton, D.D., 256–70.
Lafcadio Hearn. Helen Grierson, 271–85.
Poem: Holy Ground. Late Francis Thompson, 286.
The Changes in India and After. 287–306.
Darwin and the Theory of Natural Selection. Sir Bertram C. A. Windle, F.R.S., 307–24.
The Destiny of China. C. J. L. Gilson, 325–37.
Christian Edifices before Constantine. Mgr. A. S. Barnes, 338–52.
Home Rule for Ireland. James Fitzalan Hope, MP, 353–69.
Notes for a Reader of Dickens. Alice Meynell, 370–84.
Some Recent Books. 385–424.

JULY 1912

The Centenary of William George Ward. Canon William Barry, 1–24.
The Entail: An Appreciation. John Ayscough, 25–52.
The Story of Abbé de Salamon during the Reign of Terror. Comtesse de Courson, 53–79.
Poem: The "Titanic's" Dead. Mrs. Bellamy Storer, 80.
The Futurists. Rev. T. J. Gerrard, 81–93.
Leo XIII and Anglican Orders. Wilfrid Ward, 94–117.
The Preternatural in Early Irish Poetry. Alfred Perceval Graves, 118–40.
Some Recent Strikes. Stephen Harding, 141–54.
Music and Literature: The Work of Robert Schumann. Clement Antrobus Harris, 155–59.
The Belgian Election of 1912. M. Leon de Lantsheere, formerly Belgian Minister of Justice, and Professor of Law in the University of Louvain, 160–77.
Some Recent Books. 178–205.
Chronicle of Recent New Testament Works. Dom John Chapman, O.S.B., 206–16.

OCTOBER 1912

Reduced Christianity: Its Advocates and Its Critics. Wilfrid Ward, 217–40.
Is Darwinism Played Out? R. E. Froude, C.B., F.R.S., 241–55.
The Centenary of St. Clare. Rev. Paschal Robinson, O.S.F.C., 256–68.
English Catholic Literature. Wilfrid Ward, 269–76.
Recent Light on Jerusalem Topography. Rev. Hugh Pope, O.P., 277–98.
Poems: Las Decenne Sete. Isabel Clarke, 299.
Newborn. Dorothea Still, 299.
La Famille, l'Etat, l'Eglise, l'Ecole et l'Enfant. George Fonsegrive, 300–329.
Personal Recollections of a "Dublin" Reviewer, Dora Greenwell McChesney. Michael Barrington, 330–38.
Dean Gregory. James Britten, 339–48.
What Is a Conservative? G. K. Chesterton, 349–56.
The Entry into the Dark Ages. Hilaire Belloc, 357–69.

Labour: War or Peace? T. M. Kettle, 370–93.
Some Recent Books. 394–432.

JANUARY 1913

Disraeli. Wilfrid Ward, 1–20.
The Mental Deficiency Bill. Rev. T. J. Gerrard, 21–40.
The Religion of Mazzini. Mrs. Hamilton King, 41–67.
The Revolution in Cuba. W. M. Kennedy, 68–76.
Poem: Judgement. C. Sproxton, 77.
The Louvain Conference and Comparative Religion. Rev. C. Meli, S.J., 78–92.
The Teresa of Canada. Hon. Mrs. Maxwell Scott, 93–110.
Digby Dolben. Mrs. Warre Cornish, 111–31.
The Irish National Theatre. Charles Bewley, 132–44.
Foreign Politics of the Day. Lancelot Lawton, 145–74.
Some Recent Books. 175–214.
Catholic Truth Society Publications, 1912. 214–16.

APRIL 1913

Disraeli (concluded). Wilfrid Ward, 217–31.
The Catholic Party in the Netherlands. Lady Dorothy Acton, 232–53.
On Epitaphs, Catholic and "Catholic-Minded." Miss L. I. (Louise Imogen) Guiney, 254–68.
St John Damascene's Canon for the Repose of the Mother of God. Trans. G. R. Woodward, M.A., 269–75.
The Rheims Version of the New Testament. Rev. Hugh Pope, O.P., 276–300.
Music in Moslem Spain. J. F. Scheltema, 301–10.
Early Man. Sir Bertram Windle, F.R.S., 311–25.
The Position in Japan. E. S. (Stephen) Harding, 326–42.
A Successful Catholic Experiment in India. Saint Nihal Singh, 343–56.
Three Catholic Associations in France. Comtesse de Courson, 357–81.
Emancipation. Canon William Barry, 382–98.
Some Recent Books. 399–432.

JULY 1913

Blessed Thomas More and the Arrest of Humanism in England. J. S. Phillimore, 1–26.
Science and Philosophy at Louvain. Rev. J. G. Vance, D.D., 27–52.
Some Oxford Essays. Wilfrid Ward, 53–64.
Irish Gaelic Nature Poetry. Alfred Perceval Graves, 65–85.
The Napoleon of San Domingo. Harry Graham, 86–110.
Sonnet. Rev. Joseph M. Plunkett, 111.
The Chinese Republic and Yüan Shih-k'ai. Stephen Harding, 112–26.
The Belgian Strike. Francis McCullagh, 127–47.
"Et in Vitam Aeternam." Rev. C. C. Martindale, S.J., 148–59.
George Wyndham. Wilfrid Ward, 160–65.
Some Recent Books. 166–208.

OCTOBER 1913

Franciscan Influences in Art. Mrs. Crawford, 209–21.
The Court at Berlin in 1888. From the Diary of Princess Ouroussoff, 222–41.

The Lighting of Churches. Edwin de Lisle, 242–54.
If Home Rule Is Defeated. Charles Bewley, 255–65.
Papal Dispensation for Polygamy. Norman Hardy, 266–74.
Poem. 275.
Sir Nicholas O'Conor. Sir Mark Sykes, Bt. MP, 276–81.
Richard Wagner: A Centenarial Sketch. Donald Davidson, 282–99.
The Present Religious Situation in France. George Fonsegrive, 300–331.
An Indian Mystic: Rabindranath Tagore. Rev. C. C. Martindale, S.J., 332–52.
Charles Péguy. Lady Ashburne, 353–64.
Foreign Politics of the Day. Lancelot Lawton, 365–85.
Some Recent Books. 386–406.
Chronicle of Biblical Works. J. P. Arendzen, 406–16.

JANUARY 1914

Richard Holt Hutton. Wilfrid Ward, 1–21.
Psychology in the Concrete. Rev. C. C. Martindale, S.J., 22–32.
Frédéric Ozanam. Hon Mrs. Maxwell Scott, 33–50.
The Hero of English Fiction. E. G. Moore, 51–69.
Poem: The Divine Privilege. Alice Meynell, 70.
Notes on Recent Books by their Writers. Mary Cholmondeley, Mrs. Wilfrid Ward, John Ayscough, A. C. Benson, Robert Hugh Benson, G. K. Chesterton, 71–84.
A Neglected Aspect of Anglican Christianity. James Britten, 85–108.
Catholic Progress in the Study of Scripture. 109–23.
The Conservative Party and Agriculture. Bevil Tollemache, 124–48.
Professor Bury's History of Freedom of Thought. Hilaire Belloc, 149–71.
Some Recent Books. 172–98.
A Chronicle of Recent Philosophical Works. John Vance, 198–208.

APRIL 1914

A Visit to America. Wilfrid Ward, 209–36.
Martin Luther, Augustinian Friar. Mgr. Barnes, 237–46.
Cromwell's Nickname: "The Brewer." Miss L. I. Guiney, 247–71.
Three Ambassadors of the Victorian Age. Sir Hubert E. H. Jerningham, G.C.M.G., 272–95.
Poetry: A Sea Picture. M. Samuel Daniel, 296.
Rhythm and Colour in English Prose. Dom John Chapman, O.S.B., 297–313.
The Portuguese Republic and the Press. Francis McCullagh, 314–29.
The Lightening of Westminster Cathedral. John A. Marshall, architect to the Cathedral, 330–34.
Kikuyu. James Britten, 335–54.
Labour and Civilization. Professor T. M. Kettle, 355–71.
Some Recent Books. 372–405.
C.T.S Publications, 1913. 405–7.
Chronicle of Recent Biblical Works. J. P. Arendzen, 408–16.

JULY 1914

A Visit to America (continued). Wilfrid Ward, 1–18.
Mr Balfour on Beauty. Albert A. Cock, 19–27.
The Fruits of the "Golden Bough." Rev. C. C. Martindale, S.J., 28–41.

George Borrow in Spain. Shane Leslie, 42–59.
Poem: St. Brigid's Lullabies. Ethel Rolt-Wheeler, 60–61.
Rudolf Eucken's Philosophy. Dom Daniel Feuling, O.S.B., 62–83.
Professor Bédier and the French Epic. Prof. W. W. Comfort, 84–100.
The Confessions of a Catholic Socialist. H. [Henry Somerville], 101–15.
A Poet of the Streets. W. M. Letts, 116–24.
Cardinal Gasquet. Mgr. R. H. Benson, 125–30.
Foreign Politics of the Day. Lancelot Lawton, 131–52.
Jane Austen. Walter Moberly, 153–69.
The Budget. J. G. Snead-Cox, 170–81.
Some Recent Books. 182–207.
A Chronicle of Some Recent Philosophical Works. Rev. J. G. Vance, D.D., 208–16.

OCTOBER 1914

Pope Pius X. Wilfrid Ward, 217–25.
The Causes of the War. Lancelot Lawton, 226–56.
Roger Bacon, 1214:1914. Rev. J. G. Vance, 257–80.
The Centenary of Waverley. Wilfrid Ward, 281–304.
Poem: A Prayer before War. W. G. Hole, 305–6.
The Eighth Lord Petre. James Britten, 307–21.
Samuel Butler of "Erewhon." Canon Barry, 322–44.
A Catholic Critique of Current Social Theories. W. H. Mallock, 345–60.
The Modern French Temper. Hilaire Belloc, 361–72.
Benedict XV: An Impression. J. S. Barnes, 373–77.
Notes on the War. (September 14.) 378–99.
Some Recent Books. 400–423.
Chronicle of Recent Biblical Works. Rev. Dr. J. P. Arendzen, 424–32.

JANUARY 1915

Germany's Great Failure. Lancelot Lawton, 1–29.
The Conduct of German Soldiery. Wilfrid Ward, 30–54, with documents on 55–56.
The Letters of Jeanne d'Arc: An Epitome. I. M. (Irene Mary) Rope, 57–72.
Poem: Revenge for Rheims. Stephen Phillips, 73.
The Interpretation of Treitschke. Wilfrid Ward, 74–88.
The Lesson of Louvain. Canon Barry, D.D., 89–110.
The Economics of War. Hilaire Belloc, 111–21.
The Death of Monsignor Benson. Mrs. Warre Cornish, 122–39.
Notes on the War. L. L. [Lancelot Lawton], 140–63.
The French Awakening. F. Y. Eccles, 164–75.
Some Recent Books. 176–207.
A Chronicle of Some Recent Philosophical Works. Rev. J. G. Vance, 208–16.

APRIL 1915

Cardinal Mercier and the Martyrdom of Belgium. Wilfrid Ward, 217–26.
A View of Russia. Lancelot Lawton, 227–56.
Verhaeren: Flemish Poet and Patriot. Mrs. V. M. Crawford, 257–70.
Toynbee Hall and the Settlement Movement. James Britten, 271–87.
The Journalism of Great Englishmen. Wilfrid Ward, 288–310.

Poem: Easter Eve. M. S. Daniel, 311.
A Plea for International Law. F. F. Urquhart, 312–25.
The Submarine Myth. A. H. Pollen, 326–40.
The Plague of False Prophets. Rev. Herbert Thurston, S.J., 341–58.
The Arrest of Cardinal Mercier and His Publisher. 359–73.
Notes on the War. L. L. [Lancelot Lawton], 374–91.
Some Recent Books. 374–413.
C.T.S. Publications, 1914. 413–16.
Biblical Chronicle. Rev. J. P. Arendzen, 416–24.

JULY 1915

Father Maturin. Wilfrid Ward, 1–15.
The City of Constantine. Canon Barry, 16–37.
Disraeli. Bernard Holland, C.B., 38–54.
The Marquise de la Tour du Pin. Comtesse de Courson, 55–73.
War and the Conscience of Nations. Rev. Cuthbert O.S.F.C., 74–86.
The Submarine Campaign. A. H. Pollen, 87–102.
Anglicanism Past and Present. James Britten, 103–21.
The Effect of Waterloo. Hilaire Belloc, 122–33.
The Neutrality of the Holy See. Bishop of Northampton, 134–45.
Eleven Months of the War. Lancelot Lawton, 146–83.
Some Recent Books. 184–208.

OCTOBER 1915

Prussianism, Pacificism and Chivalry. Wilfrid Ward, 209–25.
The Early Romance of English Trade with Russia. W. H. Mallock, 226–40.
The National Temper and the Press. 241–51.
La Prière pour la France. Abbot of Farnborough [Fernand Cabrol], 252–71.
The Teutonic Knights and the Kingdom of Prussia. Mgr. Barnes, 272–83.
An American Catholic University. Wilfrid Ward, 284–94.
Religion in the French Army. 265–308.
Some American Problems. W. R. Castle, 309–23.
Who Were the Fairies? Sir Bertram Windle, 324–36.
The Significance of the Russian Retreat. Lancelot Lawton, 337–62.
The Guarantees of International Honour. Cardinal Gasquet, 363–74.
Some Recent Books. 375–407.
Chronicle of Biblical Works. J. P. Arendzen, 408–16.

JANUARY 1916

Bishop Hedley. Wilfrid Ward, 1–12.
German Catholics and the War. 13–35.
A Plea for Nationalism. Fr. Cuthbert, O.S.F.C., 36–50.
Art after the War. Rev. Thomas J. Gerrard, 51–66.
Aristocracy. Bernard Holland, C.B., 67–83.
The Use of Aircraft in the Present War. Eric Stuart Bruce, 84–102.
Catholicism and International Law. Judge Sir Geo. Sherston Baker, Bart., 103–18.
The Gifford Lectures of Mr Balfour. Rev. John Rickaby, S.J., 119–35.
Before the Hierarchy. Canon Barry, 136–56.

The Eastern Churches and the War. Rev. Sydney Smith, S.J., 157–81.
Some Recent Books. 182–208.

APRIL 1916

Spain and the War. Bishop of Southwark, 209–19.
The Memoria Apostolorum on the Appian Way. Prof. Rodolfo Lanciani, 220–29.
La Philosophie Scolastique et la Guerre. Prof. Fernand Deschamps, 230–58.
Anthologia Laureata. Rev. C. C. Martindale, 259–65.
The Religious Ideal of the Slavophils. Rev. A. Palmieri, O.S.A., 266–87.
Islam: A Christian Heresy. Mgr. Barnes, 288–306.
Letters of a Jesuit Father in the Reign of George I. Richard Cecil Wilton, 307–23.
Infant Mortality and the Population. Dr. Alice Vowe Johnson, 324–35.
A Versatile Bishop of the Fifth Century. Rev. Francis St. John Thackeray, 336–45.
Clause-Length in English Prose. Dom John Chapman, O.S.B., 346–52.
Civil Liberty in Peace and War. Rev. J. Keating, S.J., 353–78.
Some Recent Books. 379–409.
Chronicle of Some Recent Philosophical Works. John Vance, 410–16.

SELECT BIBLIOGRAPHY

MANUSCRIPT SOURCES

British Library, London—George Tyrrell Papers. Maud Petre Papers.

Downside Abbey Archives—Cardinal Gasquet Papers.

St. Andrews University Library, St. Andrews, Scotland. Wilfrid Ward Papers (WWP).

PUBLISHED SOURCES

Acton, John. "Conflicts with Rome." In *The History of Freedom and Other Essays,* ed. J. N. Figgis and R. V. Laurence, 461–91. London: Macmillan, 1907.

———. "The Catholic Press" and "The Munich Congress." In

Essays on Church and State, ed. Douglas Woodruff, 260–78 and 159–99. London: Hollis and Carter, 1952.

Adelson, Roger. *Mark Sykes: Portrait of an Amateur.* London: J. Cape, 1975.

———. *London and the Invention of the Middle East: Money, Power, and War, 1902–1922.* New Haven: Yale University Press, 1995.

Akenson, Donald Harmon. *The Church of Ireland: Ecclesiastical Reform and Revolution, 1800–1885.* New Haven: Yale University Press, 1971.

Altholz, Josef L. *The Liberal Catholic Movement in England: The "Rambler" and Its Contributors, 1848–1864.* London: Burns & Oates, 1962.

———. "The Dublin Review, 1836–1900." In *The Wellesley Index to Victorian Periodicals, 1814–1900,* vol. 2, ed. Walter E. Houghton, 11–22. Toronto: University of Toronto Press, 1972.

———. "Daniel O'Connell and the *Dublin Review.*" *Catholic Historical Review* 74 (Jan. 1988): 1–12.

———. *The Religious Press in Britain, 1760–1900.* New York: Greenwood Press, 1989.

———. "Social Catholicism in England in the Age of the Devotional Revolution." In *Piety and Power in Ireland, 1760–1960: Essays in Honour of Emmet Larkin,* ed. Stewart J. Brown and David M. Miller, 209–19. Notre Dame: University of Notre Dame Press, 2000.

Anderson, Margaret Lavinia. *Windthorst: A Political Biography.* Oxford: Clarendon Press, 1981.

———. "Kulturkampf and the Course of German History." *Central European History* 19 (1986): 82–115.

———. "Interdenominationalism, Clericalism, Pluralism: The Zentrumsstreit and the Dilemma of Catholicism in Wilhelmine Germany." *Central European History* 21 (1988): 350–78.

Appleby, R. Scott. *"Church and Age Unite": The Modernist Impulse in American Catholicism.* Notre Dame: University of Notre Dame Press, 1992.

Arnold, Matthew. "The Function of Criticism at the Present Time." In *Essays in Criticism,* 1st ser. London: Macmillan, 1902.

Arnstein, Walter L. *Protestant versus Catholic in Mid-Victorian England: Mr. Newdegate and the Nuns.* Columbia: University of Missouri Press, 1982.

Arx, Jeffrey Paul von. *Progress and Pessimism: Religion, Politics, and History in Late Nineteenth-Century Britain.* Cambridge: Harvard University Press, 1985.

Aspden, Kester. *Fortress Church: The English Roman Catholic Bishops and Politics, 1903–63.* Leominster: Gracewing, 2002.

———. "Archbishop Frederick Keating and the Catholic Social Movement, 1908–1928." *Downside Review* 120 (Jan. 2002): 11–32.

Aspinwall, Bernard. "Towards an English Catholic Social Conscience, 1829–1920." *Recusant History* 25 (May 2000): 106–19.

Aubert, Roger. *Catholic Social Teaching: An Historical Perspective.* Milwaukee: Marquette University Press, 2003.

Badeni, June. *The Slender Tree: A Life of Alice Meynell.* Padstow: Tabb House, 1981.

Bailey, Cyril. *Francis Urquhart: A Memoir.* London: Macmillan, 1936.

Barker, Dudley. *G. K. Chesterton: A Biography.* London: Stein and Day, 1973.

Barker, Nicolas. *Stanley Morison.* London: Macmillan, 1972.

Barlett, Thomas. *The Fall and Rise of the Irish Nation: The Catholic Question, 1690–1830.* Dublin: Gill and Macmillan, 1992.

Barmann, Lawrence. *Baron Friedrich von Hügel and the Modernist Crisis in England.* Cambridge: Cambridge University Press, 1972.

Barry, Michael. *By Pen and Pulpit: The Life and Times of the Author Canon Sheehan.* Fermoy, Ireland: Saturn Press, 1990.

Barry, William. *Memories and Opinions.* New York: G. P. Putnam's Sons, 1926.

Becker, Annette. "The Churches and the War." In Jean-Jacques Becker, *The Great War and the French People,* trans. Arnold Pomerans, 161–91. New York: St. Martin's Press, 1986.

———. *War and Faith: The Religious Imagination in France, 1914–1930.* Trans. Helen McPhail. New York: Berg, 1998.

Bell, P. M. H. *Disestablishment in Ireland and Wales.* London: S.P.C.K., 1969.

Bence-Jones, Mark. *The Catholic Families.* London: Constable, 1992.

Bewley, Charles. *Memoirs of a Wild Goose.* Dublin: Lilliput Press, 1989.

Biggs-Davison, John, and George Chowdharay-Best. *The Cross of St Patrick: The Catholic Unionist Tradition in Ireland.* Abbotsbrook: Kensal Press, 1984.

Blackbourn, David. *Class, Religion, and Local Politics in Wilhelmine Germany: The Centre Party in Württemberg.* New Haven: Yale University Press, 1980.

Blewett, Neal. "The Franchise in the United Kingdom: 1885–1918." *Past and Present* 32 (Dec. 1965): 27–56.

———. *The Peers and the People: The General Elections of 1910.* London: Macmillan, 1972.

Blunt, Wilfrid Scawen. *My Diaries: Being a Personal Narrative of Events, 1888–1914.* New York: Knopf, 1921.

Boardman, Brigid M. *Between Heaven and Charing Cross: A Life of Francis Thompson.* New Haven: Yale University Press, 1988.

Bossy, John. *The English Catholic Community: 1570–1850.* New York: Oxford University Press, 1976.

———. "English Catholics after 1688." In *From Persecution to Toleration: The Glorious Revolution and Religion in England,* ed. Ole Peter Grell, Jonathan I. Israel, and Nicholas Tyacke, 369–87. Oxford: Clarendon Press, 1991.

Boyer, John W. *Political Radicalism in Late Imperial Vienna: Origins of the Christian Social Movement, 1848–1897.* Chicago: University of Chicago Press, 1985.

———. *Culture and Political Crisis in Vienna: Christian Socialism in Power, 1897–1918.* Chicago: University of Chicago Press, 1995.

Bristow, Edward. "Profit-Sharing, Socialism, and Labour Unrest." In *Essays in Anti-Labour History: Responses to the Rise of Labour in Britain,* ed. Kenneth D. Brown, 262–89. London: Macmillan, 1974.

Broderick, Francis L. *Right Reverend New Dealer: John A. Ryan.* New York: Macmillan, 1963.

Brown, Alice. *Louise Imogen Guiney.* New York: Macmillan, 1921.

Brown, Alan. *The Metaphysical Society.* New York: Columbia University Press, 1947.

Brown, Kenneth D., ed. *Essays in Anti-Labour History: Responses to the Rise of Labour in Britain.* London: Macmillan, 1974.

Brown, Stewart J., and David M. Miller, eds. *Piety and Power in Ireland 1760–1960: Essays in Honour of Emmet Larkin.* Notre Dame: University of Notre Dame Press, 2000.

Brundell, Barry. "Catholic Church Politics and Evolution Theory, 1894–1902." *British Journal for the History of Science* 34 (March 2001): 81–95.

Brzezinski, Zbigniew. *Out of Control: Global Turmoil on the Eve of the 21st Century.* New York: Scribner's, 1993.

Buckland, Patrick. *Irish Unionism One: The Anglo-Irish and the New Ireland, 1885–1922.* Dublin: Gill and Macmillan, 1972.

———. *Irish Unionism Two: Ulster Unionism and the Origins of Northern Ireland, 1886–1922.* Dublin: Gill and Macmillan, 1973.

Buehrle, Marie Cecilia, *Rafael Cardinal Merry del Val.* London: St. Martin's Press, 1957.

Bull, Philip J. *Land, Politics and Nationalism: A Study of the Irish Land Question.* New York: St. Martin's Press, 1996.

Butler, Cuthbert. "Abbot Chapman." *Downside Review* 52 (Jan. 1934): 1–12.

Callahan, William J. *The Catholic Church in Spain, 1875–1998.* Washington, D.C.: Catholic University of America Press, 2000.

Candy, Catherine. *Priestly Fictions: Popular Irish Novelists of the Early 20th Century.* Dublin: Wolfhound Press, 1995.

Cannadine, David. *The Decline and Fall of the British Aristocracy.* New Haven: Yale University Press, 1990.

Caraman, Philip. *C. C. Martindale: A Biography.* London: Longmans, 1967.

Carlen, Claudia, ed. *The Papal Encyclicals: 1903–1939.* Wilmington, N.C.: McGrath, 1981.

Carpenter, James. *Gore: A Study in Liberal Catholic Thought.* London: Faith Press, 1960.

Casartelli, L. C. "The First Sixty Years." *Dublin Review* (April 1936): 192–220.

Cashman, John. "The Education Bill: Catholic Peers and Irish Nationalists." *Recusant History* 18 (Oct. 1987): 422–39.

Chapman, John. *The Spiritual Letters of John Chapman.* Edited by Roger Hudleston. London: Sheed and Ward, 1935.

Chesterton, G. K. "Wilfrid Ward (II.)." *Dublin Review* (July 1916): 23–32.

———. *The Autobiography of G. K. Chesterton.* New York: Sheed and Ward, 1936.

Chinnici, Joseph P. *The English Catholic Enlightenment: John Lingard and the Cisalpine Movement, 1780–1850.* Shepherdstown, W.Va.: Patmos Press, 1980.

Clark, Elaine. "Catholics and the Campaign for Women's Suffrage in England. *Church History* 73 (Sept. 2004): 635–65.

Clarke, Peter. *Liberals and Social Democrats.* Cambridge: Cambridge University Press, 1978.

Cleary, J. M. *Catholic Social Action in Britain, 1909–1959: A History of the Catholic Social Guild.* Oxford: Catholic Social Guild, 1961.

Collini, Stefan. *Public Moralists: Political Thought and Intellectual Life in Britain, 1850–1939.* Oxford: Clarendon Press, 1991.

Colvin, Ian. *Carson: The Statesman.* New York: Macmillan, 1935.

Connelly, Gerard. "Irish and Catholic: Myth or Reality? Another Sort of Irish and the Renewal of the Clerical Profession among Catholics in England, 1791–1918." In *The Irish in the Victorian City,* ed. Roger Swift and Sheridan Gilley, 225–54. London: Croom Helm, 1985.

Conquest, Robert. *Reflections on a Ravaged Century.* New York: W. W. Norton, 2000.

Cookey, S. J. S. *Britain and the Congo Question, 1885–1913.* New York: Humanities Press, 1968.

Crehan, Joseph. *Father Thurston: A Memoir with a Bibliography of His Writings.* New York: Sheed and Ward, 1952.

Crews, Clyde F. *English Catholic Modernism: Maude Petre's Way of Faith.* Notre Dame: University of Notre Dame Press, 1984.

Crowther, M. A. *The Workhouse System, 1834–1929: The History of an English Social Institution.* Athens: University of Georgia Press, 1982.

Cruickshank, Marjorie. *Church and State in English Education, 1870 to the Present Day.* New York: St. Martin's Press, 1963.

Curtis, Lewis Perry, Jr. *Coercion and Conciliation in Ireland, 1880–1892: A Study in Conservative Unionism.* Princeton: Princeton University Press, 1963.

———. *Anglo-Saxons and Celts: A Study of Anti-Irish Prejudice in Victorian England.* Bridgeport, Conn.: Conference on British Studies, University of Bridgeport, 1968.

———. *Apes and Angels: The Irishman in Victorian Caricature.* Washington, D.C.: Smithsonian Institution Press, 1971.

Daly, Gabriel. *Transcendence and Immanence: A Study in Catholic Modernism and Integralism.* Oxford: Clarendon Press, 1980.

Dangerfield, George. *The Damnable Question: A Study in Anglo-Irish Relations.* Boston: Little, Brown, 1976.

David, Edward. "The New Liberalism of C. F. G. Masterman, 1873–1927. In *Essays in Anti-Labour History: Responses to the Rise of Labour in Britain,* ed. Kenneth D. Brown, 17–41. London: Macmillan, 1974.

DeGroot, Gerard J. *Blighty: British Society in the Era of the Great War.* New York: Longman, 1996.

Dell, Robert. "A Liberal Catholic View of the Case of Dr. Mivart." *Nineteenth Century* 47 (April 1900): 669–84.

———. "Mr. Wilfrid Ward's Apologetics." *Nineteenth Century* 48 (July 1900): 127–36.

Dimnet, Ernest. *My Old World.* New York: Simon and Schuster, 1935.

———. *My New World.* New York: Simon and Schuster, 1937.

Dooley, D. J. *Compton Mackenzie.* New York: Twayne, 1974.

Douglas, Roy. *Land, People and Politics: A History of the Land Question in the United Kingdom, 1878–1952.* New York: St. Martin's Press, 1976.

Doyle, Peter. "The Catholic Federation, 1906–1920." In *Voluntary Religion,* ed. W. J. Sheils and Diana Wood, 461–76. Studies in Church History 23. Oxford: B. Blackwell, 1986.

———. "Charles Plater S.J. and the Origins of the Catholic Social Guild." *Recusant History* 21 (May 1993): 401–17.

Driver, Felix. *Power and Pauperism: The Workhouse System, 1834–1884.* Cambridge: Cambridge University Press, 1993.

Dwyer, J. J. "The Catholic Press, 1850–1950." In *The English Catholics: 1850–1950,* ed. George Andrew Beck, 475–514. London: Burns, Oates and Washbourne, 1950.

Edwards, Owen Dudley, and Patricia J. Storey. "The Irish Press in Victorian Britain." In

The Irish in the Victorian City, ed. Roger Swift and Sheridan Gilley, 158–78. London: Croom Helm, 1985.

Egremont, Max. *The Cousins: The Friendship, Opinions and Activities of Wilfrid Scawen Blunt and George Wyndham.* London: Collins, 1977.

Eigelsbach, Jo Ann. "The Intellectual Dialogue of Friedrich von Hügel and Wilfrid Ward." *Downside Review* 104 (July 1986): 144–57.

Eksteins, Modris. *Rites of Spring: The Great War and the Birth of the Modern Age.* Boston: Houghton Mifflin, 1989.

Emy, H. V. "The Land Campaign: Lloyd George as Social Reformer, 1909–14." In *Lloyd George: Twelve Essays,* ed. A. J. P. Taylor, 35–68. London: Hamilton, 1971.

Epstein, Klaus. *Mathias Erzberger and the Dilemma of German Democracy.* Princeton: Princeton University Press, 1959.

Erb, Peter. "Some Aspects of Modern British Catholic Literature: Apologetic in the Novels of Josephine Ward." *Recusant History* 24 (July 1999): 364–83.

Evans, Ellen Lovell. *The German Center Party, 1870–1933: A Study in Political Catholicism.* Carbondale: Southern Illinois University Press, 1981.

Fallon, Ann Connerton. *Katherine Tynan.* Boston: Twayne, 1979.

Fanning, Ronan. "'Rats' versus 'Ditchers': The Die-hard Revolt and the Parliament Bill of 1911." In *Parliament and Community,* ed. Art Cosgrove and J. I. McGuire, 191–210. Belfast: Appletree Press, 1983.

Ferguson, Niall. *The Pity of War.* New York: Basic Books, 1999.

Ferrell, William R. *George Wyndham at the Irish Office, 1900–1905.* Master's thesis, University of South Carolina, 1974.

Feske, Victor. *From Belloc to Churchill: Private Scholars, Public Culture, and the Crisis of British Liberalism, 1900–1939.* Chapel Hill: University of North Carolina Press, 1996.

Fidelis [Robert Dell]. "A Convert's Experiences of the Catholic Church." *Contemporary Review* 77 (June 1900): 817–34.

———. "The Movement for Reform within the Catholic Church." *Contemporary Review* 78 (Nov. 1900): 693–709.

Fleischmann, Ruth. *Catholic Nationalism in the Irish Revival: A Study of Canon Sheehan, 1852–1913.* New York: St. Martin's Press, 1997.

Fletcher, John R. "Early Catholic Periodicals in England." *Dublin Review* (April 1936): 284–310.

Fogarty, Gerald. *American Catholic Biblical Scholarship: A History from the Early Republic to Vatican II.* New York: Harper & Row, 1989.

Ford, D. J. "W. H. Mallock and Socialism in England, 1880–1918." In *Essays in Anti-Labour History: Responses to the Rise of Labour in Britain,* ed. Kenneth D. Brown, 317–42. London: Macmillan, 1974.

Forrest, Derek W. *Francis Galton: The Life and Work of a Victorian Genius.* New York: Taplinger, 1974.

Foster, R. F. *W. B. Yeats: A Life,* vol. 1, *The Apprentice Mage.* Oxford: Oxford University Press, 1997.

Fraser, Derek. *The Evolution of the British Welfare State: A History of Social Policy since the Industrial Revolution.* 2d ed. London: Macmillan, 1984.

Freeden, Michael. *The New Liberalism: An Ideology of Social Reform.* Oxford: Clarendon Press, 1978.

Fromkin, David. *Europe's Last Summer: Who Started the Great War in 1914.* New York: Knopf, 2004.

Gailey, Andrew. *Ireland and the Death of Kindness: The Experience of Constructive Unionism, 1890–1905*. Cork: Cork University Press, 1987.

Gasquet, Francis Aidan. *Lord Acton and His Circle*. New York: Longmans, Green, 1906.

Geehr, Richard S. *Karl Lueger: Mayor of Fin de Siècle Vienna*. Detroit: Wayne State University Press, 1990.

Gibson, William. "An Outburst of Activity in the Roman Congregations." *Nineteenth Century* (May 1899): 785–94.

Gillham, Nicholas Wright. *A Life of Sir Francis Galton: From African Exploration to the Birth of Eugenics*. Oxford: Oxford University Press, 2001.

Gilley, Sheridan. "Wilfrid Ward and His Life of Newman." *Journal of Ecclesiastical History* 29 (1978): 177–93.

———. "Vulgar Piety and the Brompton Oratory, 1850–1860." In *The Irish in the Victorian City*, ed. Roger Swift and Sheridan Gilley, 255–66. London: Croom Helm, 1985.

———. "Catholics and Socialists in Scotland, 1900–30." In *The Irish in Britain, 1815–1939*, ed. Roger Swift and Sheridan Gilley, 212–38. Savage, Md.: Barnes and Noble, 1989.

———. "An Intellectual Discipleship: Newman and the Making of Wilfrid Ward." *Louvain Studies* 15 (1990): 318–45.

———. "Father William Barry: Priest and Novelist." *Recusant History* 24 (Oct. 1999): 523–51.

———. "The Years of Equipoise, 1892–1943." In *From without the Flaminian Gate: 150 Years of Roman Catholicism in England and Wales, 1850–2000*, ed. Vincent Alan McClelland and Michael Hodgetts, 21–61. London: Darton, Longman and Todd, 1999.

Gourvish, T. R. "The Standard of Living, 1890–1914." In *The Edwardian Age: Conflict and Stability, 1900–1914*, ed. Alan O'Day, 13–34. Hamden, Conn.: Archon Books, 1979.

Gray, Edwyn. *The Killing Time*. London: Seeley, 1972.

Grayson, Janet. *Robert Hugh Benson: Life and Works*. Lanham, Md.: University Press of America, 1998.

Greaves, C. Desmond. *The Life and Times of James Connolly*. London: Lawrence and Wishart, 1972.

Greene, Dana. *The Living of Maisie Ward*. Notre Dame: University of Notre Dame Press, 1997.

Gruber, Jacob W. *A Conscience in Conflict: A Life of St. George Jackson Mivart*. New York: Columbia University Press, 1960.

Haight, Roger. "Bremond's Newman." *Journal of Theological Studies* 36 (Oct. 1985): 350–79.

Hales, E. E. Y. *Pio Nono: A Study in European Politics and Religion in the Nineteenth Century*. London: P. J. Kennedy, 1954.

Harrison, Brian. *Separate Spheres: The Opposition to Women's Suffrage in Britain*. New York: Holmes & Meier, 1978.

———. "The Act of Militancy: Violence and the Suffragettes, 1904–1914." In Brian Harrison, *Peacable Kingdom: Stability and Change in Modern Britain*, 26–81. Oxford: Clarendon Press, 1982.

Harris, Jose. *Unemployment and Politics: A Study of English Social Policy, 1886–1914*. Oxford: Clarendon Press, 1972.

———. *Private Lives, Public Spirit: A Social History of Britain, 1870–1914*. Oxford: Oxford University Press, 1993.

———. *William Beveridge: A Biography*. 2d ed. Oxford: Clarendon Press, 1997.

Hart, M. A. *Soul Ordained to Fail*. New York: Pageant Press, 1962.

Headings, Mildred J. *French Freemasonry under the Third Republic*. Johns Hopkins Studies in Historical and Political Science 66. Baltimore: Johns Hopkins University Press, 1948.

Hedley, John Cuthbert. *Evolution and Faith, with Other Essays*. London: Sheed and Ward, 1931.

Heimann, Mary. *Catholic Devotion in Victorian England*. Oxford: Clarendon Press, 1995.

Herrmann, David G. *The Arming of Europe and the Making of the First World War*. Princeton: Princeton University Press, 1996.

[Hess], Cuthbert. "Wilfrid Ward (I.)." *Dublin Review* (July 1916): 1–22.

Heyck, Thomas William. "The Genealogy of Irish Modernism: The Case of W. B. Yeats." In *Piety and Power in Ireland, 1760–1960: Essays in Honour of Emmet Larkin*, ed. Stewart J. Brown and David M. Miller, 220–51. Notre Dame: University of Notre Dame Press, 2000.

Himmelfarb, Gertrude. *Poverty and Compassion: The Moral Imagination of the Late Victorians*. New York: Knopf, 1991.

———. *The De-moralization of Society: From Victorian Virtues to Modern Values*. New York: Knopf, 1995.

Hinchliff, Peter. *God and History: Aspects of British Theology, 1875–1914*. Oxford: Clarendon Press, 1992.

Hochschild, Adam. *King Leopold's Ghost: A Story of Greed, Terror, and Heroism in Colonial Africa*. New York: Houghton Mifflin, 1998.

Hollis, Patricia. *Ladies Elect: Women in English Local Government, 1865–1914*. Oxford: Clarendon Press, 1987.

Holmes, J. Derek. "Cardinal Raphael Merry del Val—An Uncompromising Ultramontane: Gleanings from His Correspondence with England." *Catholic Historical Review* 60 (Jan. 1974): 55–64.

———. *More Roman Than Rome: English Catholicism in the Nineteenth Century*. London: Burns & Oates, 1978.

———. *The Triumph of the Holy See: A Short History of the Holy See in the Nineteenth Century*. Shepherdstown, W.Va.: Patmos Press, 1978.

Horne, John, and Alan Kramer. *German Atrocities, 1914: A History of Denial*. New Haven: Yale University Press, 2001.

Horwood, Thomas. "Public Opinion and the 1908 Eucharistic Congress." *Recusant History* 25 (May 2000): 120–32.

Howell, David. *A Lost Left: Three Studies in Socialism and Nationalism*. Chicago: University of Chicago Press, 1986.

Hügel, Friedrich von. *Baron Friedrich von Hügel: Selected Letters, 1896–1924*. Edited by Bernard Holland. London: J. M. Dent & Sons, 1927.

Hynes, Samuel. *The Edwardian Turn of Mind*. Princeton: Princeton University Press, 1968.

———. "The Chesterbelloc." In *Edwardian Occasions: Essays on English Writing in the Early Twentieth Century*, 80–90. New York: Oxford University Press, 1972.

———. *A War Imagined: The First World War and English Culture*. New York: Atheneum, 1991.

Hynes, William J. "A Hidden Nexus between Catholic and Protestant Modernism: C. A. Briggs in Correspondence with Loisy, von Hügel and Genocchi." *Downside Review* 105 (July 1987): 193–223.

Jalland, Patricia. *The Liberals and Ireland: The Ulster Question in British Politics to 1914*. New York: St. Martin's Press, 1980.

———. "Irish Home-Rule Finance: A Neglected Dimension of the Irish Question, 1910–1914." *Irish Historical Studies* 23 (May 1983): 233–53.

James, Lawrence. *Raj: The Making and Unmaking of British India*. New York: St. Martin's Press, 1997.

Jenkins, Roy. *Mr. Balfour's Poodle: An Account of the Struggle between the House of Lords and the Government of Mr. Asquith.* London: Heinemann, 1954.

Jodock, Darrell, ed. *Catholicism Contending with Modernity: Roman Catholic Modernism and Anti-Modernism in Historical Context.* Cambridge: Cambridge University Press, 2000.

Jones, Greta. *Social Darwinism and English Thought: The Interaction between Biological and Social Theory.* Brighton: Harvester Press, 1980.

Jones, Peter d'A. *The Christian Socialist Revival, 1877–1914: Religion, Class, and Social Conscience in Late-Victorian England.* Princeton: Princeton University Press, 1968.

Kane, Paula. "'The Willing Captive of Home?' The English Catholic Women's League, 1906–1920." *Church History* 60 (Sept. 1991): 331–55.

Keene, Donald. *Emperor of Japan: Meiji and His World, 1852–1912.* New York: Columbia University Press, 2002.

Kelly, James. "Experience and Transcendence: An Introduction to the Religious Philosophy of Baron von Hügel." *Downside Review* 99 (July 1981): 172–89.

Kendle, John. *Ireland and the Federal Solution: The Debate over the United Kingdom Constitution, 1870–1921.* Montreal: McGill-Queen's University Press, 1989.

Kennedy, Robert G., Mary Christine Athans, Bernard V. Brady, William C. McDonough, and Michael J. Naughton. *Religion and Public Life: The Legacy of Monsignor John A. Ryan.* Lanham, Md.: University Press of America, 2001.

Knightley, Phillip. *The First Casuality: From the Crimea to Vietnam; The War Correspondent as Hero, Propagandist, and Myth Maker.* New York: Harcourt Brace Jovanovich, 1975.

Knox, Ronald. *Some Loose Stones.* London: Longmans, Green, 1913.

———. *A Spiritual Aeneid.* London: Longmans, Green, 1918.

———. *Essays in Satire.* New York: E. P. Dutton, 1930.

Kolakowski, Leszek. *Modernity On Endless Trial,* 3–13. Chicago: University of Chicago Press, 1990.

Koss, Stephen E. *Lord Haldane: Scapegoat for Liberalism.* New York: Columbia University Press, 1969.

Mark Krameras, ed. *The Black Book of Communism: Crimes, Terror, Repression.* Trans. Jonathan Murphy and Mark Kramer. Cambridge: Harvard University Press, 1999.

Lahutsky, Nadia M. "Ward's Newman: The Struggle to be Faithful and Fair." In *Newman and the Modernists,* ed. Mary Jo Weaver, 47–67. Lanham, Md.: University Press of America, 1985.

———. "Wilfrid Ward: Roman Catholic 'Modernism' between the Modernists and the Integralists." *Downside Review* 103 (Jan. 1985): 26–40.

Larkin, Emmet. *James Larkin: Irish Labour Leader, 1876–1947.* Cambridge: Cambridge University Press, 1965.

Larkin, Maurice. *Church and State after the Dreyfus Affair: The Separation Issue in France.* London: Macmillan, 1974.

Lease, Gary. "Merry del Val and Tyrrell: A Modernist Struggle." *Downside Review* 102 (April 1984): 133–56.

———. "Newman: The Roman View." In *Newman and the Modernists,* ed. Mary Jo Weaver, 161–82. Lanham, Md.: University Press of America, 1985.

Leslie, Shane. *Mark Sykes: His Life and Letters.* London: Cassell, 1923.

———. *Cardinal Gasquet.* London: Burns & Oates, 1953.

Lightman, Bernard. "*Robert Elsmere* and the Agnostic Crises of Faith." In *Victorian Faith in Crisis: Essays on Continuity and Change in Nineteenth-Century Religious Belief,* ed.

Richard J. Helmstader and Bernard Lightman, 283–311. Stanford: Stanford University Press, 1990.
Linklater, Andro. *Compton Mackenzie: A Life.* New York: B. Blackwell, 1987.
Longford, Elizabeth. *A Pilgrimage of Passion: The Life of Wilfrid Scawen Blunt.* New York: Knopf, 1980.
Loome, Thomas Michael. "A Bibliography of the Published Writings of George Tyrrell, 1861–1909." *Heythrop Journal* 10 (1969): 280–314.
———. *Liberal Catholicism, Reform Catholicism, Modernism: A Contribution to a New Orientation in Modernist Research.* Mainz: Matthias-Grünewald Verlag, 1979.
Lyons, F. S. L. *The Irish Parliamentary Party, 1890–1910.* London: Faber and Faber, 1951.
Lyons, J. B. *The Enigma of Thomas Kettle: Irish Patriot, Essayist, Poet, British Soldier, 1880–1916.* Dublin: Glendale Press, 1983.
Macaulay, Ambrose. *Dr. Russell of Maynooth.* London: Darton, Longman and Todd, 1983.
Macdonald, Lyn. *1915: The Death of Innocence.* New York: Henry Holt, 1995.
Machin, G. I. T. "The Liberal Government and the Eucharistic Procession of 1908." *Journal of Ecclesiastical History* 34 (Oct. 1983): 559–83.
Mackail. John William, and Guy Wyndham. *The Life and Letters of George Wyndham.* 2 vols. London: Hutchinson, 1925.
Mackenzie, Compton. *My Life and Times: Octave Four, 1907–1915.* London: Chatto & Windus, 1965.
MacKenzie, N. I., and Jeanne MacKenzie. *The Fabians.* New York: Simon and Schuster, 1977.
Mallock, W. H. *Memoirs of Life and Literature.* London: Chapman and Hall, 1920.
Mansergh, Nicholas. *The Irish Question, 1840–1921.* London: Allen and Unwin, 1965.
Markel, Michael H. *Hilaire Belloc.* Boston: Twayne, 1982.
Martin, Benjamin F. *Count Albert de Mun: Paladin of the Third Republic.* Chapel Hill: University of North Carolina Press, 1978.
Martindale, C. C. *The Life of Monsignor Robert Hugh Benson.* London: Longmans, Green, 1916.
———. *Charles Dominic Plater, S.J.* London: Harding & More, 1922.
Marwick, Arthur. *The Deluge: British Society and the First World War.* Boston: Little, Brown, 1965.
Mason, Francis M. "The Newer Eve: The Catholic Women's Suffrage Society in England, 1911–1923." *Catholic Historical Review* 72 (Oct. 1986): 620–38.
Massa, Mark. "'Mediating Modernism': Charles Briggs, Catholic Modernism, and an Ecumenical 'Plot.'" *Harvard Theological Review* 81 (Oct. 1988): 413–30.
Masterman, C. F. G. *The Condition of England.* Edited by J. T. Boulton. London: Methuen, 1960.
Masterman, Lucy. *C. F. G. Masterman: A Biography.* London: Nicholson and Watson, 1939.
Mathews, P. J. *Revival: The Abbey Theatre, Sinn Féin, the Gaelic League, and the Co-operative Movement.* Notre Dame: University of Notre Dame Press, 2003.
Matthews, Edmund. "Bishop Hedley as Editor." *Dublin Review* (April 1936): 253–66.
McAvoy, Thomas Timothy. *The Americanist Heresy in Roman Catholicism, 1895–1900.* Notre Dame: University of Notre Dame Press, 1963.
McBriar, A. M. *Fabian Socialism and English Politics, 1884–1918.* Cambridge: Cambridge University Press, 1962.
McBride, Lawrence W. "Imagining the Nation in Irish Historical Fiction, c. 1870–c. 1925." In *Piety and Power in Ireland, 1760–1960: Essays in Honour of Emmet Larkin,* ed. Stewart

J. Brown and David M. Miller, 81–107. Notre Dame: University of Notre Dame Press, 2000.

McCarthy, John P. *Hilaire Belloc: Edwardian Radical.* Indianapolis: Liberty Press, 1978.

McClain, James L. *Japan: A Modern History.* New York: W. W. Norton, 2002.

McClelland, Vincent Alan. *English Catholics and Higher Education, 1830–1903.* Oxford: Clarendon Press, 1973.

———. "Bourne, Norfolk, and the Irish Parliamentarians: Roman Catholics and the Education Bill of 1906." *Recusant History* 23 (Oct. 1996): 228–56.

McCool, Gerald A. *Catholic Theology in the Nineteenth Century: The Quest for a Unitary Method.* New York: Seabury Press, 1977.

McElrath, Damian. *The Syllabus of Pius IX: Some Reactions in England.* Louvain: Bibliothèque de l'Université, Bureau de la Revue, 1964.

McEntee, Georgiana Putnam. *The Social Catholic Movement in Great Britain.* New York: Macmillan, 1927.

McLeod, Hugh. "Building the 'Catholic Ghetto': Catholic Organizations, 1870–1920." In *Voluntary Religion,* ed. W. J. Sheils and Diana Wood, 411–44. Studies in Church History 23. Oxford: B. Blackwell, 1986.

McManners, John. *Church and State in France, 1870–1914.* London: S.P.C.K., 1972.

Meacham, Standish. *Toynbee Hall and Social Reform, 1880–1914.* New Haven: Yale University Press, 1987.

Meynell, Everard. *The Life of Francis Thompson.* New York: Burns & Oates, 1913.

Meynell, Francis. *My Lives.* New York: Random House, 1971.

Meynell, Viola. *Alice Meynell, A Memoir.* London: J. Cape, 1929.

———. *Francis Thompson and Wilfrid Meynell.* London: Hollis and Carter, 1952.

Miller, David W. *Church, State, and Nation in Ireland: 1898–1921.* Pittsburgh: University of Pittsburgh Press, 1973.

Miller, Steuart N. "John Swinnerton Phillimore: A Memoir." *Dublin Review* (winter 1960–1961): 316–34 and *Wiseman Review* (spring 1961): 23–47.

Misner, Paul. *Social Catholicism in Europe: From the Onset of Industrialization to the First World War.* New York: Crossroad, 1991.

Mivart, St. George Jackson. "The Continuity of Catholicism." *Nineteenth Century* (Jan. 1900): 51–72.

———. "Some Recent Catholic Apologists." *Fortnightly Review* (Jan. 1900): 24–44.

Morgan, David. *Suffragists and Liberals: The Politics of Woman Suffrage in England.* Totowa, N.J.: Rowman & Littlefield, 1975.

Morrissey, T. J. *Towards a National University, William Delany, SJ (1835–1924): An Era of Initiative in Irish Education.* Dublin: Wolfhound Press, 1983.

———. *William J. Walsh, Archbishop of Dublin, 1841–1921: No Uncertain Voice.* Dublin: Four Courts Press, 2000.

———. *Bishop Edward Thomas O'Dwyer of Limerick, 1842–1917.* Dublin: Four Courts Press, 2003.

Mulvey, Kieran. *Hugh Pope.* London: Blackfriars Publications, 1954.

Murphy, James. *Church, State and Schools in Britain, 1800–1970.* London: Routledge & Kegan Paul, 1971.

Murray, Bruce K. *The People's Budget, 1909/10: Lloyd George and Liberal Politics.* Oxford: Clarendon Press, 1980.

Newman, John Henry. *Sermons Preached on Various Occasions.* London: Longmans, Green, 1900.

———. *The Idea of a University Defined and Illustrated (I. In Nine Discourses Delivered to the Catholics of Dublin; II. In Occasional Lectures and Essays Addressed to the Members of the Catholic University).* London: Longmans, Green, 1907.

———. *Apologia Pro Vita Sua.* Edited by Martin Svaglic. Oxford: Clarendon Press, 1967.

———. *The Letters and Diaries of John Henry Newman.* Vol. 20, ed. C. S. Dessain (London: T. Nelson, 1970); vol. 21, ed. C. S. Dessain and Edward Kelly (London: T. Nelson, 1971); vol. 31, ed. C. S. Dessain and Thomas Gornall (Oxford: Clarendon Press, 1977).

Nichols, Aidan. *From Newman to Congar: The Idea of Doctrinal Development from the Victorians to the Second Vatican Council.* Edinburgh: T. & T. Clark, 1990.

———. *The Panther and the Hind: A Theological History of Anglicanism.* Edinburgh: T. & T. Clark, 1993.

Norman, Edward R. *Anti-Catholicism in Victorian England.* New York: Barnes and Noble, 1968.

———. *The Victorian Christian Socialists.* Cambridge: Cambridge University Press, 1987.

O'Brien, Conor Cruise. "Passion and Cunning: An Essay on the Politics of W. B. Yeats." In *Passion and Cunning and Other Essays,* 8–61. London: Weidenfeld and Nicolson, 1988.

O'Conner, Ulick. *Celtic Dawn: A Portrait of the Irish Literary Renaissance.* London: Hamish Hamilton, 1984.

O'Day, Alan. *Irish Home Rule, 1867–1921.* Manchester: Manchester University Press, 1998.

O'Dwyer, Edward. *Cardinal Newman and the Encyclical Pascendi Dominici Gregis.* London: Longmans, Green, 1908.

O'Ferrall, Fergus. *Catholic Emancipation: Daniel O'Connell and the Birth of Irish Democracy, 1820–1830.* Dublin: Gill and Macmillan, 1985.

O'Tuathaigh, M. A. G. "The Irish in Nineteenth-Century Britain: Problems of Integration." In *The Irish in the Victorian City,* ed. Roger Swift and Sheridan Gilley, 13–38. London: Gill and Macmillan, 1985.

Paesta, Senia. "The Catholic Hierarchy and the Irish University Question, 1880–1908." *History* 85 (April 2000): 268–84.

Parsons, Gerald. "Victorian Roman Catholicism: Emancipation, Expansion and Achievement." In *Religion in Victorian Britain,* ed. Gerald Parsons, 1:146–83. Manchester: Manchester University Press, 1988.

Partin, Malcolm O. *Waldeck-Rousseau, Combes, and the Church: The Politics of Anticlericalism, 1899–1905.* Durham: Duke University Press, 1969.

Paul, Harry W. *The Second Ralliement: The Rapprochement between Church and State in France in the Twentieth Century.* Washington, D.C.: Catholic University of America Press, 1967.

Pauley, Bruce F. *From Prejudice to Persecution: A History of Austrian Anti-Semitism.* Chapel Hill: University of North Carolina Press, 1992.

Paz, D. G. *Popular Anti-Catholicism in Mid-Victorian England.* Stanford: Stanford University Press, 1992.

Pearce, Joseph. *Wisdom and Innocence: A Life of G. K. Chesterton.* London: Hodder & Stoughton, 1996.

Peters, Walter H. *The Life of Benedict XV.* Milwaukee: Bruce Publ. Co., 1959.

Peterson, William S. *Victorian Heretic: Mrs Humphry Ward's Robert Elsmere.* Leicester: Leicester University Press, 1976.

Petre, Maud. *Catholicism and Independence: Studies in Spiritual Liberty.* London: Longmans, Green, 1907.

Phillips, Gregory D. *The Diehards: Aristocratic Society and Politics in Edwardian England.* Cambridge: Harvard University Press, 1979.

Pollard, John F. *The Unknown Pope: Benedict XV (1914–1922) and the Pursuit of Peace.* London: Geoffrey Chapman, 1999.

Pomfret, John E. *The Struggle for Land in Ireland, 1800–1923.* Princeton: Princeton University Press, 1930.

Quinn, Dermot. *Patronage and Piety: The Politics of English Roman Catholicism, 1850–1900.* Stanford: Stanford University Press, 1993.

Radice, Lisanne. *Beatrice and Sidney Webb: Fabian Socialists.* New York: St. Martin's Press, 1984.

Rafferty, Oliver. *Catholicism in Ulster, 1603–1983: An Interpretative History.* Columbia: University of South Carolina Press, 1994.

Ray, James. "The Turin Shroud Now." *Times Literary Supplement* (Oct. 18, 1996): 3–4.

Reardon, Bernard M. G. "Roman Catholic Modernism." In *Nineteenth-Century Religious Thought in the West,* vol. 2, ed. Ninian Smart, John Clayton, Patrick Sherry, and Steven T. Katz, 141–77. Cambridge: Cambridge University Press, 1985.

Reid, Alastair J. *Social Classes and Social Relations in Britain, 1850–1914.* Basingstoke: Macmillan Education, 1992.

Rempel, Richard A. "Lord Hugh Cecil's Parliamentary Career, 1900–1914: Promise Unfulfilled." *Journal of British Studies* 11 (May 1972): 104–30.

———. *Unionists Divided: Arthur Balfour, Joseph Chamberlain and the Unionist Free Traders.* Newton Abbot: David & Charles, 1972.

Riet, Georges van. *Thomistic Epistemology: Studies Concerning the Problem of Cognition in the Contemporary School,* trans. Gabriel Franks. Vol. 1. St. Louis: B. Herder, 1963.

Robinson, John Martin. *The Dukes of Norfolk: A Quincentennial History.* Oxford: Oxford University Press, 1982.

Robinson, R. A. H. "The Religious Question and the Catholic Revival in Portugal, 1900–1930." *Journal of Contemporary History* 12 (April 1977): 345–62.

Root, John D. "The Final Apostasy of St. George Jackson Mivart." *Catholic Historical Review* 71 (Jan. 1985): 1–25.

———. "William J. Williams, Newman, and Modernism." In *Newman and the Modernists,* ed. Mary Jo Weaver, 69–95. Lanham, Md.: University Press of America, 1985.

Rope, Henry. *Benedict XV: The Pope of Peace.* London: Catholic Book Club, 1940.

Rose, Kenneth. *The Later Cecils.* New York: Harper & Row, 1975.

Ross, Ronald. *Beleaguered Tower: The Dilemma of Political Catholicism in Wilhelmine Germany.* Notre Dame: University of Notre Dame Press, 1976.

———. *The Failure of Bismarck's Kulturkampf: Catholics and State Power in Imperial Germany, 1871–1887.* Washington, D.C.: Catholic University of America Press, 1998.

Rowland, Peter. *The Last Liberal Governments: The Promised Land, 1905–1910.* London: Macmillan, 1968.

———. *The Last Liberal Governments: Unfinished Business, 1911–1914.* London: Barrie & Jenkins, 1971.

Russell, A. K. *Liberal Landslide: The General Election of 1906.* Newton Abbot: David & Charles, 1973.

Sacks, Benjamin. *The Religious Issue in the State Schools of England and Wales, 1902–1914.* Albuquerque: University of New Mexico Press, 1961.

Sagovsky, Nicholas. "'Frustration, disillusion and enduring filial respect': George Tyrrell's Debt to John Henry Newman." In *Newman and the Modernists,* ed. Mary Jo Weaver, 97–115. Lanham, Md.: University Press of America, 1985.

Samuel, Raphael. "The Roman Catholic Church and the Irish Poor." In *The Irish in the Victorian City,* ed. Roger Swift and Sheridan Gilley, 267–300. London: Croom Helm, 1985.

Schiefen, Richard J. *Nicholas Wiseman and the Transformation of English Catholicism.* Shepherdstown, W.Va.: Patmos Press, 1984.

Schoenl, William J. *The Intellectual Crisis in English Catholicism: Liberal Catholics, Modernists, and the Vatican in the Late Nineteenth and Early Twentieth Centuries.* New York: Garland, 1982.

Schultenover, David G. *George Tyrrell: In Search of Catholicism.* Shepherdstown, W.Va.: Patmos Press, 1981.

———. "George Tyrrell: 'Devout Disciple of Newman.'" *Heythrop Journal* 33 (Jan. 1992): 20–44.

———. *A View from Rome: On the Eve of the Modernist Crisis.* New York: Fordham University Press, 1993.

Scotti, Paschal. "Wilfrid Ward and the *Dublin Review.*" *Downside Review* 117 (July 1999): 191–216.

———. "Happiness in Hell: The Case of Dr Mivart." *Downside Review* 119 (July 2001): 177–90.

———. "Wilfrid Ward: A Religious Fabius Maximus." *Catholic Historical Review* 88 (Jan. 2002): 42–64.

———. "Necromancy and Monsignor Benson." *Downside Review* 121 (April 2003): 135–49.

Searle, G. R. *The Quest for National Efficiency.* Oxford: B. Blackwell, 1971.

———. *Eugenics and Politics in Britain, 1900–1914.* Leyden: Noordhoff, 1976.

———. "Critics of Edwardian Society: The Case of the Radical Right." In *The Edwardian Age: Conflict and Stability, 1900–1914,* ed. Alan O'Day, 79–96. Hamden, Conn.: Archon Books, 1979.

———. *The Liberal Party: Triumph and Disintegration, 1886–1929.* New York: St. Martin's Press, 1992.

Shannon, Catherine. *Arthur Balfour and Ireland, 1874–1922.* Washington, D.C.: Catholic University of America Press, 1988.

Shaw, G. B. "Belloc and Chesterton." *New Age,* Feb. 15, 1908.

Solow, Barbara. *The Land Question and the Irish Economy.* Cambridge: Harvard University Press, 1971.

Soloway, Richard Allen. *Birth Control and the Population Question in England, 1877–1930.* Chapel Hill: University of North Carolina Press, 1982.

———. "Eugenics and Pronatalism in Wartime Britain." In *The Upheaval of War: Family, Work and Welfare in Europe, 1914–1918,* ed. Richard Wall and Jay Winter, 369–88. Cambridge: Cambridge University Press, 1988.

———. *Demography and Degeneration: Eugenics and the Declining Birthrate in Twentieth-Century Britain.* Chapel Hill: University of North Carolina Press, 1990.

Speaight, Robert. *The Life of Hilaire Belloc.* London: Hollis and Carter, 1957.

Spence, Jonathan. *The Search for Modern China.* New York: W. W. Norton, 1990.

Strikwerda, Carl. "The Divided Class: Catholics vs. Socialists in Belgium, 1880–1914." *Comparative Studies in Society and History* 30 (April 1988): 333–59.

———. *A House Divided: Catholics, Socialists, and Flemish Nationalists in Nineteenth-Century Belgium.* Lanham, Md.: Rowman & Littlefield, 1997.

Sullivan, Alvin, ed. *British Literary Magazines.* Vol. 2, *The Romantic Age, 1789–1836.* Westport, Conn.: Greenwood Press, 1983.

Sutherland, John. *Mrs Humphry Ward: Eminent Victorian, Pre-eminent Edwardian.* Oxford: Clarendon Press, 1990.

Swift, Roger, and Sheridan Gilley, eds. *The Irish in the Victorian City.* London: Croom Helm, 1985.

———. *The Irish in Britain, 1815–1939.* Savage, Md.: Barnes and Noble, 1989.

Sykes, Alan. *Tariff Reform in British Politics, 1903–1913.* Oxford: Clarendon Press, 1979.

Taylor, Beverly. *Francis Thompson.* Boston: Twayne, 1987.

Taylor, Brian. *The Life and Writings of James Owen Hannay (George Birmingham), 1865–1950.* Lewiston, N.Y.: E. Mellen Press, 1995.

Taylor, Monica. *Sir Bertram Windle: A Memoir.* London: Longmans, Green, 1932.

Tenison, E. M. *Louise Imogen Guiney: Her Life and Her Work, 1861–1920.* London: Longmans Green, 1923.

Thompson, Francis. *The Letters of Francis Thompson.* Edited by John Walsh. New York: Hawthorn Books, 1969.

———. *Shelley,* with an introduction by George Wyndham and notes by W. M. [Wilfrid Meynell]. London: Burns & Oates, 1911.

Thompson, J. A. "The Historians and the Decline of the Liberal Party." *Albion* 22 (1990): 65–83.

Thomson, Mathew. *The Problem of Mental Deficiency: Eugenics, Democracy, and Social Policy in Britain, c. 1870–1959.* Oxford: Clarendon Press, 1998.

Toke, Leslie. "Pauperism and the Nation." *Downside Review* 9 (Nov. 1909): 197–216, and 10 (March 1910): 18–48.

Tucker, Albert V. "W. H. Mallock and Late Victorian Conservatism." *University of Toronto Quarterly* 31 (1962): 223–41.

Tucker, Maurice G. *John Neville Figgis: A Study.* London: S.P.C.K., 1950.

Tuell, Anne Kimball. *Mrs. Meynell and Her Literary Generation.* New York: E. P. Dutton, 1925.

Tulloch, Hugh. *Acton.* New York: St. Martin's Press, 1988.

Tyrrell, George. "The Recent Anglo-Roman Pastoral." *Nineteenth Century* 49 (May 1901): 736–54.

———. "Semper Eadem." In *Through Scylla and Charybdis: Or the Old Theology and the New,* 106–32. London: Longmans, Green, 1907.

———. *Letters from a "Modernist": The Letters of George Tyrrell to Wilfrid Ward, 1893–1908.* Edited by Mary Jo Weaver. Shepherdstown, W.Va.: Patmos Press, 1981.

Ullman, Joan Connelly. *The Tragic Week: A Study of Anticlericalism in Spain, 1875–1912.* Cambridge: Harvard University Press, 1968.

Valentine, Ferdinand. *Father Vincent McNabb, O.P.* Westminster, Md.: Newman Press, 1955.

Vogeler, Martha S. *Frederic Harrison: The Vocations of a Positivist.* Oxford: Clarendon Press, 1984.

Walsh, John. *Strange Harp, Strange Symphony: The Life of Francis Thompson.* New York: Hawthorn Books, 1967.

Walsh, Leo J. "William Ward and the *Dublin Review.*" Ph.D. diss., Columbia University, 1962.

Ward, Maisie. *The Wilfrid Wards and the Transition,* vol. 1, *The Nineteenth Century.* New York: Sheed and Ward, 1934.

———. "W. G. Ward and Wilfrid Ward." *Dublin Review* (April 1936): 235–52.

———. *The Wilfrid Wards and the Transition,* vol. 2, *Insurrection Versus Resurrection.* New York: Sheed and Ward, 1937.

———. *Gilbert Keith Chesterton.* New York: Sheed and Ward, 1943.

———. *Unfinished Business.* New York: Sheed and Ward, 1964.

Ward, Wilfrid. "The Healing Art in Philosophy." *Dublin Review* (Jan. 1885): 30–49.

———. *William George Ward and the Oxford Movement.* London: Macmillan, 1889.

———. "The Scholastic Movement and Catholic Philosophy." *Dublin Review* (April 1891): 255–71.

———. *William George Ward and the Catholic Revival.* London: Macmillan, 1893.

———. "New Wine in Old Bottles." In *Witnesses to the Unseen and Other Essays,* 68–97. London: Macmillan, 1893.

———. *The Life and Times of Cardinal Wiseman.* 2 vols. London: Longmans, Green, 1897.

———. "The Ethics of Religious Conformity." *Quarterly Review* (Jan. 1899): 103–36.

———. "Catholic Apologetics: A Reply." *Nineteenth Century* (June 1899): 951–61.

———. "Liberalism and Intransigeance." *Nineteenth Century* (June 1900): 960–73.

———. "The Rigidity of Rome." In *Problems and Persons,* 66–98. London: Longmans, Green, 1903.

———. "The Time-Spirit of the Nineteenth Century." In *Problems and Persons,* 1–65. London: Longmans, Green, 1903.

———. "Unchanging Dogma and Changeful Man." In *Problems and Persons,* 99–132. London: Longmans, Green, 1903.

———. "Leo XIII." In *Ten Personal Studies,* 156–97. London: Longmans, Green, 1908.

———. "A Political Fabius Maximus." In *Ten Personal Studies,* 1–47. London: Longmans, Green, 1908.

———. "The Conservative Genius of the Church: An Address to the Catholic Conference of 1900." In *Men and Matters,* 301–18. London: Longmans, Green, 1914.

———. "Doctores Ecclesiae." *Pilot* 3 (June 22, 1901): 774–76.

———. "George Wyndham: Some Impressions by a Friend." In *Men and Matters,* 70–104. London: Longmans, Green, 1914.

———. *Last Lectures by Wilfrid Ward.* Edited by Mrs. Wilfrid Ward. London: Longmans, Green, 1918.

Ward, Mrs. Wilfrid. *Three Novels.* London: Sheed and Ward, 1933.

Warwick-Haller, Sally. *William O'Brien and the Irish Land War.* Dublin: Irish Academic Press, 1990.

Wasti, Syed Razi. *Lord Minto and the Indian Nationalist Movement, 1905 to 1910.* Oxford: Clarendon Press, 1964.

Weaver, Mary Jo. "A Working Catalogue of the Ward Family Papers." *Recusant History* 15 (1979): 43–71.

———. "A Bibliography of the Published Works of Wilfrid Ward." *Heythrop Journal* 20 (Oct. 1979): 399–420.

———. "George Tyrrell and the Joint Pastoral Letter." *Downside Review* 99 (Jan. 1981): 18–39.

———. "Wilfrid Ward's Interpretation and Application of Newman." In *Newman and the Modernists,* ed. Mary Jo Weaver, 27–46. Lanham, Md.: University Press of America, 1985.

———, ed. *Letters from a "Modernist": The Letters of George Tyrrell to Wilfrid Ward, 1893–1908.* Shepherdstown, W.Va.: Patmos Press, 1981.

———. *Newman and the Modernists.* Lanham, Md.: University Press of America, 1985.

Weaver, Stewart A. *The Hammonds: A Marriage in History.* Stanford: Stanford University Press, 1997.

Weber, Ralph. *Notre Dame's John Zahm: American Catholic Apologist and Educator.* Notre Dame: University of Notre Dame Press, 1961.

Weiler, Peter. *The New Liberalism: Liberal Social Theory in Great Britain, 1889–1914.* New York: Garland, 1982.

White, C. W. "*The Strange Death of Liberal England* in Its Time." *Albion* 17 (1985): 425–47.

Wilson, A. N. *Hilaire Belloc.* New York: Atheneum, 1984.

Wilson, J. Anselm. *The Life of Bishop Hedley.* New York: P. J. Kennedy, 1930.

Winstanley, Michael J. *Ireland and the Land Question, 1800–1922.* London: Routledge, 1984.

Winter, J. M. *The Great War and the English People.* Cambridge: Harvard University Press, 1986.

Wiseman, Nicholas. *Essays on Various Subjects.* 3 vols. New York: P. O'Shea, 1853.

———. "The Present Catholic Dangers." *Dublin Review* (Dec. 1856): 441–70.

Wohl, Robert. *The Generation of 1914.* Cambridge: Harvard University Press, 1979.

Wolffe, John. *The Protestant Crusade in Great Britain, 1829–1860.* Oxford: Clarendon Press, 1991.

Wood, Peter. *Poverty and the Workhouse in Victorian Britain.* Wolfeboro Falls, N.H.: Alan Sutton Publ., 1991.

Woolf, Virginia. "Mr. Bennett and Mrs. Brown." In *The Captain's Death Bed and Other Essays,* 94–119. New York: Harcourt Brace Jovanovich, 1950.

Wraith, Barbara. "A Pre-Modern Interpretation of the Modern: The English Catholic Church and the 'Social Question' in the Early Twentieth Century." In *The Church Retrospective,* ed. R. N. Swanson, 529–45. Studies in Church History 33. Woodbridge: Boydell Press, 1997.

Yeates, Pádraig. *Lockout: Dublin 1913.* New York: St. Martin's Press, 2000.

Yeats, W. B. *Autobiographies.* London: Macmillan, 1955.

Young, Kenneth. *Arthur James Balfour.* London: G. Bell, 1963.

Zebel, Sydney. *Balfour: A Political Biography.* Cambridge: Cambridge University Press, 1973.

Zeender, John K. "The German Center Party during World War I: An Internal Study." *Catholic Historical Review* 42 (Jan. 1957): 441–68.

———. "German Catholics and the Concept of an Interconfessional Party, 1900–1920." *Journal of Central European Affairs* 23 (1964): 424–39.

———. *The German Center Party, 1890–1906.* Philadelphia: American Philosophical Society, 1976.

Zuckerman, Larry. *The Rape of Belgium: The Untold Story of World War I.* New York: New York University Press, 2004.

INDEX

Abdul Hamid II, 255
Acton, John, 40–43, 46, 51, 52, 59
Ad Beatissimi (Benedict XV), 89
Aeterni Patris (Leo XIII), 13
Africa, 237–40, 245–46, 249
Americanism, 15
Aquinas, Thomas, 10, 20, 21n59, 44, 55, 58, 71, 76
Arendzen, John, 56
Asquith, Herbert, 104, 105, 112, 113, 114, 218, 223, 272
Association Catholique de la Jeunesse Française, 131–32
Athenaeum, 28

Balfour, Arthur, 49, 83, 91–92, 93, 98, 102, 104, 110, 113, 115, 120, 140, 207, 210, 224, 272, 291
Barnes, Arthur S., 265, 291
Barrès, Maurice, 175
Barry, William, 55, 172, 189, 267
Bazin, René, 175
Beerbohm, Max, 174n20, 176
Belloc, Hilaire, 98–101, 105, 156, 175, 176–81, 235n21, 236–37, 287
Benedict XV, 89–90, 174, 281–82
Bennett, Arnold, 169–70
Benson, Robert Hugh, 176, 190–95
Bernhardi, Freidrich von, 261, 264, 265, 267, 276
Beveridge, William, 140–41, 144–45, 147
Bewley, Charles, 200–203, 221–22
biblical criticism, 9, 15, 55–56, 63–65, 68, 85
Bidwell, Mgr., 71, 73, 75, 235
Birmingham, George A., 196, 197, 198–99
Blunt, Wilfrid Scawen, 67n28, 75n48, 190
Boer War, vii, 50n62, 75, 158, 222, 246, 254
Bourne, Francis, 27, 49, 51, 65, 72–73, 75n48, 289–91
Bremond, Henri, 65n18, 69, 71
Britten, James, 26, 138–39
Broadhead, Mgr. Joseph, 78
Brunetière, Ferdinand, 175
Bury, J.B., 179–80
Bute, 3rd Marquess of, 50–51

Catholic Church: in America, 243–45; in Belgium, 241–42; in England, 29–34, 40, 46, 50–51; in France, 131–32, 226–34, 278–80; in Germany, 132–36, 240–41, 275–78; in the Netherlands, 241–42; in Portugal, 234; and socialism, 122–30; in Spain, 234–37
Catholic Disabilities Bill, 96–98
Catholic Emancipation (Catholic Relief Act of 1829), 30, 32, 96, 206
Catholic Magazine, 34–35
Catholic Settlements Association, 137–38. *See also* settlement movement
Catholic Social Guild, 131, 139, 141, 147, 281n47
Catholic Truth Society, 135, 138n36, 139, 149n53
Catholic Women's League, 118, 137, 139
Catholic Women's Suffrage Society, 118
Cecil, Lord Hugh, 54, 91, 101, 103, 114, 116, 117, 121, 122n4
Center Party. *See* Catholic Church in Germany
Challoner, Richard, 31, 33
Chamberlain, Joseph, 98, 102. *See also* tariff reform
Chapman, John, 48, 54, 56, 68n30
Chesterton, Cecil, 99
Chesterton, G. K., 4n8, 54, 82–85, 86, 99, 117, 119–20, 122, 156, 176, 181–83, 235n21, 292–93
Childers, Erskine, 222
China, 50n63, 249, 250, 251, 252, 253–54
Cisalpines, 31, 33–34, 276
Civiltà Cattolica, 16–17, 24

Cock, Albert A., 188–89
Congo Free State, 237–40
Connolly, Hugh, 56
Connolly, James, 124
Connolly, P. J., 175
Conservative Party, 91, 92, 98, 104n32, 110, 117, 120, 121, 122n4, 166, 207, 208, 210, 212, 213, 214, 219, 224, 254n66, 272,
Crawford, Virginia, 118, 141–47
Cuthbert [Hess], Fr., 3–4, 91, 284–87, 294

de Mun, Count Albert, 131, 232–33
Devas, C.S., 66, 124–28, 129, 137
Dimnet, Ernest, 228–30, 278
Disraeli, Benjamin, 51n64, 212, 245
Döllinger, Ignaz von, 34, 42, 43, 50n63
Dreyfus Affair, 18, 228, 278
Dublin Lockout, 153–55
Dublin Review: founding, 34–38; under Hedley, 44–47; under Vaughan and Moyes, 47–48; under William George Ward, 41–44; under Wiseman, 38–41

Eccles, F.Y., 99, 175, 278–79
Edinburgh Review, 37, 291
Education Bill (Birrell Bill), 92–96
Edward VII, vii, 96, 113, 156, 257
Entente Cordiale, 249, 257–58, 259
Eucharistic Congress (London), 96
eugenics, 156–65
evolution, 15–17, 44–45

Ferrer, Francisco, 236–37
Figgis, John Neville, 85–88
Fogazzaro, Antonio, 90
Fonsegrive, George, 233–34
France, Anatole, 175

Gaelic League, 195–96, 197, 198, 201, 211
Galsworthy, John, 169
Galton, Francis, 155–57, 159, 161, 162, 164
Gasquet, Francis Aidan, 48, 243–44, 284
Gerrard, T.J., 159–62
Gibson, William. 17–18, 77n5
Gilson, C.J.L., 253–54
Gladstone, William Ewart, 50n62, 112n48, 206, 207, 208, 209, 212, 217
Gore, Charles, 9. *See also Lux Mundi*
Gosse, Edmund, 6
Graves, Alfred Perceval, 196–97
Graves de communi (Leo XIII), 123n7, 124
Gravissimo (Pius X), 230
Great War: causes, 260–62; and Gallipoli, 270, 271; and French Catholics, 278–80; and German Catholics, 275–78; and prewar tensions, 249, 257–59; and the pope, 281–82, 284; and the postwar settlement, 282–87; and the press, 271, 272–73; and the submarine, 273–75; and superstition, 280–81; Ward's view of, 262–67, 272–73
Guild of the Pope's Peace, 282

Haldane, Richard, 257, 272
Halifax, 2nd Viscount, 25, 54, 55n78, 68, 106–7, 289–90
Harding, Stephen, 148–49, 250–52, 253–54
Hedley, Cuthbert, 16, 44–47, 73, 77, 293
Holland, Bernard, 117–18
Holy Office, 16, 17, 18, 68, 89, 164
Hope, James Fitzalan, 106–7, 219–21
House of Lords, 92, 95, 103, 104, 105, 106–16, 117–18, 120, 217, 218, 222, 223
Hügel, Friedrich von, 4n5, 6, 7, 19, 23, 60n8, 63–65, 66, 74n46, 77, 266, 291n10
Huysmans, Joris Karl, 175
Hyde, Douglas. *See* Gaelic League
Hynes, Samuel, viii, 176n26, 183n53, 288

India, 51n64, 246–49, 259, 287
Irish: in England, 29, 30, 31, 32–33, 51; and the Great War, 224–25, 262; Home Rule, 217–25; land reform, 208–10; Literary Revival, 199–204; literature, 149, 195–204; Party, 92, 93, 95, 105, 206–7, 211–12, 221, 225; in penal days, 205–6; Unionism, 207–8, 210–11, 218–19, 224; universities, 212–17

Japan, 171, 249–53, 254, 259
Johnson, Alice Vowe, 162
Joint Pastoral, 17, 24–26

Kent, W.H., 55n81, 195–96
Ketteler, Emmanuel Baron von, 132–33, 135
Kettle, Thomas, 148, 149–55, 221

Knox, Ronald, 88
Kolakowski, Leszek, viii
Korea, 250, 251, 259
Kulturkampf, 3, 13, 135, 240

labor disputes, 148–55
Labour Party, 92, 105, 113, 116, 120, 124, 141n42
Lamennais, Félicité, 1, 34
Lamentabili Sane Exitu (Pius X), 70
Larkin, James, 124, 153–54
Law of Separation, 228–34
Lawton, Lancelot, 226, 250–51, 252, 254, 257–59, 260–62, 268–71, 272
Leo XIII, 13, 14–15, 24n65, 123–24, 125, 130, 135, 155, 228, 235
Leopold II. *See* Congo Free State
Leroy, M.-D., 15–16
Le Sillon, 131–32
Liberal Catholicism, 7, 17, 19, 20–21, 24–27, 42–43, 52, 53, 61, 68
Liberal Party, 51n64, 92, 93, 96, 98, 99, 103–6, 107–8, 110, 112, 113, 115–16, 120, 122, 123, 141n42, 156, 167, 207, 210n11, 212, 213, 214, 216, 217, 220, 248, 249
Lingard, John, 34–35, 179, 180
living wage, 151, 153, 155
Llandaff, 1st Viscount (Henry Matthews), 50
Lloyd George, David, 104–5, 110, 156, 167, 220, 272
Loisy, Alfred, 64n15, 68, 70
Louvain, 55, 239, 267
Lueger, Karl, 242–43
Lunn, Arnold, 173
Lux Mundi, 9–10, 88

MacDonnell, John de Courcy. *See* Congo Free State
Mackenzie, Compton, 173–75
Mallock, W.H., 54, 129–30
Manning, Henry, 41, 43, 44, 45, 46, 130, 131, 141n42, 195n92
Martindale, C.C., 53, 173–75, 184n56, 189, 193n82
Masterman, C.F.G., 156
Maura, Antonio, 235–36
Mauriac, François, 175
McCullagh, Francis, 234, 241, 255–56
McNabb, Vincent, 128, 235n21
Mental Deficiency Act of 1913, 158n73, 163–65
Mercier, Désiré, 55, 267
Merry del Val, Rafael, 17n47, 22–23, 24, 49, 71, 74n46, 78, 266n10
Metaphysical Society, 5, 6, 7n18, 49n56
Meynell, Alice, 118, 183–84, 188
Meynell, Francis, 282
Meynell, Wilfrid, x, 75n48, 78n57, 184, 185, 187, 189, 282, 289, 290
Mivart, St. George Jackson, 15–16, 18–20, 21, 23, 47
modernism, 22n61, 56, 65n18, 66, 68, 70, 73n44, 75–76, 77, 78, 79, 80n59, 82, 86, 89, 233n14, 276. *See also Pascendi Dominici Gregis*
Montalembert, Count, 42, 43
Morison, Stanley, 282
Moyes, James, 47–48, 49, 185
Murphy, William Martin, 154. *See also* Dublin Lockout

New Liberalism, 123
Newman, John Henry, viii, 4, 6, 9n24, 10, 13, 27, 29–30 32, 36, 38–39, 40–42, 45, 50n62, 51–52, 58, 59–62, 63, 65n18, 67–70, 71, 73–74, 76, 78, 80, 168–69, 188, 212, 236, 290, 294
Norfolk, 15th Duke of, 6–7, 49, 50, 70, 75n48, 78n57, 97, 114, 219, 224, 289–91

O'Connell, Daniel, 32, 35, 36, 37–38, 206
O'Conor, Nicholas, 50, 255
O'Dwyer, Edward, 65n18, 66n22, 70, 71, 73, 74, 77, 214–16
Out of Due Time, 1–2, 80n63, 294
Oxford Movement, 4, 12, 30, 31–32, 36, 38, 39

Parliament Act of 1911, 106–16, 120, 217
Pascendi Dominici Gregis (Pius X), 70–79, 216
Péguy, Charles, 175
People's Budget, 104–5, 107, 110, 115, 220
Petre, Maud, 60n8, 79–80
Phillimore, John Swinnerton, 175–76
Pius IX, 2–3, 15, 43
Pius X, 22n61, 49, 70, 74, 79, 89, 132, 235, 277
Plater, Charles, 131–36

Pollen, A.H., 270, 274–75
Poor Law, 140–47
Pope, Hugh, 55–56
Providentissimus Deus (Leo XIII), 15

Quod Apostolici Muneris (Leo XIII), 123

Ralliement, 13, 227, 228
Redmond, John, 96, 211, 221, 225
Rerum Novarum (Leo XIII), 124, 130. *See also* Social Catholicism
Ripon, 1st Marquess of, 51, 96
Russell, Charles William, 37
Russell, T. W., 208–9
Russia, 50 n 63, 171, 226 n 1, 249, 250, 251, 252, 256, 258–59, 262, 268–70
Ryan, John A., 155

Salisbury, 3rd Marquess of, 50, 101n26, 210n12
Sangnier, Marc. *See Le Sillon*
settlement movement, 136–39
Shaw, G.B., 176, 181
Sheehan, Patrick Augustine, 196–98, 199
Shelley, Percy Bysshe, 184, 185–86, 188
Simpson, Richard, 5, 40–41
Singulari Quadam (Pius X), 277
Social Catholicism: in England, 130–31, 136–39; in France, 131–32; in Germany, 132–36
Social Purity Crusade, 172
Somerville, Henry, 128–29
Storer, Mrs. Bellamy, 190
Sykes, Mark, 254–55
Syllabus of Errors (Pius IX), 2–3
Synge, John Millington, 199, 200–203
Synthetic Society, 6, 66, 181, 272n30

Tablet, 16, 23, 24n65, 48, 49n58, 60n8, 71, 73n43, 128, 239
tariff reform, 98–103, 105, 113
Tennyson, Alfred, 7, 93, 169, 183, 188
Thompson, Francis, 176, 183, 184–90
Thurston, Herbert, 53, 63n14, 96–97, 280–81
Toke, Leslie, 147
Toynbee Hall, 137, 138–39, 140n40. *See also* settlement movement
Treitschke, Heinrich von, 261, 264–65, 267
Tuas Libenter (Pius IX), 43
Turkey, 50 n 63, 254–57, 268, 270
Tynan, Katherine, 199
Tyrrell, George, 4n 5, 7, 19n52, 25, 26–27, 65n18, 66–67, 73, 74n46, 77, 79–81

Ullathorne, Bernard, 45, 46
Ultramontanes, 4, 21, 33–34, 44, 46, 52
Urquhart, Francis, 248–49, 255n68, 282–84

Vaughan, Herbert, 22, 24–25, 27, 44, 45, 47, 48, 49, 131
Vehementer Nos (Pius X), 230
Vermeersch, Arthur, 239
Volksverein für das katholische Deutschland, 132, 134, 136

Ward, Leo, 13n34, 297, 291n11
Ward, Maisie, 147, 182–83, 191–92, 291–92
Ward, Mrs. Humphrey, 9, 85–87
Ward, Mrs. Wilfrid (Josephine), 1–2, 6–7, 80, 118, 181–82, 294
Ward, Wilfrid: ix, x, 1, 15, 27, 28, 31, 51, 112, 185, 186, 216, 226; on Acton, 52, 59; on adapting Christianity to the age, 8–13, 57–65, 88–89; becomes *Dublin* editor, 27, 31, 48–49; and Bourne, 72–73, 289–91; on the British empire, 245; on Bremond, 69; on Catholic literature, 168–69, 185; on Chesterton, 82–85; on the Church's "state of siege," 12, 14; death, 292–93; early life and education, 3–6; on education, 93–95; election to the Athenaeum, 28; and the French Law of Separation, 230–32; on the French Revolution, 99, 108, 114, 122; on the House of Lords, 108–12, 114–15; on von Hügel, 23; and Ireland, 213, 218, 219; and the Joint Pastoral, 24–26; and Liberal Catholics, 7, 17–22, 23; marriage, 6–7; and Mivart, 18–20, 23; Newman biography, viii, 27, 78; on *Pascendi*, 70–79; on Figgis, 85–88; personality and temperament, 6–8, 23; on Pius X, 79; and politics, 53, 91, 92, 99, 103, 117, 121–22, 147n51; retains *Dublin* editorship, 289–92; retrospective of *Dublin* editorship, 293–94; and scholasticism, 10–11, 14, 55, 58, 71, 76; on tariff reform, 98, 101–3; on

Tyrrell, 66–67, 80–81; vision for the *Dublin*, 51–54; visits to America, 244–45, 290, 291; on Williams, 68–69; on Wyndham, 211; Wiseman biography, 13, 27, 89
Ward, William George, 4–6, 39, 43–44
Wells, H.G., 170–71, 176
Wheatley, John, 124
Williams, William J., 68–69, 73, 74
Windle, Bertram, 55, 211, 216–17
Windthorst, Ludwig, 132, 133, 240
Wiseman, Nicholas, 13, 27, 34–39
women's suffrage, 118–20
Wyndham, George, 49n 56, 91, 114, 122n 4, 185, 190, 208–11, 213, 215n20, 254n 66

Yeats, William Butler, 199, 200–204
Yüan Shih-k'ai, 253–54

Zahm, John, 15–17
960

Out of Due Time was designed and composed in Adobe Garamond by Kachergis Book Design of Pittsboro, North Carolina. It was printed on 60-pound House Natural Smooth and bound by Sheridan Books, Inc., of Ann Arbor, Michigan.

www.ingramcontent.com/pod-product-compliance
Lightning Source LLC
LaVergne TN
LVHW040152080826
844660LV00014B/935/J

* 9 7 8 0 8 1 3 2 1 4 2 7 6 *